Shaw's

Directory of Courts

in the United Kingdom

2013/14

SWEET & MAXWELL

THOMSON REUTERS

Published in 2013 by Sweet & Maxwell, 100 Avenue Road, London NW3 3PF
part of Thomson Reuters (Professional) UK Limited
(Registered in England & Wales, Company No 1679046.
Registered Office and address for service:
Aldgate House, 33 Aldgate High Street, London EC3N 1DL)

*For further information on our products and services, visit
www.sweetandmaxwell.co.uk*

Typeset by
Letterpart Limited, Caterham on the Hill, Surrey CR3 5XL
Printed and bound in Great Britain by
Ashford Colour Press, Gosford, Hants.

*No natural forests were destroyed to make this product;
only farmed timber was used and re-planted.*

A CIP catalogue record for this book
is available from the British Library

ISBN 978-0-414-02892-0

CONTENTS

INTRODUCTION

Welcome to the 2013/14 edition of *Shaw's Directory of Courts in the United Kingdom*, published by Sweet and Maxwell. You may notice that this edition looks rather different to those of previous years. We have redesigned the layout for clarity and ease of use, while still keeping the same level of detail, including the historical indexes.

Part I opens with the appellate and senior courts in England and Wales, including the Supreme Court, Court of Appeal, and High Courts of Justice, followed by Northern Ireland and Scotland. Detailed information on each of the seven HMCTS regions comes next, with contact information for delivery directors as well as lists of circuit judges. All current crown, county and magistrates' courts under each region's administration are indexed within the regional listing, as well as within the relevant section of the book, for extra ease of use. An alphabetical listing of all the crown courts, including operational manager, court offices and court houses, completes Part I.

Part II contains details of all the county courts, arranged in alphabetical order, with reference to the appropriate region to which each court belongs. Entries are annotated to indicate any jurisdiction held by the court. District registries are indicated against the relevant county court office.

Part III covers all courts of summary jurisdiction in England, Wales, Northern Ireland and Scotland. The magistrates' courts in England and Wales are arranged alphabetically in clusters, grouped under the appropriate region. There is a numerical index to court codes of current and historical courts in this section, complete with details of closures and mergers. A listing of magistrates' courts in Northern Ireland follows.

The Scottish courts are arranged under sheriffdoms. Court details are followed by numerical indexes to the sheriff courts and justice of the peace courts, and historical indexes to the district courts before and after September 1, 1998. An alphabetical index to all the courts listed in it completes this part of the book.

Part IV consists of a full list of coroners and coroners' officers, with contact details, and an alphabetical index to coroners' districts.

Part V lists probate courts in England and Wales, including names, addresses and contact numbers for all registrars, as well as normal opening times.

Part VI covers the Crown Prosecution Service (CPS), including the CPS areas, together with details of the Chief Crown Prosecutor and Deputy Chief Crown Prosecutors for each one.

Part VII lists similar information for the Crown Office and Procurator Fiscal Service (Scotland).

Part VIII deals with penal establishments in the United Kingdom. Information about the National Offender Management Service (NOMS) includes headquarters contacts and regional office listings. This is followed by a key to prison categories and a full alphabetical list of penal establishments in England and Wales, with category information and contact details. Similar information for Northern Ireland and Scotland concludes this section and the book.

Changes in the listings in this book (including names, addresses, contact numbers and email addresses where possible, together with the times and places of court sittings), are published as notified to us up to the end of July 2013. As ever, I would like to thank all the people who have helped to update this information.

Helen Gough, Editor

Part I

APPELLATE COURTS, SENIOR COURTS, HMCTS REGIONS, CROWN COURTS

APPELLATE COURTS

THE JUDICIAL COMMITTEE OF THE PRIVY COUNCIL

Parliament Square, London SW1P 3BD
Tel: 020 7960 1500
Website: www.jcpc.gov.uk
Email: jcpcregistry@jcpc.gsi.gov.uk
Registrar of the Privy Council: Louise di Mambro. Tel: 020 7960 1985
Chief Clerk: Jackie Lindsay. Tel: 020 7960 1510. Email: jackie.lindsay@jcpc.gsi.gov.uk

THE SUPREME COURT OF THE UNITED KINGDOM

Westminster, London SW1P 3BD
Tel: 020 7960 1900
Fax: 020 7960 1901
Website: www.supremecourt.gov.uk
The Lord High Chancellor and Secretary of State for Justice: The Rt Hon. Chris Grayling MP
Permanent Secretary to the Lord Chancellor: Sir Suma Chakrabarti. Tel: 0203 334 3709
President of the United Kingdom Supreme Court: The Rt Hon. the Lord Neuberger of Abbotsbury
Deputy President of the United Kingdom Supreme Court: The Right Hon. the Baroness Hale of Richmond
Justices of the United Kingdom Supreme Court:

The Rt Hon. the Lord Mance
The Rt Hon. the Lord Kerr of Tonaghmore
The Rt Hon. the Lord Clarke of Stone-cum-Ebony
The Rt Hon. Lord Wilson of Culworth
The Rt Hon. Lord Sumption
The Rt Hon. Lord Reed
The Rt Hon. Lord Carnwath of Notting Hill
The Rt Hon. Lord Hughes of Ombersley
The Rt Hon. Lord Toulson
The Rt Hon. Lord Hodge
Head of Judicial Support: Ms Georgina Isaac. Tel: 020 7960 1960. Email: georgina.isaac@supremecourt.gsi.gov.uk

SENIOR COURTS

Website: www.judiciary.gov.uk

COURT OF APPEAL
Royal Courts of Justice, Strand, London WC2A 2LL
Tel: 0207 947 6000
Fax: 0207 947 6900
DX: 44451 RCJ/STRAND
The Lord High Chancellor and Secretary of State for Justice: The Rt Hon. Chris Grayling MP
The Heads of Division:

The Lord Chief Justice of England and Wales, Head of Criminal Justice: The Rt Hon. the Lord
    Judge (until 30 September 2013); The Rt Hon. Sir John Thomas (from 1 October 2013)
The Master of the Rolls and Head of Civil Justice: The Rt Hon. Lord Dyson
The President of the Queen's Bench Division: The Rt Hon. Sir (Roger) John Laugharne Thomas
The President of the Family Division and Head of Family Justice: The Rt Hon. Sir James
    Lawrence Munby
The Chancellor of the High Court: The Rt Hon. Sir Terence Michael Elkan Barnet Etherton
The Master of the Rolls: The Right Hon. Lord Dyson

Secretary: Ms Noella Roberts Tel: 0207 947 6002
Clerk: Jessica Lear Tel: 0207 947 6371
Lord and Lady Justices of Appeal:

The Rt Hon. Sir John Grant McKenzie Laws
The Rt Hon. Dame Mary Howarth Arden DBE
The Rt Hon. Sir Andrew Centlivres Longmore
The Rt Hon. Sir Maurice Ralph Kay
The Rt Hon. Sir Martin James Moore-Bick
The Rt Hon. Sir Alan George Moses
The Rt Hon. Sir Stephen Price Richards
The Rt Hon. Dame Heather Carol Hallett DBE
The Rt Hon. Sir Brian Henry Leveson
The Rt Hon. Sir Colin Percy Farquharson Rimer
The Rt Hon. Sir Rupert Matthew Jackson
The Rt Hon. Sir John Bernard Goldring
The Rt Hon. Sir Richard John Pearson Aikens
The Rt Hon. Sir Jeremy Mirth Sullivan
The Rt Hon. Sir Patrick Elias
The Rt Hon. Sir Nicholas John Patten
The Rt Hon. Sir Christopher John Pitchford
The Rt Hon. Dame Jill Margaret Black DBE
The Rt Hon. Sir Stephen Miles Tomlinson

The Rt Hon. Sir Peter Henry Gross
The Rt Hon. Dame Anne Judith Rafferty DBE
The Rt Hon. Sir Andrew Ewart McFarlane
The Rt Hon. Sir Nigel Anthony Lamert Davis
The Rt Hon. Sir Kim Martin Jordan Lewison
The Rt Hon. Sir David James Tyson Kitchin
The Rt Hon. Sir David Lloyd Jones
The Rt Hon. Sir Colman Maurice Treacy
The Rt Hon. Sir Richard George Bramwell
    McCombe
The Rt Hon. Sir Jack Beatson
The Rt Hon. Dame Elizabeth Gloster DBE
The Rt Hon. Sir Ernest Nigel Ryder
The Rt Hon. Sir Nicholas Edward Underhill
The Rt Hon. Sir Michael Townley Featherstone
    Briggs
The Rt Hon. Sir Christopher David Floyd
The Rt Hon. Sir Adrian Bruce Fulford
The Hon. Dame Julia Wendy Macur DBE

Civil Appeal Office: *Office Manager:* Tel: 0207 947 6915. Fax: 0207 947 6740
Criminal Appeal Office: Registry Enquiries: Tel: 0207 947 6011. Fax: 0207 947 6900
Office Manager: Tel: 0207 947 6011. DX: 44451 RCJ/Strand

HIGH COURT OF JUSTICE, QUEEN'S BENCH DIVISION
Royal Courts of Justice, Strand, London WC2A 2LL
Tel: 0207 947 6000
DX: 44450 STRAND WC2
The Lord Chief Justice of England and Wales: The Rt Hon. the Lord Judge (until 30 September
2013); The Rt Hon Sir John Thomas (from 1 October 2013)
Secretary: Miss Michèle Souris. Tel: 0207 947 6776
Clerk: Mrs Glenys McDonald MBE. Tel: 0207 947 6007
President of the Queen's Bench Division: The Rt Hon. Sir Roger John Laugharne Thomas
Clerk: Jean Curtin. Tel: 0207 947 6399
Judges:

The Hon. Sir Andrew David Collins
The Hon. Sir Michael John Burton
The Hon. Sir Stephen Robert Silber

The Hon. Sir Richard Henry Quixano Henriques
The Hon. Sir Andrew Charles Smith
The Hon. Sir Duncan Brian Walter Ouseley

The Hon. Sir Robert Michael Owen
The Hon. Sir Colin Crichton Mackay
The Hon. Sir John Edward Mitting
The Hon. Sir Brian Richard Keith
The Hon. Sir Jeremy Lionel Cooke
The Hon. Sir Richard Alan Field
The Hon. Sir Peregrine Charles Hugo Simon
The Hon. Sir Roger John Royce
The Hon. Dame Laura Mary Cox DBE
The Hon. Sir Michael George Tugendhat
The Hon. Sir David Michael Bean
The Hon. Sir Alan Fraser Wilkie
The Hon. Sir Paul James Walker
The Hon. Sir Christopher Simon Courtnay
    Stephenson Clarke
The Hon. Sir Charles Peter Lawford Openshaw
The Hon. Dame Caroline Jane Swift DBE
The Hon. Sir Brian Frederick James Langstaff
The Hon. Sir Vivian Arthur Ramsey
The Hon. Sir Stephen John Irwin
The Hon. Sir Nigel John Martin Teare
The Hon. Sir John Griffith-Williams
The Hon. Sir Wyn Lewis Williams
The Hon. Sir Timothy Roger Alan King
The Hon. Sir John Henry Boulton Saunders
The Hon. Sir Julian Martin Flaux
The Hon. Sir David Robert Foskett
The Hon. Sir Robert Akenhead
The Hon. Sir Nicholas John Gorrod Blake
The Hon. Sir Ross Frederick Cranston
The Hon. Sir Peter David William Coulson
The Hon. Sir William James Lynton Blair
The Hon. Sir Alistair Geoffrey MacDuff

The Hon. Sir Ian Duncan Burnett
The Hon. Sir Nigel Hamilton Sweeney
The Hon. Dame Elizabeth Ann Slade DBE
The Hon. Sir Nicholas Archibald Hamblen
The Hon. Sir Gary Robert Hickinbottom
The Hon. Sir Timothy Victor Holroyde
The Hon. Dame Victoria Madeline Sharp DBE
The Hon. Sir Andrew George Lindsay Nicol
The Hon. Sir Kenneth Blades Parker
The Hon. Sir Antony James Cobham
    Edwards-Stuart
The Rt Hon. Dame Nicola Velfor Davies DBE
The Rt Hon. Dame Kathryn Mary Thirlwall DBE
The Hon. Sir Michael Alan Supperstone
The Hon. Sir Robin Godfrey Spencer
The Hon. Sir Keith John Lindblom
The Hon. Sir Henry Bernard Eder
The Hon. Sir Henry Brian Globe
The Hon. Sir Andrew John Popplewell
The Hon. Sir Rabinder Singh
The Hon. Dame Beverley Ann Mcnaughtan Lang
The Hon. Sir Charles Anthony Haddon-Cave
The Hon. Sir Stephen Martin Males
The Hon. Sir Jeremy Hugh Stuart-Smith
The Hon. Sir George Andrew Midsomer Leggatt
The Hon. Sir Mark George Turner
The Hon. Sir Jeremy Russell Baker
The Hon. Sir Stephen Paul Stewart
The Hon. Sir Robert Maurice Jay Q.C
The Hon. Sir James Michael Dingemans
The Hon. Sir Clive Buckland Lewis
The Hon. Dame Sue Lascelles Carr DBE

Chief Clerk to QB Judges in Chambers: Tel: 0207 947 6511
Clerk of the Lists Office: Tel: 0207 947 6021

Commercial Listing: Tel: 0207 947 6826
TECHNOLOGY & CONSTRUCTION COURT
7 Rolls Building, Fetter Lane, London EC4A 1NL
Tel: 0207 947 6022
Fax: 0207 947 7428
DX: 160040 STRAND 4
Office Manager: Tel: 0207 947 7427. Fax: 0870 761 7725
Judges:

Mr Justice Akenhead (Presiding Judge)
Mr Justice Ramsay
Mr Justice Ouseley
Mr Justice Field
Mr Justice Simon
Mr Justice Christopher Clarke

Mr Justice Teare
Mr Justice Foskett
Mr Justice Coulson
Mr Justice Edwards-Stuart
Mr Justice Stuart-Smith

HIGH COURT OF JUSTICE, FAMILY DIVISION
Royal Courts of Justice, Strand, London WC2A 2LL
Tel: 0207 947 6000
Fax: 0207 947 6709
President: The Rt Hon. Sir James Lawrence Munby
Secretary: Mrs Sarah Leung. Tel: 0207 947 7216
Clerk: George Pitchley. Tel: 0207 947 6576
Judges:

The Hon. Sir Edward James Holman
The Hon. Dame Mary Claire Hogg DBE
The Hon. Sir Arthur William Hessin Charles

The Hon. Sir David Roderick Lessiter Bodey
The Hon. Sir Paul James Duke Coleridge

The Hon. Dame Anna Evelyn Hamilton Pauffley DBE
The Hon. Sir Roderic Lionel James Wood
The Hon. Dame Florence Jacquelene Baron DBE
The Hon. Sir Andrew John Gregory Moylan
The Hon. Dame Eleanor Warwick King DBE
The Hon. Dame Judith Mary Frances Parker DBE
The Hon. Sir Jonathan Leslie Baker

The Hon. Sir Nicholas Anthony Joseph Ghislain Mostyn
The Hon. Sir Peter Arthur Brian Jackson
The Hon. Dame Lucy Morgan Theis DBE
The Hon. Sir Philip Drury Moor
The Hon. Sir Stephen William Scott Cobb
The Hon. Sir Michael Joseph Keehan
The Hon. Sir Anthony Paul Hayden QC

Clerk of the Rules: Tel: 0207 947 6543

HIGH COURT OF JUSTICE, CHANCERY DIVISION

7 Rolls Building, Fetter Lane, London EC4A 1NL
Tel: 0207 947 6000
Fax: 0207 947 7345
DX: 160040 STRAND 4
President: The Lord High Chancellor and Secretary of State for Justice, The Rt Hon. Chris Grayling MP)
The Chancellor of the High Court: The Rt Hon. Sir Terence Michael Elkan Barnet Etherton
Clerk: Mrs Amanda Collins. Tel: 0207 947 6412
Secretary: Miss Elaine Herbert. Tel: 0207 947 7477
Judges:

The Hon. Sir Peter Winston Smith
The Hon. Sir David Anthony Stewart Richards
The Hon. Sir George Anthony Mann
The Hon. Sir Nicholas Roger Warren
The Hon. Sir Launcelot Dinadin James Henderson
The Hon. Sir Paul Hyacinth Morgan
The Hon. Sir Alastair Hubert Norris
The Hon. Sir Gerald Edward Barling
The Hon. Sir Phillip James Sales

The Hon. Dame Sonia Rosemary Susan Proudman DBE
The Hon. Sir Richard David Arnold
The Hon. Sir Peter Marcel Roth
The Hon. Sir Geoffrey Charles Vos
The Hon. Sir Guy Richard Newey
The Hon. Sir Robert Henry Thuroton Hildyard
The Hon. Dame Sarah Jane Asplin DBE
The Hon. Sir Colin Ian Birss
The Hon. Dame Vivien Judith Rose DBE

High Court Bankruptcy Department: Tel: 0207 947 7472
County Court Bankruptcy Department: Tel: 0207 947 6812
CHANCERY CHAMBERS
Tel: 0207 947 6754; 0207 947 7717 (Chancery Listing)
Chief Master: J.I. Winegarten
Masters

P. Teverson
N.W. Bragge
T.J. Bowles

N. Price
M. Marsh

Court Manager: Tel: 0207 947 6571

CENTRAL OFFICE OF THE SENIOR COURTS

Royal Courts of Justice, Strand, London WC2A 2LL
Tel: 0207 947 6000 (Central Switchboard)
DX: 44450 STRAND
Senior Master (QBD) and Queen's Remembrancer: S.D. Whitaker
QBD Masters:

R.R. Roberts
J.K. Kay QC
V. McCloud
J.D. Cooke

H.J. Leslie
B. Yoxall
R. Eastman
B.J.F. Fontaine

Clerk to Interim Applications Judge: Tel: 0207 947 6508

ADMINISTRATIVE COURT

Royal Courts of Justice, Strand, London WC2A 2LL
Tel: 0207 947 6655; 0121 250 6319 (Birmingham Regional Office); 029 2037 6460 (Cardiff Regional Office); 0113 306 2578 (Leeds Regional Office); 0161 240 5313 (Manchester Regional Office). Fax: 0207 947 6802

DX: 44450 RCJ/STRAND
Registrar of Criminal Appeals, Master of the Crown Office, and Queen's Coroner and Attorney: M. Egan QC
Judge in Charge of the Administrative Court: The Hon. Mr Justice Ouseley

SENIOR COURT COSTS OFFICE
Royal Courts of Justice, Strand, London WC2A 2LL
Tel: 0207 947 6423
DX: 44454 STRAND.
Senior Cost Judge: P. T. Hurst

ADMIRALTY COURT
7 Rolls Building, Fetter Lane, London EC4A 1NL
Tel: 0207 947 7228
DX: 160040 STRAND 4
Admiralty Registrar and Queen's Bench Master: J. Kay
Admiralty Marshal: Michael Parker. Tel: 0207 947 7228

COURT OF PROTECTION
Royal Courts of Justice, Strand, London WC2A 2LL
Tel: 0300 456 4600
DX: 44450 STRAND

OFFICE OF THE PUBLIC GUARDIAN
PO Box 16185, Birmingham B2 2WH
Tel: 0300 456 0300
Fax: 0870 739 5780
DX: 744240 BIRMINGHAM 79
Website: www.gov.uk/powerofattorney
Email: customerservices@publicguardian.gsi.gov.uk

OFFICIAL SOLICITOR AND PUBLIC TRUSTEE
81 Chancery Lane, London WC2A 1DD
Tel: 020 7911 7127
Fax: 020 7911 7105

OFFICIAL RECEIVER'S OFFICE
Head Office
The Insolvency Service, 21 Bloomsbury Street, London WC1B 3QW
Tel: 0845 602 9848
Estate Accounts and Insolvency Practitioner Unit (IPU)
The Insolvency Service, Cannon House, 18 Priory Queensway, Birmingham B4 6FD
Tel: 0121 698 4000

NORTHERN IRELAND

THE ROYAL COURTS OF JUSTICE
Chichester Street, Belfast BT1 3JF
Tel: 028 9023 5111
Fax: 028 9031 3508
Lord Chief Justice of Northern Ireland: The Rt Hon. Sir Declan Morgan
Judges:

The Rt Hon. Lord Justice Higgins
The Rt Hon. Lord Justice Girvan
The Rt Hon. Lord Justice Coghlin
The Hon. Mr Justice Gillen
The Hon. Mr Justice Weatherup
The Hon. Mr Justice Weir
The Hon. Mr Justice Deeny

The Hon. Mr Justice Stephens
The Hon. Mr Justice Treacy
The Hon. Mr Justice McCloskey
The Hon. Mr Justice Maguire
The Hon. Mr Justice Horner
The Hon. Mr Justice O'Hara

THE NORTHERN IRELAND COURTS AND TRIBUNALS SERVICE
Laganside House, 23–27 Oxford Street, Belfast BT1 3LA
Tel: 028 9032 8594
Fax: 028 9072 8945
The Northern Ireland Courts and Tribunals Service (NICTS) is an agency of the Department of Justice for Northern Ireland. The NICTS is responsible for the operation of 19 courthouses and and a number of tribunal centres across Northern Ireland.
Chief Executive: Jacqui Durkin
The Chief Executive of the NICTS is the head of the Agency. She is responsible for the day-to-day operation of the Agency and the leadership and management of its staff. The NICTS Board (the Board) oversees the work of the NICTS and consists of:
Chief Executive: Jacqui Durkin (who chairs the Board)
Head of Court Operations: Peter Luney
Responsible for providing administrative support for criminal, civil and family court business and the coroners service.
Head of Tribunal, Enforcement and Parole Commissioners Secretariat: Mandy Kilpatrick
Responsible for providing administrative support for the majority of tribunals, the Enforcement of Judgments Office (EJO) and Parole Commissioners Secretariat (PCS).
Head of Business Support: Elaine Topping
Head of Finance and Estates: Sharon Hetherington

NON-EXECUTIVE BOARD MEMBERS
P.J. Fitzpatrick (Chair of Agency Audit and Risk Committee)
Colm McKenna (member of Finance Committee)
Four members of the judiciary, nominated by the Lord Chief Justice, also attend the Board meetings.

JUDICIAL REPRESENTATIVES
The Hon. Mr Justice Deeny
His Hon. Judge McFarland, Recorder of Belfast
District Judge Bagnall, Presiding District Judge (Magistrates' Courts)
Mr Conall MacLynn, President of the Appeals Tribunal

SCOTLAND

COURT OF SESSION
Supreme Courts, Parliament House, 11 Parliament Square, Edinburgh EH1 1RQ
Tel: 0131 225 2595
Fax: 0131 240 6755
DX: 549306 EDINBURGH 36
Legal Post: LP1
Website: www.scotcourts.gov.uk

HIGH COURT OF JUSTICIARY
Supreme Courts, Parliament House, 11 Parliament Square, Edinburgh EH1 1RQ
Tel: 0131 225 2595
Fax: 0131 240 6915
DX: 549307 EDINBURGH 36
Legal Post: LP1

The Lord President and Lord Justice General: The Rt Hon. Lord Gill

INNER HOUSE
First Division

The Lord President (The Rt Hon. Lord Gill)
The Rt Hon. Lord Eassie
The Rt Hon. Lord Menzies
The Rt Hon. Lady Smith
The Rt Hon. Lord Brodie

Second Division

The Lord Justice Clerk (The Rt Hon. Lord Carloway)
The Rt Hon. Lady Paton
The Rt Hon. Lord Clarke
The Rt Hon. the Lord Mackay of Drumadoon
The Rt Hon. Lady Dorrian
The Rt. Hon. Lord Bracadale

OUTER HOUSE

The Hon. Lord Hodge
The Hon. Lord Glennie
The Hon. Lord Kinclaven
The Hon. Lord Turnbull
The Hon. Lady Clark of Calton
The Hon. Lord Brailsford
The Hon. Lord Uist
The Hon. Lord Malcolm
The Hon. Lord Matthews
The Hon. Lord Woolman
The Hon. Lord Pentland
The Hon. Lord Bannatyne

The Hon. Lady Stacey
The Hon. Lord Tyre
The Hon. Lord Doherty
The Hon. Lord Stewart
The Rt Hon. the Lord Boyd of Duncansby
The Hon. Lord Jones
The Hon. Lord Burns
The Hon. Lady Scott
The Hon. Lady Wise
The Hon. Lord Armstrong
The Hon. Lord Drummond Young

SCOTTISH COURT SERVICE
Saughton House, Broomhouse Drive, Edinburgh EH11 3XD
Tel: 0131 444 3300
Fax: 0131 443 2610
DX: 545309
Website: www.scotcourts.gov.uk
Chief Executive: Eric McQueen
Chief Operations Officer: Cliff Binning
Chief Finance Officer: Neil Cook
Executive Director Judicial Office for Scotland: Steve Humphreys

HMCTS REGIONS

ENGLAND AND WALES

LONDON REGION

PRESIDING JUDGES

The Hon. Mr Justice Nicol
The Hon. Mr Justice Sweeney
The Hon. Mr Justice Singh

FAMILY DIVISION LIAISON JUDGES

The Hon. Mrs Justice Pauffley DBE
The Hon. Mrs Justice Theis DBE
The Hon. Mrs Justice Parker DBE

CHANCERY SUPERVISING JUDGE

Chancellor of the High Court, Sir Terence Michael Elkan Barnet Etherton

CIRCUIT JUDGES

Crown Court

His Hon. Judge Blacksell QC
His Hon. Judge Clarke QC
His Hon. Judge Hillen
His Hon. Judge Karsten QC
His Hon. Judge Marron QC
His Hon. Judge Pillay
His Hon. Judge Richardson
His Hon. Judge Worsley
Her Hon. Judge Sullivan
His Hon. Judge Barker QC
His Hon. Judge Forrester
His Hon. Judge Gordon
His Hon. Judge Hone QC
His Hon. Judge Kramer QC
His Hon. Judge Anthony Morris QC
His Hon. Judge Moss QC
His Hon. Judge Pontius
His Hon. Judge Peter Rook QC
His Hon. Judge Thornton QC
His Hon. Judge Worsley QC
His Hon. Judge Ainley
Her Hon. Judge Barnes
Her Hon. Judge Baucher
Her Hon. Judge Downing
His Hon. Judge Flahive
His Hon. Judge McKinnon
His Hon. Judge Tanzer
His Hon. Judge Waller
His Hon. Judge Anderson
His Hon. Judge Arran
His Hon. Judge Alan Greenwood
His Hon. Judge Bishop
His Hon. Judge Burn
His Hon. Judge Chapple
His Hon. Judge Fraser MVO
His Hon. Judge Grobel
Her Hon. Judge Karu
His Hon. Judge Seed QC
His Hon. Judge Denniss

His Hon. Judge Edmunds
Her Hon. Judge Guggenheim QC
His Hon. Judge Johnson
Her Hon. Judge Kent
His Hon. Judge Lowen
His Hon. Judge Matthews
His Hon. Judge McDowall
His Hon. Judge McGregor-Johnson
His Hon. Judge Winstanley
His Hon. Judge Andrew Campbell
Her Hon. Judge Coello
His Hon. Judge Dodgson
His Hon. Judge Hopmeier
His Hon. Judge Nicholas Jones
Her Hon. Judge Matthews QC
His Hon. Judge Fergus Mitchell
His Hon. Judge Price QC
His Hon. Judge Richard Southwell
Her Hon. Judge Tapping
His Hon. Judge Birts QC
His Hon. Judge Freeland QC
His Hon. Judge Hand QC
His Hon. Judge Huskinson
Her Hon. Judge Joseph QC
Her Hon. Judge Kamill
His Hon. Judge Kennedy
His Hon. Judge Lafferty
His Hon. Judge Lamb QC
His Hon. Judge Owen
His Hon. Judge Pardoe QC
His Hon. Judge Radford
His Hon. Judge Sanders
His Hon. Judge Shanks
His Hon. Judge Wilkinson
His Hon. Judge Zeidman QC
His Hon. Judge Beddoe
His Hon. Judge Gledhill QC
His Hon. Judge Goymer
His Hon. Judge Higgins

His Hon. Judge Leonard QC
His Hon. Judge Loraine-Smith
His Hon. Judge Pitts
His Hon. Judge Price
His Hon. Judge Robbins
Her Hon. Judge Taylor
His Hon. Judge Testar
His Hon. Judge John Rylance
His Hon. Judge Ader
His Hon. Judge Browne QC
His Hon. Judge Carr
His Hon. Judge Lyons CBE
Her Hon. Judge May QC
His Hon. Judge Robert Morrison
His Hon. Judge Patrick
His Hon. Judge Pawlak
His Hon. Judge Carroll
His Hon. Judge Dawson
Her Hon. Judge Lees
His Hon. Judge Andrew Lees
His Hon. Judge Marks Moore
His Hon. Judge Murphy
His Hon. Judge Pegden QC
His Hon. Judge Shorrock
His Hon. Judge Barklem
His Hon. Judge Bavan
His Hon. Judge Blacklett

His Hon. Judge Cooke QC
His Hon. Judge Darling
His Hon. Judge Davis
Her Hon. Judge Dean
Her Hon. Judge Dhir
His Hon. Judge Dodd
His Hon. Judge Donne
His Hon. Judge Dugdale
His Hon. Judge Gold QC
His Hon. Judge Gold QC
His Hon. Judge Grieve
His Hon. Judge Hilliard QC
Her Hon. Judge Korner, CMG, QC
His Hon. Judge Kinch QC
His Hon. Judge Marks
His Hon. Judge McCreath
Her Hon. Judge Molyneux
His Hon. Judge Moore
Her Hon. Judge Paneth
His Hon. Judge Parker QC
His Hon. Judge Peters QC
Her Hon. Judge Poulet QC
Her Hon. Judge Robinson
His Hon. Judge Saggerson
His Hon. Judge Tomlinson
His Hon. Judge Topolski QC
His Hon. Judge Wide QC

County Court

Her Hon. Judge Levy
His Hon. Judge Mayer
His Hon. Judge Hornby
Her Hon. Judge Redgrave
Her Hon. Judge Caroline Wright
His Hon. Judge Powles QC
His Hon. Judge David Mitchell
His Hon. Judge Bailey
His Hon. Judge Collender QC
His Hon. Judge Dight
His Hon. Judge Mackie CBE QC
Her Hon. Judge Faber
His Hon. Judge Atkins
His Hon. Judge Ellis
His Hon. Judge Ansell
Her Hon. Judge Atkinson
His Hon. Judge Brasse
Her Hon. Judge Cox
His Hon. Judge Cryan
His Hon. Judge John Mitchell
His Hon. Judge O'Dwyer
Her Hon. Judge Pearl
Her Hon. Judge Brasse
Her Hon. Judge Jakens
Her Hon. Judge Sally Williams
His Hon. Judge Birtles
His Hon. Judge Wulwik
His Hon. Judge Welchman

His Hon. Judge Wright
His Hon. Judge Copley
His Hon. Judge Million
His Hon. Judge Altman
Her Hon. Judge Venables
Her Hon. Judge Boye
Her Hon. Judge Harris
Her Hon. Judge Corbett
Her Hon. Judge Hughes
His Hon. Judge Gerald
His Hon. Judge Wilding
Her Hon. Judge Karp
Her Hon. Judge Gardan
Her Hon. Judge Rowe

Principal Registry of the Family Division
District Judge Aitken
District Judge Bowman
District Judge Bradley
District Judge Harper
District Judge MacGregor
District Judge Reid
District Judge Robinson
District Judge Walker
District Judge Gordon-Saker
District Judge Simmonds
District Judge Gibson
District Judge Hess

DIRECTOR OF THE ROYAL COURTS OF JUSTICE
David Thompson
Director's Office, Room E331, Royal Courts of Justice, Strand, London WC2A 2LL
Tel: 0207 947 6534

Fax: 0207 947 6666
DX: 44450 STRAND

DELIVERY DIRECTOR
Sheila Proudlock
3rd Floor, Rose Court, 2 Southwark Bridge, London SE1 9HS
Tel: 020 7921 2010
DX: 154261 SOUTHWARK 12

HEAD OF CRIME
Dave Weston
3rd Floor, Rose Court, 2 Southwark Bridge, London SE1 9HS
Tel: 020 7921 2196
DX: 154261 SOUTHWARK 12

HEAD OF CIVIL, FAMILY & TRIBUNALS
Martin John
3rd Floor, Rose Court, 2 Southwark Bridge, London SE1 9HS
Tel: 020 7921 2015
DX: 154261 SOUTHWARK 12

COURT INDEX – LONDON REGION

2572 (6572)	North London LJA (Youth)	Magistrates	108
2573 (6573)	North East London LJA (Youth)	Magistrates	109
2571 (6571)	North West London LJA (Youth)	Magistrates	109
2573 (6573)	Redbridge (Youth)	Magistrates	111
2577 (6577)	Richmond (Youth)	Magistrates	107
2573 (6573)	Romford (Youth)	Magistrates	109
0453	Snaresbrook	Crown	47
2576 (6576)	South London LJA (Youth)	Magistrates	105
2575 (6575)	South East London LJA (Youth)	Magistrates	106
2577 (65770)	South West London LJA (Youth)	Magistrates	106
2577 (6577)	South Western (Youth)	Magistrates	111
0471	Southwark	Crown	47
2574 (6574)	Stratford (Youth)	Magistrates	108
2574 (6574)	Thames (Youth)	Magistrates	108
2572 (6572)	Tottenham (Youth)	Magistrates	109
356	Uxbridge	County	81
2578 (6578)	Uxbridge (Youth)	Magistrates	110
2574 (6574)	Waltham Forest (Youth)	Magistrates	108
359	Wandsworth	County	81
368	West London	County	81
2578 (6578)	West London LJA (Youth)	Magistrates	110
2570 (6570)	Westminster (Youth)	Magistrates	105
375	Willesden	County	81
2571 (6571)	Willesden (Youth)	Magistrates	109
2577 (6577)	Wimbledon (Youth)	Magistrates	107
0469	Wood Green	Crown	47
379	Woolwich	County	82
0472	Woolwich	Crown	48

MIDLANDS REGION

PRESIDING JUDGES
The Rt Hon. Lord Justice Gross, Senior Presiding Judge
The Hon. Mr Justice Flaux
The Hon. Mrs Justice Thirlwall

FAMILY DIVISION LIAISON JUDGE
The Hon. Mrs Justice King

CHANCERY SUPERVISING JUDGE
The Hon. Mr Justice Morgan

CIRCUIT JUDGES

His Hon. Judge Simon Barker QC
His Hon. Judge Barrie
His Hon. Judge Bellamy
His Hon. Judge RIW Bond
His Hon. Judge Bray
His Hon. Judge Robert Alan Brown
His Hon. Judge Simon Brown QC
His Hon. Judge Burbidge QC
His Hon. Judge Burgess
Her Hon. Judge Bush
Her Hon. Judge Butler QC
His Hon. Judge Cardinal
His Hon. Judge Peter Carr
His Hon. Judge Chambers QC
His Hon. Judge Challinor
Her Hon. Judge Bryony Clark
His Hon. Judge Anthony Cleary
His Hon. Judge David Cooke
His Hon. Judge Creed
His Hon. Judge Cullum
His Hon. Judge William Davis QC
Her Hon. Judgede Bertodano
Her Hon. Judge Deeley
His Hon. Judge Dickinson QC
Her Hon. Judge Dowding
His Hon. Judge Drew QC
His Hon. Judge Dudley
His Hon. Judge Duggan
His Hon. Judge Eades
His Hon. Judge Farrer QC
Her Hon. Judge Fisher
His Hon. Judge Fletcher CBE
His Hon. Judge Fowler
His Hon. Judge Glenn
His Hon. Judge Godsmark QC
His Hon. Judge Gosling
His Hon. Judge David Grant
His Hon. Judge Gregory
His Hon. Judge Griffith-Jones
His Hon. Judge A. Hamilton
His Hon. Judge Hammond
Her Hon. Judge Hampton
His Hon. Judge Head
His Hon. Judge Heath
His Hon. Judge Henderson
Her Hon. Judge Hindley QC

His Hon. Judge Hooper QC
Her Hon. Judge Hughes
His Hon. Judge Inglis
His Hon. Judge Melbourne Inman QC
His Hon. Judge Juckes QC
His Hon. Judge Lea
His Hon. Judge McKenna
His Hon. Judge Main QC
His Hon. Judge Marten Coates
His Hon. Judge Mayo
His Hon. Judge Milmo QC
His Hon. Judge Mithani QC
His Hon. Judge Mooncey
His Hon. Judge Sean Morris
His Hon. Judge Nawaz
His Hon. Judge Oliver-Jones QC
His Hon. Judge Onions
His Hon. Judge Orme
His Hon. Judge Orrell
His Hon. Judge Robert Owen QC
His Hon. Judge A Parker
His Hon. Judge Parker QC
His Hon. Judge Pearce-Higgins QC
His Hon. Judge Pert QC
His Hon. Judge Plunkett
His Hon. Judge Pugsley
His Hon. Judge Purle QC
His Hon. Judge Rafferty QC
His Hon. Judge Mark Rogers
His Hon. Judge Rumbelow QC
His Hon. Judge Rundell
His Hon. Judge Sampson
His Hon. Judge Stokes QC
Her Hon. Judge Swindells QC
Her Hon. Judge Tayton QC
His Hon. Judge Teare
Her Hon. Judge Thomas
His Hon. Judge Patrick Thomas QC
His Hon. Judge Tonking
His Hon. Judge Wait
His Hon. Judge Walsh
His Hon. Judge Warner
Her Hon. Judge Watson
His Hon. Judge Webb
His Hon. Judge Worster

DELIVERY DIRECTOR
Lucy Garrod
Midlands Regional Office, 6th Floor, Temple Court, Birmingham
DX: 701993 BIRMINGHAM 7

COURT INDEX – MIDLANDS REGION

Court Code	Town Name	Court Type	Page No
127	Birmingham	County	64
0404	Birmingham	Crown	39
2908	Birmingham LJA	Magistrates	121
138	Boston	County	65
1840	Bromsgrove and Redditch LJA	Magistrates	119
158	Buxton	County	67
2799	Central and South West Staffordshire LJA	Magistrates	119
171	Chesterfield	County	69
2321	Corby LJA	Magistrates	116
180	Coventry	County	70
0417	Coventry	Crown	42
2910	Coventry District LJA	Magistrates	121
185	Derby	County	71
0419	Derby	Crown	42
189	Dudley	County	71
2911	Dudley and Halesowen LJA	Magistrates	121
2085	East Lincolnshire LJA	Magistrates	116
197	Evesham	County	72
205	Grantham	County	67
220	Hereford	County	74
0762	Hereford	Crown	44
1841	Herefordshire LJA	Magistrates	119
1430	High Peak LJA	Magistrates	114
236	Kettering	County	76
2323	Kettering LJA	Magistrates	116
237	Kidderminster	County	71
1842	Kidderminster LJA	Magistrates	120
244	Leicester	County	77
0430	Leicester	Crown	45
2048	Leicester LJA	Magistrates	116
249	Lincoln	County	78
0432	Lincoln	Crown	46
2049	Loughborough LJA	Magistrates	117
257	Ludlow	County	82
263	Mansfield	County	83
2566	Mansfield LJA	Magistrates	114
2050	Market Bosworth LJA	Magistrates	117
268	Melton Mowbray	County	83
276	Newark	County	85
1432	North East Derbyshire and Dales LJA	Magistrates	114
2791	North Staffordshire LJA	Magistrates	120
2079	North West Lincolnshire LJA	Magistrates	117
282	Northampton	County	86
0442	Northampton	Crown	43
2325	Northampton LJA	Magistrates	117
286	Nottingham	County	86
0444	Nottingham	Crown	50
2568	Nottingham LJA	Magistrates	114
287	Nuneaton	County	86
289	Oswestry	County	87
306	Redditch	County	88

311	Rugby	County	89
2920	Sandwell LJA	Magistrates	122
322	Shrewsbury	County	90
0452	Shrewsbury	Crown	51
3278	Shrewsbury and North Shropshire LJA	Magistrates	120
324	Skegness	County	90
2916	Solihull LJA	Magistrates	122
2860	South East Staffordshire LJA	Magistrates	120
2084	South Lincolnshire LJA	Magistrates	118
1843	South Worcestershire LJA	Magistrates	120
1428	Southern Derbyshire LJA	Magistrates	114
333	Stafford	County	52
0455	Stafford	Crown	91
338	Stoke-on-Trent	County	92
0456	Stoke-on-Trent	Crown	52
339	Stourbridge	County	92
340	Stratford-upon-Avon	County	92
346	Tamworth	County	93
364	Telford	County	93
3273	Telford and South Shropshire LJA	Magistrates	121
358	Walsall	County	94
2917	Walsall and Aldridge LJA	Magistrates	122
361	Warwick	County	95
0463	Warwick	Crown	53
2904	Warwickshire LJA	Magistrates	122
363	Wellingborough	County	95
2328	Wellingborough LJA	Magistrates	118
378	Wolverhampton	County	97
0421	Wolverhampton	Crown	54
2919	Wolverhampton LJA	Magistrates	122
380	Worcester	County	97
0466	Worcester	Crown	54
382	Worksop	County	97
2569	Worksop and Retford LJA	Magistrates	114

NORTH EAST REGION

PRESIDING JUDGES
The Rt Hon. Lord Justice Gross, Senior Presiding Judge
The Hon. Mr Justice Coulson
The Hon. Mr Justice Globe

FAMILY DIVISION LIAISON JUDGE
The Hon. Mr Justice Moylan

CHANCERY SUPERVISING JUDGE
To be confirmed

CIRCUIT JUDGES

His Hon. Judge M.K. Mettyear
His Hon. Judge A.N.J. Briggs
His Hon. Judge T.W. Barber
Her Hon. Judge J. Davies
His Hon. Judge P.J. Cockroft
His Hon. Judge J.D.G. Walford
His Hon. Judge D.R. Wood
His Hon. Judge R.J. Moore
His Hon. Judge P.H. Bowers
His Hon. Judge M.J. Taylor
His Hon. Judge R. Bartfield
His Hon. Judge C.O.J. Behrens
His Hon. Judge D.P. Hunt
His Hon. Judge C.T. Walton
Her Hon. Judge J.P. Moir
His Hon. Judge M.J.A. Murphy QC
His Hon. Judge P.J.B. Armstrong
Her Hon. Judge A.C. Finnerty
Her Hon. Judge J. Shipley
Her Hon. Judge E.A. Carr QC
His Hon. Judge P.H.F. Jones
His Hon. Judge J. Spencer QC
His Hon. Judge P.C. Benson
His Hon. Judge M.G.C. Moorhouse
His Hon. Judge K.R. Keen QC
His Hon. Judge J. Dowse
His Hon. Judge S.W. Lawler QC
His Hon. Judge J.T. Milford QC
His Hon. Judge S.M. Jack
Her Hon. Judge S.E.M. Cahill QC
His Hon. Judge S.J. Ashurst
His Hon. Judge R.E. Thorn QC
His Hon. Judge G. Robinson
His Hon. Judge M.J. Evans
His Hon. Judge J.D. Durham Hall QC
His Hon. Judge R.G. Kaye QC
His Hon. Judge G.C. Marson QC
Her Hon. Judge P. Belcher
His Hon. Judge C. Prince
His Hon. Judge P.N. Collier QC

His Hon. Judge B.C. Forster QC
His Hon. Judge D. Tremberg
Her Hon. Judge R.L.M. Hallam
His Hon. Judge J.L. Rose
His Hon. Judge S.E. Wood
His Hon. Judge J.W. Richardson QC
Her Hon. Judge K. Buckingham
His Hon. Judge C. Batty
Her Hon. Judge R.S.M. Hudson
His Hon. Judge J. Goss QC
His Hon. Judge J. Potter
Her Hon. Judge G. Matthews QC
His Hon. Judge M. Gosnell
His Hon. Judge H.K. Crowson
His Hon. Judge C. Burn
His Hon. Judge R. Jenkins
His Hon. Judge P.J. Kelson QC
His Hon. Judge C.W. Heaton QC
His Hon. Judge G.A. Kearl QC
Her Hon. Judge R. Coe QC
His Hon. Judge N. Clark
His Hon. Judge S. Hickey
His Hon. Judge M. Bury
Her Hon. Judge P. Moreland
Her Hon. Judge S. Lynch
Her Hon. Judge P. Tyler
His Hon. Judge S.N. Bourne-Arton QC
His Hon. Judge P.K Sloan QC
His Hon. Judge T. Bayliss QC
His Hon. Judge D. Hatton QC
His Hon. Judge R. Jameson QC
His Hon. Judge R.M. Thomas QC
His Hon. Judge M. Raeside QC
His Hon. Judge A.M. Saffman
His Hon. Judge P. Watson QC
Her Hon. Judge N. Hillier
Her Hon. Judge J. Troy
Her Hon. Judge H. Anderson
His Hon. Judge J. Goose QC

DELIVERY DIRECTOR
Mark Swales
HMCTS, 11th Floor, Pinnacle, 67 Albion Street, Leeds LS1 5AA
Tel: 0113 251 1200
Fax: 0113 251 1247
DX: 724960 Leeds 56

COURT INDEX – NORTH EAST REGION

Court Code	Town Name	Court Type	Page No
118	Barnsley	County	62
2770	Barnsley LJA	Magistrates	126
2348	Berwick-upon-Tweed LJA	Magistrates	131
141	Bradford	County	65
0402	Bradford	Crown	40
2978	Bradford and Keighley LJA	Magistrates	128
2997	Calderdale LJA	Magistrates	128
183	Darlington	County	71
187	Doncaster	County	71
0420	Doncaster	Crown	71
2771	Doncaster LJA	Magistrates	126
190	Durham	County	72
0422	Durham	Crown	53
2353	East Yorkshire LJA	Magistrates	126
202	Gateshead	County	73
2850	Gateshead District LJA	Magistrates	131
208	Great Grimsby	County	73
0425	Great Grimsby	Crown	43
1940	Grimsby and Cleethorpes LJA	Magistrates	126
212	Halifax	County	73
214	Harrogate	County	74
2527	Harrogate LJA	Magistrates	128
215	Hartlepool	County	74
1247	Hartlepool LJA	Magistrates	124
228	Huddersfield	County	75
2987	Huddersfield LJA	Magistrates	128
1943	Hull and Holderness LJA	Magistrates	127
239	Kingston-upon-Hull	County	76
0403	Kingston-upon-Hull	Crown	44
243	Leeds	County	77
0429	Leeds	Crown	45
2992	Leeds District LJA	Magistrates	129
270	Middlesbrough	County	84
273	Morpeth and Berwick	County	84
278	Newcastle-upon-Tyne	County	85
0439	Newcastle-upon-Tyne	Crown	49
2851	Newcastle-upon-Tyne LJA	Magistrates	131
1583	North Durham LJA	Magistrates	124
1903	North Lincolnshire LJA	Magistrates	127
283	North Shields	County	85
2852	North Tyneside District LJA	Magistrates	131
2543	Northallerton and Richmond LJA	Magistrates	129
2994	Pontefract LJA	Magistrates	129
310	Rotherham	County	89
2772	Rotherham LJA	Magistrates	127
318	Scarborough	County	90
2536	Scarborough LJA	Magistrates	129
319	Scunthorpe	County	90
2537	Selby LJA	Magistrates	129
320	Sheffield	County	90
0451	Sheffield	Crown	51
2773	Sheffield LJA	Magistrates	127
325	Skipton	County	90
2538	Skipton LJA	Magistrates	129
1584	South Durham LJA	Magistrates	124

2349	South East Northumberland LJA	Magistrates	132
331	South Shields	County	91
2853	South Tyneside District LJA	Magistrates	132
343	Sunderland	County	92
2855	Sunderland LJA	Magistrates	132
0460	Teesside	Crown	53
1249	Teesside LJA	Magistrates	124
357	Wakefield	County	94
2995	Wakefield LJA	Magistrates	129
386	York	County	98
0467	York	Crown	54
2541	York LJA	Magistrates	130

NORTH WEST REGION

PRESIDING JUDGES
The Rt Hon. Lord Justice Gross, Senior Presiding Judge
The Hon. Mr Justice Holroyde
To be confirmed

VICE CHANCELLOR OF THE COUNTY PALATINE OF LANCASTER
To be confirmed

FAMILY DIVISION LIAISON JUDGE
The Hon. Mr Justice Peter Jackson

QUEEN'S BENCH LIAISON JUDGE
The Hon. Mr Justice Supperstone

CIRCUIT JUDGES

His Hon. Judge Gilbart QC
 (The Hon. Recorder of Manchester)
His Hon. Judge Goldstone QC
 (The Hon. Recorder of Liverpool)
His Hon. Judge Elgan Edwards DL
 (The Hon. Recorder of Chester)
His Hon. Judge Hegarty QC
His Hon. Judge Raynor QC
His Hon. Judge Stewart QC
His Hon. Judge Russell QC
 (The Hon. Recorder of Preston)
His Hon. Judge Hodge QC
His Hon. Judge Pelling QC
His Hon. Judge Waksman QC
His Hon. Judge Stephen Davies
His Hon. Judge Trigger
His Hon. Judge Roberts
Her Hon. Judge Daley
His Hon. Judge Allweis
His Hon. Judge Halbert
His Hon. Judge Hale
Her Hon. Judge Eaglestone
His Hon. Judge Clarke
His Hon. Judge Lakin
His Hon. Judge Barnett
His Hon. Judge Mort
His Hon. Judge Dutton
His Hon. Judge Adrian Smith
His Hon. Judge Lewis
His Hon. Judge Bloom QC
His Hon. Judge Stuart Baker
His Hon. Judge Henshell
His Hon. Judge Blake
His Hon. Judge Lyon
His Hon. Judge Hamilton
His Hon. Judge Atherton
His Hon. Judge Gilmour QC
Her Hon. Judge Kushner QC
His Hon. Judge Mark Brown
Her Hon. Judge Watson
Her Hon. Judge Badley
His Hon. Judge Dodds
Her Hon. Judge Lyon
Her Hon. Judge Gibson
Her Hon. Judge Newell
Her Hon. Judge Rawkins

Her Hon. Judge Butler
Her Hon. Judge O'Leary
His Hon. Judge Lancaster
His Hon. Judge Booth
His Hon. Judge Lever
His Hon. Judge Lowcock
Her Hon. Judge Case
His Hon. Judge Hull
His Hon. Judge Woodward
Her Hon. Judge Newton
Her Hon. Judge Roddy
His Hon. Judge Steiger TD QC
His Hon. Judge Armitage QC
His Hon. Judge Jeffrey Lewis
His Hon. Judge Knopf
His Hon. Judge Rumbelow QC
His Hon. Judge Cornwall
His Hon. Judge Byrne
His Hon. Judge Rudland
Her Hon. Judge Forrester
His Hon. Judge Appleby
His Hon. Judge Warnock
His Hon. Judge Batty QC
 (The Hon. Recorder of Carlisle)
His Hon. Judge Foster QC
His Hon. Judge Anthony Gee QC
Her Hon. Judge De Haas QC
His Hon. Judge Clayson
His Hon. Judge Hernandez
Her Hon. Judge Lunt
His Hon. Judge Fletcher
His Hon. Judge Thomas QC
His Hon. Judge Platts
Her Hon. Judge Nield
His Hon. Judge Aubrey QC
His Hon. Judge Wright
His Hon. Judge Wallwork
His Hon. Judge Woolman
His Hon. Judge Teague QC
His Hon. Judge Khokhar
His Hon. Judge Morrow QC
His Hon. Judge Everett
Her Hon. Judge Coppel
His Hon. Judge Hughes QC
Her Hon. Judge Lloyd
His Hon. Judge Knowles QC

His Hon. Judge Stockdale QC
Her Hon. Judge Penna
His Hon. Judge Gore QC
His Hon. Judge Leeming QC
His Hon. Judge Altham
His Hon. Judge Bird
His Hon. Judge Wood QC
Her Hon. Judge Singleton QC

His Hon. Judge Michael Leeming
His Hon. Judge Davies
His Hon. Judge Watson QC
His Hon. Judge Filed QC
His Hon. Judge Greene
His Hon. Judge Stead
His Hon. Judge Hatton
His Hon. Judge Mansell QC

DELIVERY DIRECTOR
Gill Hague
Manchester Civil Justice Centre, PO Box 4237, 1 Bridge Street West, Manchester M60 1TE
Tel: 0161 240 5800
Fax: 0161 240 5846
DX: 724780 MANCHESTER 44

HEAD OF CRIME
Paul McGladrigan
Manchester Civil Justice Centre, PO Box 4237, 1 Bridge Street West, Manchester M60 1TE
Tel: 0161 240 5913
DX: 724780 MANCHESTER 44

HEAD OF CIVIL, FAMILY & TRIBUNALS
Simon Vowles
Manchester Civil Justice Centre, PO Box 4237, 1 Bridge Street West, Manchester M60 1TE
Tel: 0161 240 5901
DX: 724780 MANCHESTER 44

ACTING HEAD OF REGIONAL SUPPORT UNIT
Lorraine Edgar
Manchester Civil Justice Centre, PO Box 4237, 1 Bridge Street West, Manchester M60 1TE
Tel: 0161 240 5908
DX: 724780 MANCHESTER 44

CLUSTER MANAGERS
Greater Manchester Civil, Family & Tribunals
Sue Curran, Manchester Civil Justice Centre, 1 Bridge Street West, Manchester M60 1TE
Tel: 0161 240 5404
DX: 724780 MANCHESTER 44
Greater Manchester Crime
Clare Beech, Manchester & Salford Magistrates' Court, 3rd Floor, Crown Square, Manchester M60 1PR
Tel: 0161 830 4244
DX: 745170 MANCHESTER 75
Lancashire
Lesley Handford, Preston Combined Court, Openshaw Place, Ringway, Preston PR1 2LL
Tel: 01772 844888
DX: 702660 PRESTON 5
Cumbria
Steve Harris, South Cumbria Magistrates' Court, Abbey Road, Barrow-in-Furness LA14 5QX
Tel: 01229 820161
DX: 65210 BARROW-IN-FURNESS 2
Cheshire & Merseyside Civil, Family & Tribunals
Shirley Brown, Liverpool Civil & Family Courts, 35 Vernon Street, Liverpool L2 2BX
Tel: 0151 296 2401
DX: 702600 LIVERPOOL 5
Cheshire & Merseyside Crime
Sarah Gebbie, Queen Elizabeth II Law Courts, Derby Square, Liverpool L2 1XA
Tel: 0151 471 1077
DX: 740880 LIVERPOOL 22

COURT INDEX – NORTH WEST REGION

Court Code	Town Name	Court Type	Page No
103	Accrington	County	61
106	Altrincham	County	61
120	Barrow-in-Furness	County	62
0751	Barrow-in-Furness	Crown	39
126	Birkenhead	County	63
130	Blackburn	County	64
131	Blackpool	County	64
137	Bolton	County	65
0470	Bolton	Crown	40
1731	Bolton LJA	Magistrates	140
154	Burnley	County	66
0409	Burnley	Crown	40
2014	Burnley, Pendle and Rossendale LJA	Magistrates	136
156	Bury	County	67
1724	Bury and Rochdale LJA	Magistrates	140
165	Carlisle	County	68
0412	Carlisle	Crown	41
170	Chester	County	69
0415	Chester	Crown	42
1998	Chorley LJA	Magistrates	136
3340	Community Justice Centre, North Liverpool	Magistrates	133
181	Crewe	County	70
1725	East Lancashire LJA	Magistrates	136
1398	Furness and District LJA	Magistrates	137
1992	Fylde Coast LJA	Magistrates	137
	Greater Manchester Public Law Family Proceedings Courts and Manchester City LJA Private Law Family Proceedings Courts	Magistrates	140
1177	Halton LJA	Magistrates	133
235	Kendal	County	76
0767	Knutsford	Crown	45
242	Lancaster	County	77
0768	Lancaster	Crown	45
2002	Lancaster LJA	Magistrates	137
251	Liverpool	County	78
0433	Liverpool	Crown	46
5730	Liverpool and Knowsley LJA	Magistrates	133
260	Macclesfield	County	82
1178	Macclesfield LJA	Magistrates	133
262	Manchester	County	83
1723	Manchester and Salford LJA	Magistrates	140
0435	Manchester (Crown Square)	Crown	48
0436	Manchester (Minshull Street)	Crown	48
1722	North Cheshire	Magistrates	134
1727	North Cumbria LJA	Magistrates	137
288	Oldham	County	86
1734	Oldham LJA	Magistrates	141
2003	Ormskirk LJA	Magistrates	137
292	Penrith	County	87
303	Preston	County	88
0448	Preston	Crown	51
2005	Preston LJA	Magistrates	138
315	St Helens	County	89
2268	St Helens LJA	Magistrates	134
1187	South Cheshire LJA	Magistrates	134

1323	South Lakeland LJA	Magistrates	138
2007	South Ribble LJA	Magistrates	138
336	Stockport	County	92
1739	Stockport LJA	Magistrates	141
112	Tameside	County	91
174	Tameside LJA	Magistrates	141
1742	Trafford LJA	Magistrates	141
360	Warrington	County	95
0462	Warrington	Crown	53
1180	Warrington LJA	Magistrates	134
1729	West Cheshire LJA	Magistrates	134
1726	West Cumbria LJA	Magistrates	138
373	West Cumbria (formerly Whitehaven)	County	96
374	Wigan	County	96
1749	Wigan and Leigh LJA	Magistrates	141
2271	Wirral LJA	Magistrates	135

SOUTH EAST REGION

PRESIDING JUDGES
The Hon. Mr Justice Nicol
The Hon. Mr Justice Sweeney
The Hon. Mr Justice Singh
The Hon. Mr Justice Spencer

FAMILY DIVISION LIAISON JUDGE
The Hon. Mrs Justice Pauffley
The Hon. Mrs Justice Parker
The Hon. Mrs Justice Theis

CHANCERY SUPERVISING JUDGE
The Right Hon. Sir Terence Michael Elkan Barnet Etherton

CIRCUIT JUDGES

Her Hon. Judge Ackner	His Hon. Judge Moloney QC
His Hon. Judge Addison	Her Hon. Judge A. Morris
His Hon. Judge Anthony	His Hon. Judge Peter Moss
His Hon. Judge Ball QC	Her Hon. Judge Mowat
His Hon. Judge Bate	His Hon. Judge Niblett
His Hon. Judge Jonathan Black	His Hon. Judge O'Mahony
His Hon. Judge Bridge	His Hon. Judge Overbury
His Hon. Judge Bright QC	His Hon. Judge Owen-Jones
His Hon. Judge Carey	His Hon. Judge Parkes
His Hon. Judge Carroll	His Hon. Judge Plumstead
Her Hon. Judge Catterson	His Hon. Judge Reddihough
His Hon. Judge Coleman	His Hon. Judge Rennie
His Hon. Judge Critchlow	His Hon. Judge Risius
His Hon. Judge Curl	His Hon. Judge Peter Ross
Her Hon. Judge Cutts	His Hon. Judge John Rylance
His Hon. Judge Davies	His Hon. Judge Scott-Gall
His Hon. Judge Devaux	Her Hon. Judge Zoe Smith
His Hon. Judge Eccles QC	His Hon. Judge St John-Stevens
His Hon. Judge Enright	His Hon. Judge Statman
His Hon. Judge Farrell	His Hon. Judge Stewart
His Hon. Judge Richard Foster	His Hon. Judge Tain
His Hon. Judge Goldstaub QC	His Hon. Judge Turner QC
His Hon. Judge Goodin	His Hon. Judge Van Der Bijl
His Hon. Judge Graham	Her Hon. Judge Walden-Smith
His Hon. Judge Grainger	His Hon. Judge Warner
His Hon. Judge Gratwicke	Her Hon. Judge A. Williams
His Hon. Judge Griffith	His Hon. Judge Wood
His Hon. Judge Griffith-Jones QC	His Hon. Judge Wood QC
His Hon. Judge Gullick	**COUNTY COURT**
His Hon. Judge Hawkesworth	His Hon. Judge Arthur
His Hon. Judge Jonathan Haworth	His Hon. Judge Caddick
His Hon. Judge Hayward	Her Hon. Judge Cameron
His Hon. Judge J. Holt	Her Hon. Judge Coates
His Hon. Judge S. Holt	His Hon. Judge Coltart
His Hon. Judge James	His Hon. Judge Corrie
His Hon. Judge John	His Hon. Judge Everall QC
His Hon. Judge Joy	His Hon. Judge Greene
His Hon. Judge Kay QC	Her Hon. Judge Hammerton
His Hon. Judge Kemp	His Hon. Charles Harris QC
His Hon. Judge Lawson QC	Her Hon. Judge Joanne Harris
His Hon. Judge Lodge	His Hon. Judge Horowitz QC
His Hon. Judge Macdonald QC	His Hon. Judge Michael Hughes
His Hon. Judge Madge	His Hon. Judge Lochrane
Her Hon. Judge Matthews QC	Her Hon. Judge Ludlow
Her Hon. Judge Mensah	His Hon. Judge McIntyre

His Hon. Judge Murdoch QC
Her Hon. Judge Murfitt
His Hon. Judge Nathan
His Hon. Judge Newton
His Hon. Judge O'Brien
Her Hon. Judge Plumstead
His Hon. Judge Polden
Her Hon. Judge Reaside
His Hon. Judge Jeremy Richards

His Hon. Judge John Rylance
His Hon. Judge Scarratt
His Hon. Judge Serota QC
His Hon. Judge Simpkiss
Her Hon. Judge Staite
Her Hon. Judge Waddicor
His Hon. Judge Wright
His Hon. Judge Yelton

DELIVERY DIRECTOR
Chris Jennings
5th Floor, Fox Court, 14 Grays Inn Road, London WC1X 8HN
Tel: 020 3206 0688

COURT INDEX – SOUTH EAST REGION

Court Code	Town Name	Court Type	Page No
111	Ashford	County	62
113	Aylesbury	County	62
0401	Aylesbury	Crown	39
114	Banbury	County	62
153	Basildon	County	62
0461	Basildon	Crown	39
124	Bedford	County	63
1051	Bedford and Mid Bedfordshire LJA	Magistrates	143
1920	Berkshire LJA	Magistrates	153
150	Brighton	County	66
1921	Buckinghamshire LJA	Magistrates	153
157	Bury St Edmunds	County	67
0754	Bury St Edmunds	Crown	40
162	Cambridge	County	68
0410	Cambridge	Crown	41
163	Canterbury	County	68
0479	Canterbury	Crown	41
1960	Central Kent LJA	Magistrates	147
167	Chelmsford	County	69
0414	Chelmsford	Crown	42
172	Chichester	County	69
0416	Chichester	Crown	42
176	Colchester	County	70
184	Dartford	County	71
1957	East Kent LJA	Magistrates	147
191	Eastbourne	County	72
196	Epsom	County	72
211	Guildford	County	73
0474	Guildford	Crown	43
213	Harlow	County	74
216	Hastings	County	74
1879	Hatfield	Magistrates	143
218	Haywards Heath	County	74
221	Hertford	County	75
223	High Wycombe	County	75
225	Hitchin	County	75
227	Horsham	County	75
229	Huntingdon	County	75
1168	Huntingdonshire LJA	Magistrates	145
233	Ipswich	County	76
0426	Ipswich	Crown	44

238	King's Lynn	County	76
0765	King's Lynn	Crown	44
247	Lewes	County	77
0431	Lewes	Crown	45
256	Lowestoft	County	82
258	Luton	County	82
0476	Luton	Crown	48
1055	Luton and South Bedfordshire LJA	Magistrates	143
261	Maidstone	County	82
0434	Maidstone	Crown	48
267	Medway	County	83
388	Milton Keynes	County	84
277	Newbury	County	85
1972	Norfolk LJA	Magistrates	149
1911	North and East Hertfordshire LJA	Magistrates	144
	North Cambridgeshire LJA	Magistrates	145
1970	North Essex LJA	Magistrates	145
2863	North East Suffolk LJA	Magistrates	149
1966	North Kent LJA (Dartford and Medway)	Magistrates	147
2849	North Surrey LJA	Magistrates	151
285	Norwich	County	86
0443	Norwich	Crown	50
291	Oxford	County	87
0445	Oxford	Crown	50
1922	Oxfordshire LJA	Magistrates	154
294	Peterborough	County	87
0473	Peterborough	Crown	50
305	Reading	County	88
0449	Reading	Crown	51
307	Reigate	County	88
313	St Albans	County	89
0450	St Albans	Crown	51
327	Slough	County	91
	South Cambridgeshire LJA	Magistrates	146
1971	South Essex LJA	Magistrates	146
2866	South East Suffolk LJA	Magistrates	149
2856	South East Surrey LJA	Magistrates	151
2848	South West Surrey LJA	Magistrates	151
329	Southend	County	91
0772	Southend	Crown	52
334	Staines	County	92
2950	Sussex (Central) LJA	Magistrates	151
2948	Sussex (Eastern) LJA	Magistrates	152
2947	Sussex (Northern) LJA	Magistrates	152
2949	Sussex (Western) LJA	Magistrates	152
348	Thanet	County	94
355	Tunbridge Wells	County	94
362	Watford	County	95
1910	West and Central Hertfordshire LJA	Magistrates	144
2867	West Suffolk LJA	Magistrates	150
838	Worthing	County	97

SOUTH WEST REGION

PRESIDING JUDGES
The Rt Hon. Lord Justice Gross, Senior Presiding Judge
The Hon. Mr Justice Burnett

FAMILY DIVISION LIAISON JUDGE
The Hon. Mr Justice Baker

CHANCERY SUPERVISING JUDGE
The Hon. Mr Justice Morgan

CIRCUIT JUDGES

Her Hon. Judge C.M.A. Hagen
His Hon. Judge G.H. Jones
His Hon. Judge G.W.A. Cottle
His Hon. Judge J.S. Wiggs
His Hon. Judge A. Rutherford DL
His Hon. Judge John Neligan
His Hon. Judge Richard Price
His Hon. Judge K.C. Cutler CBE
His Hon. Judge P. Darlow
His Hon. Judge R. Bond
His Hon. Judge P.R. Barclay
His Hon. Judge D.K. Ticehurst
His Hon. Judge M.W. Roach
His Hon. Judge Lord Meston QC
His Hon. Judge J.R. Jarvis
His Hon. Judge D.I.H. Tyzack QC
His Hon. Judge M.K. Harington
His Hon. Judge A.M. Havelock-Allan QC
His Hon. Judge F. Gilbert QC
His Hon. Judge N. Vincent
His Hon. Judge I. Hughes QC
His Hon. Judge A.D. Hope
His Hon. Judge J. Tabor QC
His Hon. Judge G. Boney QC
His Hon. Judge R. Hetherington
His Hon. Judge J.M. Harrow
His Hon. Judge P. Wassall
His Hon. Judge A.J. Barnett
His Hon. Judge J.W. Dixon
His Hon. Judge P. Lambert

His Hon. Judge I. Pearson
His Hon. Judge R. Bromilow
His Hon. Judge C. Harvey-Clark QC
Her Hon. Judge Miranda Robertshaw
His Hon. Judge N. Marston
His Hon. Judge M. Picton
His Hon. Judge D. Field
Her Hon. Judge Black
Her Hon. Judge Marshall
His Hon. Judge Ralls QC
His Hon. Judge Hart
His Hon. Judge Horton
His Hon. Judge McCahill QC
His Hon. Judge Longman
His Hon. Judge Wildblood QC
His Hon. Judge Ambrose
His Hon. Judge Burrell QC
His Hon. Judge Henry
His Hon. Judge Denyer QC
Her Hon. Judge Sullivan QC
His Hon. Judge Ford QC
Her Hon. Judge J. Miller QC
His Hon. Judge Salomonsen
His Hon. Judge P. Johnson
Her Hon. Judge S. Munro QC
Her Hon. Judge S. Evans QC
His Hon. Judge Mark V. Horton
His Hounour Geoffrey Mercer QC
His Hon. Andrew Levey
His Hon. Barry Cotter QC

DELIVERY DIRECTOR
Sandra Aston
HMCTS, Queensway House, The Hedges, St George's, Weston-super-Mare BS22 7BB
Tel: 01934 528668
Fax: 01934 528520
DX: 152360 WESTONSUPERMARE 5
Email: sandra.aston@hmcts.gsi.gov.uk

HEAD OF CRIME
Andrea Torode
Tel: 07881 501322
Email: andrea.torode1@hmcts.gsi.gov.uk

HEAD OF CIVIL, FAMILY AND TRIBUNALS
Rachel Hunt
Tel: 01722 345213
Email: rachel.hunt1@hmcts.gsi.gov.uk

CLUSTER MANAGERS
Avon, Somerset and Gloucestershire
To be confirmed
Devon, Cornwall and Dorset
Anna Munday
Tel: 01752 675443
Email: anna.munday5@hmcts.gsi.gov.uk
Wiltshire, Hampshire and Isle of Wight
Paula Bray
Tel: 02392 857932
Email: paula.bray1@hmcts.gsi.gov.uk

COURT INDEX – SOUTH WEST REGION

328	Southampton	County	91
0454	Southampton	Crown	51
1775	Southampton LJA	Magistrates	160
345	Swindon	County	91
0458	Swindon	Crown	52
347	Taunton	County	93
0459	Taunton	Crown	53
352	Torquay and Newton Abbot	County	94
354	Truro	County	94
0477	Truro	Crown	53
1523	West Dorset LJA	Magistrates	158
370	Weston-super-Mare	County	96
371	Weymouth	County	96
3021 (7021)	Wiltshire (Youth)	Magistrates	160
376	Winchester	County	97
0465	Winchester	Crown	53
385	Yeovil	County	98

HMCTS WALES

PRESIDING JUDGES
The Hon. Mr Justice John Griffith-Williams
The Hon. Mr Justice Wyn Williams

FAMILY DIVISION LIAISON JUDGE
The Hon. Mr Justice Philip Moor

CHANCERY SUPERVISING JUDGE
The Hon. Mr Justice Morgan

ADMINISTRATIVE COURT SUPERVISING JUDGE
The Hon. Mr Justice Hickinbottom

CIRCUIT JUDGES

His Hon. Judge Neil Bidder QC
His Hon. Judge Andrew Keyser QC
His Hon. Judge John Curran
His Hon. Judge Patrick Curran QC
His Hon. Judge Huw Davies QC
His Hon. Judge Mark Furness
His Hon. Judge William Gaskell
His Hon. Judge Peter Heywood
His Hon. Judge Stephen Hopkins QC
His Hon. Judge Dafydd Hughes
His Hon. Judge Merfyn Hughes QC
His Hon. Judge Philip Hughes
His Hon. Judge Milwyn Jarman QC
His Hon. Judge Terry John
His Hon. Judge Gareth Jones

His Hon. Judge Seys Llewellyn QC
His Hon. Judge Daniel Williams
Her Hon. Judge Helen Mifflin
His Hon. Judge David Wynn Morgan
His Hon. Judge Grenville Perry
Her Hon. Judge Isabel Parry
His Hon. Judge Niclas Parry
Her Hon. Judge Eleri Rees
His Hon. Judge Phillip Richards
His Hon. Judge Rhys Rowlands
His Hon. Judge Keith G. Thomas
His Hon. Judge Paul Thomas QC
His Hon. Judge Richard Twomlow
His Hon. Judge Christopher Vosper QC
Her Hon. Judge Mereid Edwards

DELIVERY DIRECTOR FOR HMCTS WALES
Luigi Strinati
Wales Support Unit, 2nd floor, Cardiff & Vale Magistrates' Court, Fitzalan Place, Cardiff CF24 0RZ
DX 743943 Cardiff 38
Email: luigi.strinati@hmcts.gsi.gov.uk

HEAD OF CRIME FOR HMCTS WALES
Nick Albrow
Wales Support Unit, 2nd floor, Cardiff & Vale Magistrates' Court, Fitzalan Place, Cardiff CF24 0RZ
DX· 121723 CARDIFF 9
Email: nick.albrow@hmcts.gsi.gov.uk

COURT INDEX – HMCTS WALES

3253 (7253)	Ceredigion & Pembrokeshire LJA (Youth)	Magistrates	161
3062	Conwy LJA	Magistrates	164
178	Conwy and Colwyn	County	70
3061	Denbighshire LJA	Magistrates	164
0758	Dolgellau	Crown	42
3059	Flintshire LJA	Magistrates	164
3270 (7270)	Glamorgan Valleys LJA (Youth)	Magistrates	166
3211	Gwent LJA	Magistrates	166
3244	Gwynedd LJA	Magistrates	164
217	Haverfordwest	County	74
0761	Haverfordwest	Crown	44
253	Llanelli	County	78
254	Llangefni	County	78
269	Merthyr Tydfil	County	84
0437	Merthyr Tydfil	Crown	49
271	Mold	County	84
0438	Mold	Crown	49
3355	Montgomeryshire LJA	Magistrates	162
274	Neath Port Talbot	County	85
3359	Neath Port Talbot LJA	Magistrates	162
3266	Newcastle and Ogmore LJA	Magistrates	166
280	Newport (Gwent)	County	85
0441	Newport (South Wales)	Crown	49
299	Pontypridd	County	87
308	Rhyl	County	89
344	Swansea	County	91
0457	Swansea	Crown	52
3360	Swansea LJA	Magistrates	163
366	Welshpool and Newtown	County	95
0774	Welshpool	Crown	53
384	Wrexham	County	97
3058	Wrexham Maelor LJA	Magistrates	165
3238	Ynys Mon/Anglesey LJA	Magistrates	165

HMCTS Estate by Region and Cluster

London Region
Central and South (Crime)
North and West (Crime)
Family
Midlands Region
Derbyshire and Nottinghamshire
Leicestershire, Rutland, Lincolnshire and Northamptonshire
Staffordshire and West Mercia
West Midlands
North East Region
Cleveland and Durham
Humber and South Yorkshire
North and West Yorkshire
Northumbria
North West Region
Cheshire and Merseyside
Cumbria and Lancashire
Greater Manchester
South East Region
Bedfordshire and Hertfordshire
Cambridgeshire and Essex
Kent
Norfolk and Suffolk
Surrey and Sussex
Thames Valley
South West Region
Devon, Cornwall and Dorset
Avon, Somerset and Gloucestershire
Hampshire, Isle of Wight and Wiltshire
HMCTS Wales
North Wales
Mid and West Wales
South East Wales

CROWN COURTS

Note: First tier centres deal with High Court civil cases and Crown Court criminal cases and are served by High Court and circuit judges. Second and third tier centres deal only with criminal cases. Second tier centres are served by High Court and circuit judges and third tier centres only by circuit judges.

ENGLAND AND WALES

0468 ACTON
CLOSED

0401 AYLESBURY (SE)
Mrs L. Autrey, Operational Manager, County Hall, Market Square, Aylesbury, Buckinghamshire HP20 1XD
Tel: 01296 434401
Fax: 01296 435665
DX: 157430 AYLESBURY 11
Court Details
County Hall, Aylesbury
Tier 3

0750 BARNSTAPLE (SW)
Exeter Crown & County Court, Southernhay Gardens, Exeter EX1 1UH
Tel: 01392 415300 (General Enquiries); 01392 415330 (Crown Enquiries/Listing); 01392 415332 (Customer Service Officer)
Fax: 01392 415642 (General Enquiries); 01392 415644 (Crown Enquiries); 01392 415644 (Customer Service Officer)
DX: 98440 EXETER 2
Court Details
The Law Courts, Civic Centre, Barnstaple EX31 1DX
Tel: 01271 340410 (when court sitting only)
Tier 3

0751 BARROW-IN-FURNESS (NW)
Graham Ainslie, Operational Manager, Preston Combined Court Centre, The Law Courts, Openshaw Place, Ring Way, Preston PR1 2LL
Tel: 01772 844700
Fax: 01772 844759
DX: 702660 PRESTON 5
Court Details
Barrow Law Courts, Abbey Road, Barrow-in-Furness, Cumbria LA14 5QX
Tel: 01229 820161
Tier 3

0461 BASILDON (SE)
Angela Robinson, Operational Manager, Basildon Combined Court, The Gore, Basildon, Essex SS14 2BU
Tel: 01268 458000
Fax: 01268 458100
DX: 97633 BASILDON 5
Email: enquiries@basildon.crowncourt.gsi.gov.uk
Court Details
The Gore, Basildon
Tier 3

0403 BEVERLEY
CLOSED

0404 BIRMINGHAM (M)
Fiona Butler, Operational Manager, Queen Elizabeth II Law Courts, 1 Newton Street, Birmingham B4 7NA
Tel: 0121 681 3300; 3360 (Listing)
Fax: 0121 681 3370

DX: 702033 BIRMINGHAM 8
Court Details
Queen Elizabeth II Law Courts, 1 Newton Street, Birmingham
Tier 1

0405 BODMIN
CLOSED *see* TRURO

0470 BOLTON (NW)
Mr T. Anderson, Operational Manager, Bolton Combined Court Centre, The Law Courts, Blackhorse Street, Bolton BL1 1SU
Tel: 01204 392881
Fax: 01204 363204 (Crown Office)
DX: 702610 BOLTON 3
Court Details
The Law Courts, Blackhorse Street, Bolton
Tier 3

0406 BOURNEMOUTH (SW)
Bournemouth Crown and County Court, Courts of Justice, Deansleigh Road, Bournemouth BH7 7DS
Tel: 01202 502800
Fax: 01202 502801
DX: 98420 BOURNEMOUTH 4
Court Details
Courts of Justice, Deansleigh Road, Bournemouth
Tier 3

0402 BRADFORD (NE)
Simon Ellis, Operational Manager, Bradford Combined Court Centre, The Law Courts, Exchange Square, Drake Street, Bradford BD1 1JA
Tel: 01274 840274
Fax: 01274 843510
DX: 702083 BRADFORD 2
Court Details
Bradford Law Courts, Exchange Square, Drake Street, Bradford
Tier 2

0753 BRIGHTON
CLOSED *see* LEWES

0408 BRISTOL (SW)
Sharon Boreham, Operational Manager, The Law Courts, Small Street, Bristol BS1 1DA
Tel: 0117 976 3030
Fax: 0117 976 3074
DX: 78128 BRISTOL
Court Details
The Law Courts, Small Street, Bristol
Tier 1

0409 BURNLEY (NW)
Graham Ainslie, Operational Manager, Burnley Combined Court Centre, The Law Courts, Hammerton Street, Burnley, Lancashire BB11 1XD
Tel: 01282 855300
Fax: 01282 414911
DX: 724940 BURNLEY 4
Court Details
The Law Courts, Hammerton Street, Burnley
Tier 3

0754 BURY ST EDMUNDS (SE)
Julie Crosby, Delivery Manager, The Court House, 1 Russell Road, Ipswich, Suffolk IP1 2AG
Tel: 01473 228585
Fax: 01473 228560
DX: 729480 IPSWICH 19
Email: enquiries@ipswich.crowncourt.gsi.gov.uk

Court Details
Shire Hall, Bury St Edmunds, Suffolk
Tier 3

0755 CAERNARFON (WAL)
Mrs Ffion Williams, Operational Manager, The Law Courts, County Civic Centre, Mold CH7 1AE
Tel: 01352 707340
Fax: 01352 753874
DX: 702521 MOLD 2
Court Details
Caernarfon Criminal Justice Centre, Llanberis Road, Caernarfon LL55 2DF
Tier 1

0410 CAMBRIDGE (SE)
Laura Bentham, Operational Manager, 83 East Road, Cambridge CB1 1BT
Tel: 01223 488321
Fax: 01223 488333
DX: 97365 CAMBRIDGE 2
Email: enquiries@cambridge.crowncourt.gsi.gov.uk
Court Details
83 East Road, Cambridge
Tier 1

0479 CANTERBURY (SE)
Gill Casey, Delivery Manager, Canterbury Combined Court Centre, The Law Courts, Chaucer Road, Canterbury CT1 1ZA
Tel: 01227 819200
Fax: 01227 819329
DX: 99710 CANTERBURY 3
Court Details
The Law Courts, Chaucer Road, Canterbury
Tier 3

0411 CARDIFF (WAL)
Tania Pendlington, Operational Manager, The Law Courts, Cathays Park, Cardiff CF10 3PG
Tel: 029 2067 8830
Goldfax: 0870 324 0261
Email: enquiries@cardiff.crowncourt.gsi.gov.uk
DX: 99450 CARDIFF 5
Court Details
The Law Courts, Cathays Park, Cardiff
Tier 1

0412 CARLISLE (NW)
Mrs A. Robinson, Delivery Manager, Carlisle Combined Court Centre, Courts of Justice, Earl Street, Carlisle CA1 1DJ
Tel: 01228 882120
Fax: 01228 590588
DX: 65331 CARLISLE 2
Court Details
Courts of Justice, Earl Street, Carlisle
Tier 1

0756 CARMARTHEN (WAL)
Tania Pendlington, Operational Manager, The Law Courts, St Helen's Road, Swansea SA1 4PF
Tel: 01792 637000
Fax: 01792 637049
DX: 99540 SWANSEA 4
Note: *Hearings only*
Court Details
The Guildhall, Camarthen
Tier 2

0413 CENTRAL CRIMINAL COURT
see LONDON

0414 CHELMSFORD (SE)
Sue Murphy, Delivery Manager, PO Box 9, New Street, Chelmsford CM1 1EL
Tel: 01245 603000
Fax: 01245 603011 (General Office); 01245 603020 (List Office); 01245 603110 (Court Clerks)
DX: 97375 CHELMSFORD 3
Email: enquiries@chelmsford.crowncourt.gsi.gov.uk
Court Details
New Street, Chelmsford
Tier 1

0415 CHESTER (NW)
Janet Dunbar, Operational Manager, The Castle, Chester CH1 2AN
Tel: 01244 317606
Fax: 01244 350773
DX: 702527 CHESTER 5
Email: chester.listing@chester.crowncourt.gsi.gov.uk; chester.enquiries@chester.crowncourt.gsi.gov.uk
Court Details
The Castle, Chester
Tier 1

0416 CHICHESTER (SE)
Melanie Kill, Delivery Manager, Chichester Combined Court Centre, Southgate, Chichester, West Sussex PO19 1SX
Court Details
The Courthouse, Southgate, Chichester, West Sussex
Tier 3

0417 COVENTRY (M)
Laverne O'Toole, Operational Manager, Coventry Combined Court Centre, 140 Much Park Street, Coventry CV1 2SN
Tel: 0300 123 557
Fax: 024 7625 1083
DX: 701580 COVENTRY 5
Court Details
140 Much Park Street, Coventry
Tier 3

0419 DERBY (M)
Alison Irons, Operational Manager,Derby Combined Court Centre, Morledge, Derby DE1 2XE
Tel: 01332 622600
Fax: 01332 622543 (County); 01322 622540 (Crown)
DX: 724060 DERBY 21
Court Details
Derby Combined Court Centre, Morledge, Derby
Tier 3

0757 DEVIZES
CASES DEALT WITH AT SWINDON

0758 DOLGELLAU (WAL)
Operational Manager: Mrs Ffion Williams, Operational Manager, The Law Courts, County Civic Centre, Mold CH7 1AE
Tel: 01352 707340
Fax: 01352 753874
DX: 702521 MOLD 2
Court Details
The County Hall, Dolgellau, Gwynedd LL40 1AU
Tier 3

0420 DONCASTER (NE)
Crown Court, College Road, Doncaster, South Yorkshire DN1 3HS
Tel: 01302 322211
Fax: 01302 329471
DX: 703001 DONCASTER 5

Court Detail
Crown Court, College Road, Doncaster
Tier 3

0407 DORCHESTER (SW)
Dorchester Crown Court, Colliton Park, Dorchester DT1 1XJ
Tel: 01305 265867
Fax: 01305 251867
DX: 8720 DORCHESTER
Court Details
County Hall, Dorchester
Tier 2

0421 DUDLEY
CLOSED

0422 DURHAM (NE)
Carole Marshall, Operational Manager, The Law Courts, Old Elvet, Durham DH1 3HW
Tel: 0191 386 6714
Fax: 0191 383 0605
DX: 65112 DURHAM 4
Email: results@durham.crowncourt.gsi.gov.uk; listing@durham.crowncourt.gsi.gov.uk;
caseprogression@durham.crowncourt.gsi.gov.uk
Court Details
The Law Courts, Old Elvet, Durham
Tier 3

0423 EXETER (SW)
Exeter Crown & County Court, Southernhay Gardens, Exeter EX1 1UH
Tel: 01392 415300 (General Enquiries); 415330 (Crown Enquiries); 415332 (Crown Listing); 415312
(Business Support)
Fax: 01392 415644 (General Enquiries); 415644 (Crown Enquiries); 415644 (Crown Listing)
DX: 98440 EXETER 2
Email: caseprogression@exeter.crowncourt.gsi.gov.uk; enquiries@exeter.crowncourt.gsi.gov.uk;
expenses@exeter.crowncourt.gsi.gov.uk; listing@exeter.crowncourt.gsi.gov.uk;
results@exeter.crowncourt.gsi.gov.uk
Court Details
Southernhay Gardens, Exeter
Tier 1

0424 GLOUCESTER (SW)
Caroline Rees, Criminal Courts Manager, 2nd Floor, Southgate House, Southgate Street, Gloucester
GL1 1UB
Tel: 01452 420100
Fax: 01452 833557
DX: 98660 GLOUCESTER 5
Court Details
ongsmith Street, Gloucester
Tier 2

0425 GREAT GRIMSBY (NE)
Great Grimsby Combined Court Centre, Town Hall Square, Grimsby DN31 1HX
Tel: 01472 265250
Fax: 01472 265251
DX: 702007 GRIMSBY 3
Email: enquiries@grimsby.crowncourt.gsi.gov.uk (General Enquiries);
caseprogression@grimsby.crowncourt.gsi.gov.uk (Case
Progression);listing@grimsby.crowncourt.gsi.gov.uk (Listing)
Court Details
The Combined Court Centre, Town Hall Square, Grimsby
Tier 3

0474 GUILDFORD (SE)
Richard Gregg, Operational Manager, Delivery Manager, Bedford Road, Guildford, Surrey GU1 4ST
Tel: 01483 468500
Fax: 01483 579545

DX: 97862 GUILDFORD 5

Court Details
Bedford Road, Guildford
Tier 3

0761 HAVERFORDWEST (WAL)
Tania Pendlington, Operational Manager, The Law Courts, St Helen's Road, Swansea SA1 4PF
Tel: 01792 637000
Fax: 01792 637049
DX: 99540 SWANSEA 4

Court Details
Penffynnon, Hawthorn Rise, Dyfed SA61 2AX
Tier 3

0762 HEREFORD (M)
Mrs Janet Struckwick, Operational Manager, Worcester Combined Court Centre, The Shirehall,
Foregate Street, Worcester WR1 1EQ
Tel: 01905 730823
Fax: 01905 730810
DX: 721120 WORCESTER 11

Court Details
The Shirehall, Hereford
Tel: 01432 276118. Fax: 01432 274350
Tier 3

HOVE
see LEWES

0763 HUDDERSFIELD
CLOSED

0440 INNER LONDON SESSIONS HOUSE
see LONDON

0426 IPSWICH (SE)
Mr Ross Taylor, Operational Manager, The Court House, 1 Russell Road, Ipswich, Suffolk IP1 2AG
Tel: 01473 228585
Fax: 01473 228560
DX: 729480 IPSWICH 19
Email: enquiries@ipswich.crowncourt.gsi.gov.uk

Court Details
The Court House, 1 Russell Road, Ipswich
Tier 2

0475 ISLEWORTH
see LONDON

0764 KENDAL
CLOSED

0765 KING'S LYNN (SE)
Tim Room, Delivery Manager, Norwich Combined Court Centre, The Law Courts, Bishopgate,
Norwich NR3 1UR
Tel: 01603 728200
Fax: 01603 760863
DX: 97385 NORWICH 5
Email: enquiries@norwich.crowncourt.gsi.gov.uk

Court Details
The Court House, College Lane, King's Lynn, Norfolk
Tel: 01553 760847. Fax: 01553 772873
Tier 3

0403 KINGSTON-UPON-HULL (NE)
Mrs S. Booth, Court Manager, Kingston-upon-Hull Combined Court Centre, Lowgate, Hull HU1 2EZ
Tel: 01482 586161 (General Office)
Fax: 01482 588527; 621197 (Bailiffs' Office)

DX: 703010 HULL 5
Court Details
Kingston-upon-Hull Combined Court Centre, Lowgate, Hull
Tier 2

0427 KINGSTON-UPON-THAMES
see LONDON

0767 KNUTSFORD (NW)
Janet Dunbar, Operational Manager, The Castle, Chester CH1 2AN
Tel: 01244 317606
Fax: 01244 350773
DX: 702527 CHESTER 5
Email: chester.listing@chester.crowncourt.gsi.gov.uk; chester.enquiries@chester.crowncourt.gsi.gov.uk
Court Details
The Sessions House, Knutsford
Tier 3

0768 LANCASTER (NW)
Graham Ainslie, Operational Manager, Preston Combined Court Centre, The Law Courts, Openshaw
Place, Ring Way, Preston PR1 2LL
Tel: 01772 844700
Fax: 01772 844759
DX: 702660 PRESTON 5
Court Details
The Castle, Lancaster
Tel: 01524 32454
Tier 3

0429 LEEDS (NE)
Carla McKee, Court Manager, Leeds Combined Court Centre, The Court House, 1 Oxford Row,
Leeds LS1 3BG
Tel: 0113 306 2800
Fax: 0113 306 2654
DX: 703016 LEEDS 6
Email: customerenquiries@leedscrowncourt.gsi.gov.uk
Court Details
Leeds Combined Court Centre, The Court House, 1 Oxford Row, Leeds
Coverdale House, 13–15 East Parade, Leeds LS1 4BJ
Tier 1

0430 LEICESTER (M)
Adrian Palmer, Operational Manager, 90 Wellington Street, Leicester LE1 6HG
Tel: 0116 222 5800
Fax: 0116 222 5888/9
DX: 10880 LEICESTER 3
Email: enquiries@leicester.crowncourt.gsi.gov.uk
Court Details
90 Wellington Street, Leicester
Tier 2

0431 LEWES (SE)
Mrs D. Phipps, Delivery Manager, Lewes Combined Court Centre, The Law Courts, High Street,
Lewes, East Sussex BN7 1YB
Tel: 01273 480400
Fax: 01273 485269
DX: 97395 LEWES 4
Court Details
The Law Courts, High Street, Lewes
sittings also at:
Hove Court Centre, The Court House, Lansdowne Road, Hove, East Sussex BN3 3BN
Tel: 01273 229200. Fax: 01273 229229. DX: 99402 HOVE 3
Brighton Magistrates Court, Edward Street, Brighton BN2 0LG
Tel: 01273 811783. Fax: 01273 811781. DX: 153460 BRIGHTON 17
Tier 1

0432 LINCOLN (M)
Rob McGrory, Operational Manager, Lincoln Crown Court, The Castle, Castle Hill, Lincoln LN1 3GA
Tel: 01522 525222
Fax: 01522 543962
DX: 722500 LINCOLN 11
Court Details
The Castle, Castle Hill, Lincoln
Tier 1

0433 LIVERPOOL (NW)
Mrs D. McLaughlin, Operational Manager, Liverpool Crown Court, The Queen Elizabeth II Law Courts, Derby Square, Liverpool L2 1XA
Tel: 0151 473 7373
Fax: 0151 471 1000
DX: 740880 LIVERPOOL 22
Email: CustomerEnquiries@liverpool.crowncourt.gsi.gov.uk
Court Details
The Queen Elizabeth II Law Courts, Derby Square, Liverpool
Tier 1

LONDON
Phillip Golding, Cluster Manager, Central Criminal Court, Old Bailey, London EC4M 7EH
DX: 46700 OLD BAILEY

0468 ACTON
CLOSED

0428 BLACKFRIARS (LON)
(formerly Knightsbridge)
1–15 Pocock Street, London SE1 0BJ
Tel: 020 7922 5800
Fax: 0870 324 0146
DX: 400800 LAMBETH 3
Email: blackfriars.enquiries@blackfriars.crowncourt.gsi.gov.uk
Court Details
Pocock Street SE1
Tier 3

0413 CENTRAL CRIMINAL COURT (LON)
Central Criminal Court, Old Bailey, London EC4M 7EH
Tel: 020 7248 3277
Fax: 020 7192 2671; 2242 (List Office)
DX: 46700 OLD BAILEY
Email: listing@central.crowncourt.gsi.gov.uk (Listing Officer); ccc.cso@hmcts.gsi.gov.uk (Customer Service); caseprogression@central.crowncourt.gsi.gov.uk (Case Progression); results@central.crowncourt.gsi.gov.uk (Results)
Court House
Central Criminal Court, Old Bailey
Tier 2

0418 CROYDON (LON)
Croydon Crown Court, The Law Courts, Altyre Road, Croydon CR9 5AB
Tel: 020 8410 4700
Fax: 020 8781 1007
DX: 97473 CROYDON 6
Email: enquiries@croydon.crowncourt.gsi.gov.uk (Enquiries); caseprogression@croydon.crowncourt.gsi.gov.uk; listing@croydon.crowncourt.gsi.gov.uk (Listing); results@croydon.crowncourt.gsi.gov.uk (Results)
Court Details
The Law Courts, Altyre Road, Croydon
Tier 3

0468 HARROW (LON)
Harrow Crown Court, Hailsham Drive, off Headstone Drive, Harrow, Middlesex HA1 4TU
Tel: 020 8424 2294
Fax: 0870 324 0149

DX: 97335 HARROW 5
Email: listing@harrow.crowncourt.gsi.gov.uk; enquiries@harrow.crowncourt.gsi.gov.uk;
results@harrow.crowncourt.gsi.gov.uk; caseprogression@harrow.crowncourt.gsi.gov.uk;
Court Details
Harrow Crown Court, Hailsham Drive, Harrow
Tier 3

0440 INNER LONDON SESSIONS HOUSE (LON)
Sessions House, Newington Causeway, London SE1 6AZ
Tel: 020 7234 3100
Fax: 020 7234 3287
DX: 97345 SOUTHWARK 3
Email: enquiries@innerlondon.crowncourt.gsi.gov.uk
Court Details
Sessions House, Newington Causeway
Tier 3

0475 ISLEWORTH (LON)
36 Ridgeway Road, Isleworth TW7 5LP
Tel: 020 8380 4500
Fax: 0870 324 0150 (General Office); 0870 324 0152 (List Office)
DX: 97420 ISLEWORTH 1
Email: enquiries@isleworth.crowncourt.gsi.gov.uk (General Enquiries);
listing@isleworth.crowncourt.gsi.gov.uk (Listing); results@isleworth.crowncourt.gsi.gov.uk (Results)
Court Details
Ridgeway Road, Isleworth
Tier 3

0427 KINGSTON-UPON-THAMES (LON)
6–8 Penrhyn Road, Kingston-upon-Thames KT1 2BB
Tel: 020 8240 2500
Fax: 020 8240 2675
DX: 97430 KINGSTON UPON THAMES 2
Court Details
Crown Court, 6–8 Penrhyn Road, Kingston-upon-Thames
Tier 3

0428 KNIGHTSBRIDGE
see BLACKFRIARS

0464 MIDDLESEX GUILDHALL
CLOSED

0453 SNARESBROOK (LON)
Snaresbrook Crown Court, 75 Hollybush Hill, Snaresbrook, London E11 1QW
Tel: 020 8530 0000 (General Office); 020 8530 0234 (List Office)
Fax: 0870 324 0165; 0870 324 0047 (List Office)
DX: 98240 WANSTEAD 2
Email: enquiries@snaresbrook.crown court.gsi.gov.uk
Court Details
Snaresbrook Crown Court, 75 Hollybush Hill, Snaresbrook
Tier 3

0471 SOUTHWARK (LON)
1 English Grounds, (off Battlebridge Lane), Southwark, London SE1 2HU
Tel: 020 7522 7200
Fax: 020 7522 7300; 020 7407 9858 (List Office)
DX: 39913 LONDON BRIDGE SOUTH
Email: enquiries@southwark.crowncourt.gsi.gov.uk; listing@southwark.crowncourt.gsi.gov.uk
Court Details
1 English Grounds, Southwark
Tier 3

0469 WOOD GREEN (LON)
Wood Green Crown Court, Woodall House, Lordship Lane, Wood Green, London N22 5LF
Tel: 020 8826 4100

Fax: 0870 324 0160 (General); 0870 324 0159 (List Office)
DX: 130346 WOOD GREEN 3
Email: listing@woodgreen.crowncourt.gsi.gov.uk; enquiries@woodgreen.crowncourt.gsi.gov.uk
Court Details
Wood Green Crown Court, Woodall House, Lordship Lane, Wood Green
Tier 3

0472 WOOLWICH (LON)
Woolwich Crown Court, 2 Belmarsh Road, London SE28 0EY
Tel: 020 8312 7000
Fax: 020 8312 7078
DX: 117650 WOOLWICH 7
Email: listing@woolwich.crowncourt.gsi.gov.uk (Listing Office);
enquiries@woolwich.crowncourt.gsi.gov.uk (General Enquiries);
results@woolwich.crowncourt.gsi.gov.uk; caseprogression@woolwich.crowncourt.gsi.gov.uk
Court Details
Woolwich Crown Court, 2 Belmarsh Road
Tier 3

0476 LUTON (SE)
Natalie Robinson-Chatterley, Delivery Manager, Delivery Manager, Luton Crown Court, 7 George Street, Luton LU1 2AA
Tel: 01582 522000
Fax: 01582 522001; 01582 522026 (List Office)
DX: 120500 LUTON 6
Court Details
Luton Crown Court, 7 George Street, Luton LU1 2AA
Tier 2

0434 MAIDSTONE (SE)
Chris Olivares, Operational Manager, Maidstone Combined Court Centre, The Law Courts, Barker Road, Maidstone, Kent ME16 8EQ
Tel: 01622 202000
Fax: 01622 202001
DX: 130065 MAIDSTONE 7
Court Details
Law Courts, Barker Road, Maidstone
Tier 2

0435 MANCHESTER (CROWN SQUARE) (NW)
Nicki Ryan, Manchester Crown Court, Crown Square, Manchester M3 3FL
Tel: 0161 954 1800
Fax: 0161 954 1705
Customer Service: Tel: 0161 954 1702/1703. Fax: 0161 954 1706
DX: 702538 MANCHESTER 11
Email: customerservice@manchester.crowncourt.gsi.gov.uk
Court Details
Manchester Crown Court, Crown Square, Manchester M3 3FL
Tel: 0161 954 1800
Tier 1

0436 MANCHESTER (MINSHULL STREET) (NW)
Mr T. Anderson, The Crown Court at Manchester, Minshull Street, Manchester M1 3FS
Tel: 0161 954 7500; 0161 954 7601 (Customer Service)
Fax: 0161 954 7600
DX: 724860 MANCHESTER 43
Email: listing@manchesterminshullstreet.crowncourt.gsi.gov.uk (Criminal Listing);
caseprogression@manchesterminshullstreet.crowncourt.gsi.gov.uk (Case Progression);
results@manchesterminshullstreet.crowncourt.gsi.gov.uk (Post Trial/Accounts);
enquiries@manchesterminshullstreet.crowncourt.gsi.gov.uk (Court Clerks/Customer Service)
Court Details
The Crown Court at Manchester, Minshull Street, Manchester
Tier 3

0437 MERTHYR TYDFIL (WAL)
Tania Pendlington, Operational Manager, Merthyr Tydfil Combined Court Centre, The Law Courts,
Glebeland Place, Merthyr Tydfil, Mid Glamorgan CF47 8BH
Tel: 01685 727600
Fax: 01685 7227702
DX: 99582 MERTHYR TYDFIL -2
Email: merthyrtydfil.enquiries@merthyrtydfil.crowncourt.gsi.gov.uk
Court Details
The Law Courts, Glebeland Place, Merthyr Tydfil
Tier 2

MIDDLESBROUGH
see TEESSIDE

0438 MOLD (WAL)
Mrs Ffion Williams, Operational Manager, The Law Courts, County Civic Centre, Mold CH7 1AE
Tel: 01352 707340
Fax: 01352 753874
DX: 702521 MOLD 2
Court Details
The Law Courts, County Civic Centre, Mold
Tier 1

0439 NEWCASTLE-UPON-TYNE (NE)
Beverley Bowery, Operational Manager, Newcastle-upon-Tyne Combined Court Centre, The Law
Courts, Quayside, Newcastle-upon-Tyne NE1 3LA
Tel: 0191 201 2000
Fax: 0191 201 2001
DX: 65127 NEWCASTLE-UPON-TYNE 2
Email: enquiries@newcastle.crowncourt.gsi.gov.uk
Court Details
(1) The Law Courts, Quayside, Newcastle-upon-Tyne
(2) The Moot Hall, Newcastle-upon-Tyne. Tel: 0191 261 5100
Tier 1

0478 NEWPORT, ISLE OF WIGHT (SW)
Tania Baxman, Delivery Manager, Crown and County Courts, The Law Courts, Quay Street, Newport,
Isle of Wight PO30 5YT
Tel: 01983 535100
Fax: 01983 554977
DX: 98460 NEWPORT (I.O.W.) 2
Court Details
The Law Courts, Quay Street, Newport, Isle of Wight
Tier 3

0441 NEWPORT (SOUTH WALES) (WAL)
Tania Pendlington, Operational Manager, Cardiff Crown Court, The Law Courts, Cathays Park, Cardiff
CF10 3PG
Tel: 029 2067 8830
Goldfax: 0870 324 0261
DX: 99450 CARDIFF 5
Email: enquiries@cardiff.crowncourt.gsi.gov.uk
Court Details
Crown Court, Faulkner Road, Newport NP20 4PR
Tier 2

0442 NORTHAMPTON (M)
Adrian Palmer, Operational Manager, Northampton Combined Court Centre, 85/87 Lady's Lane,
Northampton NN1 3HQ
Tel: 01604 470400
Fax: 01604 632728
DX: 725380 NORTHAMPTON 21
Email: enquiries@northampton.crowncourt.gsi.gov.uk

Court Details
Combined Court Centre, 85/87 Lady's Lane, Northampton
Tier 2

0443 NORWICH (SE)

Tim Room, Crown Delivery Manager, Norwich Combined Court Centre, The Law Courts, Bishopgate, Norwich NR3 1UR
Tel: 01603 728200
Fax: 01603 760863
DX: 97385 NORWICH 5
Email: enquiries@norwich.crowncourt.gsi.gov.uk

Court Details
The Law Courts, Bishopgate, Norwich
Tier 1

0444 NOTTINGHAM (M)

Alison Irons, Operational Manager, Nottingham Crown Court, The Law Courts, 60 Canal Street, Nottingham NG1 7EL
Tel: 0115 910 3551; 3556 (Listing)
Fax: 0115 910 3599
DX: 702383 NOTTINGHAM 7

Court Details
The Law Courts, 60 Canal Street, Nottingham
Tier 1

0445 OXFORD (SE)

Patricia Hicks, Delivery Manager, Oxford Combined Court Centre, St Aldates, Oxford OX1 1TL
Tel: 01865 264200
Fax: 01865 790773 (Civil; 01865 264253 (Criminal)
DX: 96450 OXFORD 4

Court Details
The Court House, St Aldate's, Oxford
Tier 1

0473 PETERBOROUGH (SE)

Graham Jones, Delivery Manager, Peterborough Combined Court Centre, Crown Buildings, Rivergate, Peterborough PE1 1EJ
Tel: 01733 349161
Fax: 01733 557348
DX: 702302 PETERBOROUGH 8
Email: enquiries@peterborough.crowncourt.gsi.gov.uk

Court Details
Crown Buildings, Rivergate, Peterborough
Tier 3

0446 PLYMOUTH (SW)

Plymouth Combined Court Centre, The Law Courts, Armada Way, Plymouth PL1 2ER
Tel: 01752 677400; 677480 (Crown Court Office)
Fax: 01752 208292
DX: 98470 PLYMOUTH 7
Email: enquiries@plymouth.crowncourt.gsi.gov.uk

Court Details
The Law Courts, Armada Way, Plymouth
Tier 2

0447 PORTSMOUTH (SW)

Eve Miller, Operational Manager, Portsmouth Combined Court Centre, The Courts of Justice, Winston Churchill Avenue, Portsmouth PO1 2EB
Tel: 023 9289 3000
Fax: 023 9201 6859
DX: 98490 PORTSMOUTH 5

Court Details
The Courts of Justice, Winston Churchill Avenue, Portsmouth
Tel: 023 9289 3000
Tier 3

0448 PRESTON (NW)
Graham Ainslie, Operational Manager, Preston Combined Court Centre, The Law Courts, Openshaw Place, Ring Way, Preston PR1 2LL
Tel: 01772 844700
Fax: 01772 844759
DX: 702660 PRESTON 5
Court Details
The Law Courts, Openshaw Place, Ring Way, Preston
The Sessions House, Lancaster Road, Preston
Tier 1

0449 READING (SE)
Jennifer Sprott, Operational Manager, The Old Shire Hall, The Forbury, Reading RG1 3EH
Tel: 0118 967 4400
Fax: 0118 967 4444
DX: 97440 READING 5
Court Details
The Old Shire Hall, The Forbury, Reading
Tier 2

0450 ST ALBANS (SE)
Sukhdev Sondh, Delivery Manager, The Court Building, Bricket Road, St Albans, Hertfordshire AL1 3JW
Tel: 01727 753220
Fax: 01727 753221
DX: 99700 ST ALBANS 3
Court Details
The Court Building, Bricket Road, St Albans
Tier 2

0480 SALISBURY (SW)
Salisbury Combined Court Centre, The Law Courts, Wilton Road, Salisbury, SP2 7EP
Tel: 01722 345200
Fax: 01722 345201: 0114 201 5130 (Family Hearing Centre)
DX: 98500 SALISBURY 2
Court Details
The Law Courts, Wilton Road, Sailsbury
Tier 3

0451 SHEFFIELD (NE)
Sheffield Combined Court Centre, The Law Courts, 50 West Bar, Sheffield S3 8PH
Tel: 0114 281 2400
Fax: 0114 281 2425
DX: 703028 SHEFFIELD 6
Court Details
The Law Courts, 50 West Bar, Sheffield
Tier 1

0452 SHREWSBURY (M)
Karen Alexander, Operational Manager, The Shirehall, Abbey Foregate, Shrewsbury SY2 6LU
Tel: 01743 260820
Fax: 01743 244236
DX: 702022 SHREWSBURY 2
Email: dianne.marrow@hmcts.gsi.gov.uk
Court Details
The Shirehall, Abbey Foregate, Shrewsbury
Tier 2

0453 SNARESBROOK
see LONDON

0454 SOUTHAMPTON (SW)
Southampton Combined Court Centre, The Courts of Justice, London Road, Southampton SO15 2XQ
Tel: 023 8021 3200
Goldfax: 0870 761 7655

DX: 111000 SOUTHAMPTON 11
Email: southamptoncrncaseprogression@hmcts.gsi.gov.uk;
southamptoncrnenquiries@hmcts.gsi.gov.uk; southamptoncrnexpenses@hmcts.gsi.gov.uk;
southamptoncrnlisting@hmcts.gsi.gov.uk; southamptoncrnresults@hmcts.gsi.gov.uk

Court Details
The Courts of Justice, London Road, Southampton
Tier 3

0772 SOUTHEND (SE)
Jeannine North, Operational Manager, Basildon Combined Court, The Gore, Basildon, Essex SS14 2BU
Tel: 01268 458000
Fax: 01268 458100
DX: 97633 BASILDON 5
Email: enquiries@basildon.crowncourt.gsi.gov.uk

Court Details
The Court House, Victoria Avenue, Southend-on-Sea, SS2 6EG
Tel: 01268 458000. Fax: 01268 458100
Tier 3

0471 SOUTHWARK
see LONDON

0455 STAFFORD (M)
Karen Alexander, Operational Manager, Stafford Combined Court Centre, Victoria Square, Stafford ST16 2QQ
Tel: 01785 610730
Fax: 01785 246786
DX: 703190 STAFFORD 4

Court Details
Combined Court Centre, Victoria Square, Stafford
Tier 1

0456 STOKE-ON-TRENT (M)
Karen Alexander, Operational Manager, Stoke-on-Trent Combined Court Centre, Bethesda Street, Hanley, Stoke-on-Trent ST1 3BP
Tel: 01782 854000
Fax: 01782 854021
DX: 703360 HANLEY 3
Email: enquiries@stoke.crowncourt.gsi.gov.uk; caseprogression@stoke.crowncourt.gsi.gov.uk;
expenses@stoke.crowncourt.gsi.gov.uk; listing@stoke.crowncourt.gsi.gov.uk;
results@stoke.crowncourt.gsi.gov.uk

Court Details
Bethesda Street, Hanley, Stoke-on-Trent
Tier 3

0457 SWANSEA (WAL)
Tania Pendlington, Operational Manager, The Law Courts, St Helen's Road, Swansea SA1 4PF
Tel: 01792 637000
Fax: 01792 637049
DX: 99540 SWANSEA 4

Court Details
The Law Courts, St Helen's Road, Swansea SA1 4PF
The Law Courts, The Guildhall, Swansea SA1 4PE
The Guildhall, Guildhall Square, Carmarthen SA31 1P3
Penffynnon (Rackhill Terrace), Hawthorn Rise, Haverfordwest SA61 2AX
Tier 1

0458 SWINDON (SW)
Sharon Graham, Swindon Combined Court Centre, The Law Courts, Islington Street, Swindon, Wiltshire SN1 2HG
Tel: 01793 690500
Fax: 01793 690535
DX: 98430 SWINDON 5
Email: enquiries@swindon.crowncourt.gsi.gov.uk

Court Details
The Law Courts, Islington Street, Swindon
Tier 3

0459 TAUNTON (SW)
Taunton Crown Court, Shire Hall, Taunton TA1 4EU
Tel: 01823 281100
Fax: 01823 322116
DX: 98411 TAUNTON 2
Court Details
Shire Hall, Taunton
Tier 3

0460 TEESSIDE (NE)
Marie Davison, Operational Manager, Teesside Combined Court Centre, Russell Street,
Middlesbrough, Cleveland TS1 2AE
Tel: 01642 340000
Fax: 01642 340002
DX: 65152 MIDDLESBROUGH 2
Court Details
Russell Street, Middlesbrough
Tier 1

0477 TRURO (SW)
Truro Crown Court, Courts of Justice, Edward Street, Truro TR1 2PB
Tel: 01872 267420
DX: 135396 TRURO 2
Email: caseprogression@truro.crowncourt.gsi.gov.uk; enquiries@truro.crowncourt.gsi.gov.uk;
expenses@truro.crowncourt.gsi.gov.uk; listing@truro.crowncourt.gsi.gov.uk;
results@truro.crowncourt.gsi.gov.uk
Court Details
Courts of Justice, Edward Street, Truro
Tier 1

0461 WAKEFIELD
CLOSED

0773 WALSALL
CLOSED

0462 WARRINGTON (NW)
Janet Dunbar, Operational Manager, c/o The Castle, Chester CH1 2AN
Tel: 01244 317606
Fax: 01244 350773
DX: 702501 WARRINGTON 3
Email: chester.listing@chester.crowncourt.gsi.gov.uk; chester.enquiries@chester.crowncourt.gsi.gov.uk
Court Details
Legh Street, Warrington, Cheshire WA1 1UR
Tier 2

0463 WARWICK (M)
Stuart Sephton, Operational Manager, Warwickshire Justice Centre, Newbold Terrace, Leamington
Spa, Warwickshire CV32 4EL
Tel: 01926 682100
Fax: 01926 682519
DX: 701964 LEAMINGTON 7
Court Details
Warwickshire Justice Centre, Leamington Spa
Tier 1

0774 WELSHPOOL
Crown Court does not currently sit at Welshpool.

0465 WINCHESTER (SW)
Winchester Combined Court Centre, The Law Courts, Winchester SO23 9EL
Tel: 01962 814100
Gold Fax: 0870 324 0125

DX: 98520 WINCHESTER 3

Court Details
The Law Courts, Winchester
Tier 1

0421 WOLVERHAMPTON (M)
Judith Jackson, Operational Manager, Wolverhampton Combined Court Centre, Pipers Row,
Wolverhampton WV1 3LQ
Tel: 01902 481000
Fax: 01902 481001
DX: 702019 WOLVERHAMPTON 4

Court Details
Combined Court Centre, Pipers Row, Wolverhampton
Tier 2

0469 WOOD GREEN
see LONDON

0466 WORCESTER (M)
Mrs Janet Strudwick, Operational Manager, Worcester Combined Court Centre, The Shirehall,
Foregate Street, Worcester WR1 1EQ
Tel: 01905 730823
Fax: 01905 730810
DX: 721120 WORCESTER 11

Court Details
Shirehall, Foregate Street, Worcester
Tier 2

0467 YORK (NE)
Andy Conboy, Operational Manager, The Castle, York YO1 9WZ
Tel: 01904 645121
Fax: 01904 611689
DX: 65162 YORK 3
Email: york.crn.cm@hmcts.gsi.gov.uk

Court Details
The Castle, York
Tier 2

THE NORTHERN IRELAND COURTS AND TRIBUNALS SERVICE

CEO: Jacqui Durkin, Laganside House, 23–27 Oxford Street, Belfast BT1 3LA.
Tel: 028 9032 8594.
Fax: 028 9072 8942

ANTRIM
The Courthouse, 30 Castle Way, Antrim BT41 4AQ
Tel: 028 9446 2661. Fax: 028 9446 3301

Court House
The Courthouse, Castle Way, Antrim

ARMAGH
Armagh Court Office, The Courthouse, The Mall, Armagh, Co. Armagh BT61 9DJ
Tel: 028 3752 2816. Fax: 028 3752 8194

Court House
Courthouse, The Mall, Armagh

BALLYMENA
Ballymena Court Office, The Courthouse, 30 Castle Way, Antrim, Co. Antrim BT41 4AQ
Tel: 028 2564 9416. Fax: 028 2565 5371

Court House
The Courthouse, Albert Place, Ballymena

BELFAST
Crown Court Office, Laganside Courts, 45 Oxford Street, Belfast BT1 3LL
Tel: 028 9032 8594. Fax: 028 9031 3771

Court House
Laganside Courts, 45 Oxford Street, Belfast BT1 3LL

COLERAINE
Coleraine Court Office, The Courthouse, 46A Mountsandel Road, Coleraine BT52 1NY

Court House
Courthouse, Mountsandel Road, Coleraine

CRAIGAVON
Craigavon Court Office, The Courthouse, Central Way, Craigavon BT64 1AP
Tel: 028 3834 1324. Fax: 028 3834 1243

Court House
Courthouse, Central Way, Craigavon

DOWNPATRICK
Downpatrick Court Office, The Courthouse, 21 English Street, Downpatrick BT30 6AD
Tel: 028 4461 4621. Fax: 028 4461 3969

Court House
Courthouse, English Street, Downpatrick

DUNGANNON
The Courthouse, 46 Killyman Road, Dungannon BT71 6DE
Tel: 028 8772 2992. Fax: 028 8772 8169

Court House
The Courthouse, Killyman Road, Dungannon

ENNISKILLEN
Enniskillen Court Office, The Courthouse, East Bridge Street, Enniskillen BT74 7BP
Tel: 028 6632 2356. Fax: 028 6632 3636

Court House
Courthouse, East Bridge Street, Enniskillen

LONDONDERRY
Londonderry Court Office, The Courthouse, Bishop Street, Londonderry BT48 6PQ
Tel: 028 7136 3448. Fax: 028 7137 2059

Court House
Courthouse, Bishop Street, Londonderry

NEWRY

The Courthouse, 23 New Street, Newry BT35 6JD
Tel: 028 3025 2040. Fax: 028 3026 9830

Court House
The Courthouse, New Street, Newry

NEWTOWNARDS

Newtonards Court Office, The Courthouse, Regent Street, Newtownards BT23 4LP

Court House
The Courthouse, Regent Street, Newtownards

OMAGH

Omagh Court Office, The Courthouse, High Street, Omagh, Co. Tyrone BT78 1DU
Tel: 028 8224 2056. Fax: 028 8225 1198

Court House
Courthouse, High Street, Omagh

Crown Court Codes

0401	Aylesbury	0452	Shrewsbury
0402	Bedford (CLOSED)	0453	Snaresbrook
0402	Bradford	0454	Southampton
0403	Beverley (CLOSED)	0455	Stafford
0403	Kingston-upon-Hull	0456	Stoke-on-Trent
0404	Birmingham	0457	Swansea
0405	Bodmin (CLOSED)	0458	Swindon
0406	Bournemouth	0459	Taunton
0407	Bradford (CLOSED)	0460	Teesside
0407	Dorchester	0461	Wakefield (CLOSED)
0408	Bristol	0461	Basildon (wef 2/1/96)
0409	Burnley	0462	Warrington
0410	Cambridge	0463	Warwick
0411	Cardiff	0464	Middlesex Guildhall (CLOSED)
0412	Carlisle	0465	Winchester
0413	Central Criminal Court (Old Bailey)	0466	Worcester
0414	Chelmsford	0467	York
0415	Chester	0468	Acton (CLOSED)
0416	Chichester	0468	Harrow
0417	Coventry	0469	Wood Green
0418	Croydon	0470	Bolton
0419	Derby	0471	Southwark
0420	Doncaster	0472	Woolwich
0421	Dudley (CLOSED)	0473	Peterborough
0421	Wolverhampton	0474	Guildford
0422	Durham	0475	Isleworth
0423	Exeter	0476	Luton
0424	Gloucester	0477	Truro
0425	Great Grimsby	0478	Newport (I.O.W.)
0426	Ipswich	0479	Canterbury
0427	Kingston-upon-Thames	0480	Salisbury
0428	Blackfriars	0750	Barnstaple
0429	Leeds	0751	Barrow-in-Furness
0430	Leicester	0752	Birkenhead (CLOSED)
0431	Lewes	0753	Brighton (CLOSED)
0432	Lincoln	0754	Bury St Edmunds
0433	Liverpool	0755	Caernarfon
0434	Maidstone	0756	Carmarthen
0435	Manchester (Crown Square)	0757	Devizes (CLOSED)
0436	Manchester (Minshull Street)	0758	Dolgellau
0437	Merthyr Tydfil	0759	Dorchester
0438	Mold	0760	Gravesend (CLOSED)
0439	Newcastle-upon-Tyne	0761	Haverfordwest
0440	Newington Causeway (Inner LondonSessions House)	0762	Hereford
0441	Newport	0763	Huddersfield (CLOSED)
0442	Northampton	0764	Kendal (CLOSED)
0443	Norwich	0765	Kings Lynn
0444	Nottingham	0766	Kingston-upon-Hull
0445	Oxford	0767	Knutsford
0446	Plymouth	0768	Lancaster
0447	Portsmouth	0769	Luton

0448	Preston	0769	Mold
0449	Reading	0772	Southend
0450	St Albans	0773	Walsall (CLOSED)
0451	Sheffield	0774	Welshpool

Part II

County Courts

HMCTS ESTATE BY REGION AND CLUSTER

London Region
Central and South (Crime)
North and West (Crime)
Family

Midlands Region
Derbyshire and Nottinghamshire
Leicestershire, Rutland, Lincolnshire, Northamptonshire
Staffordshire and West Mercia
West Midlands

North East Region
Cleveland and Durham
Humber and South Yorkshire
North and West Yorkshire
Northumbria

North West Region
Cheshire and Merseyside
Cumbria and Lancashire
Greater Manchester

South East Region
Bedfordshire and Hertfordshire
Cambridgeshire and Essex
Kent
Norfolk and Suffolk
Surrey and Sussex Thames Valley

South West Region
Avon, Somerset and Gloucestershire
Devon, Cornwall and Dorset
Hampshire, Isle of Wight and Wiltshire

HMCTS Wales
North Wales
Mid and West Wales
South East Wales

COUNTY COURTS

101 ABERDARE
Closed wef 28/7/11

102 ABERYSTWYTH (WAL)
Caroline Bevan, Edleston House, Queens Road, Aberystwyth, Ceredigion SY23 2HP
Tel: 01970 636370 (Office); 636375 (Bailiffs)
Fax: 01970 625985
DX: 99560 ABERYSTWYTH 2
Email: enquiries@aberystwyth.countycourt.gsi.gov.uk
Court Details
Edleston House, Queens Road, Aberystwyth
District Registry; Adoption Centre; Bankruptcy; Family Hearing Centre
District Judge: W.H. Godwin

103 ACCRINGTON (NW)
Mrs J. Kelly, Delivery Manager, Bradshawgate House, 1 Oak Street, Accrington, Lancashire BB5 1EQ
Tel: 01254 237490
Fax: 01254 393869
DX: 702645 ACCRINGTON 2
Court Details
1 Oak Street, Accrington
Divorce

104 ALDERSHOT AND FARNHAM (SW)
Angela Carpenter, Operations Manager, 84–86 Victoria Road, Aldershot, Hampshire GU11 1SS
Tel: 01252 796800 (General Enquiries)
Fax: 01252 345705
DX: 98530 ALDERSHOT 2
Court Details
84–86 Victoria Road, Aldershot
Divorce
District Judge: R. James, A. King

105 ALFRETON
closed wef 16/2/96 – successor courts – Chesterfield, Derby, Mansfield and Nottingham

701 ALNWICK
closed wef 15/12/97 – successor court – Morpeth and Berwick

106 ALTRINCHAM (NW)
Patrick Ward, Delivery Manager for Altrincham and Stockport County Courts, PO Box 240, Trafford Courthouse, Ashton Lane, Sale, Cheshire M33 7WX
Tel: 0161 975 4760; 4762 (Bailiffs)
Fax: 0161 975 4761
DX: 708292 SALE 6
Court Details
Trafford Courthouse, Ashton Lane, Sale
Divorce
District Judges: J. Horan, J.R. Clegg, I. Lettall, S. Jones

107 AMERSHAM
closed wef 9/1/95 – successor courts – Aylesbury, Hemel Hempstead, High Wycombe, Slough, Uxbridge and Watford

108 AMMANFORD
closed wef 27/3/97 – successor courts – Swansea, Carmarthen and Llanelli

109 ANDOVER
closed wef 30/6/97 – successor courts – Basingstoke, Salisbury and Winchester

110   ASHBY-DE-LA-ZOUCH
closed wef 1/10/84 – successor court – Burton-on-Trent

111   ASHFORD
closed wef 7/11

112   ASHTON-UNDER-LYNE AND STALYBRIDGE
renamed TAMESIDE

702   AXMINSTER AND CHARD
closed wef 5/12/94 – successor court – Yeovil

113   AYLESBURY (SE)
Marie Madeley, Delivery Manager, Walton Street, Aylesbury, Buckinghamshire HP21 7QZ
Tel: 01296 554327
Fax: 01296 554320
DX: 97820 AYLESBURY 10
Court Details
Walton Street, Aylesbury
Bankruptcy
District Judges: N. Hickman, P. Perusko, Rand, Vincent

114   BANBURY (SE)
Faith Dixey, Acting Delivery Manager, The Courthouse, Warwick Road, Banbury, Oxfordshire OX16 2AW
Tel: 01295 452090; 452093 (Bailiffs)
Fax: 01295 452051
DX: 701967 BANBURY 2
Court Details
The Courthouse, Warwick Road, Banbury
Bankruptcy
District Judge: M. Payne, V. Gatter, R. Matthews, A. Jenkins

115   BANGOR
closed wef 4/7/94 – successor court – Caernarfon

116   BARGOED
closed wef 29/12/95 – successor court – Blackwood

117   BARNET
see LONDON

118   BARNSLEY (NE)
Miss K. Angel, Barnsley County Court, Court House, Westgate, Barnsley S70 2DW
Tel: 01226 320000
Fax: 01226 320067
DX: 702080 BARNSLEY 3
Email: enquiries@barnsley.countycourt.gsi.gov.uk
Court Details
Barnsley County Court, Barnsley
District Registry; Bankruptcy; Family Hearing Centre; Divorce
District Judges: A.M. Babbington, G.M. Corkill, M.J. Young

119   BARNSTAPLE (SW)
Mandy Squire, The Law Courts, North Walk, Civic Centre, Barnstaple, Devon EX31 1DY
Tel: 01271 340412
Fax: 01271 340415
DX: 98560 BARNSTAPLE 2
Email: hearings@barnstaple.countycourt.gsi.gov.uk; family@barnstaple.countycourt.gsi.gov.uk
Court Details
7th Floor (Civic Centre), North Walk, Barnstaple
District Registry; Bankruptcy; Divorce; Family Hearing Centre
District Judge: Mark Ball

120   BARROW-IN-FURNESS (NW)
Miss T.L.Hudson, Delivery Manager, Law Courts, Abbey Road, Barrow-in-Furness, Cumbria LA14 5QX
Tel: 01229 840370; 840380 (Bailiffs)

Fax: 01229 870278
DX: 65210 BARROW-IN-FURNESS 2

Court Details
Law Courts, Abbey Road, Barrow-in-Furness
District Registry; Bankruptcy; Divorce
District Judge: C. Dodd

---

121   BARRY
closed wef 29/12/95 – successor court – Cardiff

---

153   BASILDON (SE)
Debbie Freeman, Delivery Manager, Basildon Combined Court, The Gore, Basildon, Essex SS14 2BU
Tel: 0844 892 4000
Fax: 01268 458100
DX: 97633 BASILDON 5
Email: bailiffs@basildon.countycourt.gsi.gov.uk; e-filing@basildon.countycourt.gsi.gov.uk; helpdesk@norwich.countycourt.gsi.gov.uk; hearings@basildon.countycourt.gsi.gov.uk

Court Details
The Gore, Basildon
District Judge: J.I. Collier

---

122   BASINGSTOKE (SW)
Angela Carpenter, Operations Manager, The Court House, London Road, Basingstoke RG21 4AB
Tel: 01256 318200
Fax: 01256 318217
DX: 98570 BASINGSTOKE 3

Court Details
The Court House, London Road, Basingstoke
District Registry; Family Hearing Centre
District Judges: D. Carney, M. Cooper

---

123   BATH (SW)
T. Ashley, PO Box 4302, North Parade Road, Bath BA1 0LF
Tel: 01225 476730
Fax: 01225 476724
DX: 98580 BATH 2

Court Details
The Law Courts, North Parade Road, Bath
District Registry; Bankruptcy; Divorce; Family Hearing Centre
District Judges: F. Goddard, R. Howell

---

124   BEDFORD (SE)
Luke Fusi, Acting Delivery Manager, PO Box 1405, Bedford MK40 9DN
Tel: 0844 892 0550
Fax: 01234 319026
DX: 97590 BEDFORD 11

Court Details
Shire Hall, 3 St Paul's Square, Bedford MK40 1SQ
District Registry; Bankruptcy; Divorce; Family Hearing Centre
District Judge: P.R. Ayers

---

703   BERWICK-UPON-TWEED
closed wef 15/12/97 – successor court – Morpeth and Berwick

---

704   BEVERLEY
closed wef 1/1/93 – successor court – Kingston-upon-Hull

---

126   BIRKENHEAD (NW)
Kim Halliday, Delivery Manager, 76 Hamilton Street, Birkenhead, Merseyside CH41 5EN
Tel: 0151 666 5800
Fax: 0151 666 5873
DX: 725000 BIRKENHEAD 10
Email: family@birkenhead.countycourt.gsi.gov.uk; bailiffs@birkenhead.countycourt.gsi.gov.uk; hearings@birkenhead.countycourt.gsi.gov.uk; enquiries@birkenhead.countycourt.gsi.gov.uk; e-filing@birkenhead.countycourt.gsi.gov.uk

Court Details
76 Hamilton Street, Birkenhead
District Registry; Bankruptcy; Divorce
District Judges: M.I. Peake, P.J. O'Neill, M.A. Baker, K.E. Doyle, M.M. Campbell, A. Woodburn

127 BIRMINGHAM CIVIL JUSTICE CENTRE AND FAMILY COURTS (M)
Alison Roberts, Priory Courts, 33 Bull Street, Birmingham B4 6DS
Tel: 0121 681 4441 (Civil); 0121 250 6382 (Family)
Fax: 0121 250 6386 (Family and Assessment of Costs); 6320 (Civil); 6729 (Court of Protection); 6730 (Chancery, Technology and Construction, Mercantile, Administrative Court); 681 3082 (Enforcement, Bankruptcy)
DX: 701987 BIRMINGHAM
Court Details
33 Bull Street, Birmingham
District Registry; Extended; Chancery; Mercantile, Technology and Construction; Bankruptcy; Care Centre; Race Relations; Administrative Centre; Court of Protection; Administrative Court
District Judges: D.J. Owen, D.J. O'Regan, V. Sehdev, A. Davies, M. Asokan, R. Sheldrake, D. Maughan, D. Truman, S. Dowding, S. Bull, J. Ingram, G. Baddeley, P. Griffith, R. Musgrave, S. Gailey, R. Williams, S. Hickman

128 BISHOP AUCKLAND
closed wef 7/11 – successor courts – Darlington and Durham

129 BISHOP'S STORTFORD
closed wef 1/12/97 – successor courts – Cambridge, Harlow and Colchester

130 BLACKBURN (NW)
Mrs J. Hodgkinson, Delivery Manager, 64 Victoria Street, Blackburn, Lancashire BB1 6DJ
Tel: 01254 299840
Fax: 01254 692712
DX: 702650 BLACKBURN 4
Court Details
64 Victoria Street, Blackburn
District Registry; Bankruptcy; Care Centre; Family Hearing Centre
District Judges: A. Jones, R.H. Talbot, A. Greensmith

131 BLACKPOOL (NW)
Judith Kilgallon, Delivery Manager, Blackpool County Court, The Law Courts, Chapel Street, Blackpool, Lancashire FY1 5RJ
Tel: 01253 754020
Fax: 01253 295255
DX: 724900 BLACKPOOL 10
Court Details
The Law Courts, Chapel Street, Blackpool
District Registry; Bankruptcy; Divorce
District Judges: M.E. Buckley, R. Bryce, N. Law

132 BLACKWOOD (WAL)
Mr Huw Evans, Blackwood Civil and Family Court, 8 Hall Street, Blackwood NP12 1NY
Tel: 01495 238200
Fax: 01495 238203
DX: 99470 BLACKWOOD 2
Email: blackwood.enquiries@hmcts.gsi.gov.uk
Court Details
Civil and Family Court, 8 Hall Street, Blackwood
District Registry; Bankruptcy; Divorce
District Judges: A. Fraser, G. Sandercock

133 BLETCHLEY AND LEIGHTON BUZZARD
renamed MILTON KEYNES

134 BLOOMSBURY
see LONDON

705 BLYTH
closed wef 15/12/97 – successor court – Morpeth and Berwick

136   BODMIN (SW)
Angela May, The Law Courts, Launceston Road, Bodmin, Cornwall PL31 2AL
Tel: 01208 261580
Fax: 01208 77255
DX: 136846 BODMIN 2
Court Details
The Law Courts, Launceston Road, Bodmin
Divorce
District Judges: S. Middleton, L. Thomas

137   BOLTON (NW)
Mr S. Monaghan, Delivery Manager for Bolton and Bury County Courts, Bolton Combined Court
Centre, The Law Courts, Blackhorse Street, Bolton, Lancashire BL1 1SU
Tel: 01204 392881
Fax: 01204 373706
DX: 702610 BOLTON 3
Court Details
The Law Courts, Blackhorse Street, Bolton
District Registry; Bankruptcy; Family Hearing Centre
District Judges: J. Shaw, C.M. Swindley, C. Evans

138   BOSTON (M)
Rob McGrory, Boston County Court, 55 Norfolk Street, Boston, Lincolnshire PE21 6PE
Tel: 01205 366080 (Office); 359665 (Bailiff)
Fax: 01205 311692
DX: 701922 BOSTON 2
Court Details
Boston County Court, 55 Norfolk Street, Boston
District Registry; Bankruptcy; Divorce; Family
District Judges: R.L. Hudson, R.J. Toombs, C.J. Cooper

139   BOURNEMOUTH (SW)
Bournemouth Crown and County Courts, Courts of Justice, Deansleigh Road, Bournemouth BH7
7DS
Tel: 01202 502800
Fax: 01202 502801
DX: 98420 BOURNEMOUTH 4
Court Details
Courts of Justice, Deansleigh Road, Bournemouth
District Registry; Bankruptcy; Care Centre; Family Hearing Centre
District Judges: P. Avis, J. Hurley, D. Williams, M. Dancey, A. Willis

140   BOW
see LONDON

141   BRADFORD (NE)
Karen Hardy, Bradford Combined Court Centre, The Law Courts, Exchange Square, Drake Street,
Bradford, West Yorkshire BD1 1JA
Tel: 01274 840274
Fax: 01274 840275(Civil Listing); 843510 (Criminal Listing); 843541(Case Progression)
DX: 702083 BRADFORD 2
Court Details
The Law Courts, Exchange Square, Drake Street, Bradford
District Registry; Bankruptcy; Family Hearing Centre
District Judges: G.J. Edwards, N. Hickinbottom

142   BRAINTREE
closed wef 1/12/97 – successor courts Chelmsford, Harlow and Colchester

143   BRECKNOCK (WAL)
Mark Lewis, Brecon Law Courts, Cambrian Way, Brecon, Powys LD3 7HR
Tel: 01874 622993
Fax: 01874 622441
DX: 124340 BRECON 2

Court Details
Brecon Law Courts, Cambrian Way, Brecon
District Registry; Divorce
District Judge: J. Lloyd Davies

144   BRENTFORD
see LONDON

145   BRENTWOOD
transferred to BASILDON wef 29/12/95

146   BRIDGEND (WAL)
Mark Lewis, Bridgend Law Courts, Sunnyside, Bridgend CF31 4AJ
Tel: 01656 673833
Fax: 01656 647124
DX: 99750 BRIDGEND 2

Court Details
Bridgend Law Courts, Sunnyside, Bridgend
District Registry; Bankruptcy; Divorce
District Judge: D.H. Morgan

147   BRIDGNORTH
closed wef 1/10/84 – successor court – Wellington

148   BRIDGWATER
closed wef 20/12/99 – successor court – Taunton

149   BRIDLINGTON
closed wef 24/12/97 – successor court – Scarborough

150   BRIGHTON (SE)
Barry Sutton, Delivery Manager, William Street, Brighton BN2 0RF
Tel: 01273 674421
Fax: 01273 602138
DX: 98070 BRIGHTON 3
Family Section and Care Centre: Mr L. Wales, Court Manager, Brighton Family Centre, 1 Edward
Street, Brighton BN2 2JD
Tel: 01273 811333
Fax: 01273 607638
DX: 142600 BRIGHTON 12

Court Details
William Street, Brighton
District Registry; Bankruptcy; Care Centre
District Judges: J. Merrick, M. Fawcett, P. Gamba, D. Pollard

151   BRISTOL (SW)
Helen Andrews, Operations Manager, Bristol Civil Justice Centre, 2 Redcliff Street, Bristol BS1 6GR
Tel: 0117 366 4800
Fax: 0117 366 4801; 0117 366 4802 (Family)
DX: 95903 BRISTOL 3
Email: enquiries@bristol.countycourt.gsi.gov.uk; e-filing@bristol.countycourt.gsi.gov.uk;
hearings@bristol.countycourt.gsi.gov.uk; family@bristol.countycourt.gsi.gov.uk;
bailiffs@bristol.countycourt.gsi.gov.uk; bristolchancerylisting@hmcts.gsi.gov.uk;
bristolmercantilelisting@hmcts.gsi.gov.uk; bristoltcclisting@hmcts.gsi.gov.uk

Court Details
Bristol Civil Justice Centre
**District Registry; Extended; Chancery; Administrative; Admiralty; Bankruptcy; Care Centre;
Family Hearing Centre; Mercantile Court; Patent Court (Trademarks Act 1994 only); Race
Relations; Dissolution of Civil Partnerships (Regional Court of Protection Hearing Venue);
Forced Marriage Protection Orders**
District Judges: J.A. Exton, L. Rowe, B.J. Watson, R.J. Britton, R. Howell, M. Watkins

152   BROMLEY
see LONDON

154   BURNLEY (NW)
Mrs J. Kelly, Delivery Manager, Burnley Combined Court Centre, The Law Courts, Hammerton Street,
Burnley, Lancashire BB11 1XD

Tel: 01282 855300
Fax: 01282 414911
DX: 724940 BURNLEY 4
Email: enquiries@burnley.countycourt.gsi.gov.uk
Court Details
The Law Courts, Hammmerton Street, Burnley
District Registry; Bankruptcy; Divorce
District Judges: C. Bury, T. Greensmith, D. McQueen

155   BURTON-UPON-TRENT (M)
closed wef 2013

156   BURY (NW)
Mr S. Monaghan, Delivery Manager for Bolton and Bury County Courts, The Courthouse, Tenters Street, Bury, Lancashire BL9 0HX
Tel: 0161 447 8699
Fax: 0161 763 4995
DX: 702615 BURY 2
Email: family@burycountycourt.gsi.gov.uk; bailiffs@burycountycourt.gsi.gov.uk;
e-filings@burycountycourt.gsi.gov.uk; enquiries@burycountycourt.gsi.gov.uk;
hearings@burycountycourt.gsi.gov.uk
Court Details
The Courthouse, Tenters Street, Bury
District Registry; Divorce; Insolvency
District Judges: S. Turner

157   BURY ST EDMUNDS (SE)
Graham Brewster, Delivery Manager (Interim), Triton House (Entrance B), St Andrew's Street North, Bury St Edmunds, Suffolk IP33 1TR
Tel: 0844 892 4000
Fax: 01284 702687
DX: 97640 BURY ST EDMUNDS 3
Email: e-filing@burystedmunds.countycourt.gsi.gov.uk;
family@burystedmunds.countycourt.gsi.gov.uk; hearings@burystedmunds.countycourt.gsi.gov.uk;
bailiffs@burystedmunds.countycourt.gsi.gov.uk; helpdesk@norwich.countycourt.gsi.gov.uk
Court Details
Triton House (Entrance F), St Andrew's Street North, Bury St Edmunds
District Registry; Insolvency; Divorce; Family Hearing Centre
District Judges: J. Kirby, G. Pearl, D. Hallett

158   BUXTON (M)
Judy Calderwood, Combined Court Centre, Morledge, Derby DE1 2XE
Tel: 01332 622600
Fax: 01332 622543
DX: 724060 DERBY 21
Note: This building is used only for occasional hearings. Please direct all correspondence to Derby County Court.
Court Details
Court House, Peak Buildings, Terrace Road, Buxton SK17 6DY. Tel: 01298 23951. Fax: 01298 26031
District Judges: A. G. Stark, M. Davies

159   CAERNARFON (WAL)
Lesley Hyde, Court House, Llanberis Road, Caernarfon, Gwynedd LL55 2DF
Tel: 01286 684600
Fax: 01286 678965
DX: 702483 CAERNARFON 2
Email: family@caernarfon.countycourt.gsi.gov.uk; hearings@caernarfon.countycourt.gsi.gov.uk;
e-filing@caernarfon.countycourt.gsi.gov.uk; enquiries@caernarfon.countycourt.gsi.gov.uk;
bailiffs@caernarfon.countycourt.gsi.gov.uk
Court Details
Court House, Llanberis Road, Caernarfon
District Registry; Bankruptcy; Care Centre; Family Hearing Centre
District Judges: J.G. Thomas, O.W. Williams, M. Jones-Evans

160   CAERPHILLY
closed wef 1/12/00 – successor courts – Cardiff, Blackwood

161   CAMBORNE AND REDRUTH
closed wef 24/12/98 – successor court – Penzance

162   CAMBRIDGE (SE)
Tracey Williams, Delivery Manager, 197 East Road, Cambridge CB1 1BA
Tel: 0844 892 4000
Fax: 01223 224590
DX: 97650 CAMBRIDGE 3
Email: helpdesk@norwich.countycourt.gsi.gov.uk
Court Details
197 East Road, Cambridge
District Registry; Care Centre; Family Hearing Centre; Insolvency; Race Relations; Trial Centre
District Judges: J.L.C. Kirby, P.H. Pelly, J. Taylor, G. Pearl, G. Parnell

163   CANTERBURY (SE)
Sam Doyle, Delivery Manager, Canterbury Combined Court Centre, Law Courts, Chaucer Road,
Canterbury, Kent CT1 1ZA
Tel: 01227 819200
Fax: 01227 819283
DX: 99710 CANTERBURY 3
Court Details
Law Courts, Chaucer Road, Canterbury
District Registry; Bankruptcy; Care Centre; Family Hearing Centre; Race Relations; Trial Centre
District Judges: N.E. Jackson, W. Jackson, S. Sullivan, L. Burgess, S. Gill

164   CARDIFF CIVIL JUSTICE CENTRE (WAL)
Mark Lewis, Cardiff Civil Justice Centre, 2 Park Street, Cardiff CF10 1ET
Tel: 029 2037 6400
Fax: 029 2037 6475
DX: 99500 CARDIFF 6
Email: family@cardiff.countycourt.gsi.gov.uk; bailiffs@cardiff.countycourt.gsi.gov.uk;
hearings@cardiff.countycourt.gsi.gov.uk; enquiries@cardiff.countycourt.gsi.gov.uk;
e-filing@cardiff.countycourt.gsi.gov.uk; cardiffdfjwork@hmcts.gsi.gov.uk (designated family judges);
cardiffcjcskeletons@hmcts.gsi.gov.uk; administrativecourtoffice.cardiff@hmcts.x.gsi.gov.uk;
administrativecourtofficecardiff.skeletonarguments@hmcts.x.gsi.gov.uk
Court Details
2 Park Street, Cardiff
**District Registry; Extended; Chancery; Administrative Court; Bankruptcy; Care Centre; Family
Hearing Centre; Mercantile Court; Technology and Construction Court; Adoption Centre**
District Judges: A.T. North, G.H.F. Carson, J.E. Regan, C.R. Dawson, T.M. Phillips, H.D. James

707   CARDIGAN
closed wef 29/12/95 – successor court – Carmarthen

165   CARLISLE (NW)
Mrs A. Robinson, Delivery Manager, Carlisle Combined Court Centre, Courts of Justice, Earl Street,
Carlisle CA1 1DJ
Tel: 01228 882140
Fax: 01228 590588
DX: 65331 CARLISLE 2
Court Details
Courts of Justice, Earl Street, Carlisle
**District Registry; Bankruptcy, Care Centre, Race Relations, Trial Centre, Adoption Centre,
Unified Family Administration**
District Judges: J. Park, S. Smith, C. Dodds

166   CARMARTHEN (WAL)
Caroline Bevan, Carmarthen Civil, Family, Tribunals & Probate Hearing Centre, Hill House, Picton
Terrace, Carmarthen SA31 3BS
Tel: 01267 228010
Fax: 01267 221844
DX: 99570 CARMARTHEN 2

Court Details
Guildhall, Carmarthen
District Registry; Bankruptcy; Divorce; Family Hearing Centre
District Judge: J.L. Davies

CENTRAL LONDON
see LONDON

CHARD
see AXMINSTER AND CHARD

CHATHAM
see MEDWAY

---

167   CHELMSFORD (SE)
Renuka Perera, Delivery Manager, Priory Place, New London Road, Chelmsford, Essex CM2 0PP
Tel: 0844 892 4000
Fax: 01245 295395
DX: 97660 CHELMSFORD 4
Email: enquiries@chelmsford.countycourt.gsi.gov.uk; family@chelmsford.countycourt.gsi.gov.uk;
helpdesk@norwich.countycourt.gsi.gov.uk
Court Details
Priory Place, New London Road, Chelmsford
District Registry; Bankruptcy; Care Centre
District Judges: E. Silverwood-Cope, W. F. Shanks, G. Parnell, N. Parfitt

---

168   CHELTENHAM
closed wef 30/6/11

---

169   CHEPSTOW
closed wef 1/4/02 – successor court – Newport (Gwent)

---

170   CHESTER (NW)
Pamela Akins, Delivery Manager, Trident House, Little St John Street, Chester CH1 1SN
Tel: 01244 404200; 404222 (Bailiffs)
Fax: 01244 404300
DX: 702460 CHESTER 4
Email: enquiries@chester.countycourt.gsi.gov.uk
Court Details
Trident House, Little St John Street, Chester
District Registry; Bankruptcy; Care Centre; Civil Trial Centre; Divorce; Adoption Centre; Family Hearing Centre
District Judges: C.W.F. Newman, H. Smart, I. Sanderson

---

171   CHESTERFIELD (M)
Judy Calderwood, St Mary's Gate, Chesterfield, Derbyshire S41 7TD
Tel: 01246 501200; 501201 (Bailiffs)
Fax: 01246 501205
DX: 703160 CHESTERFIELD 3
Court Details
St Mary's Gate, Chesterfield
District Registry; Bankruptcy; Divorce
District Judges: A.G. Stark, M. Wall, M. Davies, I. Lloyd Jones

---

172   CHICHESTER (SE)
Claire Hampshire, Delivery Manager, Chichester Combined Court Centre, Southgate, Chichester, West Sussex PO19 1SX
Tel: 01243 520700
Fax: 01243 533756
DX: 97460 CHICHESTER 2
Court Details
The Courthouse, Southgate, Chichester
Jays House, St Martin's Street, Chichester
District Registry; Family Hearing Centre
District Judge: S. Levinson

---

173   CHIPPENHAM
(closed wef 1/5/96 – successor courts – Swindon and Trowbridge)

353   CHIPPENHAM AND TROWBRIDGE (SW)
Jane Daniels, Business Manager, Chippenham Law Courts, Pewsham Way, Chippenham, Wiltshire SN15 3BF
Tel: 01249 463473
Fax: 01249 466246
DX: 744850 CHIPPENHAM 5
Email: enquiries@trowbridge.countycourt.gsi.gov.uk
Court Details
Chippenham Law Courts, Pewsham Way, Chippenham
(*Note:* **new divorce applications for Wiltshire are handled by Salisbury County Court wef 1/8/13**)
District Judges: D. Asplin, N. Brookes

174   CHORLEY
closed wef 9/9/11

CIRENCESTER
see SWINDON

CLERKENWELL
see LONDON

176   COLCHESTER (SE)
Renuka Perera, Delivery Manager, Falkland House, 25 Southway, Colchester, Essex CO3 3EG
Tel: 0844 892 4000
Fax: 01206 717250
DX: 97670 COLCHESTER 3
Email: helpdesk@norwich.countycourt.gsi.gov.uk
Court Details
Falkland House, 25 Southway, Colchester
Trial Centre: Norfolk House, 23 Southway, Colchester
District Registry; Bankruptcy; Family Hearing Centre; Trial Centre
District Judges: C.B. Molle, S.R. Mitchell

COLWYN BAY
see CONWY AND COLWYN

177   CONSETT
closed wef 7/11 – successor courts– Durham and Gateshead

178   CONWY AND COLWYN
closed wef 30/6/10 – administration relocated to Rhyl
County Court – hearings held at Llandudno Magistrates' Court

179   CORBY
closed wef 1/3/99 – successor courts – Kettering and Peterborough

180   COVENTRY (M)
David Biggs, Coventry Combined Court Centre, 140 Much Park Street, Coventry CV1 2SN
Tel: 0300 123 5577
Fax: 024 7652 0443
DX: 701580 COVENTRY 5
Court Details
140 Much Park Street, Coventry
District Registry; Bankruptcy; Care Centre
District Judges: T.C. Cotterill, T.R. Ridgway, P.A. Kesterton, A.S. Jones, P. Sanghera, T. Lynch

181   CREWE (NW)
Julie Burgess, Delivery Manager for Crewe and Macclesfield County Courts, The Law Courts, Civic Centre, Crewe, Cheshire CW1 2DP
Tel: 01270 539300
Fax: 01270 216344
DX: 702504 CREWE 2

Court Details
The Law Courts, Civic Centre, Crewe
District Registry; Bankruptcy; Family; Divorce Centre
District Judges: R. Pates, A. Wallace

182   CROYDON
see LONDON

183   DARLINGTON (NE)
Karen Telfer, 4 Coniscliffe Road, Darlington, County Durham DL3 7RL
Tel: 01325 463224
Fax: 01325 362829
DX: 65109 DARLINGTON 2

Court Details
4 Coniscliffe Road, Darlington
District Registry; Bankruptcy; Family Hearing Centre
District Judges: J. Mainwaring-Taylor, P. Cuthbertson, C.A. Arkless, D. Robertson

184   DARTFORD (SE)
Claire Styles, Delivery Manager, Court House, Home Gardens, Dartford, Kent DA1 1DX:
Tel: 01322 627600
Fax: 01322 270902
DX: 98090 DARTFORD 2

Court Details
Court House, Home Gardens, Dartford
Divorce; Family Hearing Centre
District Judges: P.J. Glover, A. Smith, N. Greenfield

185   DERBY (M)
Judy Calderwood, Derby Combined Court Centre, Morledge, Derby DE1 2XE
Tel: 01332 622600
Fax: 01332 622543
DX: 724060 DERBY 21

Court Details
Combined Court Centre, Morledge, Derby
District Registry; Bankruptcy; Care Centre
District Judges: D. Douce, S. Williscroft, A.G. Stark, M. Davies

DEVIZES
see TROWBRIDGE

186   DEWSBURY
closed wef 4/12

187   DONCASTER (NE)
Mr Gary Boulton, 74 Waterdale, Doncaster, South Yorkshire DN1 3BT
Tel: 01302 381730
Fax: 01302 768090
DX: 702089 DONCASTER 4

Court Details
74 Waterdale, Doncaster
District Registry; Bankruptcy; Family Hearing Centre
District Judges: S. Rodgers, P. Thompson

DORCHESTER
see WEYMOUTH

188   DOVER
closed wef 30/3/96 – successor court – Canterbury

189   DUDLEY (M)
Sharon Studholme, 7 Hagley Road, Stourbridge, West Midlands DY8 1QL
Tel: 01384 394232
Fax: 01384 441736
DX: 701889 STOURBRIDGE 2

Court Details
The Inhedge, Dudley, West Midlands DY1 1RY
District Registry; Bankruptcy; Divorce; Family Hearing Centre
District Judges: R. Jabbar, R. Lumb

190   DURHAM (NE)

Kay Graham, Civil and Family Justice Centre, Green Lane, Old Elvet, Durham DH1 3RG
Tel: 0191 375 1840
Fax: 0191 375 1844
DX: 65115 DURHAM 5

Court Details
Civil and Family Justice Centre, Green Lane, Old Elvet
District Registry; Bankruptcy; Family Hearing Centre
District Judges: P.W.J. Traynor, N.W. Goudie, D. Lascelles, D. Robertson

191   EASTBOURNE (SE)

Claire Hampshire, Delivery Manager, The Law Courts, Old Orchard Road, Eastbourne, East Sussex
BN21 4UN
Tel: 01323 727518
Fax: 01323 649372
DX: 98110 EASTBOURNE 2

Court Details
The Law Courts, Eastbourne
District Registry; Bankruptcy; Divorce
District Judge: J.T. Robinson

192   EAST GRINSTEAD
closed wef 4/1/94 – successor courts – Haywards Heath and Tunbridge Wells

194   EDMONTON
see LONDON

195   ELLESMERE PORT
closed wef 5/12/94 – successor court – Chester

196   EPSOM
closed wef 7/11

197   EVESHAM
closed wef 30/9/11 – successor court – Worcester

198   EXETER (SW)

Mandy Squire, Exeter Crown and County Court, Southernhay Gardens, Exeter, Devon EX1 1UH
Tel: 01392 415300 (General Enquiries); 415326 (Civil Listing DJ); 415354 (Civil Listing CJ); 415320
(Family); 415312 (Customer Service Officer)
Fax: 01392 415642 (General Enquiries); 415645 (Civil Listing CJ); 415642 (Customer Service Officer)
DX: 98440 EXETER 2
Email: family@exeter.countycourt.gsi.gov.uk; bailiffs@exeter.countycourt.gsi.gov.uk;
hearings@exeter.countycourt.gsi.gov.uk; enquiries@exeter.countycourt.gsi.gov.uk;
e-filing@exeter.countycourt.gsi.gov.uk

Court Details
Southernhay Gardens, Exeter
District Registry; Bankruptcy; Family Hearing Centre; Race Relations; Care Centre
District Judges: S.A. Arnold, P. Waterworth, M. Ball, J. Collins

FARNHAM
see ALDERSHOT AND FARNHAM

199   FOLKESTONE
closed wef 30/3/96 – successor court – Ashford

FROME
see TROWBRIDGE

201   GAINSBOROUGH
closed wef 1/1/93 – successor court – Lincoln

202   GATESHEAD (NE)
Gateshead Law Courts, Warwick Street, Gateshead, Tyne & Wear NE8 1DT
Tel: 0191 477 5821
DX: 742120 GATESHEAD 6
Court Details
Gateshead Law Courts, Warwick Street
Divorce
District Judges: R. Howard, P. Pescod, P. Kramer

203   GLOUCESTER AND CHELTENHAM (SW)
Caroline Rees, Family and Civil Courts, County Court Offices, Kimbrose Way, Gloucester GL1 2DE
Tel: 01452 834900
Fax: 01452 834923
DX: 98660 GLOUCESTER 5
Email: enquiries@gloucester.countycourt.gsi.gov.uk
Court Details
Kimbrose Way, Gloucester
District Registry; Bankruptcy; Family Hearing Centre
District Judges: A.B. Thomas, P. Singleton, D. Hebblethwaite

204   GOOLE
closed wef 4/11/96 – successor court – Doncaster

205   GRANTHAM
closed wef 9/11

206   GRAVESEND
closed wef 31/12/10

207   GRAYS THURROCK
closed wef 31/1/2000 – successor court – Basildon

208   GREAT GRIMSBY (NE)
Great Grimsby Combined Court Centre, Town Hall Square, Grimsby, Lincolnshire DN31 1HX
Tel: 01472 265200
Fax: 01472 265201
DX: 702007 GRIMSBY 3
Email: family@grimsby.countycourt.gsi.gov.uk; bailiffs@grimsby.countycourt.gsi.gov.uk;
enquiries@grimsby.countycourt.gsi.gov.uk
Court Details
The Combined Court Centre, Town Hall Square, Grimsby
District Registry; Bankruptcy; Divorce; Family Hearing Centre
District Judges: C. Gamwell, S.J. Richardson, L. Mcilwaine

209   GREAT MALVERN
closed wef 1/1/93 – successor court – Worcester

210   GREAT YARMOUTH
closed wef 31/1/2000 – successor court – Lowestoft, Norwich

GRIMSBY
see GREAT GRIMSBY

211   GUILDFORD (SE)
Mrs A. Wright, The Law Courts, Mary Road, Guildford, Surrey GU1 4PS
Tel: 01483 405300
Fax: 01483 300031
DX: 97860 GUILDFORD 5
Court Details
The Law Courts, Mary Road, Guildford
District Registry; Adoption Centre; Bankruptcy; Care Centre
District Judges: H.A.J. Letts, D. Beck, I. Kubiak, L. George, V. Trigg, L. Nightingale

212   HALIFAX (NE)
Alan Wraithmell, Prescott Street, Halifax, West Yorkshire HX1 2JJ
Tel: 01422 344700 (General Office); 369936 (Bailiffs)
Fax: 01422 360132
DX: 702095 HALIFAX 2

Court Details
Prescott Street, Halifax
District Registry; Bankruptcy; Family Hearing Centre
District Judge: P. Troy

HANLEY
see STOKE-ON-TRENT

---

213   HARLOW
closed wef 31/3/11

---

214   HARROGATE (NE)
Janet Smith, 2 Victoria Avenue, Harrogate, North Yorkshire HG1 1EL
Tel: 01423 503921; 527732 (Bailiffs)
Fax: 01423 528679
DX: 702098 HARROGATE 3
Email: enquiries@harrogate.countycourt.gsi.gov.uk; e-filing@harrogate.countycourt.gsi.gov.uk
Court Details
2 Victoria Avenue, Harrogate
District Registry; Bankruptcy; Family Hearing Centre
District Judges: Helen Wood

---

215   HARTLEPOOL (NE)
Law Courts, Victoria Road, Hartlepool TS24 8BS
Tel: 01429 268198
Fax: 01429 862550
DX: 65121 HARTLEPOOL 2
Court Details
Law Courts, Victoria Road, Hartlepool
District Registry; Divorce
District Judges: D.M. Robertson, P. Traynor

---

216   HASTINGS (SE)
Claire Hampshire, Delivery Manager, Law Courts, Horntye Park, Bohemia Road, Hastings, East
Sussex TN34 1QX
Tel: 01424 710280; 710290 (Listing); 710296 (Bailiffs)
Fax: 01424 421585
DX: 98150 HASTINGS 2
Court Details
Law Courts, Horntye Park, Bohemia Road, Hastings
District Registry; Bankruptcy; Divorce
District Judge: S. Hammond

---

217   HAVERFORDWEST (WAL)
Caroline Bevan, Penffynnon, Hawthorn Rise, Haverfordwest, Pembrokeshire SA61 2AX
Tel: 01437 772060; 772076 (Bailiffs)
Fax: 01437 769222
DX: 99610 HAVERFORDWEST 2
Email: enquiries@haverfordwest.countycourt.gsi.gov.uk; family@haverfordwest.countycourt.gsi.gov.uk;
bailiffs@haverfordwest.countycourt.gsi.gov.uk; hearings@haverfordwest.countycourt.gsi.gov.uk;
e-filing@haverfordwest.countycourt.gsi.gov.uk
Court Details
Penffynnon, Hawthorn Rise, Haverfordwest
District Registry; Bankruptcy; Family Hearing Centre
District Judge: W.H. Godwin

---

218   HAYWARDS HEATH
closed wef 7/11

---

219   HEMEL HEMPSTEAD
closed wef 24/12/98 – successor courts – Aylesbury, Luton and Watford

---

220   HEREFORD (M)
Mrs S. Mower, First Floor, Barclays Bank Chambers, 1/3 Broad Street, Hereford HR4 9BA
Tel: 01432 357233/264118
Fax: 01432 352593
DX: 701904 HEREFORD 2

Court Details
The Shirehall, Hereford
District Registry; Bankruptcy; Divorce
District Judges: P.R. Mackenzie, M. Parry, N. Khan

221   HERTFORD (SE)
Linda O'Connor, Delivery Manager, PO Box 373, Hertford SG13 9HT
Tel: 0844 892 0550
Fax: 01992 556535
DX: 97710 HERTFORD 2

Court Details
Shire Hall, Fore Street, Hertford SG14 1BY
Bankruptcy; Divorce
District Judge: D.M. Eynon

713   HEXHAM
closed wef 4/1/94 – successor court – Newcastle-upon-Tyne

223   HIGH WYCOMBE (SE)
Richard Keel, Delivery Manager, High Wycombe Back Office, Reading County Court, 160–163 Friar Street, Reading RG1 1HE
Tel: 0118 987 0508; 01494 651038 (Bailiffs)
Fax: 01494 651030
DX: 98010 READING 6

Court Details
The Law Courts, Easton Street, High Wycombe HP11 1LR
District Judges: S. Jones, T. Parker, K. McCulloch, P. Devlin

224   HINCKLEY
closed wef 1/10/84 – successor court – Nuneaton

225   HITCHIN
closed wef 1/7/11

226   HOLYWELL
closed wef 7/9/98 – successor courts – Rhyl and Chester

227   HORSHAM (SE)
Carol Farndale, The Law Courts, Hurst Road, Horsham, Sussex RH12 2EU
Tel: 01403 252474
Fax: 01403 258844
DX: 98170 HORSHAM 2

Court Details
The Law Courts, Hurst Road, Horsham
Divorce
District Judge: A. Taylor

228   HUDDERSFIELD (NE)
Shameem Ali-Chapman, County Court, Queensgate House, Queensgate, Huddersfield HD1 2RR
Tel: 01484 421043; 535085
Fax: 01484 426366
DX: 703013 HUDDERSFIELD 2
Email: family@huddersfield.countycourt.gsi.gov.uk; bailiffs@huddersfield.countycourt.gsi.gov.uk; hearings@huddersfield.countycourt.gsi.gov.uk; enquiries@huddersfield.countycourt.gsi.gov.uk; e-filing@huddersfield.countycourt.gsi.gov.uk

Court Details
County Court, Queensgate House, Queensgate, Huddersfield
District Registry; Bankruptcy; Family Hearing Centre
District Judges: S. Heels, H. Wood

HULL
see KINGSTON-UPON-HULL

229   HUNTINGDON
closed wef 31/3/11

230   HYDE
closed wef 31/1/87 – successor court – Tameside

231   ILFORD,
see LONDON

232   ILKESTON
closed wef 16/2/96 – successor courts – Derby and Nottingham

233   IPSWICH (SE)
Graham Brewster, Delivery Manager (Interim), 8 Arcade Street, Ipswich, Suffolk IP1 1EJ
Tel: 0844 892 4000
Fax: 01473 251797
DX: 97730 IPSWICH 3
Email: helpdesk@norwich.countycourt.gsi.gov.uk
Court Details
8 Arcade Street, Ipswich
District Registry; Bankruptcy; Care Centre
District Judges: Patrick Bazley White, Ian Evans, D. Hallett

234   KEIGHLEY
closed wef 4/12

235   KENDAL (NW)
Delivery Manager, Carlisle Combined Court Centre, Courts of Justice, Earl Street, Carlisle CA1 1DJ
Tel: 01228 882140
Fax: 01228 590588
DX: 65331 CARLISLE 2
Note: Court open Wednesdays and Fridays only. All correspondence to Lancaster County Court.
Court Details
The Court House, County Court, Burneside Road, Kendal LA9 4NF
District Registry; Bankruptcy; Divorce
District Judges: C. Dodd

236   KETTERING (M)
Martin Hirst, Dryland Street, Kettering, Northamtonshire NN16 0BH
Tel: 01536 512471
Fax: 01536 416857
DX: 701886 KETTERING 2
Court Details
Dryland Street, Kettering
District Judges: P. McHale, S. Watson, I. Murdoch

237   KIDDERMINSTER
closed wef 30/3/9/11 – successor court – Worcester

238   KING'S LYNN (SE)
Carl Poole (interim), Chequer House, 12 King Street, King's Lynn, Norfolk PE30 1ES
Tel: 0844 892 4000
Fax: 01553 769824
DX: 97740 KING'S LYNN 2
Email: helpdesk@norwich.countycourt.gsi.gov.uk
Court Details
Chequer House, 12 King Street, King's Lynn
District Registry; Bankruptcy; Divorce; Family Hearing Centre
District Judge: B.J. Rutland

239   KINGSTON-UPON-HULL (NE)
Mrs S. Booth, Kingston-upon-Hull Combined Court Centre, Lowgate, Hull HU1 2EZ
Tel: 01482 586161
Fax: 01482 588527 (General Office); 621197 (Bailiffs' Office)
DX: 703010 HULL 5
Court Details
Kingston-upon-Hull Combined Court Centre, Lowgate, Hull
District Registry; Bankruptcy; Care Centre; Divorce
District Judges: I.L. Buxton, I.P. Besford, S. Richardson

240   KINGSTON-UPON-THAMES
see LONDON

241   LAMBETH
see LONDON

714   LAMPETER
closed wef 5/12/94 – successor courts – Aberystwyth and Camarthen

242   LANCASTER (NW)
Helen Hynes, Delivery Manager for Kendal and Lancaster County Courts, 2nd Floor, Mitre House, Church Street, Lancaster LA1 1UZ
Tel: 01524 68112
Fax: 01524 846478
DX: 145880 LANCASTER 2
Court Details
County Court, 2nd Floor, Mitre House, Church Street, Lancaster
District Registry; Adoption Centre; Bankruptcy; Care Centre; Trial Centre; Unified Family Administration
District Judges: R. Forrester, M. Bland

715   LAUNCESTON
closed wef 5/12/95 – successor court – Bodmin

243   LEEDS (NE)
Fiona Quirk, Leeds Combined Court Centre, The Courthouse, 1 Oxford Row, Leeds LS1 3BG
Tel: 0113 306 2800
DX: 703016 LEEDS 6
Court Details
Leeds Combined Court Centre, The Court House, 1 Oxford Row, Leeds
Coverdale House, 13–15 East Parade, Leeds LS1 4BJ
District Registry; Extended; Chancery; Bankruptcy; Care Centre; Race Relations; Mercantile; Administrative Court
District Judges: P.G. Giles, R. Jordan, M. Glentworth, G. Lord, I. Fairwood, J. Flanagan, G. Reed, K. Woodhead, J.D. Neaves, P. Troy

244   LEICESTER (M)
Martin Hirst, 90 Wellington Street, Leicester LE1 6HG
Tel: 0116 222 5700
Fax: 0116 222 5763
DX: 17401 LEICESTER 3
Court Details
The Court House, 90 Wellington Street, Leicester
District Registry; Bankruptcy; Care Centre
District Judges: R. Hoadley, G. Reed, R. Severn, V. Stamenkovich, P. Atkinson, P. McHale

245   LEIGH
closed wef 2010 – successor court – Wigan. For Glazebury and Culcheth – Warrington

LEIGHTON BUZZARD
see BLETCHLEY AND LEIGHTON BUZZARD

246   LEOMINSTER
closed wef 1/10/84 – successor court – Hereford

247   LEWES (SE)
Anne Wright, Lewes Combined Court Centre, The Law Courts, High Street, Lewes, East Sussex BN7 1YB
Tel: 01273 480400
Fax: 01273 485270
DX: 97395 LEWES 4
Email: enquiries@lewes.countycourt.gsi.gov.uk
Court Details
Law Courts, High Street, Lewes
District Judge: To be confirmed

248   LICHFIELD
closed wef 3/7/00 – successor courts – Burton upon Trent, Stafford, Tamworth, Walsall

249   LINCOLN (M)
Rob McGrory, Lincoln County Court, 360 High Street, Lincoln LN5 7PS
Tel: 01522 551500
Fax: 01522 551551
DX: 703231 LINCOLN 6
Email: bailiffs@lincoln.countycourt.gsi.gov.uk; e-filing@lincoln.countycourt.gsi.gov.uk;
enquiries@lincoln.countycourt.gsi.gov.uk; family@lincoln.countycourt.gsi.gov.uk;
hearings@lincoln.countycourt.gsi.gov.uk
Court Details
360 High Street, Lincoln
District Registry; Adoption Centre; Bankruptcy; Care Centre; Civil Trial Centre; Family Hearing Centre
District Judges: A. Maw, R. Hudson, R. Toombs, C. Cooper

LISKEARD
see BODMIN

251   LIVERPOOL CIVIL JUSTICE CENTRE (NW)
Mr T. Allman, Liverpool Civil and Family Courts, 35 Vernon Street, Liverpool L2 2BX
Tel: 0151 296 2200; 2444 (Diary Manager CJ Listing); 2440 (DJ Listing); 2546 (Family Listing); 2472 (Enforcements and Assessments); 2251 (Family Business Manager)
Fax: 0151 296 2201
DX: 702600 LIVERPOOL 5
Court Details
35 Vernon Street, Liverpool
District Registry; Extended; Chancery; Admiralty; Adoption Centre; Bankruptcy; Care Centre; Civil Trial Centre; Family Hearing Centre; Divorce
District Judges: E. Johnson, J. Heyworth, S. Wright, J. Clark, L. Sykes, J. Henthorn, J. Coffey, P. O'Neil, M. Baker, N. Harrison, U.A. Woodburn, A.M. Bever, H. Conway, L.D. Jenkinson

143   LLANDRINDOD WELLS
closed wef 29/12/95 – successor court – Brecknock

253   LLANELLI (WAL)
Caroline Bevan, 2nd Floor, Court Buildings, Town Hall Square, Llanelli, Carmarthenshire SA15 3AL
Tel: 01554 757171
Fax: 01554 758079
DX: 99510 LLANELLI 2
Email: bailiffs@llanelli.countycourt.gsi.gov.uk; enquiries@llanelli.countycourt.gsi.gov.uk;
family@llanelli.countycourt.gsi.gov.uk; hearings@llanelli.countycourt.gsi.gov.uk;
e-filing@llanelli.countycourt.gsi.gov.uk
Court Details
2nd Floor, Court Buildings, Town Hall Square, Llanelli
Divorce
District Judges: T.J. Lewis, M.I. Taylor

254   LLANGEFNI (WAL)
Lesley Hyde, County Court Buildings, Glanhwfa Road, Llangefni, Anglesey LL77 7EN
Tel: 01248 750225
Fax: 01248 750778
DX: 702480 LLANGEFNI 2
Email: family@llangefni.countycourt.gsi.gov.uk; hearing@llangefni.countycourt.gsi.gov.uk;
enquiries@llangefni.countycourt.gsi.gov.uk; bailiffs@llangefni.countycourt.gsi.gov.uk
Court Details
County Court Buildings, Llangefni
District Registry; Bankruptcy; Family Hearing Centre
District Judges: O.W. Williams, J.G. Thomas, M. Jones-Evans

LONDON

117   BARNET (LON)
St Mary's Court, Regents Park Road, Finchley Central, London N3 1BQ
Tel: 020 8343 4272; 020 8371 7111 (family)
Fax: 020 8343 1324
DX: 122570 FINCHLEY (CHURCH END)

Email: bailiffs@barnet.countcourt.gsi.gov.uk; e-filing@barnet.countycourt.gsi.gov.uk;
enquiries@barnet.countycourt.gsi.gov.uk; family@barnet.countycourt.gsi.gov.uk;
hearings@barnet.countycourt.gsi.gov.uk

Court Details
St Mary's Court, Regents Park Road, Finchley Central
Family Hearing Centre
District Judges: M. Marin, H. Johns

134 BLOOMSBURY
combined with Westminster County Court to form Central London County Court – wef 14/8/92

140 BOW (LON)
96 Romford Road, Stratford, London E15 4EG
Tel: 020 8536 5200
Fax: 0870 324 0188
DX: 97490 STRATFORD (LONDON) 2
Email: civil@bow.countycourt.gsi.gov.uk; family@bow.countycourt.gsi.gov.uk

Court Details
96 Romford Road, Stratford
Family Hearing Centre
District Judges: C. Vokes, D. Stone, P. Dixon, N. Reeves, S. Davis, R. Clarke

144 BRENTFORD (LON)
Alexandra Road, High Street, Brentford, Middlesex TW8 0JJ
Tel: 020 8231 8940
Fax: 020 8568 2401
DX: 97840 BRENTFORD 2
Email: enquiries@brentford.countycourt.gsi.gov.uk; e-filing@brentford.countycourt.gsi.gov.uk;
bailiffs@brentford.countycourt.gsi.gov.uk; hearings@brentford.countycourt.gsi.gov.uk;
family@brentford.countycourt.gsi.gov.uk

Court Details
Alexandra Road, High Street, Brentford
Family Hearing Centre
District Judges: T. Jenkins; A. Nisa, J. Willans

152 BROMLEY (LON)
Court House, College Road, Bromley, Kent BR1 3PX
Tel: 020 8290 9620 (Main Switchboard)
Fax: 0870 761 7689
DX: 98080 BROMLEY 2
Email: enquiries@bromley.countycourt.gsi.gov.uk; e-filing@bromley.countycourt.gsi.gov.uk;
family@bromley.countycourt.gsi.gov.uk

Court Details
Court House, College Road, Bromley
Family Hearing Centre
District Judges: T. Brett, J. Wilkinson, A. Thomas, P. Brooks, S. Burn

372 CENTRAL LONDON (LON)
13–14 Park Crescent, London W1B 1HT
Tel: 020 7917 5000 (Switchboard)
Fax: 020 7917 5014
DX: 97325 REGENTS PARK 2
Email: bailiffs@centrallondon.countycourt.gsi.gov.uk; e-filing@centrallondon.countycourt.gsi.gov.uk;
enquiries@centrallondon.countycourt.gsi.gov.uk; hearings@centrallondon.countycourt.gsi.gov.uk;
djtelhearing.centrallondon@hmcts.gsi.gov.uk

Court Details
Central London Civil Justice Centre, 26 Park Crescent, London W1N 4HT. Fax: 020 7917 7940
Race Relations; Sex Discrimination; The Chancery List; Technology and Construction Court
District Judges: I. Avent, M. Langley, R. Fine, G. Jackson, B. Lightman, K. Price, H. Silverman

321 CLERKENWELL AND SHOREDITCH (LON)
The Gee Street Courthouse, 29–41 Gee Street, London EC1V 3RE
Tel: 020 7250 7200
Fax: 0870 761 7688
DX: 121000 SHOREDITCH 2

Email: bailiffs@clerkenwellandshoreditch.countycourt.gsi.gov.uk;
e-filing@clerkenwellandshoreditch.countycourt.gsi.gov.uk;
enquiries@clerkenwellandshoreditch.countycourt.gsi.gov.uk;
family@clerkenwellandshoreditch.countycourt.gsi.gov.uk;
hearings@clerkenwellandshoreditch.countycourt.gsi.gov.uk;
telephone.hearings@clerkenwellandshoreditch.countycourt.gsi.gov.uk
Court Details
29–41 Gee Street
Family Hearing Centre
District Judges: L. Sterlini, S. Cooper, H. Manners, S. Alderson

182   CROYDON (LON)
Croydon Civil and Family Court Centre, The Law Courts, Altyre Road, Croydon CR9 5AB
Tel: 0300 123 5577
Fax: 020 8760 0432
DX: 97470 CROYDON 6
Email: enquiries@croydon.countycourt.gsi.gov.uk; hearings@croydon.countycourt.gsi.gov.uk;
e-filing@croydon.countycourt.gsi.gov.uk; bailiffs@croydon.countycourt.gsi.gov.uk;
family@croydon.countycourt.gsi.gov.uk
Court Details
The Law Courts, Altyre Road, Croydon
District Registry; Bankruptcy; Family Hearing Centre
District Judges: A.J. Mills, M. Parker, K. Bishop, K. Major

194   EDMONTON (LON)
Court House, 59 Fore Street, Edmonton, London N18 2TN
Tel: 020 8884 6500
Fax: 020 8803 0564
DX: 136686 EDMONTON 3
Email: bailiffs@edmonton.countycourt.gsi.gov.uk; e-filing@edmonton.countycourt.gsi.gov.uk;
enquiries@edmonton.countycourt.gsi.gov.uk; family@edmonton.countycourt.gsi.gov.uk;
hearings@edmonton.countycourt.gsi.gov.uk
Court Details
Court House, 59 Fore Street, Upper Edmonton
Family Hearing Centre
District Judges: L. Cohen, G. Silverman, S. Morley, A. Dias

231   ILFORD
closed wef 31/3/12

240   KINGSTON-UPON-THAMES (LON)
County Court, St James's Road, Kingston-upon-Thames, Surrey KT1 2AD
Tel: 020 8972 8700
Fax: 020 8547 1426
DX: 97890 KINGSTON-UPON-THAMES 3
Email: e-filing@kingston.countycourt.gsi.gov.uk; enquiries@kingston.countycourt.gsi.gov.uk; family@
kingston.countycourt.gsi.gov.uk; hearings@ kingston.countycourt.gsi.gov.uk; bailiffs@
kingston.countycourt.gsi.gov.uk
Court Details
County Court, St James's Road, Kingston-upon-Thames
Bankruptcy; Family Hearing Centre
District Judges: A. Sturdy, S. Gold, J. Smart, S. Brown

241   LAMBETH (LON)
Court House, Cleaver Street, Kennington Road, London SE11 4DZ
Tel: 020 7091 4410
Fax: 020 7587 1951
DX: 145020 KENNINGTON 2
Email: family@lambeth.countycourt.gsi.gov.uk; bailiffs@lambeth.countycourt.gsi.gov.uk;
hearings@lambeth.countycourt.gsi.gov.uk; enquiries@lambeth.countycourt.gsi.gov.uk;
e-filing@lambeth.countycourt.gsi.gov.uk
Court Details
Court House, Cleaver Street, Kennington Road SE11 4DZ
Family Hearing Centre
District Judges: M. Zimmels, A. Worthington, L. Pearce, P. Desai

266   THE MAYOR'S AND CITY OF LONDON (LON)
Guildhall Buildings, Basinghall Street, London EC2V 5AR
Tel: 020 7796 5400
Fax: 020 7796 5424
DX: 97520 MOORGATE (EC2)
Email: e-filing@mayorsandcityoflondon.countycourt.gsi.gov.uk;
bailiffs@mayorsandcityoflondon.countycourt.gsi.gov.uk;
hearings@mayorsandcityoflondon.countycourt.gsi.gov.uk;
enquiries@mayorsandcityoflondon.countycourt.gsi.gov.uk
Court Details
Guildhall Buildings, Basinghall Street, London EC2V 5AR
District Judges: M. Trent, N. Parfitt

387   ROMFORD (LON)
2A Oaklands Avenue, Romford, Essex RM1 4DP
Tel: 01708 775353
Fax: 0870 324 0225
DX: 97530 ROMFORD 2
Email: bailiffs@romford.countycourt.gsi.gov.uk; enquiries@romford.countycourt.gsi.gov.uk;
family@romford.countycourt.gsi.gov.uk
Court Details
2A Oaklands Avenue, Romford
District Registry; Bankruptcy; Family Hearing Centre; Forced Marriage Protection Orders
District Judges: R.W. Mullis, T. P. Bowles, M. Wright, H. Kemp, J. Lewis

356   UXBRIDGE (LON)
501 Uxbridge Road, Hayes, Middlesex UB4 8HL
Tel: 020 8756 3520
Fax: 020 8561 2020
DX: 44658 HAYES (Middlesex)
Email: e-filing@uxbridge.countycourt.gsi.gov.uk; enquiries@uxbridge.countycourt.gsi.gov.uk;
bailiffs@uxbridge.countycourt.gsi.gov.uk; family@uxbridge.countycourt.gsi.gov.uk;
hearings@uxbridge.countycourt.gsi.gov.uk
Court Details
501 Uxbridge Road, Hayes
Family Hearing Centre
District Judges: J. Banks, A. Wicks, L. Wood

359   WANDSWORTH (LON)
76/78 Upper Richmond Road, Putney SW15 2SU
Tel: 020 8333 4351
Fax: 020 8877 9854
DX: 97540 PUTNEY ?
Email: enquiries@wandsworth.countycourt.gsi.gov.uk
Court Details
76/78 Upper Richmond Road, Putney
Family Hearing Centre
District Judges: L.M. Grosse, A. Rowley, T. Swan

368   WEST LONDON (LON)
Courthouse, 181 Talgarth Road, Hammersmith, London W6 8DN
Tel: 020 8600 6868
Fax: 020 8600 6860
DX: 97550 HAMMERSMITH 8
Email: enquiries@westlondon.countycourt.gsi.gov.uk
Court Details
Courthouse, 181 Talgarth Road, Hammersmith W6 8DN
District Judges: M. Nicholson, J. Ryan

369   WESTMINSTER
Combined with Bloomsbury County Court to form Central London County Court – wef 14/8/92

375   WILLESDEN (LON)
9 Acton Lane, Harlesden, London NW10 8SB
Tel: 020 8963 8200

Fax: 020 8453 0946
DX: 97560 HARLESDEN 2
Email: enquiries@willesden.countycourt.gsi.gov.uk; hearings@willesden.countycourt.gsi.gov.uk; bailiffs@willesden.countycourt.gsi.gov.uk; e-filing@willesden.countycourt.gsi.gov.uk; family@willesden.countycourt.gsi.gov.uk
Court Details
9 Acton Lane, Harlesden
Family Hearing Centre
District Judges: D.V. Steel, C. Dabezies, N. Kumrai, P. Middleton-Roy

379   WOOLWICH (LON)
The Court House, 165 Powis Street, Woolwich, London SE18 6JW
Tel: 020 8301 8700
Fax: 020 8316 4842
DX: 123450 WOOLWICH 8
Email: enquiries@woolwich.countycourt.gsi.gov.uk; bailiffs@woolwich.countycourt.gsi.gov.uk; family@woolwich.countycourt.gsi.gov.uk; hearings@woolwich.countycourt.gsi.gov.uk; efiling@woolwich.countycourt.gsi.gov.uk
Court Details
The Court House, Powis Street
Family Hearing Centre
District Judge: W. Backhouse, J. Beattie

255   LOUGHBOROUGH
closed wef 31/12/98 – successor courts – Derby, Leicester and Nottingham

256   LOWESTOFT
closed wef 31/3/11

257   LUDLOW
closed wef 9/11

258   LUTON (SE)
Luke Fusi, Acting Delivery Manager, 5th Floor, Cresta House, Alma Street, Luton, Bedfordshire LU1 2PU
Tel: 0844 892 0550
Fax: 01582 506701
DX: 97760 LUTON 4
Email: enquiries@luton.countycourt.gsi.gov.uk
Court Details
2nd & 4th Floor, Cresta House, Alma Street, Luton
District Registry; Adoption Centre; Bankruptcy; Divorce; Trial Centre; Family Court Centre
District Judges: P.S. Gill, D. Eynon, K. Wilding White

260   MACCLESFIELD (NW)
Miss Julie Burgess, Delivery Manager for Crewe and Macclesfield County Courts, 2nd Floor, Silk House, Park Green, Macclesfield SK11 7NA
Tel: 01625 412800
Fax: 01625 501262
DX: 702498 MACCLESFIELD 3
Court Details
2nd Floor, Silk House, Park Green, Macclesfield
District Registry; Bankruptcy; Divorce Centre; Family Hearing Centre; Designated Adoption, Centre
District Judge: A.A. Wallace, S. Goodchild

261   MAIDSTONE (SE)
Rebecca Humphry, Delivery Manager, Maidstone Combined Court Centre, The Law Courts, Barker Road, Maidstone, Kent ME16 8EQ
Tel: 01622 202000
Fax: 01622 202002
DX: 130065 MAIDSTONE 7
Court Details
The Law Courts, Barker Road, Maidstone
District Registry; Bankruptcy; Family Hearing Centre
District Judge: E. Millward Sullivan

719   MALDON
closed wef 30/6/92 – successor court – Chelmsford

720   MALTON
closed wef 4/1/94 – successor court – York

262   MANCHESTER (NW)
Jackie Healy, Civil Justice Centre, 1 Bridge Street West, Manchester M60 9DJ
Tel: 0161 240 5000
Fax: 0161 240 5050 (General); 5455 (Family); 5480 (Bailiffs); 5399 (High Court/Civil Listing); 5398
(Specialist Hearings); 5315 (Administrative Court)
DX: 724783 MANCHESTER 44
Email: family@manchester.countycourt.gsi.gov.uk; bailiffs@manchester.countycourt.gsi.gov.uk;
hearings@manchester.countycourt.gsi.gov.uk; e-filing@manchester.countycourt.gsi.gov.uk;
highcourtspecialisthearings@manchester.countycourt.gsi.gov.uk;
administrativecourtoffice.manchester@hmcts.x.gsi.gov.uk; plomanchestercare@hmcts.gsi.gov.uk;
manchester.mercantile@hmcts.gsi.gov.uk; manchester.qb@hmcts.gsi.gov.uk;
manchester.tcc@hmcts.gsi.gov.uk
Court Details
1 Bridge Street West, Manchester
**District Registry: Extended, Chancery/Mercantile; Bankruptcy; Care Centre; Divorce; Family
Hearing Centre; Race Relations; Administrative Court; Family Proceedings; Technology and
Construction**
District Judges: C.R. Fairclough, A.J.J. Harrison, L. Stephens, G.D. Smith, P. Richmond, C. Khan, B.
Stonier, P.O. Wheeler, A. Obodai, J. Brazier, M. Haigh, S. Iyer, R. Matharu, M. Hovington, L. Relph, J.
C. Hassall, D. Moss, A.J. Berkley

263   MANSFIELD (M)
Helen Randle, The Court House, Rosemary Street, Mansfield, Nottinghamshire NG19 6EE
Tel: 01623 451500
Fax: 01623 451502
DX: 179563 MANSFIELD 9
Court Details
The Court House, Rosemary Street, Mansfield
The Court House, 30 Potter Street, Worksop S80 2AJ
District Registry; Family Hearing Centre
District Judges: M. Wall, R. McMillan, S. Hale, M. Davies

MARGATE
see THANET

264   MARKET DRAYTON
closed wef 27/10/95 – successor courts – Shrewsbury and Stoke-on-Trent

265   MATLOCK
closed wef 16/2/96 – successor courts – Burton, Chesterfield and Derby

266   MAYOR'S AND CITY OF LONDON
see LONDON

267   MEDWAY CIVIL AND FAMILY COURT (SE)
Emma Miller, Delivery Manager, Anchorage House, 47–67 High Street, Chatham, Kent ME4 4DW
Tel: 01634 887900
Fax: 01634 811332
DX: 98180 CHATHAM 4
Court Details
Anchorage House, High Street, Chatham
District Registry; Bankruptcy; Care Centre
District Judges: G.A. Green, K. Wilkinson

268   MELTON MOWBRAY (M)
Martin Hirst, 90 Wellington Street, Leicester LE1 6HG
Tel: 0116 222 5868
Fax: 0116 222 5763
DX: 17405 LEICESTER 3

Court Details
The Court House, Norman Way, Melton Mowbray
District Judge: V. Stamenkovich

---

269   MERTHYR TYDFIL (WAL)
Mark Lewis, Merthyr Tydfil Combined Court Centre, The Law Courts, Glebeland Place, Merthyr Tydfil, Mid Glamorgan CF47 8BH
Tel: 01685 727600
Fax: 01685 727702
DX: 99582 MERTHYR TYDFIL 2
Email: enquiries@merthyrtydfil.countycourt.gsi.gov.uk
Court Details
The Law Courts, Glebeland Place, Merthyr Tydfil
District Registry; Bankruptcy
District Judge: M. Jenkins

---

270   MIDDLESBROUGH (NE)
Marie Davison, Teesside Combined Court Centre, Russell Street, Middlesbrough, Cleveland TS1 2AE
Tel: 01642 340000
Fax: 01642 340002
DX: 65152 MIDDLESBROUGH 2
Court Details
Russell Street, Middlesbrough
District Registry; Bankruptcy; Care Centre
District Judges: J.E. Mainwaring-Taylor, D. Robertson, P.W.J. Traynor, P. Cuthbertson, R. V. Hall, C.A. Arkless, S. Spencer

---

388   MILTON KEYNES (SE)
Maria Madeley, Delivery Manager, 351 Silbury Boulevard, Witan Gate East, Milton Keynes MK9 2DT
Tel: 01908 302800 (Civil Matters)
01908 302801 (Family Matters)
Fax: 01908 230063
DX: 136266 MILTON KEYNES 6
Court Details
351 Silbury Boulevard, Milton Keynes
District Registry; Bankruptcy; Care Centre
District Judges: N. Hickman, P. Perusko, L. Rand, J. Vincent

---

271   MOLD (WAL)
Lesley Hyde, Wrexham Law Courts, Bodhyfryd, Wrexham LL12 7BP
Tel: 01978 317400; 01352 707330 (Bailiff)
Fax: 01978 358213
DX: 721921 WREXHAM 4
Note: All administration details as Wrexham.
Court Details
Law Courts, County Civic Centre, Mold
Bankruptcy; Civil; District Registry; Mercantile
District Judges: J. Davies, G. Humphreys

---

272   MONMOUTH
closed wef 1/4/02 – successor court – Newport (Gwent)

---

273   MORPETH AND BERWICK (NE)
Moira Miller, Fountain House, Newmarket, Morpeth, Northumberland NE61 1LA
Tel: 01670 512221
Fax: 01670 504188
DX: 65124 MORPETH 2
Court Details
Fountain House, Newmarket, Morpeth
Divorce
The Magistrates'Court, The Court House, 40 Church Street, Berwick-upon-Tweed TD15 1EA. Tel: 01289 305053 (Wednesday 11:00–15:00)
District Judges: I. Atherton, R. Howard, P. Pescod

274 NEATH PORT TALBOT (WAL)
Caroline Bevan, Forster Road, Neath, West Glamorgan SA11 3BN
Tel: 01639 642267; 635088 (Bailiffs)
Fax: 01639 633505
DX: 99550 NEATH 2
Email: enquiries@neath.countycourt.gsi.gov.uk
Court Details
Forster Road, Neath
Bankruptcy; Divorce
District Judge: T.J. Lewis

275 NELSON
closed wef 31/1/10 – successor court – Burnley

276 NEWARK
closed wef 9/11

277 NEWBURY
Hearing centre only wef 1/7/11 – all enquiries to Reading County Court

278 NEWCASTLE-UPON-TYNE (NE)
Allison Cook, Newcastle-upon-Tyne Combined Court Centre, The Law Courts, Quayside,
Newcastle-upon-Tyne NE1 3LA
Tel: 0191 201 2000
Fax: 0191 201 2001
DX: 65128 NEWCASTLE UPON TYNE 2
Court Details
The Law Courts, Quayside, Newcastle-upon-Tyne
**District Registry; Extended; Chancery; Mercantile; Technology and Construction; Bankruptcy;
Care Centre; Family Hearing Centre; Divorce; Race Relations; Court of Protection; Forced
Marriage Act**
District Judges: P. Jackson, R. Howard, N.W. Goudie, R. Loomba, I.D. Atherton, B.D. Stapely, P.
Pescod, D. Morgan, A. Hardy, D. Grey, T. Searle, K. Malik, P. Kramer

279 NEWPORT ISLE OF WIGHT (SW)
Tania Baxman, Delivery Manager, Crown and County Courts, The Law Courts, Quay Street, Newport,
Isle of Wight PO30 5YT
Tel: 01983 535100
Fax: 01983 821039
DX: 98460 NEWPORT (I.O.W.) 2
Court Details
The Law Courts, Quay Street, Newport, Isle of Wight
District Registry; Bankruptcy; Divorce
District Judge: A. Grand

280 NEWPORT (GWENT) CIVIL & FAMILY COURT (WAL)
Mr Huw Evans, Clarence House, 5th Floor, Clarence Place, Newport, South Wales NP19 7AA
Tel: 01633 245040
Fax: 01633 245041
DX: 99480 NEWPORT GWENT 4
Court Details
The Concourse, Clarence House, Clarence Place, Newport
District Registry; Bankruptcy; Care Centre; Family Hearing Centre
District Judges: M. Jenkins, J.P. Weaver, G. Sandercock

281 NEWTON ABBOT
closed wef 30/3/96 – amalgamated with Torquay

NEWTOWN
see WELSHPOOL AND NEWTOWN

283 NORTH SHIELDS (NE)
Gillian Macnamara, 2nd Floor, Kings Court, Earl Grey Way, Royal Quays, North Shields, Tyne & Wear
NE29 6AR
Tel: 0191 298 2339
Fax: 0191 298 2337
DX: 65137 NORTH SHIELDS 2

Court Details
2nd Floor, Kings Court, Earl Grey Way, North Shields
Divorce
District Judges: P. Jackson, R. Howard, R. Loomba, D. Grey

722 NORTHALLERTON
closed wef 1/4/92 – successor court – Darlington

282 NORTHAMPTON (M)
Martin Hurst, Northampton Combined Court Centre, 85/87 Lady's Lane, Northampton NN1 3HQ
Tel: 01604 470400
Fax: 01604 232398
DX: 725380 NORTHAMPTON 21
Email: enquiries@northampton.countycourt.gsi.gov.uk
Court Details
Combined Court Centre, 85/87 Lady's Lane, Northampton
District Registry; Bankruptcy; Care Centre
District Judges: P. McHale, I. Murdoch, S. Watson, D. Flood, V. Stamenkovich

284 NORTHWICH
closed wef 29/7/11

285 NORWICH (SE)
Donna Major, Delivery Manager, Norwich Combined Court Centre, The Law Courts, Bishopgate, Norwich NR3 1UR
Tel: 0844 892 4000
Fax: 01603 760863
DX: 97385 NORWICH 5
Email: helpdesk@norwich.countycourt.gsi.gov.uk
Court Details
The Law Courts, Bishopgate, Norwich
District Registry; Bankruptcy; Care Centre; Family Hearing Centre; Trial Centre
District Judges: Martyn Royall, R.G. Sparrow, B.I. Rutland, M. Birchall, D. Pugh, P.C. Rogers, T. McLoughlin

286 NOTTINGHAM (M)
Judy Calderwood, Nottingham County Court, The Law Courts, 60 Canal Street, Nottingham NG1 7EJ
Tel: 0115 910 3500
Fax: 0115 910 3510
DX: 702380 NOTTINGHAM 7
Email: family@nottingham.countycourt.gsi.gov.uk; enquiries@nottingham.countycourt.gsi.gov.uk; bailiffs@nottingham.countycourt.gsi.gov.uk; hearings@nottingham.countycourt.gsi.gov.uk; e-filing@nottingham.countycourt.gsi.gov.uk
Court Details
The Law Courts, 60 Canal Street, Nottingham
District Registry; Bankruptcy, Care Centre, Race Relations
District Judges: D.S. Millard, D.F. Reeson, S. Hale, D. Nicole, R. McMillan, I. Lloyd-Jones, M. Wall, J. George

287 NUNEATON (M)
David Bigg, Warwickshire Justice Centre, Vicarage Street, Nuneaton CV11 4WX
Tel: 0300 123 5577
Fax: 02476 352835
DX: 701940 NUNEATON 2
Court Details
Warwickshire Justice Centre, Vicarage Street, Nuneaton
District Judge: T. Lynch

288 OLDHAM (NW)
Julie Webster, The County Court House, New Radcliffe Street, (off Rochdale Road), Oldham OL1 1NL
Tel: 0161 290 4200
Fax: 0161 290 4222
DX: 702595 OLDHAM 2
Email: bailiffs@oldham.countycourt.gsi.gov.uk; e-filing@oldham.countycourt.gsi.gov.uk; enquiries@oldham.countycourt.gsi.gov.uk; family@oldham.countycourt.gsi.gov.uk

Court Details
The County Court House, New Radcliffe Street, Oldham
District Registry; Bankruptcy; Divorce; Family Hearing Centre
District Judges: R.R.P. Ackroyd, P.S. Stockton, C. Fox, M. J. Simpson

289 OSWESTRY
closed wef 30/9/11

290 OTLEY
closed wef 2/1/96 – successor courts – Bradford, Harrogate, Leeds and Skipton

291 OXFORD (SE)
Faith Dixey, Acting Delivery Manager, Oxford Combined Court Centre, St Aldate's, Oxford OX1 1TL
Tel: 01865 264200
Fax: 01865 790773 (Civil)
01865 264253 (Criminal)
DX: 96450 OXFORD 4

Court Details
The Court House, St Aldate's, Oxford
District Registry; Bankruptcy; Care Centre; Family Hearing Centre; Race Relations; Trial Centre; Divorce
District Judges: A. Jenkins, M. Payne, R. Matthews, V. Gatter

292 PENRITH
closed wef 26/7/11

293 PENZANCE
closed wef 30/6/11

294 PETERBOROUGH (SE)
Graham Jones, Delivery Manager, Peterborough Combined Court Centre, Crown Buildings, Rivergate, Peterborough PE1 1EJ
Tel: 0844 892 4000
Fax: 01733 557348
DX: 702302 PETERBOROUGH 8
Email: family@peterborough.countycourt.gsi.gov.uk; bailiffs@peterborough.countycourt.gsi.gov.uk; hearings@peterborough.countycourt.gsi.gov.uk; e-filing@peterborough.countycourt.gsi.gov.uk; helpdesk@norwich.countycourt.gsi.gov.uk

Court Details
Crown Buildings, Rivergate, Peterborough
District Registry; Bankruptcy; Care Centre
District Judges: A. Wharton, S. Farquhar, R. Chaudhuri

296 PLYMOUTH (SW)
Plymouth Combined Court Centre, The Law Courts, Armada Way, Plymouth, Devon PL1 2ER
Tel: 01752 677400; 677490 (Bailiffs)
Fax: 0870 324 0096
DX: 98470 PLYMOUTH 7
Email: family@plymouth.countycourt.gsi.gov.uk; bailiffs@plymouth.countycourt.gsi.gov.uk; hearings@plymouth.countycourt.gsi.gov.uk; enquiries@plymouth.countycourt.gsi.gov.uk

Court Details
The Law Courts, Armada Way, Plymouth
District Registry; Admiralty; Bankruptcy; Care Centre; Divorce
District Judges: R.A.F. Griggs, E. Richards, C. Gamwell

297 PONTEFRACT
closed wef 4/12

298 PONTYPOOL
closed wef 31/7/11

299 PONTYPRIDD (WAL)
Mark Lewis, The Courthouse, Courthouse Street, Pontypridd, Mid Glamorgan CF37 1JR
Tel: 01443 490800; 490821/2 (Bailiffs)
Fax: 01443 480305
DX: 99620 PONTYPRIDD 2

Court Details
The Courthouse, Courthouse Street, Pontypridd
District Registry; Bankruptcy; Care Centre; Divorce
District Judges: J.M. Doel, A.G. Fraser

300   POOLE
closed wef 30/6/11

302   PORTSMOUTH (SW)
Eve Miller, Operational Manager, Portsmouth Combined Court Centre, The Courts of Justice,
Winston Churchill Avenue, Portsmouth PO1 2EB
Tel: 023 9289 3000
Fax: 023 9282 6385 (civil)
023 9281 6730 (family)
DX: 98490 PORTSMOUTH 5
Email: enquiries@portsmouth.countycourt.gsi.gov.uk; family@portsmouth.countycourt.gsi.gov.uk
Court Details
The Courts of Justice, Winston Churchill Avenue, Portsmouth
District Registry; Admiralty; Bankruptcy; Care Centre; Family Hearing Centre
District Judges: G. Cawood, C. Ackroyd, R. Wilson, E. Manuel, S. Veysey

PORT TALBOT
see NEATH AND PORT TALBOT

303   PRESTON (NW)
Mrs J. Kelly, Delivery Manager, Preston Combined Court Centre, The Law Courts, Openshaw Place,
Ring Way, Preston PR1 2LL
Tel: 01772 844700
Fax: 01772 844710
DX: 702660 PRESTON 5
Court Details
The Law Courts, Openshaw Place, Ring Way, Preston
District Registry; Extended; Chancery; Bankruptcy; Divorce
District Judges: M. Turner, M. Anson, I. Knifton, A. Rouine

304   RAWTENSTALL
closed wef 30/9/11

305   READING (SE)
Deborah Burgess, Delivery Manager, 160–163 Friar Street, Reading RG1 1HE
Tel: 0118 987 0500
Fax: 0118 987 0555; 959 9827
DX: 98010 READING 6
Court Details
160–163 Friar Street, Reading
District Registry; Bankruptcy; Care Centre
District Judges: G. Burgess, S. Henson, J.R. Davidson, R. Henry, C. Darbyshire

306   REDDITCH
closed wef 30/9/11 – successor court – Worcester

REDHILL
see REIGATE

REDRUTH
see CAMBORNE AND REDRUTH

307   REIGATE (SE)
Kim Smith, Law Courts, Hatchlands Road, Redhill, Surrey RH1 6BL
Tel: 01737 763637
Fax: 01737 766917
DX: 98020 REDHILL WEST
Court Details
Law Courts, Hatchlands Road, Redhill
Divorce
District Judges: L. George, H. Letts, L. Nightingale

308   RHYL (WAL)
Lesley Hyde, The Courthouse, Clwyd Street, Rhyl, Denbighshire LL18 3LA
Tel: 01745 352940
Fax: 01745 336726
DX: 702489 RHYL 2
Email: family@rhyl.countycourt.gsi.gov.uk; hearing@rhyl.countycourt.gsi.gov.uk;
enquiries@rhyl.countycourt.gsi.gov.uk; bailiffs@rhyl.countycourt.gsi.gov.uk
Court Details
The Courthouse, Clwyd Street, Rhyl
District Registry; Bankruptcy; Care Centre; Family Hearing Centre
District Judges: O.W. Williams, J.G. Thomas, M. Jones-Evans

309   ROCHDALE
closed wef 7/9/98 – successor courts – Oldham and Rawtenstall

387   ROMFORD
see LONDON

310   ROTHERHAM (NE)
Sharon Frost, Rotherham Law Courts, The Statutes, off Main Street, Rotherham S60 1YW
Tel: 01709 839339
Fax: 01709 788414
DX: 703025 ROTHERHAM 4
Email: bailiffs@rotherham.countycourt.gsi.gov.uk; enquiries@rotherham.countycourt.gsi.gov.uk;
rotherhamfamily@hmcts.gsi.gov.uk
Court Details
Rotherham Law Courts, The Statutes, off Main Street, Rotherham
Family Hearing Centre
District Judges: P.J. Bellamy, T.W. Hill, G. Corkill

311   RUGBY
closed wef 30/9/11

312   RUNCORN
closed wef 29/7/11

313   ST ALBANS (SE)
Linda O'Connor, Delivery Manager, The Court Building, Bricket Road, St Albans, Hertfordshire AL1 3JW
Tel: 0844 892 0550
Fax: 01727 753234
DX: 97770 ST ALBANS 2
Email: enquiries@stalbans.countycourt.gsi.gov.uk
Court Details
The Court Building, Bricket Road, St Albans
Bankruptcy
District Judge: G. Field

314   ST AUSTELL
closed wef 30/3/96 – successor courts – Bodmin and Truro

315   ST HELENS (NW)
Alison Keeffe, Delivery Manager for St Helens and Warrington County Courts, St Helens County Court, St Helens Courthouse, Corporation Street, St Helens WA10 1SZ
Tel: 01744 620244
Fax: 01744 627288
DX: 19488 ST HELENS
Email: sthelens.cty.ge@hmcts.gsi.gov.uk
Court Details
The Law Courts, Corporation Street, St Helens
District Registry; Divorce
District Judges: G. Fitzgerald, H. Conway

316   SALFORD
closed wef 5/8/11 – successor court – Manchester

317   SALISBURY (SW)
Salisbury Combined, Court Centre, The Law Courts, Wilton Road, Salisbury SP2 7EP
Tel: 01722 345200
Fax: 01722 345201
DX: 98500 SALISBURY 2
Court Details
The Law Courts, Wilton Road, Salisbury
District Registry; Divorce
District Judges: D. Asplin, N. Brookes

318   SCARBOROUGH (NE)
Kevin Page, Pavilion House, Valley Bridge Road, Scarborough, North Yorkshire YO11 2JS
Tel: 01723 366361
Fax: 01723 501992
DX: 65140 SCARBOROUGH 2
Court Details
Pavilion House, Valley Bridge Road, Scarborough
District Registry; Bankruptcy; Family Hearing Centre
District Judges: P. Wildsmith

319   SCUNTHORPE (NE)
Scunthorpe Court Centre, Corporation Road, Scunthorpe, Lincolnshire DN15 6QB
Tel: 01724 281100
Fax: 01724 281890
DX: 742212 SCUNTHORPE 10
Court Details
Scunthorpe Court Centre, Corporation Road, Scunthorpe
District Registry; Bankruptcy; Divorce
District Judge: S. Stephenson, S. Richardson, I. P. Besford, I.L. Buxton

723   SEVENOAKS
closed wef 5/4/94 – successor court – Tunbridge Wells

724   SHAFTESBURY
closed wef 5/12/94 – successor court – Yeovil

725   SHEERNESS
closed wef 5/4/94 – successor court – Sittingbourne

320   SHEFFIELD (NE)
Sheffield Combined Court Centre, The Law Courts, 50 West Bar, Sheffield S3 8PH
Tel: 0114 281 2400 (Switchboard); 2520/2539/2527/2550 (Family and General Enquiries); 2429
(Bailiffs' Office)
Fax: 0114 281 2425
DX: 703028 SHEFFIELD 6
Court Details
The Law Courts, 50 West Bar, Sheffield
District Registry; Bankruptcy; Care Centre
District Judges: D. Kirkham, D.A. Oldham, P. Mort, C.J. Birkby, T.W. Hill, M. Young, A.M. Barrington

321   SHOREDITCH
see LONDON

322   SHREWSBURY
closed wef 30/9/11

323   SITTINGBOURNE
closed wef 30/3/96 – successor courts – Maidstone and Medway

324   SKEGNESS
closed wef 9/11

325   SKIPTON (NE)
Kelly Marcuccio, The Law Courts, Otley Street, Skipton, North Yorkshire BD23 1RH
Tel: 01756 692650
Fax: 01756 692655
DX: 703031 SKIPTON 2

Court Details
The Law Courts, Otley Street, Skipton
Family Hearing Centre
District Judges: J.A.B. Buchan, G.Y. Lingard

326   SLEAFORD
closed wef 16/2/96 – successor courts – Boston, Grantham, Lincoln and Newark

327   SLOUGH (SE)
Richard Keel, Delivery Manager, The Law Courts, Windsor Road, Slough SL1 2HE
Tel: 01753 690300
Fax: 01753 575990
DX: 98030 SLOUGH 3
Court Details
The Law Courts, Windsor Road, Slough
Bankruptcy; Family Hearing Centre
District Judges: S. Jones, T. Parker, K. McCulloch, P. Devlin

328   SOUTHAMPTON (SW)
Southampton Combined Court Centre, The Courts of Justice, London Road, Southampton,
Hampshire SO15 2XQ
Tel: 023 8021 3200
Goldfax: 0870 761 7769 (Family); 761 7750 (Civil); 324 0112 (Bailiffs)
DX: 111000 SOUTHAMPTON 11
Email: family@southampton.countycourt.gsi.gov.uk; bailiffs@southampton.countycourt.gsi.gov.uk;
hearings@southampton.countycourt.gsi.gov.uk
Court Details
The Courts of Justice, London Road, Southampton
District Registry; Bankruptcy; Family Hearing Centre; Race Relations; Divorce; Admiralty
District Judges: J.S. Sparrow, A. Grand, M. Codlin-Tate, L. Powell, M. Stewart

329   SOUTHEND (SE)
Debbie Freeman, Delivery Manager, County Court, Tylers House, Tylers Avenue, Southend-on-Sea,
Essex SS1 2AW
Tel: 0844 892 4000
Fax: 01702 603090
DX: 97780 SOUTHEND ON SEA 2
Email: helpdesk@norwich.countycourt.gsi.gov.uk
Court Details
Tylers House, Tylers Avenue, Southend-on-Sea
District Registry; Trial Centre; Bankruptcy; Family Hearing Centre *District Judges:* R.D. Dudley, L.
Ashworth, S. Molineaux

330   SOUTHPORT
closed wef 29/7/11

331   SOUTH SHIELDS (NE)
South Tyneside Law Courts, Millbank, Secretan Way, South Shields, Tyne & Wear NE33 1RG
Tel: 0191 456 3343
Fax: 0191 427 4499
DX: 65143 SOUTH SHIELDS 3
Court Details
Law Courts, Millbank, Secretan Way
District Registry; Admiralty; Divorce
District Judges: J.R.A. Howard, D. Grey, A. Hardy, D. Morgan

332   SPALDING
closed wef 16/2/96 – successor courts – Boston, Grantham and Peterborough

333   STAFFORD (M)
Isabel Syred, Stafford Combined Court Centre, Victoria Square, Stafford ST16 2QQ
Tel: 01785 610730
Fax: 01785 213250 (County)
DX: 703190 STAFFORD 4

Court Details
District Registry; Bankruptcy; Family Hearing Centre
Combined Court Centre, Victoria Square, Stafford
District Judges: J.I. Ilsley, R. Chapman

334   STAINES (SE)
Kim Smith, The Law Courts, Knowle Green, Staines, Middlesex TW18 1XH
Tel: 01784 895900
Fax: 01784 895530
DX: 98040 STAINES 2
Court Details
The Law Courts, Knowle Green, Staines
Divorce
District Judges: V.S. Batcup, V. Trigg

335   STAMFORD
closed wef 1/10/84 – successor court – Peterborough

336   STOCKPORT (NW)
Patrick Ward, Delivery Manager for Altrincham and Stockport County Courts, Stockport Courthouse, Edward Street, Stockport SK1 3NF
Tel: 0161 477 2020
Fax: 0161 968 9733
DX: 702620 STOCKPORT 4
Email: family@stockport.countycourt.gsi.gov.uk; bailiffs@stockport.countycourt.gsi.gov.uk; hearings@stockport.countycourt.gsi.gov.uk; enquiries@stockport.countycourt.gsi.gov.uk; e-filing@stockport.countycourt.gsi.gov.uk
Court Details
Stockport Courthouse, Stockport
District Registry; Divorce; Bankruptcy; Family Hearing Centre
District Judges: S. Jones, J.P. Horan, P.S. Dignan, I. Lettall

337   STOCKTON-ON-TEES
closed wef 2/11/94 – resited to form Teeside Combined Court Centre

338   STOKE-ON-TRENT (M)
Isabel Syred, Stoke-on-Trent Combined Court Centre, Bethesda Street, Hanley, Stoke-on-Trent ST1 3BP
Tel: 01782 854 000
Fax: 01782 854 046; 854 014
DX: 703360 HANLEY 3
Email: e-filing@stoke.countycourt.gsi.gov.uk; family@stoke.countycourt.gsi.gov.uk; bailiffs@stoke.countycourt.gsi.gov.uk; hearings@stoke.countycourt.gsi.gov.uk; enquiries@stoke.countycourt.gsi.gov.uk
Court Details
Bethesda Street, Hanley, Stoke-on-Trent
District Registry; Bankruptcy; Care Centre
District Judges: L. Schroeder, J.I. Ilsley, J. Jack, P. Rank, G. Crowe

339   STOURBRIDGE
closed wef 30/9/11

340   STRATFORD-UPON-AVON
closed wef 30/9/11

341   STROUD
closed wef 4/7/94 – successor court – Gloucester

342   SUDBURY
closed wef 5/4/94 – successor courts – Bury St Edmund's, Braintree, Colchester and Ipswich

343   SUNDERLAND (NE)
Trish Banks, The Court House, 44 John Street, Sunderland SR1 1RB
Tel: 0191 568 0750
Minicom: 0191 478 1476
Fax: 0191 514 3028
DX: 65149 SUNDERLAND 2

Court Details
The Court House, John Street, Sunderland
District Registry; Bankruptcy; Care Centre; Divorce; Family Hearing Centre
District Judges: D. Lascelles, B. Stapely, R. Loomba, D. Morgan

344   SWANSEA (WAL)
Caroline Bevan, Caravella House, Quay West, Quay Parade, Swansea SA1 1SP
Tel: 01792 485800
Fax: 01792 485810
DX: 99740 SWANSEA 5
Email: enquiries@swansea.countycourt.gsi.gov.uk; e-filing@swansea.countycourt.gsi.gov.uk;
family@swansea.countycourt.gsi.gov.uk; bailiffs@swansea.countycourt.gsi.gov.uk;
hearings@swansea.countycourt.gsi.gov.uk
Court Details
Caravella House, Quay West, Quay Parade, Swansea
District Registry; Bankruptcy; Care Centre; Family Hearing Centre; Civil Justice Centre
District Judges: P. Evans, P. Llewellyn, OBE, J. Garland-Thomas, M.I. Taylor

345   SWINDON (SW)
Cheryl Hawkins, Delivery Manager, Swindon Combined Court Centre, The Law Courts, Islington
Street, Swindon, Wiltshire SN1 2HG
Tel: 01793 690500
Fax: 01793 690555
DX: 98430 SWINDON 5
Email: swindon.cty.enq@hmcts.gsi.gov.uk (Civil Enquiries); swindon.cty.fly@hmcts.gsi.gov.uk (Family
Enquiries)
Court Details
The Law Courts, Islington Street, Swindon
District Registry; Bankruptcy; Care Centre; Single Family Court for Wiltshire
(*Note:* New divorce applications for Wiltshire are handled by Salisbury County Court wef
1/8/13)
District Judges: T. Cronin, A. Ralton
Designated Family Judge: Katharine Marshall

112   TAMESIDE (NW)
Dave Whittle, Delivery Manager for Oldham and Tameside County Courts, PO Box 166, Henry
Square, Ashton-under-Lyne, Lancashire OL6 7TP
Tel: 0161 331 5614
Fax: 0161 331 5649
DX: 702625 ASHTON-U-LYNE 2
Email: tameside.cty@hmcts.gsi.gov.uk
Court Details
Henry Square, Ashton-under-Lyne
Bankruptcy; Divorce
District Judges: C. Osborne, P.S. Stockton, R.R.P. Ackroyd, C. Fox

346   TAMWORTH
closed wef 30/9/11

347   TAUNTON (SW)
Taunton County Court, Shire Hall, Taunton, Somerset TA1 4EU
Tel: 01823 281110
DX: 98410 TAUNTON 2
Email: enquiries@taunton.countycourt.gsi.gov.uk
Court Details
Shire Hall, Taunton
District Registry; Adoption Centre; Bankruptcy; Care Centre; Family Hearing Centre; Trial
Centre
District Judges: D. White, R. Prigg

364   TELFORD (M)
Telford County Court, Telford Square, Malinsgate, Town Centre, Telford, Shropshire TF3 4JP
Tel: 01952 238280
Fax: 01952 291601
DX: 701976 TELFORD 3

Court Details
Telford Square, Malinsgate, Telford
District Registry; Adoption Centre; Care Centre; Trial Centre; Divorce; Insolvency
District Judge: S. Rogers; R.D. Chapman; M. Ellery; A. Brown

348   THANET (SE)
Sam Doyle, Delivery Manager, The Court House, 2nd Floor, Cecil Square, Margate, Kent CT9 1RL
Tel: 01843 221722
Fax: 01843 222730
DX: 98210 CLIFTONVILLE 2
Court Details
The Court House, 2nd Floor, Cecil Square, Margate
District Registry; Divorce
District Judge: L. Burgess

350   THORNE
closed wef 4/1/94 – successor court – Doncaster

351   TONBRIDGE
closed wef 1/10/84 – successor court – Tunbridge Wells

727   TODMORDEN
CLOSED wef 28/10/91 – successor court – Halifax

352   TORQUAY AND NEWTON ABBOT (SW)
The Willows, Nicholson Road, Torquay, Devon TQ2 7AZ
Tel: 01803 616791; 01803 617031 (Listing)
Fax: 01803 616795
DX: 98740 TORQUAY 4
Email: hearings@torquayandnewtonabbotcountycourt.gsi.gov.uk;
family@torquayandnewtonabbotcountycourt.gsi.gov.uk;
bailiffs@torquayandnewtonabbotcountycourt.gsi.gov.uk;
civil@torquayandnewtonabbotcountycourt.gsi.gov.uk;
Court Details
Nicholson Road, Torquay
District Registry; Bankruptcy; Divorce
District Judges: P. Taylor, C. Maunder

353   TROWBRIDGE (SW)
CLOSED WEF 29/3/13 – renamed Chippenham and Trowbridge (SW)

354   TRURO (SW)
Angela May, Truro County Court, Courts of Justice, Edward Street, Truro, Cornwall TR1 2PB
Tel: 01872 267460
DX: 135396 TRURO 2
Court Details
Courts of Justice, Edward Street, Truro
District Registry; Bankruptcy; Care Court; Family Hearing Centre
District Judges: P. Mitchell, L. Thomas, S. Middleton

356   UXBRIDGE
see LONDON

357   WAKEFIELD (NE)
Michelle Dunderdale, Wakefield Civil Justice Centre, Emerald House, 1 Mulberry Way, Wakefield WF1 2QN
Tel: 01924 370268; 291257 (Bailiffs); 299161 (Court Manager)
Fax: 01924 200818
DX: 703040 WAKEFIELD 3
Court Details
Wakefield Civil Justice Centre, Emerald House, Wakefield
District Registry; Bankruptcy; Family Hearing Centre
District Judges: K. Woodhead, G. Reed

358   WALSALL (M)
Sharon Studholme, Bridge House, Bridge Street, Walsall, West Midlands WS1 1JQ
Tel: 01922 728855

Fax: 01922 728891
DX: 701943 WALSALL 2

Court Details
Bridge House, Bridge Street, Walsall
District Registry; Bankruptcy; Family Hearing Centre; Civil Trial Centre
District Judges: D. Crowley, D. England, P. Watson, R. Hearne

359   WANDSWORTH
see LONDON

360   WARRINGTON (NW)
Paul Mulraney, Law Courts, Legh Street, Warrington WA1 1UR
Tel: 01925 256700
Fax: 01925 413335
DX: 702501 WARRINGTON 3

Court Details
Law Courts, Legh Street, Warrington
District Registry; Bankruptcy; Care Centre; Family Hearing Centre
District Judges: C. Gilham, G. Little, S. Rogers

361   WARWICK (M)
Ian Wilkinson, Warwickshire Justice Centre, Newbold Terrace, Leamington Spa, Warwickshire CV32 4EL
Tel: 0300 123 5577
Fax: 01926 682517
DX: 701964 LEAMINGTON 7

Court Details
Warwickshire Justice Centre, Leamington Spa
Bankruptcy
District Judge: A.S. Jones

362   WATFORD (SE)
Linda O'Connor, Delivery Manager, Cassiobury House, 11–19 Station Road, Watford, Hertfrodshire WD17 1EZ
Tel: 0844 892 0550
Fax: 01923 699479
DX: 122740 WATFORD 5
Email: family@watford.countycourt.gsi.gov.uk; bailiffs@watford.countycourt.gsi.gov.uk; hearings@watford.countycourt.gsi.gov.uk; enquiries@watford.countycourt.gsi.gov.uk; e-filing@watford.countycourt.gsi.gov.uk

Court Details
Cassiobury House, 11–19 Station Road, Watford
Care Centre; Family Proceedings Court
District Judges: P. Carr, J. Rhodes, S. Sethi, S. Cooper

363   WELLINGBOROUGH
closed wef 30/9/11

364   WELLINGTON
renamed TELFORD

WELLS
see BRISTOL

366   WELSHPOOL AND NEWTOWN (WAL)
Lesley Hyde, Wrexham Law Courts, Bodhyfryd, Wrexham LL2 7BP
Tel: 01978 317400
01352 707330 (Bailiff)
Fax: 01978 358213
DX: 721921 WREXHAM 4
Note: All administration details as Wrexham.

Court Details
The Mansion House, 24 Severn Street, Welshpool
District Registry; Bankruptcy; Civil; Mercantile; Divorce
District Judges: J. Davies, G. Humphreys

367   WEST BROMWICH
(closed wef 24/12/98 – successor courts – Birmingham, Dudley and Walsall)

373   WHITEHAVEN
see 373 WEST CUMBRIA

373   WEST CUMBRIA (NW)
Pauline Croall, Delivery Manager, West Cumbria County Court, Hall Park, Ramsey Brow, Workington
CA14 4AS
Tel: 01900 609609
Fax: 01900 609636
DX: 743420 WORKINGTON 5
Email: enquiries@westcumbria.countycourt.gsi.gov.uk
Court Details
West Cumbria County Court, Workington
District Registry; Bankruptcy;Divorce
District Judges: J.K. Park, S.C.W. Smith

368   WEST LONDON
see LONDON

369   WESTMINSTER
see LONDON

370   WESTON-SUPER-MARE (SW)
The Hedges, St George's, Weston-super-Mare BS22 7BB
Tel: 01934 528686
Fax: 01934 528594
DX: 152361 WESTON-SUPER-MARE 5
Court Details
The Hedges, St George's, Weston-super-Mare
Divorce; Family Hearing Centre
District Judge: S. Cope

371   WEYMOUTH (SW)
Weymouth & Dorchester Combined Court Centre, Westwey House, Westwey Road, Weymouth,
Dorset DT4 8TE
Tel: 01305 752510
Fax: 01305 788293
DX: 98820 WEYMOUTH 3
Court Details
Westwey House, Westwey Road, Weymouth
County Hall, Dorchester
District Registry; Bankruptcy; Divorce; Family Hearing Centre
District Judge: A. Willis, D. Williams

730   WHITBY
closed wef 4/1/94 – successor court – Scarborough

374   WIGAN (NW)
Mr M. Williams, Delivery Manager, Wigan & Leigh Courthouse, Darlington Street, Wigan, Lancashire
WN1 1DW
Tel: 01942 405405
Fax: 01942 405499
DX: 724820 WIGAN 9
Email: hearings@wigan.countycourt.gsi.gov.uk; bailiffs@wigan.countycourt.gsi.gov.uk;
e-filing@wigan.countycourt.gsi.gov.uk; family@wigan.countycourt.gsi.gov.uk;
enquiries@wigan.countycourt.gsi.gov.uk
Court Details
Darlington Street, Wigan
District Registry; Bankruptcy; Divorce
District Judges: S. Jackson, M. Mornington, E. Gordon

375   WILLESDEN
see LONDON

376   WINCHESTER (SW)
Winchester Combined Court Centre, The Law Courts, Winchester, Hampshire SO23 9EL
Tel: 01962 814100
Fax: 01962 814260
DX: 98520 WINCHESTER 3
Court Details
The Law Courts, Winchester
District Registry; Bankruptcy; Divorce
District Judge: M. Stewart

377   WISBECH
closed wef 29/9/95 – successor court – King's Lynn

378   WOLVERHAMPTON (M)
Sharon Studholme, Wolverhampton Combined Court Centre, Pipers Row, Wolverhampton, West
Midlands WV1 3LQ
Tel: 01902 481000
Fax: 01902 481001
DX: 702019 WOLVERHAMPTON 4
Court Details
Combined Court Centre, Pipers Row, Wolverhampton
**District Registry; Bankruptcy; Care Centre incorporating Black Country; Family Proceedings
Unit**
District Judges: R. Hearne, M. Ellery, D. England, P. Watson

379   WOOLWICH
see LONDON

380   WORCESTER (M)
Janet Strudwick, Worcester Combined Court Centre, The Shirehall, Foregate Street, Worcester WR1
1EQ
Tel: 01905 730807 (Civil & Enforcements); 730805 (Divorce); 730831 (Family); 732003 (Civil & Family
Listing)
Fax: 01905 730830 (Civil & Enforcement, Divorce); 730801 (Family); 730826 (Civil & Family Listing)
DX: 721120 WORCESTER 11
Court Details
The Shirehall, Foregate Street, Worcester
**District Registry; Bankruptcy; Care Centre (incorporating Herefordshire and Worcestershire
Family Proceedings Courts Administration); Trial Centre**
District Judges: M. Parry, P. Mackenzie, N. Khan, R. Savage

381   WORKINGTON
closed wef 2/1/01 – successor court – West Cumbria (formerly Whitehaven)

382   WORKSOP
closed wef 9/11

383   WORTHING (SE)
Claire Hampshire, Delivery Manager, The Law Courts, Christchurch Road, Worthing, West Sussex
BN11 1JD
Tel: 01903 221920
Fax: 01903 235559
DX: 98230 WORTHING 4
Court Details
Law Courts, Christchurch Road, Worthing
District Registry; Divorce
District Judges: C. Edwards, H. Clarke

384   WREXHAM (WAL)
Lesley Hyde, Wrexham Law Courts, Bodhyfryd, Wrexham LL12 7BP
Tel: 01978 317400; 01978 317407 (Bailiff)
Fax: 01978 358213
DX: 721921 WREXHAM 4
Court Details
Wrexham Law Courts, Bodhyfryd

District Registry; Adoption Centre; Bankruptcy; Care Centre; Divorce; Family Hearing Centre; Race Relations; Trial Centre
District Judges: J. Davies, G. Humphreys

385   YEOVIL (SW)
22 Hendford, Yeovil, Somerset BA20 2QD
Tel: 01935 382150
Fax: 01935 410004
DX: 98830 YEOVIL 2
Court Details
22 Hendford, Yeovil
District Registry; Bankruptcy; Divorce; Family Hearing Centre
District Judge: Peter Corrigan

386   YORK (NE)
Janet Allsopp, Piccadilly House, 55 Piccadilly, York YO1 9WL
Tel: 01904 688550
Fax: 01904 679963
DX: 65165 YORK 4
Court Details
Piccadilly House, 55 Piccadilly, York
District Registry; Bankruptcy; Care Centre
District Judges: P.J.E. Wildsmith, M.F. Handley, C. Dodd, R. Hill, H. Wood

NORTHERN IRELAND

ARDS
Mrs K. Coey, Newtownards Court Office, The Courthouse, Regent Street, Newtownards, County Down BT23 4LP
Tel: 028 9181 4343
Fax: 028 9181 8024
Court Houses: Newtownards; Downpatrick

ARMAGH AND SOUTH DOWN
Mrs G. Campbell, Newry Court Office, The Courthouse, 23 New Street, Newry BT35 6AD
Tel: 028 3025 2040
Fax: 028 3026 9830
Court Houses: Armagh; Newry

BELFAST (BELFAST RECORDER'S COURT)
Mrs P. McCourt, Business Manager, Belfast Combined Courts, Laganside Courts, 45 Oxford Street, Belfast BT1 3LL
Tel: 028 9072 4515
Fax: 028 9031 5219
Court Houses: Laganside Courts, 45 Oxford Street, Belfast; Old Town Hall, Victoria Street, Belfast

FERMANAGH AND TYRONE
Mrs S. Hughes, Omagh Court Office, The Courthouse, High Street, Omagh, County Tyrone BT78 1DU
Tel: 028 8224 2056
Fax: 028 8225 1198
Court Houses: Omagh; Dungannon; Enniskillen; Strabane

LONDONDERRY (LONDONDERRY RECORDER'S COURT)
Mr L. Millar, Londonderry Court Office, The Courthouse, Bishop Street, Londonderry BT48 6PQ
Tel: 028 7136 3448
Fax: 028 7137 2059
Court Houses: Londonderry; Limavady; Magherafelt

ANTRIM
Mr M. Little, Ballymena Court Office, The Courthouse, 30 Castle Way, Antrim, County Antrim BT41 4AQ
Tel: 028 2564 9416
Fax: 028 2565 5371
Court Houses: Ballymena; Coleraine; Antrim

CRAIGAVON
Mr D. Harkin, Craigavon Court Office, The Courthouse, Central Way, Craigavon BT64 1AP
Tel: 028 3834 1324
Fax: 028 3834 1243
Court Houses: Craigavon; Lisburn

Part III

COURTS OF SUMMARY JURISDICTION

ABBREVIATIONS

CPS	Crown Prosecution Service
DDC	Dedicated Drugs Court
Dir	Directions
Enf	Enforcement
FPC	Family Proceedings Court
JP	Justice of the Peace
Misc	Miscellaneous
NP	Non-police
RTC	Road Traffic Court
SDVC	Special Domestic Violence Court
SIC	Sensitive Issues Court
TFOs	Transfer of Fine Orders
VC	Video Court
YC	Youth Court

LONDON REGION

Delivery Director: Sheila Proudlock, 3rd Floor, Rose Court, 2 Southwark Bridge, London SE1 9HS. Tel: 020 7921 2010. DX: 154261 SOUTHWARK 12.

LOCAL JUSTICE AREAS IN THE GREATER LONDON AREA

LONDON – CENTRAL AND SOUTH (CRIME)

Cluster Manager: Jan Hartnett, South West London Administration Centre, Lavender Hill Magistrates' Court, 176A Lavender Hill, Battersea, London SW11 1JU. DX: 58559 CLAPHAM JUNCTION

Justices' Clerk, London Central and South Clerkship: Kevin Griffiths, City of London Magistrates' Court, 1 Queen Victoria Street, London EC4N 4XY

Justices' Clerk, London West Clerkship: Julien Vantyghem, City of London Magistrates' Court, as above

Fines, fixed penalties and maintenance enforcement enquiries: see London Collection and Compliance Centre, p 113

Legal aid enquiries: Legal Aid Office, PO Box 2919, Romford RM7 1NZ. Tel: 01708 794228/9. DX: 743412 ROMFORD 15

CENTRAL LONDON LJA (ADULT COURT 2570, YOUTH COURT 6570)

WESTMINSTER MAGISTRATES' COURT
Central London Administration Centre, Westminster Magistrates' Court, 181 Marylebone Road, London NW1 5BR
Tel: 020 3126 3050 (Listing); 3040 (Legal Aid); 3020 (Applications); 3030 (Post Court); 3010 (International Jurisdiction)
Fax: 020 3126 3051 (Listing); 3041 (Legal Aid); 3031 (Applications/Post Court); 3011 (International Jurisdiction)
DX: 120551 MARYLEBONE 9
Email: westminster.mc@hmcts.gsi.gov.uk (General); westminster.lt@hmcts.gsi.gov.uk (Listing); gl-cow.legalaid@hmcts.gsi.gov.uk (Legal Aid); westminster.go@hmcts.gsi.gov.uk (Applications/Post Court)

Courts and times
Westminster Magistrates' Court, 181 Marylebone Road, London NW1 5BR
Times on application

CITY OF LONDON MAGISTRATES' COURT
All correspondence and telephone enquiries to: Central London Administration Centre, Westminster Magistrates' Court, 181 Marylebone Road, London NW1 5BR
Tel: 020 3126 3355 (Westminster); 3040 (Legal Aid)
Fax: 020 7332 1493
DX: 120551 MARYLEBONE 9
Email: westminster.mc@hmcts.gsi.gov.uk

Courts and times
City of London Magistrates' Court, 1 Queen Victoria Street, London EC4N 4XY
Times on application

HAMMERSMITH MAGISTRATES' COURT
All correspondence to: Hammersmith Magistrates' Court, 181 Talgarth Road, Hammersmith, London W6 8DN
Tel: 020 8700 9360 (Customer Services/Post Court/Resulting); 9350 (Listing/Pre Court)
Fax: 020 8700 9344 (Listing/Pre Court); 9355 (Post Court)
DX: 124800 HAMMERSMITH 8
Email: hammersmith.mc@hmcts.gsi.gov.uk

Courts and times
Hammersmith Magistrates' Court, 181 Talgarth Road, Hammersmith, London W6 8DN
Times on application

SOUTH LONDON LJA (ADULT COURT 2576, YOUTH COURT 6576)

CAMBERWELL GREEN MAGISTRATES' COURT
South London Administration Centre, Camberwell Green Magistrates' Court, 15 D'Eynsford Road, Camberwell Green, London SE5 7UP
Tel: 020 7805 9851/60 (Customer Services); 9852 (Legal Aid)
Fax: 020 7805 9898
DX: 157730 CAMBERWELL GREEN 3
Email: gl-camberwellmcenq@hmcts.gsi.gov.uk

Courts and times
Camberwell Green Magistrates' Court, 15 D'Eynsford Road, Camberwell Green, London SE5 7UP
Times on application

TOWER BRIDGE MAGISTRATES' COURT
Court closed. All correspondence to: South London Administration Centre, Camberwell Green Magistrates' Court, 15 D'Eynsford Road, Camberwell Green, London SE5 7UP

CROYDON MAGISTRATES' COURT
The Magistrates Court, Barclay Road, Croydon CR9 3NG. All correspondence to: South London Administration Centre, Camberwell Green Magistrates' Court, 15 D'Eynsford Road, Camberwell Green, London SE5 7UP
Tel: 020 8686 8680
Fax: 020 8680 9801
DX: 97474 CROYDON 6
Email: gl-croydonmcenq@hmcts.gsi.gov.uk
Courts and times
The Magistrates Court, Barclay Road, Croydon CR9 3NG
Times on application

SOUTH EAST LONDON LJA (ADULT COURT 2575, YOUTH COURT 6575)

BROMLEY MAGISTRATES' COURT
South East London Administration Centre, The Court House, London Road, Bromley, Kent BR1 71RA
Tel: 020 8437 3585/3500/3618
Fax: 0870 324 0223
DX: 156800 BROMLEY 10
Email: gl-bromleymclist@hmcts.gsi.gov.uk
Courts and times
Bromley Magistrates' Court, The Court House, London Road, Bromley, Kent BR1 71RA
Times on application

BEXLEY MAGISTRATES' COURT
All correspondence to: South East London Administration Centre, The Court House, London Road, Bromley, Kent BR1 71RA
Tel: 020 8437 3585/3500/3618
Fax: 0870 324 0223
DX: 156800 BROMLEY 10
Email: gl-bromleymclist@hmcts.gsi.gov.uk
Courts and times
Bexley Magistrates' Court, Norwich Place, Bexleyheath DA6 7NB
Times on application

GREENWICH MAGISTRATES' COURT
All correspondence to: South East London Administration Centre, The Court House, London Road, Bromley, Kent BR1 71RA
Tel: 020 8437 3585/3500/3618
Fax: 0870 324 0223
DX: 156800 BROMLEY 10
Email: gl-bromleymclist@hmcts.gsi.gov.uk
Courts and times
Greenwich Magistrates' Court, 9 Blackheath Road, Greenwich SE10 8PG
Belmarsh Magistrates' Court, 4 Belmarsh Road, London SE28 0HA
Times on application

SOUTH WEST LONDON LJA (ADULT COURT 2577, YOUTH COURT 6577)

LAVENDER HILL MAGISTRATES' COURT
South West London Administration Centre, 176A Lavender Hill, Battersea, London SW11 1JU
Tel: 020 7805 1445 (Main); 1447 (Listing); 1493/1479 (Post Court/Resulting); 1452 (Youth Listing)
Fax: 020 7805 1448; (Main) 1461 (Listing); 1437 (Youth Listing)
DX: 58559 CLAPHAM JUNCTION

Email: gl-swesternmcenq@hmcts.gsi.gov.uk

Courts and times
Lavender Hill Magistrates' Court, 176A Lavender Hill, Battersea, London SW11 1JU
Times on application

RICHMOND MAGISTRATES' COURT
All correspondence to: South West London Administration Centre, 176A Lavender Hill, Battersea, London SW11 1JU
Tel: 020 7805 1445 (Main, Lavender Hill); 1447 (Listing, Lavender Hill); 1493/79 (Post Court/Resulting, Lavender Hill); 1452 (Youth Listing, Lavender Hill); 020 8126 3040 (Legal Aid)
Fax: 020 7805 1448 (Main); 1461 (Listing); 1437 (Youth Listing) (Lavender Hill Magistrates' Court)
DX: 58559 CLAPHAM JUNCTION
Email: gl-swesternmcenq@hmcts.gsi.gov.uk

Courts and times
The Court House, Parkshot, Richmond
Times on application

WIMBLEDON MAGISTRATES' COURT
All correspondence to: South West London Administration Centre, 176A Lavender Hill, Battersea, London SW11 1JU
Tel: 020 7805 1445 (Main, Lavender Hill); 1447 (Listing, Lavender Hill); 1493/1479 (Post Court/Resulting, Lavender Hill); 1452 (Youth Listing, Lavender Hill)
Fax: 020 7805 1448 (Main); 1461 (Listing); 1437 (Youth Listing) (Lavender Hill Magistrates' Court)
DX: 58559 CLAPHAM JUNCTION
Email: gl-swesternmcenq@hmcts.gsi.gov.uk

Courts and times
The Law Courts, Alexandra Road, Wimbledon
Times on application

BEXLEY MAGISTRATES' COURT
see **2575/6575 South East London LJA**

BROMLEY MAGISTRATES' COURT
see **2575/6575 South East London LJA**

CITY OF LONDON MAGISTRATES' COURT
see **2570/6570 Central London LJA**

CITY OF WESTMINSTER MAGISTRATES' COURT
see **2570/6570 Central London LJA**

CROYDON MAGISTRATES' COURT
see **2576/6576 South London LJA**

GREENWICH MAGISTRATES' COURT
see **2575/6575 South East London LJA**

WOOLWICH MAGISTRATES' COURT
closed wef 1/7/11

CAMBERWELL GREEN MAGISTRATES' COURT
see **2576/6576 South London LJA**

GREENWICH, LEWISHAM & SOUTHWARK YOUTH COURTS
see **6576 South London LJA**

TOWER BRIDGE MAGISTRATES' COURT
closed wef 2013

SUTTON MAGISTRATES' COURT
closed wef 3/6/11

LONDON – NORTH AND WEST (CRIME)

Cluster Manager: Jenny Taylor, North West London Administration Centre, Willesden Magistrates' Court, 448 High Road, London NW10 2DZ. DX: 110850 WILLESDEN 2

Justices' Clerk (London North and East Clerkship): Tom Ring, City of London Magistrates' Court, 1 Queen Victoria Street, London EC4N 4XY

Justices' Clerk (London West Clerkship): Julien Vantyghem, City of London Magistrates' Court, as above

Fines, fixed penalties and maintenance enforcement enquiries: see London Collection and Compliance Centre, p 113

Legal aid enquiries: Legal Aid Office, PO Box 2919, Romford RM7 1NZ. Tel: 01708 794228/9. DX: 743412 ROMFORD 15

EAST LONDON LJA (ADULT COURT 2574, YOUTH COURT 6574)

THAMES MAGISTRATES' COURT
58 Bow Road, London E3 4DJ
Administration and adult remand centre, including adult sentencing, for East London LJA; Hackney, Newham, Tower Hamlets and Waltham Forest boroughs
Tel: 020 8271 1530/1533 (Customer Service Unit); 1207 (Pre Court Case Progression Officers)
Fax: 020 8271 1241
DX: 157540 Bow 3
Email: gl-thamesmclist@hmcts.gsi.gov.uk

Courts and times
Thames Magistrates' Court, 58 Bow Road, London E3 4DJ
Times on application

STRATFORD MAGISTRATES' COURT
389–397 High Street, London E15 4SB
Adult and youth trial centre and youth remand centre for East London LJA; Hackney, Newham, Tower Hamlets and Waltham Forest boroughs
Tel: 020 8437 6066
Fax: 020 8271 1241
DX: 157540 Bow 3
Note: All enquiries and correspondence to Administration Centre, Thames Magistrates' Court, 58 Bow Road, London E3 4DJ

Courts and times
Stratford Magistrates' Court, 389–397 High Street, London E15 4SB
Times on application

WALTHAM FOREST MAGISTRATES' COURT
The Court House, 1 Farnan Avenue, Walthamstow, London E17 4NX
Traffic gateway centre for East, North and North East London LJAs
Tel: 020 8272 4113
Fax: 020 8271 124
DX: 157540 Bow 3
Note: All enquiries and correspondence to Administration Centre, Thames Magistrates' Court, 58 Bow Road, London E3 4DJ

Courts and times
The Court House, 1 Farnan Avenue, Walthamstow, London E17 4NX
Times on application

NORTH LONDON LJA (ADULT COURT 2572, YOUTH COURT 6572)

HIGHBURY CORNER MAGISTRATES' COURT
51 Holloway Road, London N7 8JA
Postal address: North London Administration Centre, PO Box 52693, London N7 1AF
Administration centre for North London LJA
Tel: 020 7506 3100/3156/3221
Fax: 020 7506 3190
DX: 153700 HIGHBURY 4

Email: gl-hcornermcenq@hmcts.gsi.gov.uk

Courts and times
Highbury Corner Magistrates' Court, 51 Holloway Road, London N7 8JA
Times on application

TOTTENHAM MAGISTRATES' COURT
All correspondence to: North London Administration Centre, PO Box 52693, London N7 1AF
Tel: 020 7506 3100/3156/3221
Fax: 020 7506 3190
DX: 153700 HIGHBURY 4
Email: gl-hcornermcenq@hmcts.gsi.gov.uk

Courts and times
Tottenham Magistrates Court, The Court House, Lordship Lane, Tottenham, London N17 6RT
Times on application

NORTH EAST LONDON LJA (ADULT COURT 2573, YOUTH COURT 6573)

BARKINGSIDE MAGISTRATES' COURT
850 Cranbrook Road, Barkingside, Ilford, Essex IG6 1HW
Administration Centre for North East London LJA
Tel: 020 8437 6525 (General Enquiries and Results)
Fax: 020 8437 6561
DX: 156842 ILFORD 9
Email: gl-barkingsidemcenq@hmcts.gsi.gov.uk; gl-centralisedlegalaidofficeenquiries@hmcts.gsi.gov.uk
(Legal Aid Enquiries)

Courts and times
Barkingside Magistrates' Court, 850 Cranbrook Road, Barkingside, Ilford, Essex IG6 1HW
Times on application

ROMFORD MAGISTRATES' COURT
All correspondence to: North East London Administration Centre, Barkingside Magistrates' Court,
850 Cranbrook Road, Barkingside, Ilford, Essex IG6 1HW
Tel: 020 8437 6525 (General Enquiries and Results, Barkingside)
Fax: 01708 794270
DX: 156842 ILFORD 9
Email: gl-barkingsidemcenq@hmcts.gsi.gov.uk

Courts and times
Romford Magistrates' Court, Main Road, Romford, Essex RM1 3BH
Times on application

NORTH WEST LONDON LJA (ADULT COURT 2571, YOUTH COURT 6571)

WILLESDEN MAGISTRATES' COURT
North West London Administration Centre, Willesden Magistrates' Court, 448 High Road, Willesden,
London NW10 2DZ PS
Administration centre for North West London LJA and West London LJA
Tel: 020 8955 0555 (General Enquiries); 0679 (Pre Court); 0856 (Listing); 0544 (Post Court/Resulting)
Fax: 0870 324 0240
Minicom: 020 8988 0550
DX: 110850 WILLESDEN 2
Email: gl-brentmcenq@hmcts.gsi.gov.uk

Courts and times
Willesden Magistrates' Court, 448 High Road, Willesden, London NW10 2DZ
Times on application

HENDON MAGISTRATES' COURT
All correspondence to: North West London Administration Centre, Willesden Magistrates' Court, 448
High Road, Willesden, London NW10 2DZ
Tel: 020 8955 0555 (General Enquiries); 0679 (Pre Court, Willesden); 0856 (Listing, Willesden); 0544
(Post Court/Resulting, Willesden)
Fax: 0870 324 0240

Minicom: 020 8988 0550
DX: 110850 WILLESDEN 2
Email: gl-brentmcenq@hmcts.gsi.gov.uk

Courts and times
Hendon Magistrates' Court, The Court House, Hendon
Times on application

WEST LONDON LJA (ADULT COURT 2578, YOUTH COURT 6578)

EALING MAGISTRATES' COURT
North West & West London Administration Centre, Willesden Magistrates' Court, 448 High Road,
Willesden, London NW10 2DZ
Tel: 020 8955 0555 (General Enquiries); 020 8437 4707 (Ealing); 0679 (Pre Court, Willesden); 0856
(Listing, Willesden); 0544 (Post Court/Resulting, Willesden)
Fax: 0870 324 0240
Minicom: 020 8988 0550
DX: 110850 WILLESDEN 2
Email: gl-brentmcenq@hmcts.gsi.gov.uk

Courts and times
Ealing Magistrates' Court, The Court House: Green Man Lane, Ealing
Times on application

FELTHAM MAGISTRATES' COURT
All correspondence to: North West & West London Administration Centre, Willesden Magistrates'
Court, 448 High Road, Willesden, London NW10 2DZ
Tel: 020 8955 0555 (General Enquiries); 0679 (Pre Court, Willesden); 0856 (Listing, Willesden); 0544
(Post Court/Resulting, Willesden)
Fax: 0870 324 0240
Minicom: 020 8988 0550
DX: 110850 WILLESDEN 2
Email: gl-brentmcenq@hmcts.gsi.gov.uk

Courts and times
Feltham Magistrates' Court, Hanworth Road, Feltham
Times on application

UXBRIDGE MAGISTRATES' COURT
All correspondence to: North West & West London Administration Centre, Willesden Magistrates'
Court, 448 High Road, Willesden, London NW10 2DZ
Tel: 020 8955 0555 (General Enquiries); 0679 (Pre Court, Willesden); 0856 (Listing, Willesden); 0544
(Post Court/Resulting, Willesden)
Fax: 0870 324 0240
Minicom: 020 8988 0550
DX: 110850 WILLESDEN 2
Email: gl-brentmcenq@hmcts.gsi.gov.uk

Courts and times
Uxbridge Magistrates' Court, The Court House, Harefield Road, Uxbridge UB8 1PQ
Times on application.

BARKING MAGISTRATES' COURT
closed wef 30/9/11

HENDON MAGISTRATES' COURT
see **2571/6571 North West London LJA**

BRENT MAGISTRATES' COURT
see **2578/6578 West London LJA**

HIGHBURY CORNER MAGISTRATES' COURT
see **2572/6572 North London LJA**

EALING MAGISTRATES' COURT
see **2578/6578 West London LJA**

ACTON MAGISTRATES' COURT
closed wef 28/4/11

ENFIELD MAGISTRATES' COURT
see **2572/6572 North London LJA**

THAMES MAGISTRATES' COURT
see **2574/6574 East London LJA**

WEST LONDON MAGISTRATES' COURT
see **2570/6570 Central London LJA**

HARINGEY MAGISTRATES' COURT
see **2572/6572 North London LJA.**

HARROW MAGISTRATES' COURT
closed wef 30/6/11

HAVERING MAGISTRATES' COURT
see **2573/6573 North East London LJA**

UXBRIDGE MAGISTRATES' COURT
see **2578/6578 West London LJA**

BRENTFORD MAGISTRATES' COURT
closed wef 30/12/11

FELTHAM MAGISTRATES' COURT
see **2578/6578 West London LJA**

LAMBETH AND WANDSWORTH YOUTH COURTS (BALHAM YOUTH COURT)
closed wef 30/12/11

KINGSTON-UPON-THAMES MAGISTRATES' COURT
closed wef 30/6/11

WIMBLEDON MAGISTRATES' COURT
see **London – Central and South (Crime) – 2577/6577 South West London LJA**

STRATFORD MAGISTRATES' COURT
see **2574/6574 East London LJA**

REDBRIDGE MAGISTRATES' COURT
see **2573/6573 North East London LJA**

RICHMOND-UPON-THAMES MAGISTRATES' COURT
see **London – Central and South (Crime) – 2577/6577 South West London LJA**

WALTHAM FOREST MAGISTRATES' COURT
see **2574/6574 East London LJA**

SOUTH WESTERN MAGISTRATES' COURT
see **London – Central and South (Crime) – 2577/6577 South West London LJA**

HIGHGATE MAGISTRATES' COURT
closed wef 2013

LONDON – FAMILY

Justices' Clerk, London Family: John Baker, City of London Magistrates' Court, 1 Queen Victoria Street, London EC4N 4XY

Fines, fixed penalty and maintenance enforcement enquiries: see London Collection and Compliance Centre, p 113

INNER LONDON FAMILY PROCEEDINGS COURT
59–65 Wells Street, London W1A 3AE
Tel: 020 7805 3400
Fax: 020 7805 3490
DX: 160000 SOHO SQUARE 6

Courts and times
Inner London Family Proceedings Court, 59–65 Wells Street, London W1A 3AE
FPC: Weekdays 09:00–17:00

PRINCIPAL REGISTRY OF THE FAMILY DIVISION (PRFD)
First Avenue House, 42–49 High Holborn, London WC1V 6NP
Tel: 0207 947 6000
DX: 610010 KINGSWAY 7
Probate Manager: Tel: 0207 947 6945

District Judges
District Judge Aitken; District Judge Bowman; District Judge Bradley; District Judge Harper; District Judge MacGregor; District Judge Reid; District Judge Robinson; District Judge Walker; District Judge Gordon-Saker; District Judge Simmonds; District Judge Gibson; District Judge Hess

LONDON COLLECTION & COMPLIANCE CENTRE

Fines enquiries: Tel: 020 7556 8500 (all areas); or by post/DX as below.

Bexley, Bromley, Camberwell Green, City of London, City of Westminster, Croydon, Greenwich, Tower Bridge: London Collection & Compliance Centre, Central & South East, PO Box 31090 (Metropolitan Police); or PO Box 31089 (City of London Police), London SW1P 3WQ. DX: London Collection & Compliance Centre Central & South East 154264 SOUTHWARK 12

Brent, Enfield, Haringey, Hendon, Highbury Corner, Uxbridge: London Collection & Compliance Centre, North West, PO Box 31091 (Metropolitan Police); or PO Box 31089 (City of London Police), London SW1P 3WR. DX: London Collection & Compliance Centre North West 154264 SOUTHWARK 12

Acton, Brentford, Ealing, Feltham, Richmond-upon-Thames, South Western, Wimbledon, West London: London Collection & Compliance Centre, South West, PO Box 31089 (Metropolitan Police); or PO Box 31089 (City of London Police), London SW1P 3WP. DX: London Collection & Compliance Centre South West 154264 SOUTHWARK 12

Havering, Redbridge, Stratford, Thames, Waltham Forest: London Collection & Compliance Centre, North East, PO Box 31092 (Metropolitan Police); or PO Box 31089 (City of London Police), London SW1P 3WS. DX: London Collection & Compliance Centre North East 154264 SOUTHWARK 12

Maintenance enforcement enquiries

Tel: 020 7556 8506; or by post to PO Box 31093 (Metropolitan Police); or PO Box 31089 (City of London Police), London SW1P 3WT

Fixed penalty enquiries

Tel: 020 7556 8555 (Metropolitan Police); 020 7556 8787 (City of London Police); 020 7556 8777 (British Transport Police); or by post to PO Box 31093, London SW1P 3WT

MIDLANDS REGION

DERBYSHIRE AND NOTTINGHAMSHIRE

Delivery Director: Lucy Garrod, Midlands Regional Office, 6th Floor, Temple Court, Birmingham. DX: 701993 BIRMINGHAM 7

1430 HIGH PEAK LJA
Graham Hooper, Justices' Clerk, Peak Buildings, Terrace Road, Buxton, Derbyshire SK17 6DY
Tel: 01298 23951 (General Enquiries)
Fax: 01298 26031
DX: 701980 BUXTON 2
Note: All enquiries regarding payment of fines and maintenance and all TFOs should be directed to Southern Derbyshire Magistrates' Court

Courts and times
Court House, Peak Buildings, Terrace Road, Buxton
Adult: Monday and Wednesday 10:00 (except bank holidays), Tuesday 10:00
YC: Thursday 10:00
FPC: Friday 10:00 (dates specified annually)

2566 MANSFIELD LJA
Graham Hooper, Justices' Clerk, Mansfield Magistrates' Court, Rosemary Street, Mansfield, Nottinghamshire NG19 6EE
Tel: 01623 451500
Fax: 01623 45164
DX: 179560 MANSFIELD 9

Courts and times
Mansfield Magistrates' Court, Rosemary Street, Mansfield
Adult: Weekdays 10:00 and 14:15
YC: Tuesday
FPC: Thursday and Friday 10:00

2567 NEWARK AND SOUTHWELL LJA
closed wef 30/9/11

1432 NORTH EAST DERBYSHIRE AND DALES LJA
Graham Hooper, Justices' Clerk, Court House, Tapton Lane, Chesterfield, Derbyshire S41 7TW
Tel: 01246 224040
Fax: 01246 246492
DX: 742041 CHESTERFIELD 7

Courts and times
Court House, Tapton Lane, Chesterfield
Adult: Weekdays 10:00
YC: Tuesday and Friday 10:00
FPC: Thursday 10:00

2568 NOTTINGHAM LJA
Graham Hooper, Justices' Clerk, Nottingham Magistrates' Court, Carrington Street, Nottingham NG2 1EE
Tel: 0115 955 8111
Fax: 0115 955 8139
DX: 719030 NOTTINGHAM 32

Courts and times
Nottingham Magistrates' Court, Carrington Street, Nottingham NG2 1EE
Adult: Weekdays 10:00 and 14:15, occasional courts 10:00
YC: Weekdays 10:00 and 14:15
FPC: Wednesday, Thursday, Friday 10:00, Monday, Friday 14:15

1428 SOUTHERN DERBYSHIRE LJA
Graham Hooper, Justices' Clerk, The Court House, St Mary's Gate, Derby DE1 3JR
Tel: 01332 362000
Fax: 01332 333183
DX: 707570 DERBY 8

Courts and times
The Court House, St Mary's Gate, Derby
Adult: Weekdays 10:00 and 14:15
YC: Weekdays 10:00 and 14:15
FPC: Tuesday and Wednesday 10:00 and 14:15

2569 WORKSOP AND RETFORD LJA
Graham Hooper, Justices' Clerk, The Court House, 30 Potter Street, Worksop, Nottinghamshire S80 2AJ
Tel: 01909 486111
Fax: 01909 473521
DX: 743240 WORKSOP 4

Courts and times
The Court House, Potter Street, Worksop
Adult: Monday, Wednesday and Thursday 10:00 and 14:15
YC: Friday 10:00 and 14:15
FPC: Tuesday 10:00 and 14:15
Private Prosecutions: Wednesday (every four weeks) 10:00 and 14:15

LEICESTERSHIRE, RUTLAND, LINCOLNSHIRE, NORTHAMPTONSHIRE

Delivery Director: Lucy Garrod, Midlands Regional Office, 6th Floor, Temple Court, Birmingham. DX: 701993 BIRMINGHAM 7

2047 ASHBY-DE-LA-ZOUCH LJA
closed wef 31/7/11

2073 BOSTON LJA
combined with **2082 SKEGNESS LJA** to form **2085 EAST LINCOLNSHIRE LJA**

2321 CORBY LJA
Nick Watson, Justices' Clerk, Regent's Pavilion, Summerhouse Road, Moulton Park, Northampton NN3 6AS
Tel: 01604 497000
Fax: 01604 497010; 497020
DX: 151720 NORTHAMPTON 27

Courts and times
The Court House, Elizabeth Street, Corby
Adult: Thursday and Friday 10:00
FPC: Every four weeks 10:00

2322 DAVENTRY LJA
closed wef 31/3/11

2085 EAST LINCOLNSHIRE LJA
Nick Watson, Justices' Clerk, The Court House, Park Avenue, Skegness PE25 1BH
Tel: 01754 898848
Fax: 01754 767318
DX: 743030 SKEGNESS 3

Courts and times
Law Courts, Norfolk Street, Boston
Court House, Park Avenue, Skegness
Adult: Boston: Alternate Mondays, Wednesday, alternate Fridays 10:00; **Skegness:** Monday, Wednesday, alternate Fridays 10:00
YC: Boston: Alternate Thursdays 10:00; **Skegness:** Alternate Thursdays 10:00
FPC: Boston: One Thursday a month 10:00; **Skegness:** One Thursday a month 10:00

2076 ELLOES, BOURNE AND STAMFORD LJA
combined with **2077 GRANTHAM AND SLEAFORD LJA** to form **2084 SOUTH LINCOLNSHIRE LJA**

2075 GAINSBOROUGH LJA
closed wef 31/7/11

2077 GRANTHAM AND SLEAFORD LJA
combined with **2076 ELLOES, BOURNE AND STAMFORD LJA** to form **2084 SOUTH LINCOLNSHIRE LJA**

2323 KETTERING LJA
Nick Watson, Justices' Clerk, Regent's Pavilion, Summerhouse Road, Moulton Park, Northampton NN3 6AS
Tel: 01604 497000
Fax: 01604 497010 497020
DX: 151720 NORTHAMPTON 27

Courts and times
The Court House, London Road, Kettering
Adult: Wednesday 10:00
YC: Friday 10:00
FPC: Every four weeks 10:00

2048 LEICESTER LJA
Nick Watson, Justices' Clerk, 15 Pocklingtons Walk, Leicester LE1 6BT
Tel: 0116 255 3666
Fax: 0116 254 5851

DX: 10828 LEICESTER

Courts and times
15 Pocklingtons Walk, Leicester
Wellington Street, Leicester
Adult: Pocklingtons Walk: Weekdays 10:00 and 14:00
YC: Combined Youth Panel for Leicestershire: Pocklingtons Walk: Monday, Wednesday, Friday 10:00 and 14:00
Enf: Pocklingtons Walk: Weekdays 10:00
FPC: Wellington Street: Monday, Wednesday, Thursday, Friday

2079 LINCOLN DISTRICT LJA
now **2083 NORTH WEST LINCOLNSHIRE LJA**

2049 LOUGHBOROUGH LJA
Nick Watson, Justices' Clerk, The Court House, 60 Pinfold Gate, Loughborough, Leicestershire LE11 1AZ
Tel: 01509 215715
Fax: 01509 261714
DX: 716116 LOUGHBOROUGH 4

Courts and times
The Court House, 60 Pinfold Gate, Loughborough
Adult: Monday, Wednesday, Friday 10:00 and 14:00, Tuesday 14:00
YC: Combined Youth Panel for Leicestershire: Friday 10:00 and 14:00
FPC: Monday, Tuesday, Wednesday 10:00

2050 MARKET BOSWORTH LJA
Nick Watson, Justices' Clerk, The Court House, 60 Pinfold Gate, Loughborough, Leicestershire LE11 1AZ
Tel: 01509 215715
Fax: 01509 261714
DX: 716116 LOUGHBOROUGH 4

Courts and times
Court House, Upper Bond Street, Hinckley
Adult: Tuesday and Thursday 10:00 and 14:00
YC: Combined Youth Panel for Leicestershire: Tuesday 14:00

2051 MARKET HARBOROUGH AND LUTTERWORTH LJA
closed wef 31/7/11

2045 MELTON, BELVOIR AND RUTLAND LJA
closed wef 31/7/11

2083 NORTH WEST LINCOLNSHIRE LJA
Nick Watson, Justices' Clerk, Magistrates' Clerk's Office, The Court House, 358 High Street, Lincoln LN5 7QA
Tel: 01522 528218; 551528 (Family Admin); 582803 (Fines)
Fax: 01522 525832
DX: 703232 LINCOLN 6
Email: li-lincoln@hmcts.gsi.gov.uk

Courts and times
The Court House, 358 High Street, Lincoln
Adult: Weekdays 10:00
YC: Thursday 10:00
FPC: Wednesday 10:00 and 14:15, Friday 10:00

2325 NORTHAMPTON LJA
Nick Watson, Justices' Clerk, Regent's Pavilion, Summerhouse Road, Moulton Park, Northampton NN3 6AS
Tel: 01604 497000
Fax: 01604 497010; 497020
DX: 151720 NORTHAMPTON 27

Courts and times
The Court House, Campbell Square, Northampton
Adult: Weekdays 10:00
YC: Monday and Wednesday 10:00
FPC: Tuesday 10:00

2082 SKEGNESS LJA (FORMERLY SPILSBY AND SKEGNESS DIVISION)
combined with **2073 BOSTON LJA** to form **2085 EAST LINCOLNSHIRE LJA**

2084 SOUTH LINCOLNSHIRE LJA
Nick Watson, Justices' Clerk, The Court House, Harlaxton Road, Grantham NG31 7SB
Tel: 01476 563438
Fax: 01476 567200
DX: 711100 GRANTHAM 4

Courts and times
Magistrates' Court, Harlaxton Road, Grantham
Sessions House, Spalding
Adult: Grantham: Monday, Wednesday, Thursday, Friday 10:00; **Spalding:** Tuesday, Thursday 10:00, Wednesday twice a month 10:00
YC: Grantham: Tuesday twice a month 10:00; **Spalding:** Wednesday twice a month 10:00
FPC: Grantham: Tuesday once a month 10:00; **Spalding:** Monday twice a month 10:00

2327 TOWCESTER LJA
closed wef 31/3/11

2328 WELLINGBOROUGH LJA
Nick Watson, Justices' Clerk, Regent's Pavilion, Summerhouse Road, Moulton Park, Northampton NN3 6AS
Tel: 01604 497000
Fax: 01604 497010; 497020
DX: 151720 NORTHAMPTON 27

Courts and times
The Court House, Midland Road, Wellingborough
Adult: Monday and Tuesday 10:00
FPC: Friday 10:00

STAFFORDSHIRE AND WEST MERCIA

Delivery Director: Lucy Garrod, Midlands Regional Office, 6th Floor, Temple Court, Birmingham. DX: 701993 BIRMINGHAM 7

West Mercia Central Finance & Enforcement Unit: Tel: 01562 514000. Fax: 01562 514091

Fine and maintenance payments: West Mercia, PO Box 6267, The Court House, Bryans Lane, Rugeley WS14 4GX. Tel: 01889 503500 option 3

Enquiries relating to enforcement of fines and maintenance accounts: PO Box 6088, Kidderminster DY11 9DD

Enquiries relating to administration and enforcement of maintenance accounts for Hereford and Worcester: Tel: 01905 730800 (Monday–Friday 09:00–13:00)

Enquires relating to administration and enforcement of maintenance accounts for Shropshire: Tel: 01952 238280

Reciprocal enforcement enquiries: Kidderminster Magistrates' Court. Tel: 01562 514000

Fixed penalty payments and enquiries: PO Box 2642, Kidderminster DY10 1WZ

Family proceedings enquiries: Hereford & Worcester Family Team, Worcester Combined Court, The Shirehall, Foregate Street, Worcester WR1 1EQ

Staffordshire Central Finance & Enforcement Unit: Tel: 01889 503500. Fax: 01889 503535. DX: 720990 RUGELEY 2

Fines and maintenance payments: Central Finance & Enforcement Unit, The Court House, Bryans Lane, Rugeley WS15 2FX

Enquiries relating to enforcement of fines and maintenance accounts: Central Finance & Enforcement Unit, The Court House, as above

Fixed penalty payments and enquiries: PO Box 1778, Rugeley WS15 2WX.

TFOs and fixed penalty registration: Central Finance & Enforcement Unit, The Court House, as above

---

1840 BROMSGROVE AND REDDITCH LJA

Stephen Abbott, Justices' Clerk, The Magistrates' Courts, Comberton Place, Kidderminster, Worcestershire DY10 1QQ
Tel: 01562 514000
Fax: 01562 514323

Courts and times
Magistrates' Court, Grove Street, Redditch
Adult: Weekdays 10:00 and 13:30
YC: Thursday 10:00
FPC: Wednesday and Friday 10:00
Enf: Tuesday (every four weeks) 10:00

2799 CENTRAL AND SOUTH WEST STAFFORDSHIRE LJA

Stephen Abbott, Justices' Clerk, The Court House, South Walls, Stafford ST16 3DW
Tel: 01785 223144
Fax: 01785 275735
DX: 14575 STAFFORD-1

Courts and times
The Court House, Wolverhampton Road, Cannock
The Court House, South Walls, Stafford
Stafford County Court
Adult: Cannock: Weekdays 10:00
YC: Cannock: Wednesday 10:00
FPC: South Walls: Wednesday and Thursday 10:00
Private Prosecutions: South Walls: Wednesday 10:00
Dir: Stafford County Court: Friday
DV: Cannock: Monday

1841 HEREFORDSHIRE LJA

Stephen Abbott, Justices' Clerk, The Magistrates' Court, Bath Street, Hereford HR1 2HE
Tel: 01562 514000
Fax: 01562 514111

Courts and times
The Court House, Bath Street, Hereford
Adult: Weekdays 10:00

YC: Tuesday 10:00
FPC: Thursday 10:00 and 14:00
Enf: Monday 10:00 and 14:00

1842 KIDDERMINSTER LJA
Stephen Abbott, Justices' Clerk, The Magistrates' Courts, Comberton Place, Kidderminster, Worcestershire DY10 1QQ
Tel: 01562 514000
Fax: 01562 514097
Courts and times
Comberton Place, Kidderminster
Adult: Monday, Tuesday, Thursday, Friday 10:00 and 13:30
YC: Wednesday 10:00
FPC: Monday 10:00
Enf: Friday (every four weeks) 10:00

2791 NORTH STAFFORDSHIRE LJA
Stephen Abbott, Justices' Clerk, Ryecroft, Newcastle-under-Lyme, Staffordshire ST5 2DT
Tel: 01782 741641
Fax: 01782 741729
DX: 708600 NEWCASTLE UNDER LYME 3
Courts and times
The Court House, Ryecroft, Newcastle-under-Lyme
Stoke-on-Trent Combined Court Centre, Betheseda Street, Hanley, Stoke-on-Trent
Adult: Newcastle-under-Lyme: Weekdays 10:00 and 14:00
YC: Newcastle-under-Lyme: Monday, Wednesday, Friday 10:00
FPC: Stoke-on-Trent: Monday, Tuesday, Wednesday, Friday 10:00
DV: Newcastle-under-Lyme: Thursday 10:00
Private Prosecutions: Newcastle-under-Lyme: Weekdays 14:00
Enf: As required

3278 SHREWSBURY AND NORTH SHROPSHIRE LJA
Stephen Abbott, Justices' Clerk, Court Office, Preston Street, Shrewsbury SY2 5NX
Tel: 01743 458500 (Switchboard); 458503 (Court Support)
Fax: 01743 458502
Note: Market Drayton Magistrates' Court closed wef 1/4/11. Oswestry Magistrates' Court closed wef 1/4/11
Courts and times
The Court House, Preston Street, Shrewsbury
Adult: Monday, Tuesday, Wednesday, Thursday 10:00
VC: Tuesday 10:00
YC: Friday 10:00
FPC: Thursday 10:00
Enf: As required

2860 SOUTH EAST STAFFORDSHIRE LJA
Stephen Abbott, Justices' Clerk, The Court House, South Walls, Stafford ST16 3DW
Tel: 01785 223144
Fax: 01785 275735
DX: 14575 STAFFORD-1
Courts and times
Magistrates' Court, Horninglow Street, Burton-upon-Trent
Adult: Weekdays 10:00
YC: Wednesday 10:00
FPC: Monday, Tuesday, Thursday, Friday 10:00
DV: Friday 10:00
Private Prosecutions: Tuesday, Wednesday 14:00

1843 SOUTH WORCESTERSHIRE LJA
Stephen Abbott, Justices' Clerk, Castle Street, Worcester WR1 3QZ
Tel: 01905 743200
Fax: 01905 743346
Courts and times
Magistrates' Courts, Castle Street, Worcester
Adult: Weekdays 10:00

YC: Wednesday 10:00
FPC: Monday and Tuesday 10:00
Enf: Alternate Tuesdays 10:00

3273 TELFORD AND SOUTH SHROPSHIRE LJA
Stephen Abbott, Justices' Clerk, Court Office, Telford Square, Malinsgate, Telford TF3 4HX
Tel: 01952 204500 (Switchboard)
Fax: 01952 204554

Courts and times
Magistrates' Court, Telford Square, Malinsgate, Telford
Adult: Weekdays 10:00 and 14:00
YC: Wednesday 10:00
FPC: Tuesday, Thursday, Friday 10:00

WEST MIDLANDS AND WARWICKSHIRE

Delivery Director: Lucy Garrod, Midlands Regional Office, 6th Floor, Temple Court, Birmingham. DX: 701993 BIRMINGHAM 7.
Payments, account enquiries and correspondence (including TFOs and fixed penalty registrations): Central Finance Unit, Department 05CY, Victoria Law Courts, Corporation Street, Birmingham B4 6QF

2908 BIRMINGHAM LJA
Michael Seath, Justices' Clerk, Victoria Law Courts, Corporation Street, Birmingham B4 6QA
Tel: 0121 212 6600; 250 6189/93 (Family Courts Centre)
Fax: 0121 212 6771 (Post-Court); 6613 (Listing Pre-Court); 0121 250 6183 (Family Courts Centre)
DX: 715206 BIRMINGHAM 39 (Central Finance Unit); DX: 715205 BIRMINGHAM 39 (Birmingham Magistrates and Youth Court)

Courts and times
Victoria Law Courts, Corporation Street, Birmingham
Youth Courts, Steelhouse Lane, Birmingham (correspondence to Victoria Law Courts)
Birmingham Family Courts Centre, Level 5, Priory Courts, Bull Street, Birmingham B4 6JX
Adult: Victoria Law Courts: Weekdays 10:00 and 14:00
YC: Youth Courts: Weekdays 10:00 and 14:00
FPC: Birmingham Family Courts Centre: Weekdays 10:00 and 14:00

2910 COVENTRY DISTRICT LJA
Michael Seath, Justices' Clerk, Magistrates' Court, Little Park Street, Coventry CV1 2SQ
Tel: 024 7663 0666
Fax: 024 7650 0699
DX: 701583 COVENTRY 5

Courts and times
Magistrates' Court, Little Park Street, Coventry
Adult: Weekdays 10:00 and 14:00
YC: Weekdays 10:00
FPC: Monday, Tuesday, Wednesday, Friday 10:00, Tuesday, Wednesday, Friday 14:00

2911 DUDLEY LJA
combined with **2912 STOURBRIDGE AND HALESOWEN LJA** to form **2921 DUDLEY AND HALESOWEN LJA**

2921 DUDLEY AND HALESOWEN LJA
Michael Seath, Justices' Clerk, Magistrates' Clerk's Office, Magistrates' Courts, The Inhedge, Dudley DY1 1RY
Tel: 01384 211411
Fax: 01384 211415
DX: 12769
Note: Halesowen Magistrates' Court closed wef 28/4/11

Courts and times
Magistrates' Courts, The Inhedge, Dudley
Adult: Weekdays
YC: Tuesday, Wednesday, Thursday
FPC: Monday, Wednesday, Thursday, Friday (am only)

2920 SANDWELL LJA
Michael Seath, Justices' Clerk, The Court House, Oldbury Ringway, Oldbury, West Midlands B69 4JN
Tel: 0121 511 2222
Fax: 0121 544 8492
DX: 708330 OLDBURY 3
Note: West Bromwich Magistrates' Court closed wef 15/4/11

Courts and times
The Court House, Oldbury
Adult: Weekdays 10:00 and 14:00
YC: Tuesday and Thursday 10:00
FPC: Monday, Tuesday, Wednesday, Friday 10:00
Dir: Friday 10:00 and 14:00

2916 SOLIHULL LJA
Michael Seath, Justices' Clerk, The Court House, Homer Road, Solihull, West Midlands B91 3RD
Tel: 0121 705 8101
Fax: 0121 711 2045
DX: 708350 SOLIHULL 14

Courts and times
The Court House, Solihull
Adult: Weekdays 10:00 and 14:00
YC: Tuesday and Thursday 10:00 and 14:00
FPC: Monday, Wednesday, Friday 10:00

2912 STOURBRIDGE AND HALESOWEN LJA
combined with **2911 DUDLEY LJA** to form **2921 DUDLEY AND HALESOWEN LJA**

2909 SUTTON COLDFIELD LJA
closed wef 30/6/11

2917 WALSALL AND ALDRIDGE LJA
Michael Seath, Justices' Clerk, Magistrates' Court, Stafford Street, Walsall WS2 8HA
Tel: 01922 638222
Fax: 01922 635657
DX: 12118 WALSALL 1

Courts and times
Magistrates' Court, Stafford Street, Walsall
Adult: Weekdays 10:00
Youth: Thursday and Friday 10:00
FPC: Tuesday, Wednesday, Thursday 10:00
SDVC: Monday 10:00

2914 WARLEY LJA
combined with **2915 WEST BROMWICH LJA** to form **2920 SANDWELL LJA**

2904 WARWICKSHIRE LJA
Michael Seath, Justices' Clerk, Magistrates' Court, Warwickshire Justice Centre, PO Box 10, Newbold Terrace, Leamington Spa CV32 4EL
Tel: 01926 429133
Fax: 01926 426217
DX: 701966 LEAMINGTON SPA 7
Note: Rugby Magistrates' Court closed wef 29/7/11. Stratford Courthouse closed wef 9/11

Courts and times
Warwickshire Justice Centre – Leamington Spa, PO Box 10, Newbold Terrace, Leamington Spa CV32 4EL
Warwickshire Justice Centre – Nuneaton, PO Box 3878, Vicarage Street, Nuneaton CV11 4WX
Adult: Leamington Spa: Weekdays 10:00; Nuneaton: Weekdays 10:00
YC: Leamington Spa: Tuesday 10:00; **Nuneaton:** Wednesday 10:00
FPC: Leamington Spa: Monday and Thursday 10:00; **Nuneaton:** Wednesday, Thursday, Friday 10:00

2915 WEST BROMWICH LJA
combined with **2914 WARLEY LJA** to form **2920 SANDWELL LJA**

2919 WOLVERHAMPTON LJA
Michael Seath, Justices' Clerk, Law Courts, North Street, Wolverhampton WV1 1RA
Tel: 01902 773151
Fax: 01902 427875
DX: 10419
Courts
The Law Courts, North Street, Wolverhampton
Adult: Weekdays 10:00
YC: Monday, Thursday, Friday 10:00
FPC: Monday, Wednesday, Thursday, Friday 10:00
Fine Dflt: Thursday 10:00

CLEVELAND AND DURHAM

Delivery Director: Mark Swales, HMCTS, NE Regional Support Unit, 11th Floor Pinnacle, Albion Street, Leeds LS1 5AA. Tel: 0113 251 1200. Fax: 0113 251 1247. DX: 724960 LEEDS 56
Regional Payment Centre: PO Box 135, Morley LS27 7ZT Tel: 0113 307 6600. DX: 743920 MORLEY 5
Central Finance Unit (North and South Durham): PO Box 107, Darlington DL1 1ZD Fax: 01325 376639. DX: 712818 DARLINGTON 8. Email: du-durhammcfinance@hmcts.gsi.gov.uk

1585/5585 COUNTY DURHAM AND DARLINGTON LJA
North Admin: Mr R. Burton, Justices' Clerk/Mr G. Garbutt, Deputy Justices' Clerk, Magistrates' Court, Newcastle Road, Chester-le-Street, County Durham DH3 3UA
Tel: 0191 387 0700
Fax: 0191 387 0746
DX: 721663 CHESTER-LE-STREET 2
Email: du-durhammcnorthenq@hmcts.gsi.gov.uk
South Admin: Mr R. Burton, Justices' Clerk/Mr G. Garbutt, Deputy Justices' Clerk, Magistrates' Court, Central Avenue, Newton Aycliffe, County Durham DL5 5RT
Tel: 01325 318114
Fax: 01325 327697
DX: 63808 NEWTON AYCLIFFE
Email: du-durhammcsouthenq@hmcts.gsi.gov.uk
Courts and times
NORTH
Magistrates' Court, Ashdale Road, Consett
Magistrates' Court, St Aidan's Way, Peterlee
Durham Civil & Family Justice Centre, Old Elvet, Durham DH1 3HW
Adult: Consett: Monday, Tuesday, Thursday; **Peterlee:** Weekdays
YC: Consett: Friday; **Peterlee:** Thursday
FPC: Durham Civil & Family Justice Centre: Tuesday and Thursday
SOUTH
Magistrates' Court, Central Avenue, Newton Aycliffe
Magistrates' Court, Parkgate, Darlington
Adult: Newton Aycliffe: Weekdays; **Darlington:** Tuesday and Thursday
Adult SIC: Newton Aycliffe: Wednesday pm; **Darlington:** Thursday pm
Adult Private: Darlington: Tuesday and Wednesday
YC: Newton Aycliffe: Monday and Friday; **Darlington:** Monday and Friday
FPC: Newton Aycliffe: Tuesday; **Darlington:** Monday and Wednesday

1247 HARTLEPOOL LJA
Mr R. Burton, Justices' Clerk/Mrs K. Embleton, Deputy Justices' Clerk, The Law Courts, Victoria Road, Hartlepool TS24 8BS
Tel: 01429 271451 (4 lines); 01642 230600 (Admin)
Fax: 01429 866696
DX: 68706 HARTLEPOOL 2
Email: postboxhp@hmcts.gsi.gov.uk
Courts and times
The Law Courts, Victoria Road, Hartlepool
Adult: Weekdays 10:00 and 14:15
YC: Thursday 10:00
FPC: Tuesday 10:00

1248 LANGBAURGH EAST LJA
closed wef 1/12

1583 NORTH DURHAM LJA
combined with **1584 SOUTH DURHAM LJA** to form **1585 and 5585 COUNTY DURHAM AND DARLINGTON LJA**

1584 SOUTH DURHAM LJA
combined with **1583 NORTH DURHAM LJA** to form **1585 and 5585 COUNTY DURHAM AND DARLINGTON LJA**

1249 TEESSIDE LJA
Mr R. Burton, Justices' Clerk/Mrs K. Embleton, Deputy Justices' Clerk, Teesside Law Courts, Victoria Square, Middlesbrough TS1 2AS
Tel: 01642 240301
Fax: 01642 224010
DX: 60562 MIDDLESBROUGH
Email: postbox@hmcts.gsi.gov.uk

Courts and times
Magistrates' Court, Teesside Law Courts, Victoria Square, Middlesbrough
Youth Court, Law Courts, Albert Road, Middlesbrough
Adult: Magistrates' Court, Middlesbrough: Weekdays 10:00 and 14:15
YC: Youth Court, Middlesbrough: Weekdays 10:00 and 14:15
FPC: Magistrates' Court, Middlesbrough: Weekdays 10:00 and 14:15

HUMBER AND SOUTH YORKSHIRE

Delivery Director: Mark Swales, HMCTS, NE Regional Support Unit, 11th Floor Pinnacle, Albion Street, Leeds LS1 5AA. Tel: 0113 251 1200. Fax: 0113 251 1247. DX: 724960 LEEDS 56

Regional Payment Centre: PO Box 135, Morley LS27 7ZT. Tel: 0113 307 6600. DX: 743920 MORLEY 5

Enforcement Unit: Sheffield Magistrates' Court, Castle Street, Sheffield S3 8LU. Tel: 0114 252 1833. Fax: 0114 252 1843. DX: 10599 SHEFFIELD 1

2770 BARNSLEY LJA

Alison Watts, Justices' Clerk, Court House, PO Box 17, Barnsley, South Yorkshire S70 2DW
Tel: 01226 320032 (Criminal Listing); 320013 (Administration/General Enquiries); 320005/58 (Family and Maintenance); 320024 (Legal Aid); 320000 (Switchboard)
Fax: 01226 320044 (Administration)
DX: 702080 BARNSLEY 3

Courts and times
Court House, Westgate, Barnsley
Adult: Weekdays 10:00 and 14:00
YC: Tuesday and Friday 10:00
FPC: Monday and Wednesday 10:00

1942 BEVERLEY AND THE WOLDS LJA
combined with **1941 BRIDLINGTON LJA** to form **2353 EAST YORKSHIRE LJA**

1941 BRIDLINGTON LJA
combined with **1942 BEVERLEY AND THE WOLDS LJA** to form **2353 EAST YORKSHIRE LJA**

2771 DONCASTER LJA

Alison Watts, Justices' Clerk, PO Box 49, The Law Courts, College Road, Doncaster, South Yorkshire DN1 3HT
Tel: 01302 366711
Fax: 01302 347359
DX: 742840 DONCASTER 20

Courts and times
The Law Courts, College Road, Doncaster
Adult: Weekdays 10:00 and 14:15
YC: Tuesday and Thursday 10:00 and 14:15
FPC: Tuesday, Wednesday, Thursday, Friday 10:00 (other times by arrangement)

2352 EAST YORKSHIRE LJA

Alison Watts, Justices' Clerk, Beverley Magistrates' Court, Champney Road, Beverley, East Yorkshire HU17 9EJ
Tel: 01482 861607
Fax: 01482 882004

Courts and times
The Court House, Champney Road, Beverley
The Court House, Quay Road, Bridlington
Adult: Beverley: Weekdays 09:30; **Bridlington:** Weekdays 09:30
YC: Beverley: Tuesday 09:30; **Bridlington:** Thursday 09:30
FPC: Beverley: Monday 09:30; **Bridlington:** Wednesday 09:30
Non-CPS: Beverley: Wednesday 09:30; **Bridlington:** Thursday 09:30

1928 GOOLE AND HOWDENSHIRE LJA
closed wef 12/11

1940 GRIMSBY AND CLEETHORPES LJA

Alison Watts, Justices' Clerk, Victoria Street, Grimsby, North East Lincolnshire DN31 1NH
Tel: 01472 320444
Fax: 01472 320440
DX: 707680 GRIMSBY 5

Courts and times
Magistrates' Court, Victoria Street, Grimsby
Adult: Weekdays 09:30; Monday, Tuesday, Wednesday, Thursday 14:15
YC: Monday, Wednesday, Friday 09:30 and 14:15

FPC: Wednesday 09:30 and 14:15
Dir: Thursday 10:00

1943 HULL AND HOLDERNESS LJA

Alison Watts, Justices' Clerk, PO Box 2, Market Place, Kingston-upon-Hull HU1 2AD
Tel: 01482 328914
Fax: 01482 219790
DX: 742160 HULL 20

Courts and times
The Courthouse, Market Place, Kingston-upon-Hull
Adult: Weekdays 10:00
YC: Monday, Tuesday, Wednesday 10:00
FPC: Weekdays 10:00

1903 NORTH LINCOLNSHIRE LJA

Alison Watts, Justices' Clerk, Court Centre Office, Corporation Road, Scunthorpe DN15 6QB
Tel: 01724 281100
Fax: 01724 281890
DX: 742212 SCUNTHORPE 10
Email: hu-scunmcadmin@hmcts.gsi.gov.uk

Courts and times
Scunthorpe Court Centre, Laneham Street, Scunthorpe
Adult: Weekdays 10:00, Wednesday 14:15
YC: Thursday 10:00 and 14:15
FPC: Monday and Friday 10:00 and 14:15
Dir: Friday 14:15

2772 ROTHERHAM LJA

Alison Watts, Justices' Clerk, The Law Courts, The Statutes, PO Box 15, Rotherham, South Yorkshire S60 1YW
Tel: 01709 839339
Fax: 01709 370082 (General); 788414 (Family)
DX: 703025 ROTHERHAM 4
Email: rotherhamfamily@hmcts.gsi.gov.uk (Family)

Courts and times
The Statutes, Rotherham
Adult: Weekdays 10:00 and 14:15, Saturday 10:00
YC: Monday and Thursday 10:00
FPC: Tuesday 10:00 and 14:15, Wednesday 10:00

2773 SHEFFIELD LJA

Alison Watts, Justices' Clerk, Magistrates' Court, Castle Street, Sheffield S3 8LU
Tel: 0114 276 0760
Fax: 0114 252 1860
DX: 10599 SHEFFIELD 1

Courts and times
Magistrates' Court, Castle Street, Sheffield
Adult: Weekdays 10:00 and 14:15
YC: Weekdays 10:00
FPC: Monday and Thursday 14:15, Tuesday, Wednesday, Friday 10:00 (other times by arrangement)

NORTH AND WEST YORKSHIRE

Delivery Director: Mark Swales, HMCTS, NE Regional Support Unit, 11th Floor Pinnacle, Albion Street, Leeds LS1 5AA. Tel: 0113 251 1200. Fax: 0113 251 1247. DX: 724960 LEEDS 56

Central Finance Office (North Yorkshire): PO Box 87, Northallerton DL7 8GF. Tel: 01609 783539. Fax: 01609 760918

Collection & Enforcement Centre (West Yorkshire): PO Box 135, Morley LS27 7ZT. Tel: 0113 307 6600. DX: 743920 MORLEY 5

Regional Payment Centre: PO Box 135, Morley LS27 7ZT. Tel: 0113 307 6600. DX: 743920 MORLEY 5

2996 BATLEY AND DEWSBURY LJA
closed wef 4/12

2978 BRADFORD AND KEIGHLEY LJA
Sam Goozée, Justices' Clerk, North & West Yorkshire/Gordon Airy, Deputy Justices' Clerk, The Court Office, PO Box 187, The Tyrls, Bradford, West Yorkshire BD1 1JL
Tel: 01274 390111
Fax: 01274 391731
DX: 743850 BRADFORD 25

Courts and times
The Tyrls, Bradford
Civil and Family Justice Centre, Combined Court Centre, The Law Courts, Drake Street, Bradford
Adult: The Tyrls: Weekdays 10:00 and 14:00
YC: The Tyrls: Weekdays 10:00 and 14:00
FPC: Civil and Family Justice Centre: Monday 10:00 and 14:00, Thursday and Friday 14:00
Dir: Civil and Family Justice Centre: Tuesday 10:00 and 14:00; **The Tyrls:** As required

2997 CALDERDALE LJA
Sam Goozée, Justices' Clerk, North & West Yorkshire/Gordon Airy, Deputy Justices' Clerk, The Court Office, PO Box 32, Harrison Road, Halifax, West Yorkshire HX1 2AN
Tel: 01422 360695
Fax: 01422 347874
DX: 743870 HALIFAX 5
Email: wy-halifaxmags@hmcts.gsi.gov.uk

Courts and times
Harrison Road, Halifax
Adult: Weekdays 10:00
YC: Monday and Wednesday 10:00
FPC: Monday and Thursday 10:00

2527 HARROGATE AND SKIPTON LJA
Sam Goozée, Justices' Clerk, North & West Yorkshire/Christine Gardner, Deputy Justices' Clerk, The Court House, PO Box 72, Victoria Avenue, Harrogate, North Yorkshire HG1 1LS; Skipton Law Courts, Otley Street, Skipton, North Yorkshire BD23 1RH
Tel: 01423 722000/02 (Maintenance Office); 01756 692670 (Skipton)
Fax: 01423 722001; 01756 701169 (Skipton)
DX: 742910 HARROGATE 3; 703031 SKIPTON 2

Courts and times
Court House, Victoria Avenue, Harrogate
Skipton Law Courts, Otley Street, Skipton
Adult: Harrogate: Monday–Thursday 10:00; **Skipton:** Friday 10:00
YC: Harrogate: Wednesday 10:00
FPC: Harrogate: Monday 10:00
Trial Courts: Skipton: Alternate Mondays 10:00

2987 HUDDERSFIELD LJA
see **2987 KIRKLEES LJA**

2979 KEIGHLEY LJA
closed wef 4/12

2987 KIRKLEES LJA
Sam Goozée, Justices' Clerk, North & West Yorkshire/David Jackson, Deputy Justices' Clerk,The Court Office, Civic Centre, Huddersfield, West Yorkshire HD1 2NH
Tel: 01484 423552
Fax: 01484 430085
DX: 743880 HUDDERSFIELD 20

Courts and times
Court House, Civic Centre, Huddersfield
Adult: Weekdays 10:00 and 14:00
YC: Monday and Tuesday 10:00 and 14:00
FPC: Monday, Wednesday, Thursday 10:00 and 14:00

2992 LEEDS DISTRICT LJA
Sam Goozée, Justices' Clerk, North & West Yorkshire/Graham Bishop, Deputy Justices' Clerk,The Court House, PO Box No. 97, Westgate, Leeds LS1 3JP
Tel: 0113 245 9653
Fax: 0113 244 4700
DX: 743890 LEEDS (Westgate)

Courts and times
The Court House, Westgate, Leeds
Adult: Weekdays 10:00 and 14:00
YC: Monday and Friday 10:00 and 14:00, Thursday 10:00
FPC: Weekdays 10:00

2543 NORTHALLERTON AND RICHMOND LJA
Sam Goozée, Justices' Clerk, North & West Yorkshire/Christine Gardner, Deputy Justices' Clerk,3 Racecourse Lane, Northallerton, North Yorkshire DL7 8QZ
Tel: 01609 788200 (General Enquiries)
Fax: 01609 783509
DX: 742420 NORTHALLERTON

Courts and times
3 Racecourse Lane, Northallerton
Adult: Monday and Friday 10:00
YC: Alternate Tuesdays 10:00
FPC: Alternate Mondays 10:00
RTC: Tuesday

2994 PONTEFRACT LJA
CLOSED wef 3/2013 *see* **2995 WAKEFIELD AND PONTEFRACT LJA**

2536 SCARBOROUGH LJA
Sam Goozée, Justices' Clerk/Christine Gardner, Deputy Justices' Clerk, Law Courts, Northway, Scarborough, North Yorkshire YO12 7AE
Tel: 01723 505000
Fax: 01723 353250
DX: 68893 SCARBOROUGH

Courts and times
Law Court, Northway, Scarborough
Adult: Monday, Wednesday, Thursday, Friday 10:00 and 14:00
YC: Tuesday 10:00
FPC: Thursday, 10:00

2537 SELBY LJA
CLOSED wef 3/2013 *see* **2541 YORK AND SELBY LJA**

2538 SKIPTON LJA
see **2527 HARROGATE AND SKIPTON LJA**

2995 WAKEFIELD AND PONTEFRACT LJA
Sam Goozée, Justices' Clerk, North and West Yorkshire/David Jackson, Deputy Justices' Clerk, The Court Office, Cliff Parade, Wakefield WF1 2TW
Tel: 01924 231100
Fax: 01924 231146
DX: 743910 WAKEFIELD 20

Courts and times
Court House, Cliff Parade, Wakefield
Adult: Weekdays 10:00 and 14:00
YC: Wednesday 10:00 and 14:00
FPC: Tuesday 10:00

2541   YORK AND SELBY LJA
Sam Goozée, North and West Yorkshire/Christine Gardner, Deputy Justices' Clerk,Law Courts,
Clifford Street, York YO1 9RE
Tel: 01904 818300
Fax: 01904 818301
DX: 744330 YORK 41

Courts and times
Law Courts, Clifford Street, York
County Court, Piccadilly House, 55 Piccadilly, York YO1 9WL
Adult: Law Courts: Weekdays 10:00
YC: Law Courts: Tuesday 10:00
FPC: County Court: Monday and Friday 10:00

NORTHUMBRIA

Delivery Director: Mark Swales, HMCTS, NE Regional Support Unit, 11th Floor Pinnacle, Albion Street, Leeds LS1 5AA. Tel: 0113 251 1200. Fax: 0113 251 1247. DX: 724960 LEEDS 56

Regional Payment Centre: PO Box 135, Morley LS27 7ZT. Tel: 0113 307 6600. DX: 743920 MORLEY 5.

Northumbria Central Enforcement Unit: PO Box 826, North Shields NE29 1DZ. Tel: 0191 298 2280. Fax: 0191 298 2281. DX: 65137 NORTH SHIELDS 2. Email: no-ceu-admin@hmcts.gsi.gov.uk

2347 ALNWICK LJA
closed wef 31/3/11 – successor courts – South East Northumberland and Berwick-upon-Tweed

2348 BERWICK-UPON-TWEED LJA
Ms L. Brenkley, 40 Church Street, Berwick-upon-Tweed, Northumberland TD15 1DX
Tel: 01289 306885
Goldfax: 0870 324 0209
DX: 551540 BERWICK3 TD
Email: no_berwick@hmcts.gsi.gov.uk
Courts
40 Church Street, Berwick-upon-Tweed
Adult: Tuesday and Thursday 10:00
YC: Alternate Mondays pm
FPC: Alternate Mondays pm

2850 GATESHEAD DISTRICT LJA
Ms J. Brenkley, Gateshead Magistrates' Court, Warwick Street, Gateshead, Tyne-and-Wear NE8 1DT
Tel: 0191 477 5821
Fax: 0191 478 7825
DX: 742120 GATESHEAD 6
Email: no_gatesheadcourt@hmcts.gsi.gov.uk (Listing and General Office);
gatesheadfamily@hmcts.gsi.gov.uk
Courts and times
Gateshead Law Courts, Warwick Street, Gateshead
Adult: Weekdays 10:00 and 14:00
YC: Tuesday 10:00 and 14:00
FPC: Monday 10:00 and 14:00

2854 HOUGHTON-LE-SPRING LJA
closed wef 31/3/11. Enquiries to Sunderland Magistrates' Court Tel: 0191 514 1621

2851 NEWCASTLE-UPON-TYNE LJA
Ms L. Brenkley, Magistrates' Courts, PO Box 839, Market Street, Newcastle-upon-Tyne NE99 1AU
Tel: 0191 232 7326
Fax: 0191 221 0025
DX: 61098 NEWCASTLE UPON TYNE
Email: no_newcastle@hmcts.gsi.gov.uk
Courts and times
Magistrates' Court, Market Street, Newcastle-upon-Tyne
Combined Court Centre, The Quayside, Newcastle-upon-Tyne
Adult: Magistrates' Court: Weekdays 10:00, 11:00, 14:15, Saturdays and bank holidays 09:30
YC: Magistrates' Court: Tuesday 10:00 and 11:00, Wednesday 10:00 and 14:15, Friday 10:00, 11:00 and 14:15
FPC: Combined Court Centre: Thursday 09:30
SIC: Magistrates' Court: Tuesday 10:00 and 14:15
DDC: Magistrates' Court: Thursday 10:00, reviews 14:15

2852 NORTH TYNESIDE DISTRICT LJA
Ms L. Brenkley, The Courthouse, Tynemouth Road, North Shields, Tyne-and-Wear NE30 1AG
Tel: 0191 296 0099; 298 2320 (Family Proceedings)
Fax: 0191 272 8010; 298 2337 (Family Proceedings)
DX: 744750 NORTH SHIELDS 6
Email: no-ntmclistcpo@hmcts.gsi.gov.uk

Courts and times
The Court House, Tynemouth Road, North Shields
Kings Court, Earl Grey Way, Royal Quays, North Shields
Adult: The Court House: Weekdays 10:00 and 14:00
YC: The Court House: Monday, Tuesday, Friday 10:00 and 14:00
FPC: Kings Court: Weekdays 09:30 and 14:00

2349 SOUTH EAST NORTHUMBERLAND LJA
Ms L. Brenkley, Magistrates' Clerk's Office, The Law Courts, Bedlington, Northumberland NE22 7LX
Tel: 01670 531100; 01670 512221 (Family Proceedings)
Fax: 01670 820133
DX: 62705 BEDLINGTON
Email: no_sen@hmcts.gsi.gov.uk
Courts and times
The Law Courts, Bedlington
Morpeth & Berwick County Court, Fountain House, Morpeth
Adult: Bedlington: Weekdays 10:00
YC: Bedlington: Friday 10:00
FPC: Morpeth: Tuesday, Wednesday, Thursday

2853 SOUTH TYNESIDE DISTRICT LJA
Ms L. Brenkley, South Tyneside Magistrates' Court, Millbank, Secretan Way, South Shields NE33 1RG
Tel: 0191 455 8800
Fax: 0191 427 4499
DX: 65143 SOUTH SHIELDS 3

Courts and times
Magistrates' Court, Millbank, South Shields
Adult: Weekdays 10:00 and 14:00
Private Prosecutions: Tuesday and Friday 14:00, alternate Fridays 10:00
YC: Wednesday 10:00 and 14:00
FPC: Thursday 10:00 and 14:00
Dir: Thursday 10:00 and 14:00, alternate Fridays 14:00
Enf: Fines: Tuesday 10:00; **Maintenance Arrears:** Thursday 10:00
CT: Alternate Tuesdays 14:00

2855 SUNDERLAND LJA
Ms L. Brenkley, Magistrates' Courts, Gillbridge Avenue, Sunderland SR1 3AP
Tel: 0191 514 1621
Fax: 0191 565 8564
DX: 742740 SUNDERLAND 17

Courts and times
Magistrates' Courts, Gillbridge Avenue, Sunderland
Adult: Weekdays 10:00
YC: Thursday 10:00
FPC: Tuesday 10:00

2346 TYNEDALE LJA
closed wef 31/3/11. Enquiries to Newcastle-upon-Tyne Magistrates' Court Tel: 0191 232 7326

CHESHIRE AND MERSEYSIDE

Delivery Director: Gill Hague, Manchester Civil Justice Centre, PO Box 4237, 1 Bridge Street West, Manchester M60 1TE. Tel: 0161 240 5800. Fax: 0161 240 5846. DX: 724780 MANCHESTER 44

Justices' Clerk for Cheshire & Merseyside: Keith Townend, QEII Law Courts, Derby Square, Liverpool L2 1XA. Tel: 0151 471 1079. DX 74080 Liverpool 22

Regional Enforcement Lead: Chris Flanagan, Manchester Civil Justice Centre, 1 Bridge Street West, Manchester M60 1TE. Tel: 0161 240 5844. DX: 724783 MANCHESTER 44

Fines Unit: Accounts Enforcement Central Payments Office, PO Box 104, Runcorn, Cheshire WA7 2GE. Tel: 0845 200 2078 (09:00–17:00). Fax: 01928 703356

1188 CHESTER, ELLESMERE PORT AND NESTON LJA
see **1729 WEST CHESHIRE LJA**

3340 COMMUNITY JUSTICE CENTRE, NORTH LIVERPOOL
Richard Holland, Deputy Justices' Clerk, Community Justice Centre, North Liverpool, Boundary Street, Kirkdale, Liverpool L5 2QD
Tel: 0151 298 3600
Fax: 0151 298 3601/3725 (Main Office); 0151 298 3721 (Community Engagement)
Courts and times
Community Justice Centre, North Liverpool
Adult: Weekdays 09:45, Monday and Wednesday 14:00
YC: Tuesday and Thursday 14:00
Crown Court: One day a month 14:00

1177 HALTON LJA
combined with **1180 WARRINGTON LJA** to form **1722 NORTH CHESHIRE LJA**

2266 KNOWSLEY LJA
closed wef 12/11

2267 LIVERPOOL LJA
see **5730 LIVERPOOL AND KNOWSLEY LJA**

5730 LIVERPOOL AND KNOWSLEY LJA
Sarah Pemberton, Deputy Justices' Clerk, City Magistrates' Courts, Dale Street, Liverpool L2 2JQ
Tel: 0151 243 5500; 0151 243 5532 (Youth); 0151 296 2200 (Family)
Fax: 0151 243 5555
DX: 707900 LIVERPOOL 8
Courts and times
Magistrates' Courts, Dale Street, Liverpool
Youth Courts, QEII Law Courts, Derby Square, Liverpool L2 1XA
Civil and Family Courts, 35 Vernon Street, Liverpool L2 2BX
Adult: Magistrates' Courts: Weekdays 10:00 and 14:00
YC: Youth Courts: Weekdays 10:00 and 14:00
FPC: Civil and Family Courts: Weekdays 10:00 and 14:00

1178 MACCLESFIELD LJA
Andrew Ball, Deputy Justices' Clerk, The Law Courts, Civic Centre, Crewe, Cheshire CW1 2DT
Tel: 01270 655922
Fax: 01270 589357
DX: 702504 CREWE 2
Email: ch-crewemcadmin@hmcts.gsi.gov.uk
Courts and times
The Law Courts, Hibel Road, Macclesfield
2nd Floor, Silk House, Park Green, Macclesfield SK11 7NA
Adult: The Law Courts: Weekdays 10:00
YC: The Law Courts: Fourth Tuesday in month 10:00
FPC: Silk House: Tuesday and Friday 10:00

1722 NORTH CHESHIRE LJA
Andrew Ball, Deputy Justices' Clerk, Winmarleigh Street, Warrington, Cheshire WA1 1PB
Tel: 01925 236 250
DX: 17793 WARRINGTON 1
Email: ch-warrmcadmin@hmcts.gsi.gov.uk
Courts and times
Warrington Magistrates' Court, Arpley Street, Warrington WA1 1LQ
Runcorn Magistrates' Court, Runcorn WA7 2GE
Adult: Weekdays 10:00
YC: Alternate Thursdays 10:00
FPC: Tuesday, Thursday, Friday 10:00

2269 NORTH SEFTON DISTRICT LJA
closed wef 9/11

2268 ST HELENS LJA
Richard Holland, Deputy Justices' Clerk, The Court House, Corporation Street, St Helens,
Merseyside WA10 1SZ
Tel: 01744 620244
Fax: 01744 627249
DX: 19488 ST HELENS
Courts and times
The Court House, St Helens
Civil and Family Courts, 35 Vernon Street, Liverpool L2 2BX
Adult: The Court House: Weekdays 10:00 and 14:00
YC: The Court House: Tuesday and Thursday 10:00
FPC: Civil and Family Courts: Weekdays 10:00 and 14:00

1728 SEFTON LJA
Richard Holland, Deputy Justices' Clerk, The Magistrates' Court, Merton Road, Bootle, Merseyside
L20 3XX
Tel: 0151 933 6999
Fax: 0151 922 4285
DX: 707620 BOOTLE
Courts and times
Magistrates' Courts, Merton Road, Bootle
Adult: Weekdays 10:00 and 14:00
YC: Tuesday and Thursday 10:00

1187 SOUTH CHESHIRE LJA
Andrew Ball, Deputy Justices' Clerk, Law Courts, Civic Centre, Crewe, Cheshire CW1 2DT
Tel: 01270 655920
Fax: 01270 589357
DX: 702504 CREWE 2
Email: h-crewemcadmin@hmcts.gsi.gov.uk
Courts and times
Law Courts, Civic Centre, Crewe
Adult: Weekdays 10:00
YC: Thursday 10:00
FPC: Monday, Wednesday, Thursday 10:00

2270 SOUTH SEFTON DISTRICT LJA
see **1728 SEFTON LJA**

1179 VALE ROYAL LJA
closed wef 9/11

1180 WARRINGTON LJA
combined with **1177 HALTON LJA** to form **1722 NORTH CHESHIRE LJA**

1729 WEST CHESHIRE LJA
Andrew Ball, Deputy Justices' Clerk, Chester Magistrates' Court, Grosvenor Street, Chester CH1
2XA
Tel: 0870 162 6261
Fax: 01244 405843

Courts and times
Chester Magistrates' Court, Grosvenor Street, Chester
Chester Civil Justice Centre, Trident House, Little St John Street, Chester CH1 1SN
Adult: Chester Magistrates' Court: Weekdays 10:00 and 14:00
YC: Chester Magistrates' Court: Tuesday 10:00 and 14:00
FPC: Chester Civil Justice Centre: Wednesday and Thursday 10:00 and 14:00

2271 WIRRAL LJA
Sarah Pemberton, Deputy Justices' Clerk, The Sessions Courts, Chester Street, Birkenhead,
Merseyside CH41 5HW
Tel: 0151 285 4100
Fax: 0151 285 4111
DX: 17888 BIRKENHEAD

Courts and times
Birkenhead
MC: Weekdays 10:00 and 14:00
YC: Monday, Tuesday, Thursday 10:00

CUMBRIA AND LANCASHIRE

Delivery Director: Gill Hague, Manchester Civil Justice Centre, PO Box 4237, 1 Bridge Street West, Manchester M60 1TE. Tel: 0161 240 5800. Fax: 0161 240 5846. DX: 724780 MANCHESTER 44

Justices' Clerk for Cumbria and Lancashire: David Greensmith, Justices' Clerk Office, Preston Magistrates' Court, Preston, Lancashire PR1 2QT. Tel: 01722 208015

Regional Enforcement Lead: Chris Flanagan, Manchester Civil Justice Centre, 1 Bridge Street West, Manchester M60 1TE. Tel: 0161 240 5844. DX: 724783 MANCHESTER 44

Cumbria Central Payments Unit (including Fixed Penalty Office): Burneside Road, Kendal LA9 4TJ. Tel: 01539 720478. Fax: 01539 740502. DX: 70780 KENDAL 4. Email: cm-kendalmcenq@hmcts.gsi.gov.uk

Lancashire Fines Unit: PO Box 64, Colne Road, Reedley, Lancashire BB10 2NQ. Tel: 01282 610000. Fax: 01282 610034

2012 BLACKBURN, DARWEN AND RIBBLE VALLEY LJA
see 1725 EAST LANCASHIRE LJA

2014 BURNLEY, PENDLE AND ROSSENDALE LJA
Helen Meanwell, Deputy Justices' Clerk, The Court House, Parker Lane, Burnley BB11 2BS
Tel: 01282 800100
Fax: 01282 800101
DX: 745300 BURNLEY 11
Email: in-reedleymcenq@hmcts.gsi.gov.uk
Note: Rawtenstall Magistrates' Court closed wef 30/3/2011

Courts and times
Court House, Parker Lane, Burnley
Court House, Colne Road, Reedley, near Burnley
Adult: Burnley: Weekdays 10:00 and 14:00
YC: Burnley: Monday 10:00
Comb FPC: Reedley: Friday 10:00

1322 CARLISLE AND DISTRICT LJA
see 1727 NORTH CUMBRIA LJA

1998 CHORLEY LJA
David Greensmith, Cumbria and Lancashire Justices' Clerk, Court House, St Thomas's Square, Chorley, Lancashire PR7 1RZ
Tel: 01257 240500
Fax: 01257 261948
DX: 707530 CHORLEY 5
Email: in-chorleymcenq@hmcts.gsi.gov.uk

Courts and times
Court House, St Thomas's Square, Chorley
Court House, Lancastergate, Leyland
Adult: Chorley: Monday, Wednesday, Thursday, Friday 09:30, Wednesday 14:30
FPC: Leyland: Tuesday 09:30
Enf: Chorley: Thursday 11:00

1725 EAST LANCASHIRE LJA
Helen Meanwell, Deputy Justices' Clerk, Court House, Northgate, Blackburn, Lancashire BB2 1AA
Tel: 01254 687500 (General Listings); 687510 (Listings)
Fax: 01254 687524
DX: 742020 BLACKBURN 10
Email: In-blackburnmcenq@hmcts.gsi.gov.uk

Courts and times
Court House, Northgate, Blackburn
Law Courts, Manchester Road, Accrington
Adult: Blackburn: Weekdays 10:00 and 14:00
YC: Blackburn: Tuesday 10:00
Comb FPC: Accrington: Friday 10:00

1324 EDEN LJA
closed wef 1/12

1398 FURNESS AND DISTRICT LJA
David Greensmith, Cumbria and Lancashire Justices' Clerk, South Cumbria Magistrates' Court, Abbey Road, Barrow-in-Furness, Cumbria LA14 5QX
Tel: 01229 820161
Fax: 01229 870287
DX: 65210 BARROW-IN-FURNESS 2
Email: cumbria.south.magistrates@hmcts.gsi.gov.uk
Courts and times
Magistrates' Court, Abbey Road, Barrow-in-Furness
Adult: Monday, Tuesday, Wednesday, Thursday 10:00 and 14:00
YC: Friday 10:00
FPC: Wednesday and Friday 10:00
Enf: Tuesday once a month 10:00 or 14:00
NP: Tuesday once a month 10:00 and 14:00

1992 FYLDE COAST LJA
Mark Adamson, Deputy Justices' Clerk, The Magistrates' Court, Civic Centre, Chapel Street, Blackpool, Lancashire FY1 5DQ
Tel: 01253 757000
Fax: 01253 757024 757014
DX: 741861 BLACKPOOL 16
Note: all correspondence should be sent to Blackpool Magistrates' Court
Courts and times
Chapel Street, Blackpool
11 The Esplanade, Fleetwood FY7 6AT
Adult: Blackpool: Weekdays 10:00 and 14:00; **Fleetwood:** Tuesday and Wednesday 10:00 and 14:00
YC: Blackpool: Monday and Thursday 10:00 and 14:00
FPC: Fleetwood: Tuesday, Thursday, Friday 10:00 and 14:00

2010 HYNDBURN LJA
see **1725 EAST LANCASHIRE LJA**

2002 LANCASTER LJA
Mark Adamson, Deputy Justices' Clerk, Magistrates' Court, George Street, Lancaster LA1 1XZ
Tel: 01524 597000
DX: 741320 LANCASTER 5
Email: in-lancastermcenq@hmcts.gsi.gov.uk
Courts and times
Magistrates' Court, George Street, Lancaster
Adult: Weekdays 10:00 and 14:00
YC: Tuesday 10:00 and 14:00
FPC: Wednesday 10:00 and 14:00
NP: Thursday and Friday 14:00

1727 NORTH CUMBRIA LJA
David Greensmith, Cumbria and Lancashire Justices' Clerk, North Cumbria Magistrates' Court, Rickergate, Carlisle, Cumbria CA3 8QH
Tel: 01228 518800
Fax: 01228 518844
DX: 63018 CARLISLE
Email: cumbria.north.magistrates@hmcts.gsi.gov.uk
Courts and times
The Court House, Rickergate, Carlisle
Adult: Weekdays 10:00 and 14:00
YC: Wednesday 09:15
FPC: Wednesday 10:00

2003 ORMSKIRK LJA
David Greensmith, Cumbria and Lancashire Justices' Clerk, Court House, St Thomas's Square, Chorley, Lancashire PR7 1RZ
Tel: 01257 240500
Fax: 01257 261948

DX: 707530 CHORLEY 5
Email: in-chorleymcenq@hmcts.gsi.gov.uk

Courts and times
The Court House, Derby Street, Ormskirk
Adult: Monday, Tuesday, Friday 09:30
YC: Thursday 09:30
FPC: Wednesday (fortnightly) 09:30

2005 PRESTON LJA

David Greensmith, Cumbria and Lancashire Justices' Clerk, Magistrates' Court, PO Box 52, Lawson Street, Preston, Lancashire PR1 2RD
Tel: 01772 208000
DX: 702663 PRESTON 5
Email: in-prestonmcenq@hmcts.gsi.gov.uk

Courts and times
Magistrates' Court, Lawson Street, Preston
South Ribble Magistrates' Court, Lancastergate, Leyland PR25 2EX
Adult: Preston: Weekdays 10:00 and 14:00
YC: Preston: Weekdays 10:00
FPC: Leyland: Tuesday 10:00

1323 SOUTH LAKELAND LJA

David Greensmith, Cumbria and Lancashire Justices' Clerk, South Cumbria, Magistrates' Court, Abbey Road, Barrow-in-Furness, Cumbria LA14 5QX
Tel: 01229 820161
Fax: 01229 870287
DX: 65210 BARROW-IN-FURNESS 2
Email: cumbria.south.magistrates@hmcts.gsi.gov.uk
Note: Please send all correspondence to Furness & District Magistrates' Court.

Courts and times
The Court House, Burneside Road, Kendal
Adult: Monday, alternate Tuesdays, Thursday 10:00 and 14:00
YC: Alternate Mondays 10:00 and 14:00
FPC: Friday once a month
Enf: Monthly
NP: Alternate Tuesdays

2007 SOUTH RIBBLE LJA

David Greensmith, Cumbria and Lancashire Justices' Clerk, Court House, St Thomas's Square, Chorley, Lancashire PR7 1RZ
Tel: 01257 240500
Fax: 01257 261948
DX: 707530 CHORLEY 5
Email: in-chorleymcenq@hmcts.gsi.gov.uk
Note: Please send all correspondence to Chorley Magistrates' Court.

Courts and times
Court House, Lancastergate, Leyland
Adult: Monday 09:30, Thursday 09:30 and 14:00
FPC: Tuesday 09:30

1325 WEST ALLERDALE AND KESWICK LJA
see **1726 WEST CUMBRIA LJA**

1726 WEST CUMBRIA LJA

David Greensmith , Cumbria and Lancashire Justices' Clerk, West Cumbria Magistrates' Courts, West Cumbria Court House, Hall Park, Ramsay Brow, Workington, Cumbria CA14 4AS
Tel: 01900 62244
Fax: 01900 68644
DX: 743420 WORKINGTON 5

Courts and times
West Cumbria Magistrates' Courts, Ramsay Brow, Workington
Adult: Weekdays 10:00
YC: Tuesday 10:00
FPC: Tuesday 10:00

1375 WHITEHAVEN LJA
closed wef 6/11 (see **1726 WEST CUMBRIA LJA**)

GREATER MANCHESTER

Delivery Director: Gill Hague, Manchester Civil Justice Centre, PO Box 4237, 1 Bridge Street West, Manchester M60 1TE. Tel: 0161 240 5800. Fax: 0161 240 5846. DX: 724780 MANCHESTER 44

Justices' Clerk: Norman Draper, Manchester City Magistrates' Court, Crown Square, Manchester M60 1PR. Tel: 0161 830 4250

Regional Enforcement Lead: Chris Flanagan, Manchester Civil Justice Centre, PO Box 4237, 1 Bridge Street West, Manchester M60 1TE. Tel: 0161 240 5800. Fax: 0161 240 5846. DX: 724780 MANCHESTER 44

Greater Manchester Central Accounts & Enforcement Unit: PO Box 4372, Crown Square, Manchester M61 0EQ. Tel: 0161 830 4381 (Accounts); 4389 (Fixed Penalties); 4396 (Fines Support); 4212 (Enforcement). Fax: 0161 830 4237 (Accounts and Fixed Penalties); 4225 (Fines Support)

1731 BOLTON LJA
Jackie Lowe, Deputy Justices' Clerk, The Courts, Civic Centre, Le Mans Crescent, Bolton BL1 1UA
Tel: 01204 558200
Fax: 01204 366978
DX: 745180 BOLTON 22

Courts and times
The Courts, Civic Centre, Bolton
Adult: Weekdays 10:00 and 14:00
YC: Wednesday 14:00
FPC: Monday, alternate Wednesdays 10:00

1732 BURY LJA
see **1724 BURY AND ROCHDALE LJA**

1724 BURY AND ROCHDALE LJA
Jackie Lowe, Deputy Justices' Clerk, Magistrates' Court, The Courthouse, Tenters Street, Bury BL9 0HX
Tel: 0161 447 8600
Fax: 0161 447 8630
DX: 707370 BURY 4

Courts and times
Magistrates' Court, Tenters Street, Bury
Adult: Weekdays 10:00 and 14:00
YC: Thursday 10:00 and 14:00
FPC: Tuesday 10:00 and 14:00
Dir: Tuesday am

1747 CITY OF SALFORD LJA
closed wef 12/11

GREATER MANCHESTER PUBLIC LAW FAMILY PROCEEDINGS COURTS AND MANCHESTER CITY LJA PRIVATE LAW FAMILY PROCEEDINGS COURTS
Simon Dodgshon, Deputy Justices' Clerk (Family), Civil Justice Centre, 1 Bridge Street West, Manchester M3 3FX
Tel: 0161 240 5000
Fax: 0161 240 5132

Courts and times
Civil Justice Centre, 1 Bridge Street West, Manchester M3 3FX
FPC: Weekdays 10:00 and 14:00

1723 MANCHESTER AND SALFORD LJA
Anita Bhardwaj, Deputy Justices' Clerk, City Magistrates' Court, Crown Square, Manchester M60 1PR
Tel: 0161 830 4200; 240 5421 (Family Listings)
Fax: 0161 240 5455 (Family Listings); 830 4210 (Pre-court); 830 4206 (Listings)
DX: 745170 MANCHESTER 75

Courts and times
Magistrates' Court, Crown Square, Manchester
Manchester Civil Justice Centre, 1 Bridge Street West, Manchester M60 9DJ
Adult: Magistrates' Court: Weekdays 10:00
YC: Magistrates' Court: Weekdays 10:00
FPC: Manchester Civil Justice Centre: Weekdays 10:00

1733 MANCHESTER CITY LJA
see **1723 MANCHESTER AND SALFORD LJA**

1734 OLDHAM LJA
Ruth Salem, Deputy Justices' Clerk, Magistrates' Court, St Domingo Place, West Street, Oldham
OL1 1QE
Tel: 0161 620 2331
Fax: 0161 652 0172
DX: 745190 OLDHAM 8
Courts and times
Magistrates' Court, St Domingo Place, Oldham
Adult: Monday, Tuesday, Wednesday, Thursday 10:00 and 14:00, Friday 10:00
YC: Friday 10:00 and 14:00
FPC: Wednesday 10:00 and 14:00
Dir (Private Law): Wednesday 14:00

1750 ROCHDALE, MIDDLETON AND HEYWOOD LJA
closed wef 12/11 (see **1724 BURY AND ROCHDALE LJA**)

1739 STOCKPORT LJA
Ruth Salem, Deputy Justices' Clerk, The Courthouse, Stockport Magistrates' Court, PO Box 155,
Edward Street, Stockport SK1 3NF
Tel: 0161 477 2020
Fax: 0161 968 9679
DX: 702620 STOCKPORT 4
Courts and times
The Courthouse, Edward Street, Stockport
Adult: Weekdays 10:00 and 14:00
YC: Wednesday
FPC: Tuesday and Thursday 10:00

1748 TAMESIDE LJA
Ruth Salem, Deputy Justices' Clerk, Magistrates' Court, Henry Square, Ashton-under-Lyne OL6 7TP
Tel: 0161 330 2023
Fax: 0161 343 1498
DX: 702625 ASHTON UNDER LYNE 2
Courts and times
Magistrates' Court, Henry Square, Ashton-under-Lyne
Adult: Weekdays 10:00
YC: Tuesday 10:00
FPC: Friday 10:00

1742 TRAFFORD LJA
Ruth Salem, Deputy Justices' Clerk, Magistrates' Court, PO Box 13, Ashton Lane, Sale, Cheshire
M33 7NR
Tel: 0161 976 3333
Fax: 0161 975 4673
DX: 708290 SALE 6
Courts and times
Magistrates' Court, Ashton Lane, Sale
Adult: Weekdays 10:00
YC: Wednesday 10:00
FPC: Monday 10:00

1749 WIGAN AND LEIGH LJA
Jackie Lowe, Deputy Justices' Clerk, Magistrates' Court, Darlington Street, Wigan WN1 1DW
Tel: 01942 405405
Fax: 01942 405444/69
DX: 724820 WIGAN 9

Courts and times
Darlington Street, Wigan
Adult: Weekdays 10:00 and 14:00
YC: Thursday 10:00 and 14:00
FPC: Tuesday 10:00 and 14:00
Dir: Wednesday 10:00

SOUTH EAST REGION

BEDFORDSHIRE AND HERTFORDSHIRE

Delivery Director: Chris Jennings, 5th Floor, Fox Court, 14 Grays Inn Road, London WC1X 8HN. Tel: 020 3206 0688

Justices' Clerk (Bedfordshire): Suzanne Gadd, South Bedfordshire Magistrates' Court, Stuart Street, Luton LU1 5BL. Tel: 01582 524232. Fax: 01582 524252. DX: 151660 LUTON 16.

Justices' Clerk (Hertfordshire): Suzanne Gadd, HMCTS, Bayley House, Sish Lane, Stevenage SG1 3SS. Tel: 01438 730431. Fax: 01438 730413. DX: 153620 OLD STEVENAGE 2

Listings enquiries: Bedfordshire and Hertfordshire Case Management Unit (CMU). Tel: 01438 730412

Legal Aid enquiries: Bedfordshire and Hertfordshire Legal Aid Unit (LAPU). Tel: 01438 730415

Payments: Central Accounting Unit, Bayley House, Sish Lane, Stevenage SG1 3SS. Tel: 01438 730400. DX: 153620 OLD STEVENAGE

Transfer of fines and FP registration: Enforcement Unit, 3 St Paul's Square, Bedford MK40 1SQ. Tel: 01234 319081. DX: 729420 BEDFORD 10

Home (UK) orders: SE Regional Maintenance Unit, PO Box 936, Luton LU1 5TJ. Tel: 01582 524307. DX: 151660 LUTON 16

Reciprocal orders: SE Regional Reciprocal Maintenance Unit, Bury St Edmunds Magistrates' Court, Shire Hall, Bury St Edmunds IP33 1HF. Tel: 01284 778000. DX: 741460 BURY ST EDMUNDS 7

1051 BEDFORD AND MID BEDFORDSHIRE LJA

Suzanne Gadd, Justices' Clerk, 3 St Paul's Square, Bedford MK40 1SQ
Tel: 01234 319100; 01234 319060 (Fixed Penalty); 01582 524200 (Court Administration); 01234 319081 (Enforcement)
Fax: 01234 319114
DX: 729420 BEDFORD 10
Email: bd-bedfordmcenq@hmcts.gsi.gov.uk (General enquiries); bd-bedfordmclist@hmcts.gsi.gov.uk (Listing)

Courts and times
Shire Hall, Bedford
Adult: Weekdays 10:00
YC: Wednesday 10:00
FPC: Weekdays 10:00

1892 CENTRAL HERTFORDSHIRE LJA
combined with **1893 WEST HERTFORDSHIRE LJA** to form **1910 WEST** and **CENTRAL HERTFORDSHIRE LJA**

1888 EAST HERTFORDSHIRE LJA
combined with **1889 NORTH HERTFORDSHIRE LJA** to form **1911 NORTH** and **EAST HERTFORDSHIRE LJA**

1879 HATFIELD MAGISTRATES' COURT
Comet Way, Hatfield, Hertfordshire AL10 9SJ
Tel: 01923 297500
Fax: 01923 297528

Courts and times
Hatfield Magistrates' Court, Comet Way, Hatfield
Overnight cases for Hertfordshire: Monday to Sunday and bank holidays 09:30

1055 LUTON AND SOUTH BEDFORDSHIRE LJA
Suzanne Gadd, Justices' Clerk, Luton and South Bedfordshire Magistrates' Courts, Stuart Street, Luton LU1 5BL
Tel: 01582 524200; 01234 319060 (Fixed Penalty); 01582 524200 (Court Administration); 01234 319081 (Enforcement)
Fax: 01582 524252
DX: 151660 LUTON 16
Email: bd-lutonmcenq@hmcts.gsi.gov.uk (General enquiries); bd-lutonmclist@hmcts.gsi.gov.uk (Listing)

Courts and times
Luton Magistrates' Court, Stuart Street, Luton
Luton County Court, Cresta House, Alma Street, Luton LU1 2PU. Tel: 01582 506700
Adult: Luton Magistrates' Court: Weekdays 10:00
YC: Luton Magistrates' Court: Wednesday 10:00
FPC: Luton County Court: Weekdays 10:00

1889 NORTH HERTFORDSHIRE LJA
combined with **1888 EAST HERTFORDSHIRE LJA** to form **1911 NORTH AND EAST HERTFORDSHIRE LJA**

1911 NORTH AND EAST HERTFORDSHIRE LJA
Suzanne Gadd, Justices' Clerk, Bayley House, Sish Lane, Stevenage SG1 3SS
Tel: 01923 297500 (Admin); 0844 892 0550 (Family); 01234 319081 (Central Enforcement Unit)
Fax: 01923 297528 (Admin)
DX: 153620 OLD STEVENAGE 2
Note: overnight cases are dealt with at Hatfield

Courts and times
Bayley House, Sish Lane, Stevenage
Shire Hall, Fore Street, Hertford
Adult: Stevenage: Monday, Tuesday, Wednesday and Friday 10:00; **Hertford:** Weekdays (trials and road traffic) 10:00
YC: Hertford: Tuesday 10:00
SDVC: Stevenage: Tuesday 10:00
FPC: Stevenage: Tuesday and Thursday (and as required)

1893 WEST HERTFORDSHIRE LJA
combined with **1892 CENTRAL HERTFORDSHIRE LJA** to form **1910 WEST AND CENTRAL HERTFORDSHIRE LJA**

1910 WEST AND CENTRAL HERTFORDSHIRE LJA
Suzanne Gadd, Justices' Clerk, The Court House, Clarendon Road, Watford WD17 1ST
Tel: 01923 297500; 01234 319081 (Central Enforcement Unit)
Fax: 01923 297528
DX: 51509 WATFORD 2
Note: overnight cases are dealt with at Hatfield

Courts and times
Court House, St Peter's Street, St Albans AL1 3LB
The Court House, Clarendon Road, Watford
Adult: St Albans: Weekdays 10:00; **Watford (trials and road traffic):** Weekdays 10:00
YC: St Albans: Wednesday 10:00
SDVC: St Albans: Thursday 10:00; **Watford:** Thursday 10:00
FPC: St Albans: Wednesday 10:00; **Watford:** Monday and Friday 10:00 and 14:00

CAMBRIDGESHIRE AND ESSEX

Delivery Director: Chris Jennings, 5th Floor, Fox Court, 14 Grays Inn Road, London WC1X 8HN. Tel: 020 3206 0688.

Justices' Clerk (Essex and Cambridgeshire): Siân E. Jones, Peterborough Magistrates' Court, Bridge Street, Peterborough PE1 1ED. Tel: 01733 201301 (Cambridgeshire); 01245 313300 (Essex). Fax: 01733 313749 (Cambridgeshire); 01245 313396 (Essex). DX: 742250 PETERBOROUGH 23 (Cambridgeshire); 151020 CHELMSFORD 17 (Essex). Email: northessexbench@hmcts.gsi.gov.uk; southessexbench@hmcts.gsi.gov.uk

Payments and Accounts (including TFOs and Fixed Penalty Registrations): Central Accounts and Enforcement Office, North East Suffolk Magistrates' Court, Old Nelson Street, Lowestoft NR32 1HJ. Tel: 01502 501060. Fax: 01502 513875. DX: 97760 LOWESTOFT 2.

Home (UK) orders: SE Regional Maintenance Unit, PO Box 936, Luton LU1 5TJ. Tel: 01582 524307. DX: 151660 LUTON 16.

Reciprocal orders: SE Regional Reciprocal Maintenance Unit, Bury St Edmunds Magistrates' Court, Shire Hall, Bury St Edmunds IP33 1HF. Tel: 01284 778000. DX: 741460 BURY ST EDMUNDS 7.

1165 CAMBRIDGE LJA
combined with **1166 EAST CAMBRIDGESHIRE LJA** to form **SOUTH CAMBRIDGESHIRE LJA** – wef 1/1/12

1166 EAST CAMBRIDGESHIRE LJA
combined with **1165 CAMBRIDGE LJA** to form **SOUTH CAMBRIDGESHIRE LJA** – wef 1/1/12

1167 FENLAND LJA
combined with **1162 PETERBOROUGH** to form **NORTH CAMBRIDGESHIRE LJA** – wef 1/1/12

1168 HUNTINGDONSHIRE LJA
Siân E. Jones, Justices' Clerk, Magistrates' Court, Bridge Street, Peterborough PE1 1ED
Tel: 0845 310 0575
Fax: 01733 313749
DX: 742250 PETERBOROUGH 23

Courts and times
Law Courts, Walden Road, Huntingdon PE29 3DW
Adult: Monday, Tuesday, Wednesday, Thursday 10:00
YC: (Combined with North Cambridgeshire LJA) Tuesday 10:00

1612 MID-NORTH ESSEX LJA
combined with **1613 NORTH-EAST ESSEX LJA** and **1619 NORTH WEST ESSEX LJA** to form **1970 NORTH ESSEX LJA**

1610 MID-SOUTH ESSEX LJA
combined with **1629 SOUTH-EAST ESSEX LJA** and **1626 SOUTH-WEST ESSEX LJA** to form **1971 SOUTH ESSEX LJA**

NORTH CAMBRIDGESHIRE LJA
Siân E. Jones, Justices' Clerk, Magistrates' Court, Bridge Street, Peterborough PE1 1ED
Tel: 0845 310 0575
Fax: 01733 313749
DX: 742250 PETERBOROUGH 23

Courts and times
Magistrates' Court, Peterborough
Adult: Weekdays 10:00
YC: Monday and Thursday 10:00
FPC: Monday, Tuesday, Thursday, Friday 10:00

1613 NORTH-EAST ESSEX LJA
combined with **1612 MID-NORTH ESSEX LJA** and **1619 NORTH-WEST ESSEX LJA** to form **1970 NORTH ESSEX LJA**

1970 NORTH ESSEX LJA
Siân E. Jones, Justices' Clerk, Essex Magistrates' Courts Business Centre, PO Box 10754, Chelmsford CM1 9PZ

Tel: 01245 313300
Fax: 01245 313396
DX: 151020 Chelmsford 17
Email: es-osprey.general@hmcts.gsi.gov.uk

Courts and times
10 New Street, Chelmsford CM1 1NT
St Botolph's Circus, Magdalen Street, Colchester CO2 7EF
The High, Harlow CM20 1HH
Adult: Chelmsford: Weekdays 10:00; **Colchester:** Weekdays 10:00; **Harlow:** Wednesday, Thursday 10:00
YC: Chelmsford: Friday 10:00; **Colchester:** Wednesday 10:00
FPC: Chelmsford: Thursday 10:00; **Colchester:** Monday 10:00

1619 NORTH-WEST ESSEX LJA
combined with **1612 MID-NORTH ESSEX LJA** and **1613 NORTH EAST ESSEX LJA** to form **1970 NORTH ESSEX LJA**

1162 PETERBOROUGH LJA
combined with **1167 FENLAND** to form **NORTH CAMBRIDGESHIRE LJA** – wef 1/1/12

SOUTH CAMBRIDGESHIRE LJA
Siân E. Jones, Justices' Clerk, Bridge Street, Peterborough PE1 1ED
Tel: 0845 310 0575
Fax: 01223 376094
DX: 131966 CAMBRIDGE 6

Courts and times
The Courthouse, 12 St Andrew's Street, Cambridge CB2 1ED
Adult: Weekdays 10:00
YC: Wednesday 10:00
FPC: (Combined with North Cambridgeshire LJA) Alternate Tuesdays 10:00

1971 SOUTH ESSEX LJA
Siân E. Jones, Justices' Clerk, Essex Magistrates' Courts Business Centre, PO Box 10754, Chelmsford CM1 9PZ
Tel: 01245 313300
Fax: 01245 313396
DX: 151020 Chelmsford 17
Email: Siân E. Jones, Justices' Clerk,es-osprey.general@hmcts.gsi.gov.uk

Courts and times
Great Oaks, Basildon SS14 1EH
80 Victoria Avenue, Southend-on-Sea SS2 6EU
Adult: Basildon: Weekdays 10:00; **Southend-on-Sea:** Weekdays 10:00
YC: Basildon: Tuesday 10:00; **Southend-on-Sea:** Thursday 10:00
FPC: Basildon: Friday 10:00; **Southend-on-Sea:** Tuesday 10:00

1629 SOUTH-EAST ESSEX LJA
combined with **1610 MID-SOUTH ESSEX LJA** and **1626 SOUTH WEST ESSEX LJA** to form **1971 SOUTH ESSEX LJA**

1626 SOUTH-WEST ESSEX LJA
combined with **1610 MID-SOUTH ESSEX LJA** and **1629 SOUTH-EAST ESSEX LJA** to form **1971 SOUTH ESSEX LJA**

KENT

Delivery Director: Chris Jennings, 5th Floor, Fox Court, 14 Grays Inn Road, London WC1X 8HN. Tel: 020 3206 0688.

Kent Clerk to the Justices: Malcolm Dodds, Gail House, Lower Stone Street, Maidstone ME15 6NB. Tel: 01622 680050. Fax: 01622 680078. DX: 141482 MAIDSTONE 12.

Kent, Surrey & Sussex Finance Centre: PO Box 2989, Brighton BN2 0TF. Tel: 01273 811660. Fax: 01273 811773. DX: 153460 BRIGHTON 17.

Kent, Surrey & Sussex Enforcement Business Centre: PO Box 1288, Maidstone ME14 9PG. Tel: 01622 680070. Fax: 01622 68008.1 DX: 141482 MAIDSTONE 12

Home (UK) Orders: SE Regional Maintenance Unit, PO Box 936, Luton LU1 5TJ. Tel: 01582 524307.

Reciprocal Orders: SE Regional Reciprocal Maintenance Unit, Bury St Edmunds Magistrates' Court, Shire Hall, Bury St Edmunds IP33 1HF. Tel: 01284 778000. DX: 741460 BURY ST EDMUNDS 7.

Kent Fixed Penalty Office: PO Box 925, Maidstone ME16 8YA. Tel: 01622 656380. Fax: 01622 680081. DX: 141482 MAIDSTONE 12.

1960 CENTRAL KENT LJA

Malcolm Dodds, Kent Clerk to the Justices, Maidstone Magistrates' Court, The Courthouse, Palace Avenue, Maidstone ME15 6LL
Tel: 01622 671041
Fax: 01622 691800
DX: 152303 MAIDSTONE 19 (Maidstone Magistrates' Court)

Courts and times
Maidstone Magistrates' Court, Maidstone
The Courthouse, Morewood Close, London Road, Sevenoaks TN13 2HT
Medway County Court, Anchorage House, 47–67 High Street, Chatham ME4 4DW
Medway Magistrates' Court, The Court House, The Brook, Chatham ME4 4JZ
Adult: Maidstone: Weekdays 10:00; **Sevenoaks:** Weekdays 10:00
YC: Maidstone: Monday 10:00; **Sevenoaks:** Thursday 10:00
FPC: Medway CC and Medway Magistrates' Court: Weekdays 10:00; **Sevenoaks:** Monday and Friday 10:00

1965 EAST KENT LJA

Malcolm Dodds, Kent Clerk to the Justices, Court Admin Office, The Magistrates' Court, Pencester Road, Dover CT16 1BS
Tel: 01304 218600
Fax: 01304 213819 (Admin)
DX: 154700 DOVER 6
Email: KE-dovermcenq@hmcts.gsi.gov.uk (Resulting); KE-dovermclist@hmcts.gsi.gov.uk (Listing); KE-okfinanceenq@hmcts.gsi.gov.uk (Finance); KE-confiscationregse@hmcts.gsi.gov.uk (Confiscation)

Courts and times
The Magistrates' Court, Broad Street, Canterbury CT1 2GD
The Magistrates' Court, Pencester Road, Dover
The Law Courts, Castle Hill Avenue, Folkestone CT20 2GS
The Court House, Cecil Square, Margate CT9 1RL
Adult: Canterbury: Weekdays 10:00; **Dover:** Thursday and Friday 10:00; **Folkestone:** Weekdays 10:00; **Margate:** Weekdays 10:00
YC: Canterbury: Tuesday 10:00; **Folkestone:** Tuesday 10:00; **Margate:** Wednesday 10:00
FPC: Dover: Weekdays 10:00

1966 NORTH KENT LJA (DARTFORD AND MEDWAY)

Malcolm Dodds, Kent Clerk to the Justices, Court Admin Office, PO Box CH 4, The Court House, The Brook, Chatham ME4 4JZ
Tel: 01634 830232
Fax: 01634 847400
DX: 157180 CHATHAM 13

Courts and times
Sessions House, Highfield Road, Dartford DA12 2JW
The Court House, Chatham
Medway County Court, Anchorage House, 47–67 High Street, Chatham ME4 4DW
Adult: Dartford: Monday and Tuesday 10:00 and 14:15; **Chatham:** Weekdays 10:00 and 14:15

YC: Dartford: Tuesday 10:00 and 14:15; **Chatham:** Tuesday 10:00 and 1415
Unified Family Service: Medway CC: Wednesday, Thursday, Friday 10:00 and 14:15

NORFOLK AND SUFFOLK

Delivery Director: Chris Jennings, 5th Floor, Fox Court, 14 Grays Inn Road, London WC1X 8HN. Tel: 020 3206 0688.

Justices' Clerk (Suffolk): David Ratcliffe, Bury St Edmunds Magistrates' Court, The Shire Hall, Honey Hill, Bury St Edmunds IP33 1HF. Tel: 01284 778000. Fax: 01284 778020. DX: 741460 BURY ST EDMUNDS 7.

Justices' Clerk (Norfolk): David Ratcliffe, Norwich Magistrates' Court, Bishopgate, Norwich NR3 1UP. Tel: 01603 679500. Fax: 01603 663263. DX: 97389 NORWICH 5.

Payments and Accounts (including TFOs and Fixed Penalty Registrations): CENS Payments & Accounts Office, North East Suffolk Magistrates' Court, Old Nelson Street, Lowestoft NR32 1HJ. Tel: 01502 501060. Fax: 01502 513875. DX: 97750 LOWESTOFT 2.

Home (UK) orders: SE Regional Maintenance Unit, PO Box 936, Luton LU1 5TJ. Tel: 01582 524307. DX: 151660 LUTON 16.

Reciprocal orders: SE Regional Reciprocal Maintenance Unit, Bury St Edmunds Magistrates' Court, Shire Hall, Bury St Edmunds IP33 1HF. Tel: 01284 778000. DX: 741460 BURY ST EDMUNDS 7.

1442 CENTRAL NORFOLK LJA
combined with **1443 GREAT YARMOUTH LJA, 1444 NORTH NORFOLK LJA, 1445 NORWICH LJA, 1446 SOUTH NORFOLK LJA, 1447 WEST NORFOLK LJA** to form **1972 NORFOLK LJA**

1443 GREAT YARMOUTH LJA
combined with **1442 CENTRAL NORFOLK LJA, 1444 NORTH NORFOLK LJA, 1445 NORWICH LJA, 1446 SOUTH NORFOLK LJA, 1447 WEST NORFOLK LJA** to form **1972 NORFOLK LJA**

2863 NORTH EAST SUFFOLK LJA
David Ratcliffe, Justices' Clerk, The Magistrates' Court, Old Nelson Street, Lowestoft NR32 1HJ
Tel: 01502 501060
Fax: 01502 513875
DX: 97750 LOWESTOFT 2

Courts and times
The Magistrates' Court, Old Nelson Street, Lowestoft
Adult: Monday, Tuesday, alternate Wednesdays, Thursday 10:00 and 14:15
YC: Wednesday 10:00
FPC: Tuesday 10:00

1444 NORTH NORFOLK LJA
combined with **1442 CENTRAL NORFOLK LJA, 1443 GREAT YARMOUTH LJA, 1445 NORWICH LJA, 1446 SOUTH NORFOLK LJA, 1447 WEST NORFOLK LJA** to form **1972 NORFOLK LJA**

1445 NORFOLK LJA
combined with **1442 CENTRAL NORFOLK LJA, 1443 GREAT YARMOUTH LJA, 1445 NORWICH LJA, 1446 SOUTH NORFOLK LJA, 1447 WEST NORFOLK LJA** to form **1972 NORFOLK LJA**

1972 NORFOLK LJA
David Ratcliffe, Justices' Clerk, The Magistrates' Court, Bishopgate, Norwich NR3 1UP
Tel: 01603 679500
Fax: 01603 663263
DX: 97389 NORWICH 5
Email: norwich.court@hmcts.gsi.gov.uk

Courts and times
The Magistrates' Court, Bishopgate, Norwich
The Magistrates' Court, North Quay, Great Yarmouth
The Magistrates' Court, College Lane, King's Lynn
Adult: Norwich: Weekdays 10:00 and 14:15; **Great Yarmouth:** 10:00 and 14:15; **King's Lynn:** Weekdays 10:00
YC: Norwich: Weekdays 10:00; **Great Yarmouth:** Thursday 10:00; **King's Lynn:** Tuesday 10:00
FPC: Norwich: Weekdays 10:00; **Great Yarmouth:** Wednesday 10:00; **King's Lynn:** Friday 10:00

2866 SOUTH EAST SUFFOLK LJA
David Ratcliffe, Justices' Clerk, The Magistrates' Court, Elm Street, Ipswich IP1 2AP
Tel: 01473 217261
Fax: 01473 231249

DX: 3232 IPSWICH

Courts and times
The Magistrates' Court, Elm Street, Ipswich
Adult: Weekdays 10:00
YC: Alternate Thursdays 10:00
FPC: Wednesday 10:00

1446 SOUTH NORFOLK LJA
combined with **1442 CENTRAL NORFOLK LJA, 1443 GREAT YARMOUTH LJA, 1444 NORTH NORFOLK LJA, 1445 NORWICH LJA, 1447 WEST NORFOLK LJA** to form **1972 NORFOLK LJA**

1447 WEST NORFOLK LJA
combined with **1442 CENTRAL NORFOLK LJA, 1443 GREAT YARMOUTH LJA, 1444 NORTH NORFOLK LJA, 1445 NORWICH LJA, 1446 SOUTH NORFOLK LJA** to form **1972 NORFOLK LJA**

2867 WEST SUFFOLK LJA
David Ratcliffe, Justices' Clerk, Shire Hall, Bury St Edmunds IP33 1HF
Tel: 01284 778000
Fax: 01284 778020

Courts and times
The Courthouse, Shire Hall, Bury St Edmunds
Bury St Edmunds County Court, St Andrew's Street North, Bury St Edmunds
Adult: The Courthouse, Shire Hall: Weekdays 10:00 and 14:00
YC: The Courthouse, Shire Hall: Alternate Wednesdays 10:00
FPC: Bury St Edmunds County Court: Friday 10:00

SURREY AND SUSSEX

*Delivery Director:*Chris Jennings, 5th Floor, Fox Court, 14 Grays Inn Road, London WC1X 8HN. Tel: 020 3206 0688.

Surrey Clerk to the Justices: Ian Matthews (interim), Guildford Law Courts, Mary Road, Guildford GU1 4AS. Tel: 01483 405372. DX: 97865 GUILDFORD 5

Sussex Clerk to the Justices: Ian Matthews (interim), Horsham Law Courts, Hurst Road, Horsham RH12 2EU. Tel: 01403 252474. DX: 98170 HORSHAM 2

Surrey & Sussex Finance Centre: PO Box 2989, Brighton BN2 0TF. Tel: 01273 811660. Fax: 01273 811773. DX: 153460 BRIGHTON 17

Surrey & Sussex Enforcement Business Centre: PO Box 1288, Maidstone ME14 9PG Tel: 01622 680070. Fax: 01622 68008.1 DX: 141482 MAIDSTONE 12

Home (UK) Orders: SE Regional Maintenance Unit, PO Box 936, Luton LU1 5TJ. Tel: 01582 524307

Reciprocal Orders: SE Regional Reciprocal Maintenance Unit, Bury St Edmunds Magistrates' Court, Shire Hall, Bury St Edmunds IP33 1HF. Tel: 01284 778000. DX: 741460 BURY ST EDMUNDS 7

Regional Fixed Penalty Office: PO Box 5992, Southend-on-Sea SS1 9PX. Tel: 01702 283860. Fax: 01702 283896. DX: 97585 SOUTHEND 3

2849 NORTH SURREY LJA

Ian Matthews (interim), Justices' Clerk, PO Box 5, The Law Courts, Knowle Green, Staines, Middlesex TW18 1XR

Tel: 01784 895500; 01784 895590 (Family Administration Unit)

Fax: 01784 895510 (Office); 895579 (Ushers); 895520 (Family Administration Unit for the County)

DX: 98045 STAINES 2

Courts and times

The Law Courts, Knowle Green, Staines

Adult: Weekdays 10:00

YC: Alternate Wednesdays 10:00

FPC: Monday, Tuesday, Wednesday 10:00

2857 NORTH WEST SURREY LJA

closed wef 31/12/11

2856 SOUTH EAST SURREY LJA

Ian Matthews (interim), Justices' Clerk, The Law Courts, Hatchlands Road, Redhill RH1 6DH

Tel: 01737 765581

Fax: 01737 778372 (Office); 764972 (Ushers)

DX: 98021 REDHILL WEST

Courts and times

The Law Courts, Hatchlands Road, Redhill

Magistrates' Court, Mary Road, Guildford

Adult: Redhill: Weekdays 10:00

YC: Redhill: Alternate Wednesdays 10:00

FPC: Guildford: Monday, Tuesday, Wednesday 10:00

2848 SOUTH WEST SURREY LJA

Ian Matthews (interim), Justices' Clerk, PO Box 36, Guildford GU1 4AS

Tel: 01483 405300

Fax: 01483 461791 (Office); 405375 (Ushers)

DX: 97865 GUILDFORD 5

Courts and times

Magistrates' Court, Mary Road, Guildford

Adult: Weekdays 10:00

YC: Alternate Wednesdays 10:00

FPC: Monday, Tuesday, Wednesday 10:00

2950 SUSSEX (CENTRAL) LJA

Ian Matthews (interim), Justices' Clerk, Brighton Magistrates' Court, The Law Courts, Edward Street, Brighton BN2 0LG

Tel: 01273 670888 (General Enquiries); 811620 (Listing); 811640 (Court Support)

Fax: 01273 811770 (Listing and Court Support); 811772 (Licensing)

DX: 153460 BRIGHTON 17

Courts and times
Law Courts, Edward Street, Brighton
Brighton Youth and Family Suite, John Street, Brighton
Adult: Law Courts: Weekdays 10:00 and 14:15
YC: Brighton Youth and Family Suite: Tuesday 10:00 and 14:15
FPC: Brighton Youth and Family Suite: Tuesday, Wednesday, Thursday, Friday
FPC (Lewes): See Brighton County Court for details

2948 SUSSEX (EASTERN) LJA

Ian Matthews (interim), Justices' Clerk, Hastings Magistrates' Court, The Law Courts, Horntye Park,
Bohemia Road, Hastings TN34 1ND
Tel: 01424 437644
Fax: 01424 429878
DX: 98152 HASTINGS 2

Courts and times
The Law Courts, Horntye Park, Bohemia Road, Hastings
The Law Courts, Old Orchard Road, Eastbourne BN21 4UN
Adult: Hastings: Monday, Tuesday, Wednesday, Friday 10:00 and 14:15; **Eastbourne:** Wednesday
and Thursday 10:00 and 14:15
YC: Eastbourne: Tuesday 10:00 and 14:15
FPC: Hastings: Tuesday, Wednesday, Thursday 10:00 and 14:15

2947 SUSSEX (NORTHERN) LJA

Ian Matthews (interim), Justices' Clerk, Brighton Magistrates' Court, The Law Courts, Edward Street,
Brighton BN2 0LG
Tel: 01273 670888 (Main Switchboard)
Fax: 01273 811770 (Court Support/Listing)
DX: 153460 BRIGHTON 17

Courts and times
The Court House, County Buildings, Woodfield Road, Crawley (no postal facilities)
Magistrates' Court, Hurst Road, Horsham
Adult: Crawley: Tuesday, Wednesday, Thursday, Friday 10:00; **Horsham:** Monday, Thursday, Friday
10:00
YC: Crawley: Alternate Tuesdays 10:00
FPC: Horsham: Tuesday and Wednesday 10:00

2949 SUSSEX (WESTERN) LJA

P. T. A. Vahey, Worthing Magistrates' Court, The Law Courts, PO Box 199, Christchurch Road,
Worthing BN11 1JE; Chichester Magistrates' Court, 6 Market Avenue, Chichester PO19 1YE
Tel: 01903 210981 (General Enquiries); 210981 (Listing); 01243 520705 (Family Section)
Fax: 01903 820746 (General Enquiries); 820746 (Listing); 01243 817022 (Chichester Office); 01243
839234 (Chichester Usher)
DX: 98233 WORTHING 4; DX: 97463 CHICHESTER 2

Courts and times
The Law Courts, Christchurch Road, Worthing
Magistrates' Court, 6 Market Avenue, Chichester
Adult: Worthing: Weekdays 10:00; **Chichester:** Tuesday and Wednesday 10:00
YC: Worthing: Thursdays 10:00; **Chichester:** Wednesday 10:00
FPC: Worthing: Tuesday 10:00; **Chichester:** Thursday 10:00
Remand: Chichester: Wednesday

THAMES VALLEY

Delivery Director: Chris Jennings, 5th Floor, Fox Court, 14 Grays Inn Road, London WC1X 8HN. Tel: 020 3206 0688

Justices' Clerk (Thames Valley): David Richmond, Bicester Magistrates' Court, Waverley House, Queen's Avenue, Bicester, Oxfordshire OX26 2NZ. Tel: 01869 853100. Fax: 01869 853114

Listings Enquiries: Case Management Unit (CMU). Tel: 01295 452010 (Oxfordshire); 01295 452000 (Berkshire); 01295 452020 (Buckinghamshire)

Fine Account Enquiries: Enforcement Business Centre (EBC), PO Box 267, Bicester, Oxfordshire OX25 4ZD. Tel: 0845 300 4239

Home (UK) Orders: SE Regional Maintenance Unit, PO Box 936, Luton LU1 5TJ. Tel: 01582 524307. DX: 151660 LUTON 16

Reciprocal Orders: SE Regional Reciprocal Maintenance Unit, Bury St Edmunds Magistrates' Court, Shire Hall, Bury St Edmunds IP33 1HF. Tel: 01284 778000. DX: 741460 BURY ST EDMUNDS 7I

1920 BERKSHIRE LJA
Nick Wattam, Reading Magistrates' Court, Civic Centre, Reading RG1 7TQ
Tel: 0118 980 1800
Fax: 0118 980 1830
DX: 151160 READING 25

Courts and times
The Law Courts, Chalvey Park, off Windsor Road, Slough SL1 2HJ
Magistrates' Court, Bridge Road, Maidenhead SL6 8PB (correspondence to Slough)
Magistrates' Court, Civic Centre, Reading
The Court House, Mill Lane, Newbury RG14 5QS
Adult: Maidenhead, Newbury, Reading, Slough: Monday, Tuesday, Wednesday, Thursday 10:00–17:00, Friday 09:00–16:30
YC: Maidenhead, Reading: Wednesday and Thursday 10:00–17:00, Friday 10:00–16:30
FPC: Newbury, Reading: Monday, Tuesday, Wednesday, Thursday 10:00–17:00, Friday 10:00–16:30

1921 BUCKINGHAMSHIRE LJA
Colin Webster, Aylesbury Magistrates' Court, The Law Courts, Walton Street, Aylesbury HP21 7QZ
Tel: 01296 554330
Fax: 01296 554340

Courts and times
The Law Courts, Walton Street, Aylesbury HP21 7QZ. Tel: 01908 451145
Magistrates' Court, 301 Silbury Boulevard, Witan Gate East, Milton Keynes MK9 2AJ. Tel: 01908 451146
The Law Courts, Easton Street, High Wycombe HP11 1LR. Tel: 01908 451145
Adult: Aylesbury: Tuesday 10:00–17:00; **High Wycombe, Milton Keynes:** Monday, Tuesday, Wednesday, Thursday 10:00–17:00, Friday 10:00–16:30
YC: High Wycombe: Tuesday and Friday 10:00; **Milton Keynes:** Tuesday 10:00
FPC: High Wycombe, Milton Keynes: Thursday and Friday 10:00

1129 CENTRAL BUCKINGHAMSHIRE LJA
combined with **1129 CENTRAL BUCKINGHAMSHIRE LJA** and **1130 WYCOMBE AND BEACONSFIELD LJA** to form **1921 BUCKINGHAMSHIRE LJA**

1072 EAST BERKSHIRE LJA
combined with **1075 WEST BERKSHIRE LJA** and **1076 READING LJA** to form **1920 BERKSHIRE LJA**

1124 MILTON KEYNES LJA
combined with **1129 CENTRAL BUCKINGHAMSHIRE LJA** and **1130 WYCOMBE AND BEACONSFIELD LJA** to form **1921 BUCKINGHAMSHIRE LJA**

2775 NORTHERN OXFORDSHIRE LJA
combined with **2777 OXFORD LJA** and **2774 SOUTHERN OXFORDSHIRE LJA** to form **1922 OXFORDSHIRE LJA**

2777 OXFORD LJA
combined with **2775 NORTHERN OXFORDSHIRE LJA** and **2774 SOUTHERN OXFORDSHIRE LJA** to form **1922 OXFORDSHIRE LJA**

1922 OXFORDSHIRE LJA
Sue Walton, Oxford Magistrates' Court, Speedwell Street, Oxford OX1 1XP
Tel: 01865 448014
Fax: 01865 448024
Courts and times
Oxford Magistrates' Court, Speedwell Street, Oxford OX1 1XP. Tel: 01865 448020
Banbury Magistrates' Court, The Courthouse, Warwick Road, Banbury OX16 2AW. Tel: 01865 448020
Adult: Oxford: Monday, Tuesday, Thursday, Friday 10:00; **Banbury:** Monday, Wednesday and Friday 10:00
YC: Oxford: Wednesday 10:00; **Banbury:** Thursday 10:00
FPC: Oxford: Second and fourth Monday in month, Wednesday, Friday 10:00; **Banbury:** Second and fourth Tuesday in month 10:00

1076 READING LJA
combined with **1072 EAST BERKSHIRE LJA** and **1075 WEST BERKSHIRE LJA** to form **1920 BERKSHIRE LJA**

2774 SOUTHERN OXFORDSHIRE LJA
combined with **2777 OXFORD LJA** and **2775 NORTHERN OXFORDSHIRE LJA** to form **1922 OXFORDSHIRE LJA**

1075 WEST BERKSHIRE LJA
combined with **1072 EAST BERKSHIRE LJA** and **1076 READING LJA** to form **1920 BERKSHIRE LJA**

1130 WYCOMBE AND BEACONSFIELD LJA
combined with **1124 MILTON KEYNES LJA** and **1129 CENTRAL BUCKINGHAMSHIRE LJA** to form **1921 BUCKINGHAMSHIRE LJA**

AVON, SOMERSET AND GLOUCESTERSHIRE

Cluster Manager: To be confirmed, HMCTS, Queensway House, The Hedges, St George's, Weston-super-Mare BS22 7BB. Tel: 01934 528668. Fax: 01934 528520. DX: 152360 WESTON SUPER MARE 5.

1022 BATH AND WANSDYKE LJA
see **1030 SOMERSET LJA**

1013 BRISTOL LJA
Mrs R. Davies, Magistrates' Court, Marlborough Street, Bristol BS1 3NU
Tel: 0117 930 2400
Fax: 0117 930 2487
DX: 78126 BRISTOL
Email: av-bristol.mc@hmcts.gsi.gov.uk
Courts and times
Marlborough Street, Bristol
Adult: Weekdays 10:00
YC: Monday, Friday 10:00

1698 GLOUCESTERSHIRE LJA
Mrs R. Davies, 2nd Floor, Southgate House, Southgate Street, Gloucester GL1 1UB
Tel: 01452 420100
DX: 98665 GLOUCESTER 5
Courts and times
Magistrates' Court, St George's Road, Cheltenham
The Courthouse, Barbican Way, Gloucester
The Courthouse, Parliament Street, Stroud
Adult: Cheltenham: Weekdays 10:00 and 14:00; **Gloucester:** Monday, Tuesday, Friday 10:00 and 14:00; **Stroud:** Monday and Wednesday 10:00 and 14:00

5698 GLOUCESTERSHIRE YOUTH COURT
Mrs R. Davies, PO Box 9051, Gloucester GL1 2XG
Family Proceedings Section: PO Box 9050, Gloucester GL1 2WG
Courts and times
The Courthouse, Barbican Way, Gloucester
The Courthouse, St George's Road, Cheltenham
Kimbrose Way, Gloucester
YC: The Courthouse, Gloucester: County Panel: Thursday 10:00 and 14:00; **Cheltenham:** Thursday 10:00
FPC: Kimbrose Way, Gloucester: County Panel: Tuesday, Wednesday, Thursday

1021 NORTH AVON LJA
Mrs R. Davies, Magistrates' Court, Kennedy Way, Yate, South Gloucestershire BS37 4PY
Tel: 01454 310505; 338201 (Family)
Fax: 01454 319404 (General); 315745 (Family)
DX: 743500 YATE 2
Email: av-yate.mc@hmcts.gsi.gov.uk
Courts and times
Magistrates' Court, Kennedy Way, Yate
Adult: Weekdays 10:00 and 14:15
YC: Tuesday 10:00
FPC: Thursday 10:00

1023 NORTH SOMERSET LJA
see **1030 SOMERSET LJA**

2706 SEDGEMOOR LJA
closed wef 4/12

1030 SOMERSET LJA
Mrs R. Davies, Magistrates' Court, The Law Courts, North Parade Road, Bath BA1 0LF
Tel: 01225 463281

Fax: 01225 420255
DX: 741420 BATH 9
Email: av-bath.mc@hmcts.gsi.gov.uk
Courts and times
Magistrates' Court, North Parade Road, Bath
Magistrates' Court, St John's Road, Taunton TA1 4AX. Tel: 01823 257084. Fax: 01823 335195. DX: 122473 TAUNTON 7. Email: av-taunton.mc@hmcts.gsi.gov.uk
North Somerset Courthouse, The Hedges, St George's, Weston-super-Mare BS22 7BB. Tel: 01934 528700. Fax: 01934 528599. DX: 152361 WSM5. Email: av-weston.mc@hmcts.gsi.gov.uk
The Law Courts, Petters Way, Yeovil BA20 1SW; Yeovil County Court, 22 Hendford, Yeovil BA20 2QD. Tel: 01935 426281. Fax: 01935 431022. DX: 100537 YEOVIL. Email: av-yeovil.mc@hmcts.gsi.gov.uk
Adult: Bath: Weekdays 10:00 and 14:15; **Taunton:** weekdays 10:00; **Weston-super-Mare:** weekdays 10:00; **Yeovil:** Monday, Thursday, Friday 10:00
YC: Bath: Thursday 10:00; **Taunton:** Tuesday 10:00; **Weston-super-Mare:** Wednesday 10:00; **Yeovil:** Wednesday 10:00
FPC: Bath: Wednesday 10:00; **Taunton:** Tuesday, Friday 10:00; **Weston-super-Mare:** Thursday 10:00; **Yeovil County Court:** Wednesday 10:00

2716 SOUTH SOMERSET AND MENDIP LJA
see **1030 SOMERSET LJA**

2709 TAUNTON DEANE AND WEST SOMERSET LJA
see **1030 SOMERSET LJA**

DEVON, CORNWALL AND DORSET

Cluster Manager: Anna Munday. Tel: 01752 675443. Email: anna.munday5@hmcts.gsi.gov.uk
Central Finance Unit: Magistrates' Court, St Andrew Street, Plymouth PL1 2DP

1292 CENTRAL DEVON LJA
combined with **1291 NORTH DEVON LJA** to form **1292 NORTH AND EAST DEVON LJA**

1301 CORNWALL LJA
T.A.M. Smith, Justices' Clerk, The Law Courts, Launceston Road, Bodmin, Cornwall PL31 2AL
Tel: 01208 262700
Fax: 01208 269965
DX: 740535 BODMIN4PL
Email: dcmcc.eastcornwall@hmcts.gsi.gov.uk
The Magistrates' Court, Tremorvah Wood Lane, Mitchell Hill, Truro TR1 1HZ
Tel: 01872 321900
Fax: 01872 276227
DX: 140880 TRURO 5
Email: westcornwall@hmcts.gsi.gov.uk
Notes:
Family Court Administration Department is located at The Truro County Court, Courts of Justice, Edward Street, Truro TR1 2PB. Tel: 01872 267460. DX: 135396 TRURO 2.

Courts and times
The Law Courts, Launceston Road, Bodmin
The Magistrates' Court, Tremorvah Wood Lane, Mitchell Hill, Truro
Old Wesleyan Chapel, Garrison Lane, Hugh Town, St Mary's, Isles of Scilly
Adult: Bodmin: Weekdays 10:00; **Truro:** Weekdays 10:00; **Isles of Scilly:** Quarterly as required 10:00
YC: Bodmin: Alternate Mondays 10:00; **Truro:** Alternate Fridays 10:00
FPC: Bodmin: Thursday 10:00; **Truro:** Tuesday and Wednesday 10:00

DORSET COMBINED FAMILY PANEL AND UNIFIED FAMILY OFFICE
T.A.M. Smith, Justices' Clerk, or Mr S. Rover, Deputy Clerk to the Justices (Family), The Combined Court, Deansleigh Road, Bournemouth BH7 7DS
Tel: 01202 502800
Fax: 01202 502801
DX: 98420 BOURNEMOUTH 4

Courts and times
The Family Court Suite at The Law Courts, Stafford Road, Bournemouth
The Law Courts, Westwey Road, Weymouth
Dates and venues as required

5522/5523 DORSET COMBINED YOUTH PANEL
T.A.M. Smith, Justices' Clerk, The Law Courts, Westwey Road, Weymouth, Dorset DT4 8BS
Tel: 01305 783891
Fax: 01305 761418
DX: 98820 WEYMOUTH 3

Courts
The Law Courts, Park Road, Poole
The Law Courts, Westwey Road, Weymouth
Dates and venues as required

1289 EAST CORNWALL LJA
combined with **1288 WEST CORNWALL LJA** to form **1301 CORNWALL LJA**

1522 EAST DORSET LJA
T.A.M. Smith, Justices' Clerk, The Law Courts, Stafford Road, Bournemouth, Dorset BH1 1LA
Tel: 01202 745309
Fax: 01202 711999
DX: 157500 BOURNEMOUTH 24

Courts and times
The Law Courts, Stafford Road, Bournemouth
The Law Courts, Park Road, Poole
Adult: Bournemouth: Weekdays 10:00; **Poole:** As required

YC: See Dorset Combined Youth Panel
FPC: See Dorset Combined Family Panel

1291 NORTH DEVON LJA
combined with **1292 CENTRAL DEVON LJA** to form **1292 NORTH AND EAST DEVON LJA**

1292 NORTH AND EAST DEVON LJA
T.A.M. Smith, East Devon Magistrates' Courts, Southernhay Gardens, Exeter EX1 1UH
Tel: 01392 415594 (Admin); 415320 (Family)
Fax: 01392 415593
DX: 98440 EXETER 2
The Law Courts, Civic Centre, Barnstaple, Devon EX31 1DX
Tel: 01271 340410; 01271 340412
Fax: 01271 340415
DX: 98563 BARNSTAPLE 2
Email: de-barnstaplemcadm@hmcts.gsi.gov.uk; family@barnstaple.countycourt.gsi.gov.uk
Courts and times
Court House, Heavitree Road, Exeter
Crown and County Buildings, Southernhay Gardens, Exeter
The Law Courts, Civic Centre, Barnstaple
Adult: Heavitree Road: Alternate Thursdays 10:00; **Barnstaple:** Alternate Tuesdays 10:00
YC: Heavitree Road: Thursday 10:00; **Barnstaple:** Tuesday 10:00
FPC: Southernhay Gardens: Monday, Tuesday, Wednesday 10:00; **Barnstaple:** Thursday 10:00

1290 PLYMOUTH DISTRICT LJA
T.A.M. Smith, Magistrates' Court, St Andrew Street, Plymouth PL1 2DP
Tel: 01752 206200
Fax: 01752 206194
Courts and times
Magistrates' Court, St Andrew Street, Plymouth
Adult: Weekdays 10:00 and 14:00
YC: Weekdays 10:00 and 14:00
FPC: Wednesday and Friday 10:00

1293 SOUTH DEVON LJA
T.A.M. Smith, c/o Torquay & Newton Abbott County Court, The Willows, Nicholson Road, Torquay, Devon TQ2 7AZ
Tel: 01803 616365; 614295 (Listing)
Fax: 01803 616795
DX: 98740 TORQUAY 4
Email: southdevonmc@hmcts.gsi.gov.uk
Courts and times
The Court House, Union Street, Torquay
Court House, Newton Abbot
Torquay and Newton Abbot County Court, Nicholson Road, Torquay
Adult: Union Street: Weekdays 10:00; **Newton Abbot:** Monday, Tuesday, Thursday, Friday 10:00
YC: **Newton Abbot:** Tuesday 14:00
FPC: Torquay and Newton Abbot County Court: Monday 10:00

1288 WEST CORNWALL LJA
combined with **1289 EAST CORNWALL LJA** to form **1301 CORNWALL LJA**

1523 WEST DORSET LJA
T.A.M. Smith, The Law Courts, Westwey Road, Weymouth, Dorset DT4 8BS
Tel: 01305 783891
Fax: 01305 761418
DX: 98820 WEYMOUTH 3
Courts and times
The Law Courts, Westwey Road, Weymouth
Adult: Dates and venues as required
YC: See Dorset Combined Youth Panel
FPC: See Dorset Combined Family Panel

HAMPSHIRE, ISLE OF WIGHT AND WILTSHIRE

Cluster Manager: Paula Bray. Tel: 02392 857932. Email: paula.bray1@hmcts.gsi.gov.uk

1945 ISLE OF WIGHT LJA
Christine Murray, Justices' Clerk, The Magistrates' Court, The Law Courts, Quay Street, Newport, Isle of Wight PO30 5YT
Tel: 01983 535100
Fax: 01983 554977
DX: 98460 NEWPORT IW 2
Courts and times
Magistrates' Court, The Law Courts, Quay Street, Newport, Isle of Wight
Adult: Monday, Tuesday, Thursday, Friday 09:30
YC: Alternate Wednesday 09:30
FPC: Wednesday 09:30

1779 NEW FOREST LJA
closed wef 1/04/11

1305 NORTH HAMPSHIRE LJA
5305 (YC)
Christine Murray, Justices' Clerk, Angela Carpenter, Operations Manager, Basingstoke Magistrates' Court, The Court House, London Road, Basingstoke RG21 4AB
Tel: 01252 366000
Fax: 01256 81122
Aldershot Magistrates' Court, The Court House, Civic Centre, Aldershot GU11 1NY
Tel: 01252 366000; 366033 (Accounts)
Fax: 01252 330877
DX: 98570 BASINGSTOKE 3
Courts and times
The Court House, London Road, Basingstoke
The Court House, Civic Centre, Aldershot
The Court House, Normandy Street, Alton
Adult: Basingstoke: Monday, Tuesday, Thursday, Friday 10:00 and 14:00; **Aldershot:** Weekdays 10:00 and 14:00; **Alton:** As required
YC: Basingstoke: Wednesday 10:00 and 14:00; **Alton:** As required
FPC: Basingstoke: As required; **Alton:** As required

1780 NORTH EAST HAMPSHIRE LJA
combined with **1781 NORTH WEST HAMPSHIRE LJA** to form **1305/5305 NORTH HAMPSHIRE LJA**

1781 NORTH WEST HAMPSHIRE LJA
combined with **1780 NORTH EAST HAMPSHIRE LJA** to form **1305/5305 NORTH HAMPSHIRE LJA**

3026 NORTH WEST WILTSHIRE LJA
See **3012 WILTSHIRE LJA**

1782 SOUTH EAST HAMPSHIRE LJA
Christine Murray, Justices' Clerk, The Law Courts, Winston Churchill Avenue, Portsmouth, Hampshire PO1 2DQ
Tel: 023 9281 9421
Fax: 023 9229 3085
DX: 98494 PORTSMOUTH 5
Courts and times
The Law Courts, Winston Churchill Avenue, Portsmouth
The Court House, Trinity Street, Fareham (closed Mondays)
Adult: Portsmouth: Weekdays 10:00
YC: Fareham: (Combined with South Hampshire LJA): Tuesday to Friday 10:00
FPC: Portsmouth: (Combined with South Hampshire LJA): Tuesday to Friday 10:00

3027 SOUTH EAST WILTSHIRE LJA
See **3012 WILTSHIRE LJA**

1783 SOUTH HAMPSHIRE LJA
Christine Murray, Justices' Clerk, The Law Courts, Winston Churchill Avenue, Portsmouth, Hampshire
PO1 2DQ
Tel: 023 9281 9421
Fax: 023 9229 3085
DX: 98494 PORTSMOUTH 5

Courts and times
The Court House, Trinity Street, Fareham
The Law Courts, Winston Churchill Avenue, Portsmouth
Adult: Fareham: Weekdays 10:00
YC: Fareham: (Combined with South East Hampshire LJA): Weekdays 10:00
FPC: Portsmouth: (Combined with South East Hampshire LJA): Weekdays 10:00

1775 SOUTHAMPTON LJA
See **1304 WEST HAMPSHIRE LJA**

3015 SWINDON LJA
See **3012 WILTSHIRE LJA**

1304 WEST HAMPSHIRE LJA
Christine Murray, Justices' Clerk, Southampton Magistrates' Court, 100 The Avenue, Southampton
SO17 1EY
Tel: 023 8038 4200
Fax: 023 8038 4203
DX: 135986 SOUTHAMPTON 32

Courts and times
Southampton Magistrates' Court, 100 The Avenue, Southampton
Southampton Combined Court Centre, London Road, Southampton
Adult: Southampton Magistrates' Court: Weekdays 10:00 and 14:00
YC: Southampton Magistrates' Court: Monday, Thursday 10:00 and 14:00
FPC: Southampton Combined Court Centre: Weekdays

3021 WILTSHIRE LJA
    7021 (YC)
Christine Murray, Justices' Clerk, Swindon Magistrates' Court, Princes Street, Swindon, Wiltshire
SN1 2JB
Tel: 01793 699800
Fax: 01793 699863
DX: 118725 SWINDON 7

Courts and times
Chippenham Magistrates' Court, The Court House, Pewsham Way, Chippenham SN15 3BF
Salisbury Magistrates' Court, Salisbury Law Courts, Wilton Road, Salisbury SP2 7EP
Swindon Magistrates' Court, Princes Street, Swindon
Adult: Chippenham: Monday, Tuesday, Wednesday, Thursday; **Salisbury:** Monday, Wednesday,
Thursday, Friday; **Swindon:** Monday, Tuesday, Wednesday, Friday
YC: Chippenham: Alternate Tuesdays; **Salisbury:** Alternate Thursdays; **Swindon:** Alternate Tuesdays
FPC: Chippenham: Friday; **Salisbury:** Friday; **Swindon:** Thursday

Thank you for purchasing The Directory of Courts in the UK 2013/2014.

☑ **Don't miss important updates**

So that you have all the latest information, **the Directory of Courts in the UK** is published annually. Sign up today for a Standing Order to ensure you receive the updating copies as soon as they publish. Setting up a Standing Order with Sweet & Maxwell is hassle-free, simply tick, complete and return this FREEPOST card and we'll do the rest.

You may cancel your Standing Order at any time by writing to us at Thomson Reuters, PO Box 1000, Andover, SP10 9AH stating the Standing Order you wish to cancel.

Alternatively, if you have purchased your copy of **the Directory of Courts in the UK** from a bookshop or other trade supplier, please ask your supplier to ensure that you are registered to receive the new editions.

All goods are subject to our 30 day Satisfaction Guarantee (applicable to EU customers only)

Yes, please send me new editions of **the Directory of Courts in the UK** of Title to be invoiced on publication, until I cancel the standing order in writing.

☐ All new editions

Title .... Name ....

Organisation ....

Job title ....

Address ....

....

Postcode ....

Telephone ....

Email ....

S&M account number (if known) ....

PO number ....

All orders are accepted subject to the terms of this order form and our Terms of Trading. (see www.sweetandmaxwell.co.uk). By submitting this order form I confirm that I accept these terms and I am authorised to sign on behalf of the customer.

Signed .... Job Title ....

Print Name .... Date ....

UK VAT Number: GB 900 5487 43. Irish VAT Number: IE 9513874E. For customers in an EU member state (except UK & Ireland) please supply your VAT Number. VAT No [   ]

(BC007) V9 (07.2013) LC / JK

SWEET & MAXWELL

THOMSON REUTERS

THOMSON REUTERS

FREEPOST

PO BOX 1000

ANDOVER

SP10 9AH

UNITED KINGDOM

HMCTS WALES

MID AND WEST WALES

Delivery Director for HMCTS Wales: Luigi Strinati. Email: luigi.strinati@hmcts.gsi.gov.uk
Head of Crime for HMCTS Wales: Nick Albrow. Email: nick.albrow@hmcts.gsi.gov.uk
Wales Support Unit, 2nd Floor, Cardiff & Vale Magistrates' Court, Fitzalan Place, Cardiff CF24 0RZ. DX: 743943 CARDIFF 38.
Wales Enforcement Contact/Compliance Centre: PO Box 84, Cwmbran NP44 1ZP. Tel: 01633 645112.
Wales Enforcement & Accounts Office: Port Talbot Justice Centre, Harbourside Road, Port Talbot SA13 1SB. Tel: 01633 645112.
Wales Fixed Penalty Office: Port Talbot Justice Centre, Harbourside Road, Port Talbot SA13 1SB. Tel: 01639 605784.

3250 BRECKNOCK AND RADNORSHIRE LJA
7250 (YC)
Clerk to the Justices, Magistrates' Court, The Law Courts, Glebeland Place, Merthyr Tydfil CF47 8BH
Tel: 01685 727600
Fax: 01685 727705
DX: 99582 MERTHYR TYDFIL 2
Note: All fine payments and accounts enquiries to the Wales Enforcement & Accounts Office, as above. All fixed penalty enquiries to the Wales Fixed Penalty Office, as above.
Courts and times
Brecon Law Courts, Cambrian Way, Brecon
Justice Centre, Noyadd Park, Llandrindod Wells, Powys LD1 5DF
Adult: Brecon: Second Wednesday in month, first and third Thursday in month, second, third and fourth Friday in month 10:00; **Llandrinod Wells:** Third Wednesday in month, second and fourth Thursday in month, first Friday in month
Youth: Brecon: Fourth Wednesday in month 10:00
FPC: Brecon: First Friday in month 10:00; **Llandrinod Wells:** Third Friday in month 10:00
Enf & Misc: Llandrinod Wells: First Wednesday in month 10:00

3138 CARMARTHEN LJA
combined with **3140 DINEFWR AND 3122 LLANELLI LJAS** to form **3252 CARMARTHENSHIRE LJA**

3252 CARMARTHENSHIRE LJA
J. Hehir, Justices' Clerk, Llanelli Magistrates' Court, Town Hall Square, Llanelli SA15 3AW
Tel: 01554 757201
Fax: 01554 779986
DX: 99512 LLANELLI 2
Note: All fine payments and accounts enquiries to the Wales Enforcement & Accounts Office, as above. All fixed penalty enquiries to the Wales Fixed Penalty Office, as above.
Courts and times
The Guildhall, Guildhall Square, Carmarthen
Town Hall Square, Llanelli
Adult: Carmarthen: Wednesday, second, third, fourth Thursday and Friday in month 09:30; **Llanelli:** Monday, Wednesday, Thursday and Friday 10:00
YC: Carmarthen: Second Tuesday in month 10:00; **Llanelli:** First, third, fourth, fifth Tuesday in month 10:00
FPC: Carmarthen: Second and fourth Monday in month 10:00; **Llanelli:** Alternate Tuesdays
Enf: Llanelli: Second Monday in month 10:00
Misc: Carmarthen: First and third Monday in month 10:00

3135 CEREDIGION LJA
combined with **3356 PEMBROKESHIRE LJA** to form **3253 CEREDIGION AND PEMBROKESHIRE LJA**

3253 CEREDIGION AND PEMBROKESHIRE LJA
7253 (YC)
J. Hehir, Justices' Clerk, Aberystwyth Justice Centre, Y Lanfa, Trefechan, Aberystwyth, Ceredigion SY23 1AS
Tel: 01970 621250

Fax: 01970 621251
DX: 99560 ABERYSTWYTH 2
Haverfordwest Law Courts, Penffynnon, Hawthorn Rise, Haverfordwest SA61 2AX
Tel: 01437 772090
Fax: 01437 771399
DX: 99613 HAVERFORDWEST 2
Note: All fine payments and accounts enquiries to the Wales Enforcement & Accounts Office, as above. All fixed penalty enquiries to the Wales Fixed Penalty Office, as above.

Courts and times
Aberystwyth Justice Centre, Y Lanfa, Trefechan, Aberystwyth
Magistrates' Court, Penffynnon, Haverfordwest
Adult: Aberystwyth: Monday, Wednesday, Thursday 10:00; **Haverfordwest:** Monday, Tuesday, Wednesday, Thursday 10:00
YC: Aberystwyth: Alternate Tuesdays 10:00; **Haverfordwest:** First, second, third and fifth Friday in the morning 10:00
FPC: Aberystwyth: Alternate Tuesdays 10:00; **Haverfordwest:** Friday 10:00
Enf: Aberystwyth: Monday every four weeks 10:00; **Haverfordwest:** First Tuesday in month
Misc: Haverfordwest: Third Monday in month
TV: Haverfordwest: Fourth Friday in month

3350 DE BRYCHEINIOG LJA
combined with **3357 RADNORSHIRE AND NORTH BRECKNOCK LJA** to form **3250 BRECKNOCK AND RADNORSHIRE LJA**

3140 DINEFWR LJA
combined with **3138 CARMARTHEN AND 3122 LLANELLI LJAS** to form **3252 CARMARTHENSHIRE LJA**

3122 LLANELLI LJA
combined with **3138 CARMARTHEN AND 3140 DINEFWR LJAS** to form **3252 CARMARTHENSHIRE LJA**

3355 MONTGOMERYSHIRE LJA
J. Hehir, Justices' Clerk, Mansion House, 24 Severn Street, Welshpool, Powys SY21 7UX
Tel: 01938 555968
Fax: 01938 554593
DX: 702535 WELSHPOOL 2
Note: All fine payments and accounts enquiries to the Wales Enforcement & Accounts Office, as above. All fixed penalty enquiries to the Wales Fixed Penalty Office, as above.

Courts and times
Mansion House, Welshpool
Adult: Monday, Tuesday, second, fourth and fifth Wednesday in month 10:00
YC: First and third Wednesday in month 10:00
FPC: Second and fourth Friday in month 10:00
Misc: Third Friday in month 10:00
Enf: Third Tuesday in month 14:00

3359 NEATH PORT TALBOT LJA
S. Whale, Justices' Clerk, Magistrates' Clerk's Office, Fairfield Way, Neath SA11 1RF
Tel: 01639 765900
Fax: 01639 765954
Note: All fine payments and accounts enquiries to the Wales Enforcement & Accounts Office, as above. All fixed penalty enquiries to the Wales Fixed Penalty Office, as above. Matters involving Maintenance Enforcement should be addressed to Swansea Magistrates' Court.

Courts and times
The Court House, Fairfield Way, Neath
Neath County Court
Port Talbot Justice Centre
Adult: The Court House: Weekdays 10:00 and 14:15
YC: The Court House: Wednesday 11:00
FPC: Neath County Court or Port Talbot Justice Centre: Thursday 10:00

3356 PEMBROKESHIRE LJA
combined with **3135 CEREDIGION LJA** to form **3253 CEREDIGION AND PEMBROKESHIRE LJA**

3351 RADNORSHIRE AND NORTH BRECKNOCK LJA
combined with **3350 DE BRYCHEINIOG** to for **3250 BRECKNOCK AND RADNORSHIRE LJA**

3360 SWANSEA LJA
S. Whale, Justices' Clerk, Magistrates' Court, Grove Place, Swansea SA1 5DB
Tel: 01792 478300; 485853 (Family)
Fax: 01792 478352
DX: 40605 SWANSEA 17
Note: All fine payments and accounts enquiries to the Wales Enforcement & Accounts Office, as above. All fixed penalty enquiries to the Wales Fixed Penalty Office, as above. Swansea Magistrates' Court deals with Maintenance Enforcement for Swansea, Neath and Port Talbot.

Courts and times
Magistrates' Court, Grove Place, Swansea
Magistrates' Court, Dynevor Place, Swansea
Adult: Grove Place: Weekdays 10:00 and 14:15
YC: Dynevor Place: Friday 10:00
FPC: Dynevor Place: Monday 14:15, Tuesday, Wednesday, Thursday 10:00 and 14:15

NORTH WALES

Delivery Director for HMCTS Wales: Luigi Strinati. Email: luigi.strinati@hmcts.gsi.gov.uk
Head of Crime for HMCTS Wales: Nick Albrow. Email: nick.albrow@hmcts.gsi.gov.uk
Wales Support Unit, 2nd Floor, Cardiff & Vale Magistrates' Court, Fitzalan Place, Cardiff CF24 0RZ. DX: 743943 CARDIFF 38.
Wales Enforcement Contact/Compliance Centre: PO Box 84, Cwmbran NP44 1ZP. Tel: 01633 645112.
Wales Enforcement & Accounts Office: Port Talbot Justice Centre, Harbourside Road, Port Talbot SA13 1SB. Tel: 01633 645112.
Wales Fixed Penalty Office: Port Talbot Justice Centre, as above. Tel: 01639 605784.

3062 CONWY LJA
J. Hehir, Justices' Clerk, The Courthouse, Conwy Road, Llandudno LL30 1GA
Tel: 01492 871333
Fax: 01492 872321 (Admin); 879203 (Listing)
DX: 11365 LLANDUDNO
Note: All fine payments and accounts enquiries to the Wales Enforcement & Accounts Office, as above. All fixed penalty enquiries to the Wales Fixed Penalty Office, as above. All enquiries regarding administrative work for the Family Proceedings Court should be made to The Courthouse, Clwyd Street, Rhyl, Denbighshire LL18 3LA. Tel: 01745 352940.

Courts and times
The Courthouse, Conwy Road, Llandudno
Adult: Weekdays 10:00
YC: First, third and fourth Tuesday in month 10:00
FPC: First, second and third Wednesday in month 10:00
NP: Monday 11:00

3061 DENBIGHSHIRE LJA
J. Hehir, Justices' Clerk, The Courthouse, Conwy Road, Llandudno LL30 1GA
Tel: 01492 871333
Fax: 01492 872321 (Admin); 879203 (Listing)
DX: 11365 LLANDUDNO
Note: All fine payments and accounts enquiries to the Wales Enforcement & Accounts Office, as above. All fixed penalty enquiries to the Wales Fixed Penalty Office, as above. All enquiries regarding administrative work for the Family Proceedings Court should be made to The Courthouse, Clwyd Street, Rhyl, Denbighshire LL18 3LA. Tel: 01745 352940.

Courts and times
The Courthouse, Victoria Road, Prestatyn
Adult: Weekdays 10:00
YC: First, third and fourth Friday in month 10:00
FPC: First, second and fourth Thursday in month 10:00
NP: Wednesday 11:00

3059 FLINTSHIRE LJA
J. Hehir, Justices' Clerk, Justices' Clerk's Office, The Law Courts, Mold, Flintshire CH7 1AE
Tel: 01352 707330 (Admin/Listing)
Fax: 01352 707333 (Admin/Listing)
Note: All fine payments and accounts enquiries to the Wales Enforcement & Accounts Office, as above. All fixed penalty enquiries to the Wales Fixed Penalty Office, as above. All enquiries regarding administrative work for the FPC should be made to Law Courts, Bodhyfryd, Wrexham LL12 7BP. Tel: 01978 317400

Courts and times
The Law Courts, Mold
Adult: Weekdays 10:00
YC: Wednesday 10:00
FPC: Friday 10:00
NP: Second and fourth Friday in month 10:00

3244 GWYNEDD LJA
J. Hehir, Justices' Clerk, Criminal Justice Centre, Llanberis Road, Caernarfon, Gwynedd LL55 2DF
Tel: 01286 669700
Fax: 01286 669798

DX: 744382 CAERNARFON 6
Note: All fine payments and accounts enquiries to the Wales Enforcement & Accounts Office, as above. All fixed penalty enquiries to the Wales Fixed Penalty Office, as above. All enquiries regarding administrative work for the FPC should be made to Caernarfon County Court, Llanberis Road, Caernarfon LL55 2DF. Tel: 01286 684600.

Courts and times
Criminal Justice Centre, Caernarfon
The Shire Hall, Dolgellau
Caernarfon County Court
Adult: Caernarfon: Weekdays 10:00; **Dolgellau:** Monday 10:00
YC: Caernarfon: Second and fourth Friday in month 10:00; **Dolgellau:** First Thursday in month 10:00
FPC: Caernarfon County Court: 10:00
NP: Caernarfon County Court: Third Thursday 10:00; **Dolgellau:** Fourth Thursday in month 11:00

3058 WREXHAM MAELOR LJA
J. Hehir, Justices' Clerk, Justices' Clerk's Office, The Law Courts, Mold, Flintshire CH7 1AE
Tel: 01352 707330 (Admin/Listing)
Fax: 01352 707333 (Admin/Listing)
Note: All fine payments and accounts enquiries to the Wales Enforcement & Accounts Office, as above. All fixed penalty enquiries to the Wales Fixed Penalty Office, as above. All enquiries regarding administrative work for the FPC should be made to Law Courts, Bodhyfryd, Wrexham LL12 7BP.

Courts and times
Law Courts, Bodhyfryd, Wrexham
Adult: Weekdays 10:00
YC: Tuesday 10:00
FPC: Thursday 10:00

3238 YNYS MON/ANGLESEY LJA
J. Hehir, Justices' Clerk, Criminal Justice Centre, Llanberis Road, Caernarfon, Gwynedd LL55 2DF
Tel: 01286 669700
Fax: 01286 669798
DX: 744382 CAERNARFON 6
Note: All fine payments and accounts enquiries to the Wales Enforcement & Accounts Office, as above. All fixed penalty enquiries to the Wales Fixed Penalty Office, as above. All enquiries regarding administrative work for the FPC should be made to Caernarfon County Court, Llanberis Road, Caernarfon LL55 2DF. Tel: 01286 684600.

Courts and times
The Law Courts, Holyhead
Adult: Thursday 10:00
YC: First and third Friday in month
NP: Second and fourth Tuesday in month 10:00

SOUTH EAST WALES

Delivery Director for HMCTS Wales: Luigi Strinat. Email: luigi.strinati@hmcts.gsi.gov.uk
Head of Crime for HMCTS Wales: Nick Albrow. Email: nick.albrow@hmcts.gsi.gov.uk
Wales Support Unit, 2nd Floor, Cardiff & Vale Magistrates' Court, Fitzalan Place, Cardiff CF24 0RZ. DX: 743943 CARDIFF 38.
Wales Enforcement Contact/Compliance Centre: PO Box 84, Cwmbran NP44 1ZP. Tel: 01633 645112.
Wales Enforcement & Accounts Office: Port Talbot Justice Centre, Harbourside Road, Port Talbot SA13 1SB. Tel: 01633 645112.
Wales Fixed Penalty Office: Port Talbot Justice Centre, Harbourside Road, Port Talbot SA13 1SB. Tel: 01639 605784.

3348 CARDIFF LJA
combined with **3349 VALE OF GLAMORGAN LJA** to form **3251 CARDIFF AND THE VALE OF GLAMORGAN LJA**

3251 CARDIFF AND THE VALE OF GLAMORGAN LJA
7251 (YC)
Stephen Whale, Justices' Clerk, The Magistrates' Court, Fitzalan Place, Cardiff CF24 0RZ
Tel: 029 2046 3040
Fax: 0870 324 0236
Note: All fine payments and accounts enquiries to the Wales Enforcement & Accounts Office, as above. All fixed penalty enquiries to the Wales Fixed Penalty Office, as above.

Courts and times
Magistrates' Court, Cardiff
Cardiff Civil Justice Centre
Adult: Magistrates' Court: Monday to Friday 10:00. Saturday 09:30
YC: Magistrates' Court: Tuesday, Wednesday, Thursday 10:00
FPC: Cardiff Civil Justice Centre: Monday, Tuesday, Wednesday, Thursday, Friday 10:00

3262 CYNON VALLEY
combined with **3264 MERTHYR TYDFIL LJA** and **3265 MISKIN LJA** to form **3270 GLAMORGAN VALLEYS LJA**

3270 GLAMORGAN VALLEYS LJA
7270 (YC)
Stephen Whale, Justices' Clerk, Magistrates' Court, Law Courts, Glebeland Place, Merthyr Tydfil CF47 8BH
Tel: 01685 727600
Fax: 01685 727703
Note: All fine payments and accounts enquiries to the Wales Enforcement & Accounts Office, as above. All fixed penalty enquiries to the Wales Fixed Penalty Office, as above.

Courts and times
Union Street, Pontypridd
Law Courts, Merthyr Tydfil
Adult: Pontypridd: Weekdays 10:00; **Merthyr Tydfil:** Weekdays 10:00
YC: Pontypridd: Wednesday 10:00; **Merthyr Tydfil:** Tuesday 10:00
FPC: County Court, Pontypridd: Monday, Tuesday 10:00; **Merthyr Tydfil:** Wednesday 10:00

3211 GWENT LJA
Stephen Whale, Justices' Clerk, PO Box 83, Cwmbran NP44 1ZW
Tel: 01633 645000
Fax: 01633 645179
DX: 43665 CWMBRAN

Courts and times
Magistrates' Court, Tudor Street, Abergavenny
Magistrates' Court, Tudor Road, Cwmbran
The Court House, Mountain Road, Caerphilly
County Court, Clarence House, Newport
County Court, Hall Street, Blackwood
Adult: Abergavenny: Monday, Tuesday, Friday 10:00; **Cwmbran:** Monday, Wednesday, Thursday, Friday 10:00; **Caerphilly:** Weekdays 10:00

YC: Cwmbran: Tuesday 10:00
FPC: Newport: Monday, Tuesday, Wednesday, Friday 10:00; **Blackwood:** Friday 10:00

3264 MERTHYR TYDFIL LJA
combined with **3262 CYNON VALLEY LJA** and **3265 MISKIN LJA** to form **GLAMORGAN VALLEYS LJA**

3265 MISKIN LJA
combined with **3262 CYNON VALLEY LJA** and **3264 MERTHYR TYDFIL LJA** to form **3270 GLAMORGAN VALLEYS LJA**

3266 NEWCASTLE AND OGMORE LJA
Stephen Whale, Justices' Clerk, The Magistrates' Court, The Law Courts, Sunnyside, Bridgend CF31 4AJ
Tel: 01656 673800
Fax: 01656 668981
Note: All fine payments and accounts enquiries to the Wales Enforcement & Accounts Office, as above. All fixed penalty enquiries to the Wales Fixed Penalty Office, as above.

Courts and times
Magistrates' Court, Sunnyside, Bridgend
Adult: Weekdays 09:30
YC: Wednesday 09:30
FPC: Tuesday and Wednesday 10:00

3349 VALE OF GLAMORGAN LJA
combined with **3348 CARDIFF LJA** to form **3251 CARDIFF AND THE VALE OF GLAMORGAN LJA**

ENGLAND

1012 BATH DIVISION
combined with 1018 WANSDYKE DIVISION to form **1022 BATH AND WANSDYKE DIVISION**

1013 BRISTOL LJA
see **AVON, SOMERSET AND GLOUCESTERSHIRE** .... p. 155

1014 LAWFORD'S GATE DIVISION
combined with 1016 SODBURY DIVISION to form **1020 AVON NORTH DIVISION**

1015 LONG ASHTON DIVISION
combined with 1019 WESTON-SUPER-MARE DIVISION to form **1023 WOODSPRING DIVISION**

1016 SODBURY DIVISION
combined with 1014 LAWFORD'S GATE DIVISION to form **1020 AVON NORTH DIVISION**

1017 THORNBURY DIVISION
combined with 1020 AVON NORTH DIVISION to form **1021 NORTH AVON DIVISION**

1018 WANSDYKE DIVISION
combined with 1012 BATH DIVISION to form **1022 BATH AND WANSDYKE DIVISION**

1019 WESTON-SUPER-MARE DIVISION
combined with 1015 LONG ASHTON DIVISION to form **1023 WOODSPRING DIVISION**

1020 AVON NORTH DIVISION
combined with 1017 THORNBURY DIVISION to form **1021 NORTH AVON DIVISION**

1021 NORTH AVON LJA
see **AVON, SOMERSET AND GLOUCESTERSHIRE** ....p. 155

1022 BATH AND WANSDYKE LJA
see **1030 SOMERSET LJA**

1023 NORTH SOMERSET LJA
see **1030 SOMERSET LJA**

1030 SOMERSET LJA
see **AVON, SOMERSET AND GLOUCESTERSHIRE** . . . p. 155

1050 AMPTHILL DIVISION
combined with 1051 BEDFORD DIVISION, 1052 BIGGLESWADE DIVISION, 1053 DUNSTABLE DIVISION (Part) and 1054 LEIGHTON BUZZARD DIVISION (Part) to form **1051 BEDFORD AND MID BEDFORDSHIRE DIVISION**

1051 BEDFORD DIVISION
(formerly North Bedfordshire Division) combined with 1050 AMPTHILL DIVISION, 1052 BIGGLESWADE DIVISION, 1053 DUNSTABLE DIVISION (Part) and 1054 LEIGHTON BUZZARD DIVISION (Part) to form **1051 BEDFORD AND MID BEDFORDSHIRE DIVISION**

1051 BEDFORD AND MID BEDFORDSHIRE LJA
see **BEDFORDSHIRE AND HERTFORDSHIRE** ....p. 143

1052 BIGGLESWADE DIVISION
combined with 1050 AMPTHILL DIVISION, 1051 BEDFORD DIVISION, 1053 DUNSTABLE DIVISION (Part) and 1054 LEIGHTON BUZZARD DIVISION (Part) to form **1051 BEDFORD AND MID BEDFORDSHIRE DIVISION**

1053 DUNSTABLE DIVISION
Parish of Harlington combined 1050 AMPTHILL DIVISION, 1051 BEDFORD DIVISION, 1052 BIGGLESWADE DIVISION and 1054 LEIGHTON BUZZARD DIVISION (Part) to form **1051 BEDFORD AND MID BEDFORDSHIRE DIVISION**. *Remaining parishes combined with 1054 LEIGHTON BUZZARD (Part) and 1055 LUTON DIVISION to form* **1055 LUTON AND SOUTH BEDFORDSHIRE DIVISION**

1054 LEIGHTON BUZZARD DIVISION
Part combined with 1050 AMPTHILL DIVISION, 1051 BEDFORD DIVISION, 1052 BIGGLESWADE DIVISION, 1053 DUNSTABLE DIVISION (Parish of Harlington) to form **1051 BEDFORD AND BEDFORDSHIRE DIVISION**. *Remainder combined with 1053 DUNSTABLE DIVISION (except Harlington) and 1055 LUTON DIVISION to form* **1055 LUTON AND SOUTH BEDFORDSHIRE DIVISION**

1055 LUTON DIVISION
combined with 1053 DUNSTABLE DIVISION, (except Harlington), and 1054 LEIGHTON BUZZARD DIVISION to form **1055 LUTON AND SOUTH BEDFORDSHIRE DIVISION**

1055 LUTON AND SOUTH BEDFORDSHIRE LJA
see **BEDFORDSHIRE AND HERTFORDSHIRE** p.143

1065 BRADFIELD AND SONNING DIVISION
combined with 1071 READING DIVISION to form **1076 READING AND SONNING DIVISION**

1066 FOREST DIVISION
combined with 1068 MAIDENHEAD DIVISION, 1072 SLOUGH DIVISION and 1074 WINDSOR DIVISION to form **072 EAST BERKSHIRE DIVISION**

1067 HUNGERFORD AND LAMBOURN DIVISION
combined with 1069 NEWBURY DIVISION to form **1075 WEST BERKSHIRE DIVISION**

1068 MAIDENHEAD DIVISION
combined with 1066 FOREST DIVISION, 1072 SLOUGH DIVISION and 1074 WINDSOR DIVISION to form **1072 EAST BERKSHIRE DIVISION**

1069 NEWBURY DIVISION
combined with 1067 HUNGERFORD AND LAMBOURN DIVISION to form **1075 WEST BERKSHIRE DIVISION**

1070 NEW WINDSOR DIVISION
combined with 1073 WINDSOR COUNTY DIVISION to form **1074 WINDSOR DIVISION**

1071 READING DIVISION
combined with 1065 BRADFIELD AND SONNING DIVISION to form **1076 READING AND SONNING DIVISION**

1072 SLOUGH DIVISION
combined with 1066 FOREST DIVISION, 1068 MAIDENHEAD DIVISION and 1074 WINDSOR DIVISION to form **1072 EAST BERKSHIRE DIVISION**

1072 EAST BERKSHIRE LJA
combined with 1075 WEST BERKSHIRE LJA and 1076 READING LJA to form **1920 BERKSHIRE LJA**

1073 WINDSOR COUNTY DIVISION
combined with 1070 NEW WINDSOR DIVISION to form **1074 WINDSOR DIVISION**

1074 WINDSOR DIVISION
combined with 1066 FOREST DIVISION, 1068 MAIDENHEAD DIVISION and 1072 SLOUGH DIVISION to form **1072 EAST BERKSHIRE DIVISION**

1075 WEST BERKSHIRE LJA
combined with 1072 EAST BERKSHIRE LJA and 1076 READING LJA to form **1920 BERKSHIRE LJA**

1076 READING AND SONNING DIVISION
renamed **1076 READING PSA**

1076 READING LJA
combined with 1072 EAST BERKSHIRE LJA and 1075 WEST BERKSHIRE LJA to form **1920 BERKSHIRE LJA**

1110 AMERSHAM DIVISION
combined with 1115 CHESHAM DIVISION to form **1128 CHILTERN DIVISION**

1111 AYLESBURY DIVISION
combined with 1112 BRILL DIVISION and 1118 LINSLADE DIVISION to form **1125 AYLESBURY DIVISION**

1112 BRILL DIVISION
combined with 1111 AYLESBURY DIVISION and 1118 LINSLADE DIVISION to form **1125 AYLESBURY DIVISION**

1113 BUCKINGHAM DIVISION
combined with 1122 WINSLOW DIVISION to form **126 BUCKINGHAM DIVISION**

1114 BURNHAM DIVISION
combined with 1127 WYCOMBE DIVISION to form **1130 WYCOMBE AND BEACONSFIELD DIVISION**

1115 CHESHAM DIVISION
combined with 1110 AMERSHAM DIVISION to form **1128 CHILTERN DIVISION**

1116 FENNY STRATFORD DIVISION
combined with 1120 NEWPORT PAGNELL DIVISION and 1121 STONY STRATFORD DIVISION to form **1124 MILTON KEYNES DIVISION**

1117 HIGH WYCOMBE DIVISION
combined with 1119 MARLOW DIVISION and 1123 WYCOMBE (COUNTY) DIVISION to form **1127 WYCOMBE DIVISION**

1118 LINSLADE DIVISION
combined with 1111 AYLESBURY DIVISION and 1112 BRILL DIVISION to form **1125 AYLESBURY DIVISION**

1119 MARLOW DIVISION
combined with 1117 HIGH WYCOMBE DIVISION and 1123 WYCOMBE (COUNTY) DIVISION to form **1127 WYCOMBE DIVISION**

1120 NEWPORT PAGNELL DIVISION
combined with 1116 FENNY STRATFORD DIVISION and 1121 STONY STRATFORD DIVISION to form **1124 MILTON KEYNES DIVISION**

1121 STONY STRATFORD DIVISION
combined with 1116 FENNY STRATFORD DIVISION and 1120 NEWPORT PAGNELL DIVISION to form **1124 MILTON KEYNES DIVISION**

1122 WINSLOW DIVISION
combined with 1113 BUCKINGHAM DIVISION to form **1126 BUCKINGHAM DIVISION**

1123 WYCOMBE (COUNTY) DIVISION
combined with 1117 HIGH WYCOMBE DIVISION and 1119 MARLOW DIVISION to form **1127 WYCOMBE DIVISION**

1124 MILTON KEYNES LJA
combined with 1129 CENTRAL BUCKINGHAMSHIRE LJA and 1130 WYCOMBE & BEACONSFIELD LJA to form **1921 BUCKINGHAMSHIRE LJA**

1125 AYLESBURY DIVISION
combined with 1126 BUCKINGHAM DIVISION and 1128 CHILTERN DIVISION to form **1129 CENTRAL BUCKINGHAMSHIRE DIVISION**

1126 BUCKINGHAM DIVISION
combined with 1125 AYLESBURY DIVISION and 1128 CHILTERN DIVISIION to form **1129 CENTRAL BUCKINGHAMSHIRE DIVISION**

1127 WYCOMBE DIVISION
combined with 1114 BURNHAM DIVISION to form **1130 WYCOMBE AND BEACONSFIELD DIVISION**

1128 CHILTERN DIVISION
combined with 1125 AYLESBURY DIVISION and 1126 BUCKINGHAM DIVISION to form **1129 CENTRAL BUCKINGHAMSHIRE DIVISION**

1129 CENTRAL BUCKINGHAMSHIRE LJA
combined with 1125 MILTON KEYNES LJA and 1130 WYCOMBE & BEACONSFIELD LJA to form **1921 BUCKINGHAMSHIRE LJA**

1130 WYCOMBE AND BEACONSFIELD LJA
combined with 1124 MILTON KEYNES LJA and 1129 CENTRAL BUCKINGHAMSHIRE LJA to form **1921 BUCKINGHAMSHIRE LJA**

1133 ARRINGTON AND MELBOURN DIVISION
combined with 1134 BOTTISHAM DIVISION, 1159 CAXTON DIVISION and 1141 LINTON DIVISION to form **1163 SOUTH CAMBRIDGESHIRE DIVISION**

1134 BOTTISHAM DIVISION
combined with 1133 ARRINGTON AND MELBOURN DIVISION, 1141 LINTON DIVISION and 1159 CAXTON DIVISION to form **1163 SOUTH CAMBRIDGESHIRE DIVISION**

1135 CAMBRIDGE DIVISION
combined with 1137 CAXTON DIVISION to form **1159 CAXTON DIVISION**

1136 CAMBRIDGE CITY DIVISION
combined with 1163 SOUTH CAMBRIDGESHIRE DIVISION to form **1165 CAMBRIDGE DIVISION**

1137 CAXTON DIVISION
combined with 1135 CAMBRIDGE DIVISION to form **1159 CAXTON DIVISION**

1138 ELY DIVISION
combined with 1164 NEWMARKET DIVISION to form **1166 EAST CAMBRIDGESHIRE DIVISION**

1140 HURSTINGSTONE DIVISION
combined with 1157 HUNTINGDON AND NORMAN CROSS DIVISION and 1145 RAMSEY DIVISION to form **1161 HUNTINGDON DIVISION**

1141 LINTON DIVISION
combined with 1133 ARRINGTON AND MELBOURN DIVISION, 1134 BOTTISHAM DIVISION and 1159 CAXTON DIVISION to form **1163 SOUTH CAMBRIDGESHIRE DIVISION**

1142 NEWMARKET DIVISION
combined with part of 1134 BOTTISHAM DIVISION to form **1164 NEWMARKET (CAMBS) DIVISION**

1143 NORMAN CROSS DIVISION
see **1157 HUNTINGDON AND NORMAN CROSS**

1144 NORTH WITCHFORD DIVISION
combined with 1160 WISBECH DIVISION to form **1167 FENLAND DIVISION**

1145 RAMSEY DIVISION
combined with 1157 HUNTINGDON AND NORMAN CROSS DIVISION and 1140 HURSTINGSTONE DIVISION to form **1161 HUNTINGDON DIVISION**

1147 TOSELAND DIVISION
combined with 1161 HUNTINGDON DIVISION to form **1168 HUNTINGDONSHIRE DIVISION**

1148 WHITTLESEY DIVISION
combined with 1158 SOKE OF PETERBOROUGH DIVISION to form **1162 PETERBOROUGH DIVISION**

1149 WISBECH (BOROUGH) DIVISION
combined with 1150 WISBECH (ISLE) DIVISION to form **1160 WISBECH DIVISION**

1150 WISBECH (ISLE) DIVISION
combined with 1149 WISBECH (BOROUGH) DIVISION to form **1160 WISBECH DIVISION**

1157 HUNTINGDON AND NORMAN CROSS DIVISION
combined with 1140 HURSTINGSTONE DIVISION and 1145 RAMSEY DIVISION to form **1161 HUNTINGDON DIVISION**

1158 SOKE OF PETERBOROUGH DIVISION
combined with 1148 WHITTLESEY DIVISION **to form 1162 PETERBOROUGH DIVISION**

1159 CAXTON DIVISION
combined with 1133 ARRINGTON AND MELBOURN DIVISION, 1134 BOTTISHAM DIVISION AND 1141 LINTON DIVISION to form **1163 SOUTH CAMBRIDGESHIRE DIVISION**

1160 WISBECH DIVISION
combined with 1144 NORTH WITCHFORD DIVISION to form **1167 FENLAND DIVISION**

1161 HUNTINGDON DIVISION
combined with 1147 TOSELAND DIVISION to form **1168 HUNTINGDONSHIRE DIVISION**

1162 PETERBOROUGH LJA
combined with 1167 FENLAND LJA to form **NORTH CAMBRIDGESHIRE LJA** *– wef 1/1/12*

1163 SOUTH CAMBRIDGESHIRE DIVISION
combined with 1136 CAMBRIDGE CITY DIVISION to form **1166 EAST CAMBRIDGESHIRE DIVISION**

1164 NEWMARKET (CAMBS) DIVISION
combined with 1138 ELY DIVISION to form **1166 EAST CAMBRIDGESHIRE DIVISION**

1165 CAMBRIDGE LJA
combined with 1166 EAST CAMBRIDGESHIRE LJA to form **SOUTH CAMBRIDGESHIRE LJA** – *wef 1/1/12*

1166 EAST CAMBRIDGESHIRE LJA
combined with 1165 CAMBRIDGE LJA to form **SOUTH CAMBRIDGESHIRE LJA** – *wef 1/1/12*

1167 FENLAND LJA
combined with 1162 PETERBOROUGH LJA to form **NORTH CAMBRIDGESHIRE LJA**

1168 HUNTINGDONSHIRE LJA
see **CAMBRIDGESHIRE, ESSEX, NORFOLK AND SUFFOLK** ....p. 145

1173 CHESTER PSA
combined with 1176 ELLESMERE PORT AND NESTON PSA to form **1188 CHESTER, ELLESMERE PORT AND NESTON PSA**

1174 CONGLETON DIVISION
combined with 1175 CREWE AND NANTWICH DIVISION to form **1187 SOUTH CHESHIRE DIVISION**

1175 CREWE AND NANTWICH DIVISION
combined with 1174 CONGLETON DIVISION to form **1187 SOUTH CHESHIRE DIVISION**

1176 ELLESMERE PORT AND NESTON PSA
combined with 1173 CHESTER PSA to form **1188 CHESTER, ELLESMERE PORT AND NESTON PSA**

1177 HALTON LJA
combined with 1180 WARRINGTON LJA to form **1722 NORTH CHESHIRE LJA**

1178 MACCLESFIELD LJA
see **CHESHIRE AND MERSEYSIDE** ....p. 133

1179 VALE ROYAL LJA
CLOSED wef 9/11

1180 WARRINGTON LJA
combined with 1177 HALTON LJA to form **1722 NORTH CHESHIRE LJA**

1187 SOUTH CHESHIRE LJA
see **CHESHIRE AND MERSEYSIDE** ....p. 133

1188 CHESTER, ELLESMERE PORT AND NESTON LJA
see **1729 WEST CHESHIRE LJA**

1247 HARTLEPOOL LJA
see **CLEVELAND AND DURHAM** ....p. 124

1248 LANGBAURGH EAST LJA
CLOSED wef 1/12

1249 TEESSIDE LJA
see **CLEVELAND AND DURHAM** ....p. 124

1260 BODMIN AND TRIGG DIVISION
combined with 1269 LESNEWTH DIVISION, 1273 POWDER TYWARDREATH DIVISION and 1278 WADEBRIDGE DIVISION to form **1279 BODMIN DIVISION**

1261 DUNHEVED DIVISION
combined with 1276 STRATTON DIVISION to form **1284 DUNHEVED AND STRATTON DIVISION**

1262 EAST MIDDLE DIVISION
combined with 1265 EAST SOUTH DIVISION and 1270 LISKERRETT DIVISION to form **1280 SOUTH EAST CORNWALL DIVISION**

1263 EAST PENWITH PSA
*combined with 1268 ISLES OF SCILLY PSA, PENWITH PSA, FALMOUTH AND KERRIER PSA, 1282
TRURO AND SOUTH POWDER PSA and the parishes of Cubert and St Newlyn East in 1274 PYDAR
PSA to form* **1288 WEST CORNWALL PSA**

1264 EAST POWDER PSA
*combined with 1274 PYDAR PSA (except the parishes of Cubert and St Newlyn East), 1279 BODMIN
PSA, 1284 DUNHEVED AND STRATTON., and 1280 SOUTH EAST CORNWALL to form* **1289 EAST
CORNWALL PSA**

1265 EAST SOUTH DIVISION
combined with 1262 EAST MIDDLE DIVISION and 1270 LISKERRETT DIVISION to form **1280
SOUTH EAST CORNWALL DIVISION**

1266 FALMOUTH DIVISION
combined with 1271 PENRYN DIVISION to form **1281 FALMOUTH-PENRYN DIVISION**

1267 HELSTON AND KERRIER DIVISION
combined with 1281 FALMOUTH-PENRYN DIVISION to form **1283 FALMOUTH AND KERRIER
DIVISION**

1268 ISLES OF SCILLY PSA
*combined with 1272 PENWITH PSA, 1283 FALMOUTH AND KERRIER PSA, 1282 TRURO AND
SOUTH POWDER PSA, and the Parishes of Cuber and St Newlyn East in 1274 PYDAR PSA to form*
1288 WEST CORNWALL PSA

1269 LESNEWTH DIVISION
*combined with 1260 BODMIN AND TRIGG DIVISION, 1273 POWDER TYWARDREATH DIVISION and
1278 WADEBRIDGE DIVISION to form* **1279 BODMIN DIVISION**

1270 LISKERRETT DIVISION
combined with 1262 EAST MIDDLE DIVISION and 1265 EAST SOUTH DIVISION to form **1280 EAST
CORNWALL DIVISION**

1271 PENRYN DIVISION
combined with 1266 FALMOUTH DIVISION to form **1281 FALMOUTH-PENRYN DIVISION**

1272 PENWITH PSA
*combined with 1268 ISLES OF SCILLY PSA, 1263 EAST PENWITH PSA, 1283 FALMOUTH AND
KERRIER PSA, 1282 TRURO AND SOUTH POWDER PSA and the Parishes of Cubert and St Newlyn
East in 1274 PYDAR PSA to form* **1288 WEST CORNWALL DIVISION**

1273 POWDER TYWARDREATH DIVISION
*combined with 1260 BODMIN AND TRIGG DIVISION, 1269 LESNEWTH DIVISION and 1278
WADEBRIDGE DIVISION to form* **1279 BODMIN DIVISION**

1274 PYDAR PSA
*Parishes of Cubert and St Newlyn East combined with 1268 ISLES OF SCILLY PSA, 1272 PENWITH
PSA, 1263 EAST PENWITH PSA, 1283 FALMOUTH AND KERRIER PSA and 1282 TRURO AND
SOUTH POWDER PSA to form* **1288 WEST CORNWALL PSA** *.Remainder combined with 1279
BODMIN PSA, 1264 EAST POWDER PSA 1284 DUNHEVED AND STRATTON PSA, and 1280
SOUTH EAST CORNWALL PSA to form* **1289 EAST CORNWALL PSA**

1275 SOUTH POWDER DIVISION
combined with 1277 TRURO AND WEST POWDER DIVISION to form **1282 TRURO AND SOUTH
POWDER DIVISION**

1276 STRATTON DIVISION
combined with 1261 DUNHEVED DIVISION to form **1284 DUNHEVED AND STRATTON DIVISION**

1277 TRURO AND WEST POWDER DIVISION
combined with 1275 SOUTH POWDER DIVISION to form **1282 TRURO AND SOUTH POWDER
DIVISION**

1278 WADEBRIDGE DIVISION
*combined with 1260 BODMIN AND TRIGG DIVISION, 1269 LESNEWTH DIVISION and 1273
POWDER TYWARDREATH DIVISION to form* **1279 BODMIN DIVISION**

1279 BODMIN P.S.A.
combined with 1274 PYDAR PSA (except the parishes of Cubert and St Newlyn East) 1264 EAST POWDER PSA, 1284 DUNHEVED AND STRATTON PSA and 1280 SOUTH EAST CORNWALL to form **1289 EAST CORNWALL**

1280 SOUTH EAST CORNWALL PSA
combined with 1274 PYDAR PSA (except the parishes of Cubert and St Newlyn East), 1279 BODMIN PSA, 1264 EAST POWDER PSA and 1284 DUNHEVED AND STRATTON PSA to form **1289 EAST CORNWALL PSA**

1281 FALMOUTH-PENRYN DIVISION
combined with 1267 HELSTON AND KERRIER DIVISION to form **1283 FALMOUTH AND KERRIER DIVISION**

1282 TRURO AND SOUTH POWDER PSA
combined with 1268 ISLES OF SCILLY PSA, 1272 PENWITH PSA, 1263 EAST PENWITH PSA, 1283 FALMOUTH AND KERRIER PSA and the Parishes of Cubert and St Newlyn East in 1274 PYDAR PSA to form **1288 WEST CORNWALL PSA**

1283 FALMOUTH AND KERRIER PSA
combined with 1268 ISLES OF SCILLY PSA, 1272 PENWITH PSA, 1263 EAST PENWITH PSA, 1282 TRURO AND SOUTH POWDER PSA and the Parishes of Cuber and St Newlyn East in 1274 PYDAR PSA to form **1288 WEST CORNWALL PSA**

1284 DUNHEVED AND STRATTON PSA
combined with 1274 PYDAR PSA (except the parishes of Cubert and St Newlyn East) 1279 BODMIN PSA, 1263 EAST POWDER PSA and 1280 SOUTH EAST CORNWALL PSA to form **1289 EAST CORNWALL PSA**

1288 WEST CORNWALL LJA
combined with 1289 East Cornwall LJA to form **1301 CORNWALL LJA**

1289 EAST CORNWALL LJA
combined with 1288 West Cornwall LJA to form **1301 CORNWALL LJA**

1290 PLYMOUTH DISTRICT LJA
see **DEVON, CORNWALL AND DORSET** ....p. 157

1291 NORTH DEVON LJA
combined with 1292 Central Devon LJA to form **1292 NORTH AND EAST DEVON LJA**

1292 NORTH AND EAST DEVON LJA
see **DEVON, CORNWALL AND DORSET** ....p. 157

1292 CENTRAL DEVON LJA
combined with 1291 North Devon LJA to form **1292 NORTH AND EAST DEVON LJA**

1293 SOUTH DEVON LJA
see **DEVON, CORNWALL AND DORSET** ....p. 157

1301 CORNWALL LJA
see **DEVON, CORNWALL AND DORSET LJA** . . . p. 157

1304 WEST HAMPSHIRE LJA
see **HAMPSHIRE, ISLE OF WIGHT AND WILTSHIRE** . . . p. 159

1305 NORTH HAMPSHIRE LJA (ADULT)
see **HAMPSHIRE, ISLE OF WIGHT AND WILTSHIRE** ....p. 159

1322 CARLISLE AND DISTRICT LJA
see **1727 NORTH CUMBRIA LJA**

1323 SOUTH LAKELAND LJA
see **CUMBRIA AND LANCASHIRE** ....p. 136

1324 EDEN LJA
CLOSED wef 1/12

1325 WEST ALLERDALE AND KESWICK LJA
see **1726 WEST CUMBRIA LJA**

1360 ALSTON DIVISION
combined with 1373 PENRITH DIVISION to form **1378 PENRITH AND ALSTON DIVISION**

1361 AMBLESIDE AND WINDERMERE DIVISION
combined with 1367 HAWKSHEAD DIVISION to form **1381 SOUTH LAKES DIVISION**

1362 BARROW-IN-FURNESS DIVISION
combined with 1363 BOOTLE DIVISION to form **1380 BARROW WITH BOOTLE DIVISION**

1363 BOOTLE DIVISION
combined with 1362 BARROW-IN-FURNESS DIVISION to form **1380 BARROW WITH BOOTLE DIVISION**

1364 CARLISLE PSA
combined with 1376 WIGTON PSA to form **1322 CARLISLE AND DISTRICT PSA**

1365 COCKERMOUTH DIVISION
combined with 1371 MARYPORT DIVISION and 1377 WORKINGTON DIVISION to form **1379 WEST ALLERDALE DIVISION**

1366 EAST WARD DIVISION
combined with portions of 1374 WEST WARD DIVISION to form **1383 APPLEBY DIVISION**

1367 HAWKSHEAD DIVISION
combined with 1361 AMBLESIDE AND WINDERMERE DIVISION to form **1381 SOUTH LAKES DIVISION**

1368 KENDAL DIVISION
combined with 1370 LONSDALE WARD DIVISION to form **1382 KENDAL AND LONSDALE DIVISION**

1369 KESWICK PSA
(except for the Parish of Threlkeld) combined with 1379 WEST ALLERDALE PSA to form **1325 WEST ALLERDALE AND KESWICK PSA**

1370 LONSDALE WARD DIVISION
combined with 1368 KENDAL DIVISION to form **1382 KENDAL AND LONSDALE DIVISION**

1371 MARYPORT DIVISION
combined with 1365 COCKERMOUTH DIVISION and 1377 WORKINGTON DIVISION to form **1379 WEST ALLERDALE DIVISION**

1372 NORTH LONSDALE DIVISION
combined with 1380 BARROW WITH BOOTLE DIVISION to form **1398 FURNESS AND DISTRICT DIVISION**

1373 PENRITH DIVISION
combined with 1360 ALSTON DIVISION to form **1378 PENRITH AND ALSTON DIVISION**

1374 WEST WARD DIVISION
abolished – part absorbed into **1383 APPLEBY DIVISION** *and remainder into* **1384 PENRITH AND ALSTON DIVISION**

1375 WHITEHAVEN LJA
CLOSED wef 6/11 – see **1726 WEST CUMBRIA LJA**

1376 WIGTON PSA
combined with 1364 CARLISLE PSA to form **1322 CARLISLE AND DISTRICT PSA**

1377 WORKINGTON DIVISION
combined with 1365 COCKERMOUTH DIVISION and 1371 MARYPORT DIVISION to form **1379 WEST ALLERDALE DIVISION**

1378 PENRITH AND ALSTON DIVISION
combined with portions of 1374 WEST WARD DIVISION to form **1384 PENRITH AND ALSTON DIVISION**

1379 WEST ALLERDALE PSA
combined with 1369 KESWICK PSA (except for the Parish of Threlkeld) to form **1325 WEST ALLERDALE AND KESWICK PSA**

1380 BARROW WITH BOOTLE DIVISION
combined with portions of 1372 NORTH LONSDLAE DIVISION to form **1398 FURNESS AND DISTRICT DIVISION**

1381 SOUTH LAKES PSA
combined with 1382 KENDAL AND LONSDALE PSA to form **1323 SOUTH LAKELAND PSA**

1382 KENDAL AND LONSDALE PSA
combined with 1381 SOUTH LAKES PSA to form **1323 SOUTH LAKELAND PSA**

1383 APPLEBY PSA
combined with 1384 PENRITH AND ALSTON PSA and the Parish of Threlkeld in 1369 KESWICK PSA to form **1324 EDEN PSA**

1384 PENRITH AND ALSTON PSA
combined with 1383 APPLEBY PSA and the Parish of Threlkeld in 1369 KESWICK PSA to form **1324 EDEN PSA**

1385 NORWICH DIVISION
subjected to boundary adjustments and renumbered **1445 NORWICH DIVISION**

1386 DOWNHAM MARKET DIVISION
combined with 1389 FAKENHAM DIVISION, 1394 HUNSTANTON DIVISION and 1392 KING'S LYNN DIVISION to form (after boundary adjustment) **1447 WEST NORFOLK DIVISION**

1387 DISS DIVISION
combined with 1396 THETFORD DIVISION to form **1446 SOUTH NORFOLK DIVISION**

1388 EAST DEREHAM DIVISION
combined with 1395 SWAFFHAM DIVISION and 1390 WYMONDHAM DIVISION to form **1442 CENTAL NORFOLK DIVISION**

1389 FAKENHAM DIVISION
combined with 1386 DOWNHAM MARKET DIVISION, 1394 HUNSTANTON DIVISION and 1392 KING'S LYNN DIVISION to form (after boundary adjustment) **1447 WEST NORFOLK DIVISION**

1390 WYMONDHAM DIVISION
combined with 1388 EAST DEREHAM DIVISION and 1395 SWAFFHAM DIVISION to form **1442 CENTRAL NORFOLK DIVISION**

1391 GREAT YARMOUTH DIVISION
subjected to boundary adjustments and renumbered **1443 GREAT YARMOUTH DIVISION**

1392 KING'S LYNN DIVISION
combined with 1386 DOWNHAM MARKET DIVISION, 1398 FAKENHAM DIVISION and 1394 HUNSTANTON DIVISION to form (after boundary adjustment) **1447 WEST NORFOLK DIVISION**

1393 CROMER DIVISION
combined with 1397 NORTH WALSHAM DIVISION to form (after boundary adjustment) **1444 NORTH NORFOLK DIVISION**

1394 HUNSTANTON DIVISION
combined with 1386 DOWNHAM MARKET DIVISION, 1389 FAKENHAM DIVISION and 1392 KING'S LYNN DIVISION to form (after boundary adjustment) **1447 WEST NORFOLK DIVISION**

1395 SWAFFHAM DIVISION
combined with 1388 EAST DEREHAM DIVISION and 1390 WYMONDHAM DIVISION to form **1442 CENTRAL NORFOLK DIVISION**

1396 THETFORD DIVISION
combined with 1387 DISS DIVISION to form **1446 SOUTH NORFOLK DIVISION**

1397 NORTH WALSHAM DIVISION
combined with 1393 CROMER DIVISION to form (after boundary adjustment) **1444 NORTH NORFOLK DIVISION**

1398 FURNESS AND DISTRICT LJA
see **CUMBRIA AND LANCASHIRE** ....p. 136

1414 ALFRETON DIVISION
combined with 1417 BELPER DIVISION to form (after boundary adjustments) **1426 ALFRETON AND BELPER DIVISION**

1415 ASHBOURNE DIVISION
combined with 1416 BAKEWELL DIVISION and 1424 MATLOCK DIVISION to form (after boundary adjustments) **1428 WEST DERBYSHIRE DIVISION**

1416 BAKEWELL DIVISION
combined with 1415 ASHBOURNE DIVISION and 1424 MATLOCK DIVISION to form (after boundary adjustments) **1428 WEST DERBYSHIRE DIVISION**

1417 BELPER DIVISION
combined with 1414 ALFRETON DIVISION to form (after boundary adjustments) **1426 ALFRETON AND BELPER DIVISION**

1418 CHESTERFIELD PSA
combined with Part of 1420 WEST DERBYSHIRE to form **1432 NORTH EAST DERBYSHIRE AND DALES PSA**

1419 DERBY DIVISION
combined with 1420 DERBY COUNTY AND APPLETREE DIVISION and 1425 SOUTH DERBYSHIRE DIVISION to form (after boundary adjustments) **1427 DERBY AND SOUTH DERBYSHIRE DIVISION**

1420 DERBY COUNTY AND APPLETREE DIVISION
combined with 1419 DERBY DIVISION and 1425 SOUTH DERBYSHIRE DIVISION to form (after boundary adjustments) **1427 DERBY AND SOUTH DERBYSHIRE DIVISION**

1421 GLOSSOP PSA
combined with 1422 HIGH PEAK PSA to form **HIGH PEAK PSA**

1422 HIGH PEAK PSA
combined with 1421 GLOSSOP PSA to form **HIGH PEAK PSA**

1423 ILKESTON DIVISION
combined with 1426 ALFRETON AND BELPER DIVISION to form **1429 EAST DERBYSHIRE DIVISION**

1424 MATLOCK DIVISION
combined with 1415 ASHBOURNE DIVISION and 1416 BAKEWELL DIVISION to form (after boundary adjustments) **1428 WEST DERBYSHIRE DIVISION**

1425 SOUTH DERBYSHIRE DIVISION
combined with 1419 DERBY DIVISION and 1420 DERBY COUNTY AND APPLETREE DIVISION to form (after boundary adjustments) **1427 DERBY AND SOUTH DERBYSHIRE DIVISION**

1426 ALFRETON AND BELPER DIVISION
combined with 1423 ILKESTON DIVISION to form **1429 EAST DERBYSHIRE DIVISION**

1427 DERBY AND SOUTH DERBYSHIRE PSA
combined with Part of 1428 WEST DERBYSHIRE PSA to form **1431 DERBY AND SOUTH DERBYSHIRE PSA**

1428 SOUTHERN DERBYSHIRE LJA
see **DERBYSHIRE AND NOTTINGHAMSHIRE** ....p. 114

1429 EAST DERBYSHIRE PSA
combined with 1431 DERBY AND SOUTH DERBYSHIRE PSA to form **1431 SOUTHERN DERBYSHIRE PSA**

1430 HIGH PEAK LJA
see **DERBYSHIRE AND NOTTINGHAMSHIRE** ....p. 114

1431 DERBY AND SOUTH DERBYSHIRE PSA
combined with 1429 EAST DERBYSHIRE PSA to form **1428 SOUTHERN DERBYSHIRE PSA**

1432 NORTH EAST DERBYSHIRE AND DALES LJA
see **DERBYSHIRE AND NOTTINGHAMSHIRE** ....p. 114

1442 CENTRAL NORFOLK LJA
combined with 1443, 1444, 1445, 1446, 1447 to form **1972 NORFOLK LJA**

1443 GREAT YARMOUTH LJA
combined with 1442, 1444, 1445, 1446, 1447 to form **1972 NORFOLK LJA**

1444 NORTH NORFOLK LJA
combined with 1442, 1443, 1445, 1446, 1447 to form **1972 NORFOLK LJA**

1445 NORWICH LJA
combined with 1442, 1443, 1444, 1446, 1447 to form **1972 NORFOLK LJA**

1446 SOUTH NORFOLK LJA
combined with 1442, 1443, 1444, 1445, 1447 to form **1972 NORFOLK LJA**

1447 WEST NORFOLK LJA
combined with 1442, 1443, 1444, 1445, 1446 to form **1972 NORFOLK LJA**

1475 AXMINSTER DIVISION
combined with 1481 HONITON DIVISION to form **1493 AXMINSTER AND HONITON DIVISION**

1476 BARNSTAPLE DIVISION
combined with 1486 SOUTH MOLTON DIVISION to form **1494 BARNSTAPLE AND SOUTH MOLTON DIVISION**

1477 BIDEFORD AND GREAT TORRINGTON PSA
combined with part of 1495 WEST DEVON PSA and 1494 BARNSTAPLE AND SOUTH MOLTON PSA (except Chawleigh, Eggesford and Thelbridge) to form **1291 NORTH DEVON PSA**

1478 CULLOMPTON PSA
combined with Chawleigh, Eggesford and Thelbridge in 1494 BARNSTAPLE AND SOUTH MOLTON, Part of 1495 WEST DEVON PSA, 1493 AXMINSTER AND HONITON PSA, 1478 CULLOMPTON PSA, 1489 TIVERTON PSA, 1497 EXETER AND WONFORD PSA and 1480 EXMOUTH PSA to form **1292 CENTRAL DEVON PSA**

1479 EXETER DIVISION
combined with 1492 WONFORD DIVISION to form **1497 EXETER AND WONFORD DIVISION**

1480 EXMOUTH PSA
combined with Chawleigh, Eggesford and Thelbridge in 1494 BARNSTAPLE AND SOUTH MOLTON PSA, Part of 1495 WEST DEVON PSA, 1493 AXMINSTER AND HONITON PSA, 1478 CULLOMPTON PSA, 1489 TIVERTON PSA, and 1497 EXETER AND WONFORD PSA to form **1292 CENTRAL DEVON PSA**

1481 HONITON DIVISION
combined with 1475 AXMINSTER DIVISION to form **1493 AXMINSTER AND HONITON DIVISION**

1482 KINGSBRIDGE DIVISION
combined with 1485 PLYMPTON DIVISION and 1491 TOTNES DIVISION to form **1496 SOUTH HAMS DIVISION**

1483 OKEHAMPTON DIVISION
combined with 1487 TAVISTOCK DIVISION to form **1495 WEST DEVON DIVISION**

1484 PLYMOUTH PSA
combined with part of 1495 WEST DEVON PSA to form **1290 PLYMOUTH DISTRICT PSA**

1485 PLYMPTON DIVISION
combined with 1482 KINGSBRIDGE DIVISION and 1491 TOTNES DIVISION to form **1496 SOUTH HAMS DIVISION**

1486 SOUTH MOLTON DIVISION
combined with 1476 BARNSTAPLE DIVISION to form **1494 BARNSTAPLE AND SOUTH MOLTON DIVISION**

1487 TAVISTOCK DIVISION
combined with 1476 OKEHAMPTON DIVISION to form **1495 WEST DEVON DIVISION**

1488 TEIGNBRIDGE PSA
combined with 1496 SOUTH HAMS PSA and 1490 TORBAY PSA to form **1293 SOUTH DEVON PSA**

1489 TIVERTON PSA
combined with Chawleigh, Eggesford and Thelbridge in 1494 BARNSTAPLE AND SOUTH MOLTON PSA, Part of 1495 WEST DEVON PSA 1493 AXMINSTER AND HONITON PSA, 1478 CULLOMPTON PSA, 1497 EXETER AND WOMFORD PSA and 1480 EXMOUTH PSA to form **1292 CENTRAL DEVON PSA**

1490 TORBAY PSA
combined with 1488 TEIGNBRIDGE PSA and 1496 SOUTH HANTS PSA to form **1293 SOUTH DEVON PSA**

1491 TOTNES DIVISION
combined with 1482 KINGSBRIDGE DIVISION and 1485 PLYMPTON DIVISION to form **1496 SOUTH HAMS DIVISION**

1492 WONFORD DIVISION
combined with 1479 EXETER DIVISION to form **1497 EXETER AND WONFORD DIVISION**

1493 AXMINSTER AND HONITON PSA
combined with Chawleigh, Eggesford and Thelbridge in 1494 BARNSTAPLE AND SOUTH MOLTON PSA, Part of 1495 WEST DEVON PSA, 1478 CULLOMPTON PSA, 1489 TIVERTON PSA, 1497 EXETER AND WONFORD PSA to form **1292 CENTRAL DEVON PSA**

1494 BARNSTAPLE AND SOUTH MOLTON PSA
(except Chawleigh, Eggesford and Thelbridge) combined with 1477 BIDEFORD AND GREAT TORRINGTON PSA and Part of 1495 WEST DEVON PSA to form **1291 NORTH DEVON PSA** *Chawleigh, Eggesford and Thelbridge combined with part of 1495 WEST DEVON PSA and 1493 AXMINSTER AND HONNINGTON PSA, 1478 CULLOMPTON PSA, 1489 TIVERTON PSA, 1497 EXETER AND WONFORD PSA and 1480 EXMOUTH PSA to form* **1292 CENTRAL DEVON PSA**

1495 WEST DEVON PSA
Part combined with 1484 PLYMOUTH PSA to form **1290 PLYMOUTH PSA** *Part combined with 1477 BIDEFORD AND GREAT TORRINGTON PSA and 1494 BARNSTAPLE AND SOUTH MOLTON PSA (except Chawleigh, Eggesford and Thelbridge) to form* **1291 NORTH DEVON PSA,** *and remaining part combined with Chawleigh, Eggesford and Thelbridgein 1494 BARNSTAPLE AND SOUTH MOLTON PSA together with 1493 AXMINSTER AND HONITON PSA, 1478 CULLOMPTON PSA, 1489 TIVERTON PSA, 1479 EXETER AND WONFORD PSA and* **1480 EXMOUTH** *PSA to form* **1292 CENTRAL DEVON**

1496 SOUTH HAMS PSA
combined with 1488 TEIGNBRIDGE PSA and 1490 TORBAY PSA to form **1293 SOUTH DEVON PSA**

1497 EXETER AND WONFORD PSA
combined with Chawleigh, Eggesford and Thelbridge in 1494 BARNSTAPLE AND SOUTH MOLTON PSA, Part of 1495 WEST DEVON PSA, 1493 AXMINSTER AND HONITON PSA, 1478 CULLOMPTON PSA, 1489 TIVERTON PSA, 1497 EXETER AND WONFORD PSA and EXMOUTH PSA to form **1292 CENTRAL DEVON PSA**

1500 BLANDFORD DIVISION
combined with 1508 STURMINSTER DIVISION to form (after boundary adjustments) **1512 BLANDFORD AND STURMINSTER DIVISION**

1501 BOURNEMOUTH DIVISION
combined with 1503 CHRISTCHURCH DIVISION to form **1514 BOURNEMOUTH AND CHRISTCHURCH DIVISION**

1502 BRIDPORT DIVISION
combined with 1504 DORCHESTER DIVISION and 1507 SHERBORNE DIVISION to form **1516 WEST DORSET DIVISION**

1503 CHRISTCHURCH DIVISION
combined with 1501 BOURNEMOUTH DIVISION to form **1514 BOURNEMOUTH AND CHRISTCHURCH DIVISION**

1504 DORCHESTER DIVISION
combined with 1502 BRIDPORT DIVISION and 1507 SHERBORNE DIVISION to form **1516 WEST DORSET DIVISION**

1505 POOLE PSA
combined with 1514 BOURNEMOUTH AND CHRISTCHURCH PSA and 1515 CENTRAL DORSET PSA (except for the area of the North Dorset District Council) to form **1522 EAST DORSET PSA**

1506 SHAFTESBURY DIVISION
combined with 1508 STURMINSTER DIVISION to form **1513 SHAFTESBURY DIVISION**

1507 SHERBORNE DIVISION
combined with 1502 BRIDPORT DIVISION and 1504 DORCHESTER DIVISION to form **1516 WEST DORSET DIVISION**

1508 STURMINSTER DIVISION
abolished – majority absorbed into **1512 BLANDFORD AND STURMINSTER DIVISION** *and remainder into* **1513 SHAFTESBURY DIVISION**

1509 WAREHAM DIVISION
combined with **1512 BLANDFORD AND STURMINSTER DIVISION, 1513 SHAFTESBURY DIVISION** *and 1511 WIMBORNE DIVISION to form* **1515 CENTRAL DORSET DIVISION**

1510 WEYMOUTH AND PORTLAND PSA
combined with 1516 WEST DORSET DIVISION and the area of the North Dorset District Council within 1515 CENTRAL DORSET PSA **to form 1523 WEST DORSET PSA**

1511 WIMBORNE DIVISION
combined with **1512 BLANDFORD AND STURMINSTER DIVISION, 1513 SHAFTESBURY DIVISION** *and 1509 WAREHAM DIVISION to form* **1515 CENTRAL DORSET DIVISION**

1512 BLANDFORD AND STURMINSTER DIVISION
combined with 1513 SHAFTESBURY DIVISION, 1509 WAREHAM DIVISION and 1511 WIMBORNE DIVISION to form **1515 CENTRAL DORSET DIVISION**

1513 SHAFTESBURY DIVISION
combined with 1512 BLANDFORD AND STURMINSTER DIVISION, 1509 WAREHAM DIVISION and 1511 WIMBORNE DIVISION to form **1515 CENTRAL DORSET DIVISION**

1514 BOURNEMOUTH AND CHRISTCHURCH PSA
combined with 1505 POOLE PSA and 1515 CENTRAL DORSET PSA (except for the area of North Dorset District Council) to form **1522 EAST DORSET PSA**

1515 CENTRAL DORSET PSA
(Except for the area of the North Dorset District Council) combined with 1514 BOURNEMOUTH AND CHRISTCHURCH PSA and 1505 POOLE PSA to form **1522 EAST DORSET PSA** *– The area of the North Dorset District Council combined with 1516 WEST DORSET PSA and 1510 WEYMOUTH AND PORTLAND PSA to form* **1523 WEST DORSET PSA**

1516 WEST DORSET PSA
combined with 1510 WEYMOUTH AND PORTLAND PSA and the area of the North Dorset District Council within 1515 CENTRAL DORSET PSA to form **1523 WEST DORSET PSA**

1522 EAST DORSET LJA
see **DEVON, CORNWALL AND DORSET** ....p. 157

1523 WEST DORSET LJA
see **DEVON, CORNWALL AND DORSET** ....p. 157

1576 CHESTER-LE-STREET PSA
combined with 1579 DURHAM PSA, 1576 DERWENTSIDE PSA and 1580 EASINGTON PSA to form **1583 NORTH DURHAM PSA**

1577 DARLINGTON PSA
combined with 1581 SEDGEFIELD PSA and 1582 TEESDALE AND WEAR VALLEY to form **1584 SOUTH DURHAM PSA**

1578 DERWENTSIDE PSA
combined with 1579 DURHAM PSA, 1576 CHESTER-LE-STREET PSA and 1580 EASINGTON PSA to form **1583 NORTH DURHAM PSA**

1579 DURHAM PSA
combined with 1578 DERWENTSIDE PSA, 1576 CHESTER-LE-STREET PSA and 1580 EASINGTON PSA to form **1583 NORTH DURHAM PSA**

1580 EASINGTON PSA
combined with 1579 DURHAM PSA, 1578 DERWENTSIDE PSA and 1576 CHESTER-LE-STREET PSA to form **1583 NORTH DURHAM PSA**

1581 SEDGEFIELD PSA
combined with 1577 DARLINGTON PSA and 1582 TEESDALE AND WEAR VALLEY PSA to form **1584 SOUTH DURHAM PSA**

1582 TEESDALE AND WEAR VALLEY PSA
combined with 1581 SEDGFIELD PSA and 1577 DARLINGTON PSA to form **1584 SOUTH DURHAM PSA**

1583 NORTH DURHAM LJA
combined with 1584 South Durham LJA to form **1585/5585 COUNTY DURHAM AND DARLINGTON LJA**

1584 SOUTH DURHAM LJA
combined with 1583 North Durham LJA to form **1585/5585 COUNTY DURHAM AND DARLINGTON LJA**

1585 COUNTY DURHAM AND DARLINGTON LJA
see **CLEVELAND AND DURHAM** ....p. 124

1595 BATTLE AND RYE DIVISION
combined with 1596 BEXHILL DIVISION and 1601 HASTINGS DIVISION to form **1606 HASTINGS AND ROTHER DIVISION**

1596 BEXHILL DIVISION
combined with 1595 BATTLE AND RYE DIVISION and 1601 HASTINGS DIVISION to form **1606 HASTINGS AND ROTHER DIVISION**

1597 BRIGHTON DIVISION
combined with 1602 HOVE DIVISION to form **1604 BRIGHTON AND HOVE DIVISION**

1598 CROWBOROUGH DIVISION
combined with 1603 LEWES DIVISION to form **1607 LEWES AND CROWBOROUGH DIVISION**

1599 EASTBOURNE DIVISION
combined with 1600 HAILSHAM DIVISION to form **1605 EASTBOURNE AND HAILSHAM DIVISION**

1600 HAILSHAM DIVISION
combined with 1599 EASTBOURNE DIVISION to form **1605 EASTBOURNE AND HAILSHAM DIVISION**

1601 HASTINGS DIVISION
combined with 1595 BATTLE AND RYE DIVISION and 1596 BEXHILL DIVISION to form **1606 HASTINGS AND ROTHER DIVISION**

1602 HOVE DIVISION
combined with 1597 BRIGHTON DIVISION to form **1604 BRIGHTON AND HOVE DIVISION**

1603 LEWES DIVISION
combined with 1596 CROWBOROUGH DIVISION to form **1607 LEWES AND CROWBOROUGH DIVISION**

1604 BRIGHTON AND HOVE PSA
combined with 1607 LEWES AND CROWBOROUGH PSA to form **2950 SUSSEX (CENTRAL) PSA**

1605 EASTBOURNE AND HAILSHAM PSA
combined with 1606 HASTINGS AND ROTHER PSA to form **2948 SUSSEX (EASTERN) PSA**

1606 HASTINGS AND ROTHER PSA
combined with 1605 EASTBOURNE AND HAILSHAM PSA to form **2948 SUSSEX (EASTERN) PSA**

1607 LEWES AND CROWBOROUGH PSA
combined with 1604 BRIGHTON AND HOVE PSA to **form 2950 SUSSEX (CENTRAL) PSA**

1610 BASILDON DIVISION
(formerly Billericay Division) – renamed **MID-SOUTH ESSEX DIVISION**

1610 MID-SOUTH ESSEX LJA
combined with 1629 SOUTH-EAST ESSEX LJA and 1626 SOUTH-WEST LJA to form **1971 SOUTH ESSEX LJA**

1611 BRENTWOOD DIVISION
combined with 1626 THURROCK DIVISION to form **1626 SOUTH-WEST ESSEX DIVISION**

1612 CHELMSFORD DIVISION
combined with 1630 MALDON AND WITHAM DIVISION and (after boundary adjustment) 1631 BRAINTREE AND HALSTEAD DIVISION to form **1612 MID-NORTH ESSEX DIVISION**

1612 MID-NORTH ESSEX LJA
combined with 1613 NORTH-EAST ESSEX LJA and 1619 NORTH-WEST ESSEX LJA to form **1970 NORTH ESSEX LJA**

1613 COLCHESTER DIVISION
combined with 1620 HARWICH DIVISION, 1625 TENDRING DIVISION and part of 1631 BRAINTREE AND HALSTEAD DIVISION to form **1613 NORTH-EAST ESSEX DIVISION**

1613 NORTH-EAST ESSEX LJA
combined with 1612 MID-NORTH ESSEX LJA and 1619 NORTH-WEST ESSEX LJA to form **1970 NORTH ESSEX LJA**

1614 DENGIE AND MALDON DIVISION
combined with 1627 WITHAM DIVISION to form **1630 MALDON AND WITHAM DIVISION**

1615 DUNMOW DIVISION
combined with 1623 SAFFRON WALDEN DIVISION to form **1632 DUNMOW AND SAFFRON WALDEN DIVISION**

1616 EPPING AND ONGAR DIVISION
combined with 1632 DUNMOW AND SAFFRON WALDEN DIVISION and 1619 HARLOW DIVISION to form **1619 NORTH-WEST ESSEX DIVISION**

1617 FRESHWELL AND SOUTH HINCKFORD DIVISION
combined with 1628 HALSTEAD AND HEDINGHAM DIVISION to form **1631 BRAINTREE AND HALSTEAD DIVISION**

1618 HALSTEAD DIVISION
combined with 1621 NORTH HINCKFORD DIVISION to form **1628 HALSTEAD AND HEDINGHAM DIVISION**

1619 HARLOW DIVISION
combined with 1616 EPPING AND ONGAR DIVISION and 1632 DUNMOW AND SAFFRON WALDEN DIVISION to form **1619 NORTH-WEST ESSEX DIVISION**

1619 NORTH-WEST ESSEX LJA
combined with 1612 MID-NORTH ESSEX LJA and 1613 NORTH-EAST ESSEX LJA to form **1970 NORTH ESSEX LJA**

1620 HARWICH DIVISION
combined with 1613 COLCHESTER DIVISION, 1625 TENDRING DIVISION and part of 1631 BRAINTREE AND HALSTEAD DIVISION to form **1613 NORTH-EAST ESSEX DIVISION**

1621 NORTH HINCKFORD DIVISION
combined with 1618 HALSTEAD DIVISION to form **1628 HALSTEAD AND HEDINGHAM DIVISION**

1622 ROCHFORD DIVISION
combined with 1624 SOUTHEND-ON-SEA DIVISION to form **1629 ROCHFORD AND SOUTHEND-ON-SEA DIVISION**

1623 SAFFRON WALDEN DIVISION
combined with 1615 DUNMOW DIVISION to form **1632 DUNMOW AND SAFFRON WALDEN DIVISION**

1624 SOUTHEND-ON-SEA DIVISION
combined with 1622 ROCHFORD DIVISION to form **1629 ROCHFORD AND SOUTHEND-ON-SEA DIVISION**

1625 TENDRING DIVISION
combined with 1613 COLCHESTER DIVISION, 1620 HARWICH DIVISION and part of BRAINTREE AND HALSTEAD DIVISION to form **1613 NORTH-EAST ESSEX DIVISION**

1626 THURROCK DIVISION
combined with 1611 BRENTWOOD DIVISION to form **1626 SOUTH-WEST ESSEX DIVISION**

1626 SOUTH-WEST ESSEX LJA
combined with 1610 MID-SOUTH ESSEX LJA and 1629 SOUTH-EAST ESSEX LJA to form **1971 SOUTH ESSEX LJA**

1627 WITHAM DIVISION
combined with DENGIE AND MALDON DIVISION to form **1630 MALDON AND WITHAM DIVISION**

1628 HALSTEAD AND HEDINGHAM DIVISION
combined with 1617 FRESHWELL AND SOUTH HINCKFORD DIVISION to form **1631 BRAINTREE AND HALSTEAD DIVISION**

1629 ROCHFORD AND SOUTHEND-ON-SEA DIVISION
renamed **SOUTH-EAST ESSEX DIVISION**

1629 SOUTH-EAST ESSEX LJA
combined with 1610 MID-SOUTH ESSEX LJA and 1626 SOUTH-WEST ESSEX LJA to form **1971 SOUTH ESSEX LJA**

1630 MALDON AND WITHAM DIVISION
combined with 1612 CHELMSFORD DIVISION and (after boundary adjustment) 1631 BRAINTREE AND HALSTEAD DIVISION to form **1612 MID-NORTH ESSEX DIVISION**

1631 BRAINTREE AND HALSTEAD DIVISION
combined (after boundary adjustment) with 1612 CHELMSFORD DIVISION AND 1630 MALDON AND WITHAM DIVISION to form **1612 MID-NORTH ESSEX DIVISION**

1632 DUNMOW AND SAFFRON WALDEN DIVISION
combined with 1616 EPPING AND ONGAR DIVISION and 1619 HARLOW DIVISION to form **1619 NORTH-WEST ESSEX DIVISION**

1670 BERKELEY DIVISION
combined with 1675 DURSLEY DIVISION to form **1691 BERKELEY AND DURSLEY DIVISION**

1671 CAMPDEN DIVISION
combined with 1682 NORTHLEACH DIVISION, 1983 STOW-ON-THE-WOLD DIVISION and 1688 WINCHCOMBE DIVISION to form **1694 NORTH COTSWOLD DIVISION**

1672 CHELTENHAM DIVISION
combined with 1694 NORTH COTSWOLD DIVISION and 1686 TEWKSBURY DIVISION to form **1696 NORTH GLOUCESTERSHIRE DIVISION**

1673 CIRENCESTER DIVISION
combined with 1676 FAIRFORD DIVISION and 1685 TETBURY DIVISION to form **1689 CIRENCESTER, FAIRFORD AND TETBURY DIVISION**

1674 COLEFORD DIVISION
combined with 1679 LYDNEY DIVISION and 1681 NEWNHAM DIVISION to form **1695 FOREST OF DEAN DIVISION**

1675 DURSLEY DIVISION
combined with 1670 BERKELEY DIVISION to form **1691 BERKELEY AND DURSLEY DIVISION**

1676 FAIRFORD DIVISION
combined with 1673 CIRENCESTER DIVISION and 1685 TETBURY DIVISION to form **1689 CIRENCESTER, FAIRFORD AND TETBURY DIVISION**

1677 GLOUCESTER (CITY) DIVISION
combined with 1690 GLOUCESTER COUNTY DIVISION to form **1692 GLOUCESTER DIVISION**

1678 GLOUCESTER (COUNTY) DIVISION
combined with 1680 NEWENT DIVISION to form **1690 GLOUCESTER COUNTY DIVISION**

1679 LYDNEY DIVISION
combined with 1674 COLEFORD DIVISION and 1681 NEWNHAM DIVISION to form **1695 FOREST OF DEAN DIVISION**

1680 NEWENT DIVISION
combined with 1678 GLOUCESTER (COUNTY) DIVISION to form **1690 GLOUCESTER COUNTY DIVISION**

1681 NEWNHAM DIVISION
combined with 1674 COLEFORD DIVISION and 1679 LYDNEY DIVISION to form **1695 FOREST OF DEAN DIVISION**

1682 NORTHLEACH DIVISION
combined with 1671 CAMPDEN DIVISION, 1683 STOW-ON-THE-WOLD DIVISION and 1688 WINCHCOMBE DIVISION to form **1694 NORTH COTSWOLD DIVISION**

1683 STOW-ON-THE-WOLD DIVISION
combined with 1671 CAMPDEN DIVISION, 1682 NORTHLEACH DIVISION and 1688 WINCHCOMBE DIVISION to form **1694 NORTH COTSWOLD DIVISION**

1684 STROUD DIVISION
combined with 1691 BERKELEY AND DURSLEY DIVISION and 1687 WHITMINSTER DIVISION to form **1693 SOUTH GLOUCESTERSHIRE DIVISION**

1685 TETBURY DIVISION
combined with 1673 CIRENCESTER DIVISION and 1676 FAIRFORD DIVISION to form **1689 CIRENCESTER, FAIRFORD AND TETBURY DIVISION**

1686 TEWKSBURY DIVISION
combined with 1672 CHELTENHAM DIVISION and 1694 NORTH COTSWOLD DIVISION to form **1696 NORTH GLOUCESTERSHIRE DIVISION**

1687 WHITMINSTER DIVISION
combined with 1691 BERKELEY AND DURSLEY DIVISION and 1684 STROUD DIVISION to form **1693 SOUTH GLOUCESTERSHIRE DIVISION**

1688 WINCHCOMBE DIVISION
combined with 1671 CAMPDEN DIVISION, 1682 NORTHLEACH DIVISION and 1683 STOW-ON-THE-WOLD DIVISION to form **1694 NORTH COTSWOLD DIVISION**

1689 CIRENCESTER, FAIRFORD AND TETBURY PSA
renamed and renumbered **1698 CIRENCESTER LJA**

1690 GLOUCESTER COUNTY DIVISION
combined with 1677 GLOUCESTER (CITY) DIVISION to form **1692 GLOUCESTER DIVISION**

1691 BERKELEY AND DURSLEY DIVISION
combined with 1684 STROUD DIVISION and 1687 WHITMINSTER DIVISION to form **1693 SOUTH GLOUCESTERSHIRE DIVISION**

1692 GLOUCESTER PSA
renamed and renumbered **1698 GLOUCESTERSHIRE LJA**

1693 SOUTH GLOUCESTERSHIRE PSA
renamed and renumbered **1698 STROUD LJA**

1694 NORTH COTSWOLD DIVISION
combined with 1672 CHELTENHAM DIVISION and 1686 TEWKSBURY DIVISION to form **1696 NORTH GLOUCESTERSHIRE DIVISION**

1695 FOREST OF DEAN PSA
renamed and renumbered **1698 CIRENCESTER LJA**

1696 NORTH GLOUCESTERSHIRE PSA
renamed and renumbered **1698 GLOUCESTERSHIRE LJA**

1729 WEST CHESHIRE LJA
see **CHESHIRE AND MERSEYSIDE** ....p. 133

1731 BOLTON LJA
see **GREATER MANCHESTER** ....p. 140

1732 BURY LJA
see **1724 BURY AND ROCHDALE LJA**

1733 MANCHESTER CITY LJA
see **1723 MANCHESTER AND SALFORD LJA**

1734 OLDHAM LJA
see **GREATER MANCHESTER** ....p. 140

1735 MIDDLETON AND HEYWOOD DIVISION
combined with 1736 ROCHDALE DIVISION to form **1750 ROCHDALE, MIDDLETON AND HEYWOOD DIVISION**

1736 ROCHDALE DIVISION
combined with 1735 MIDDLETON AND HEYWOOD DIVISION to form **1750 ROCHDALE, MIDDLETON AND HEYWOOD DIVISION**

1737 ECCLES DIVISION
combined with 1738 SALFORD DIVISION to form **1747 CITY OF SALFORD DIVISION**

1738 SALFORD DIVISION
combined with 1737 ECCLES DIVISION to form **1747 CITY OF SALFORD DIVISION**

1739 STOCKPORT LJA
see **GREATER MANCHESTER** ....p. 140

1740 ASHTON-UNDER-LYNE DIVISION
combined with 1741 SOUTH TAMESIDE DIVISION to form **1748 TAMESIDE DIVISION**

1741 SOUTH TAMESIDE DIVISION
combined with 1740 ASHTON-UNDER-LYNE DIVISION to form **1748 TAMESIDE DIVISION**

1742 TRAFFORD LJA
see **GREATER MANCHESTER** ....p. 140

1743 LEIGH PSA
combined with 1746 WIGAN PSA to form **1749 WIGAN AND LEIGH PSA**

1744 MAKERFIELD DIVISION
combined with 1745 WIGAN DIVISION to form **1746 WIGAN DIVISION**

1745 WIGAN DIVISION
combined with 1744 MAKERFIELD DIVISION to form **1746 WIGAN DIVISION**

1746 WIGAN PSA
combined with 1743 LEIGH PSA to form **1749 WIGAN AND LEIGH PSA**

1747 CITY OF SALFORD LJA
CLOSED wef 12/11

1748 TAMESIDE LJA
see **GREATER MANCHESTER** ....p. 140

1749 WIGAN AND LEIGH LJA
see **GREATER MANCHESTER** ....p. 140

1750 ROCHDALE, MIDDLETON AND HEYWOOD LJA
CLOSED wef 12/11 see **1724 BURY AND ROCHDALE LJA**

1760 ALTON DIVISION
combined with 1771 PETERSFIELD DIVISION to form **1778 ALTON AND PETERSFIELD DIVISION**

1761 ANDOVER DIVISION
combined with 1762 BASINGSTOKE DIVISION and 1777 WINCHESTER DIVISION to form **1781 NORTH WEST HAMPSHIRE DIVISION**

1762 BASINGSTOKE DIVISION
combined with 1761 ANDOVER DIVISION and 1777 WINCHESTER DIVISION to form **1781 NORTH WEST HAMPSHIRE DIVISION**

1763 DROXFORD DIVISION
combined with 1764 EASTLEIGH DIVISION, 1765 FAREHAM DIVISION and 1766 GOSPORT DIVISION to form **1783 SOUTH HAMPSHIRE DIVISION**

1764 EASTLEIGH DIVISION
combined with 1763 DROXFORD DIVISION, 1765 FAREHAM DIVISION and 1766 GOSPORT DIVISION to form **1783 SOUTH HAMPSHIRE DIVISION**

1765 FAREHAM DIVISION
combined with 1763 DROXFORD DIVISION, 1764 EASTLEIGH DIVISION and 1766 GOSPORT DIVISION to form **1783 SOUTH HAMPSHIRE DIVISION**

1766 GOSPORT DIVISION
combined with 1763 DROXFORD DIVISION, 1764 EASTLEIGH DIVISION and 1765 FAREHAM DIVISION to form **1783 SOUTH HAMPSHIRE DIVISION**

1767 HAVANT DIVISION
combined with 1772 PORTSMOUTH DIVISION to form **1782 EAST HAMPSHIRE DIVISION**

1768 HYTHE DIVISION
combined with 1769 LYMINGTON DIVISION, 1773 RINGWOOD DIVISION, 1774 ROMSEY DIVISION and 1776 TOTTON AND NEW FOREST DIVISION to form **1779 NEW FOREST DIVISION**

1769 LYMINGTON DIVISION
combined with 1768 HYTHE DIVISION, 1773 RINGWOOD DIVISION, 1774 ROMSEY DIVISION and 1776 TOTTON AND NEW FOREST DIVISION to form **1779 NEW FOREST DIVISION**

1770 ODIHAM DIVISION
combined with 1778 ALTON AND PETERSFIELD DIVISION to form **1780 NORTH EAST HAMPSHIRE DIVISION**

1771 PETERSFIELD DIVISION
combined with 1760 ALTON DIVISION to form **1778 ALTON AND PETERSFIELD DIVISION**

1772 PORTSMOUTH DIVISION
combined with 1767 HAVANT DIVISION to form **1782 SOUTH EAST HAMPSHIRE DIVISION**

1773 RINGWOOD DIVISION
combined with 1768 HYTHE DIVISION, 1769 LYMINGTON DIVISION, 1774 ROMSEY DIVISION and 1776 TOTTON AND NEW FOREST DIVISION to form **1779 NEW FOREST DIVISION**

1774 ROMSEY DIVISION
combined with 1768 HYTHE DIVISION, 1769 LYMINGTON DIVISION, 1773 RINGWOOD DIVISION and 1776 TOTTON AND NEW FOREST DIVISION to form **1779 NEW FOREST DIVISION**

1775 SOUTHAMPTON LJA
see **1304 WEST HAMPSHIRE LJA**

1776 TOTTON AND NEW FOREST DIVISION
TOTTON AND NEW FOREST DIVISION – combined with 1768 HYTHE DIVISION, 1769 LYMINGTON DIVISION, 1773 RINGWOOD DIVISION and 1774 ROMSEY DIVISION to form **1779 NEW FOREST DIVISION**

1777 WINCHESTER DIVISION
combined with 1761 ANDOVER DIVISION and 1762 BASINGSTOKE DIVISION to form **1781 NORTH WEST HAMPSHIRE DIVISION**

1778 ALTON AND PETERSFIELD DIVISION
combined with 1770 ODIHAM DIVISION to form **1780 NORTH EAST HAMPSHIRE DIVISION**

1779 NEW FOREST LJA
CLOSED wef 1/04/11

1780 NORTH EAST HAMPSHIRE LJA
combined with 1781 NORTH WEST HAMPSHIRE LJA to form **1305/5305 NORTH HAMPSHIRE LJA**

1781 NORTH WEST HAMPSHIRE LJA
combined with 1780 NORTH EAST HAMPSHIRE LJA to form **1305/5305 NORTH HAMPSHIRE LJA**

1782 SOUTH EAST HAMPSHIRE LJA
see **HAMPSHIRE, ISLE OF WIGHT AND WILTSHIRE** ....p. 159

1783 SOUTH HAMPSHIRE LJA
see **HAMPSHIRE, ISLE OF WIGHT AND WILTSHIRE** ....p. 159

1837 HAVERING MAGISTRATES' COURT
see **2573/6573 NORTH EAST LONDON LJA** ....p. 109

1840 BROMSGROVE AND REDDITCH LJA
see **STAFFORDSHIRE AND WEST MERCIA** ....p. 119

1841 HEREFORDSHIRE LJA
see **STAFFORDSHIRE AND WEST MERCIA** ....p. 119

1842 SEVERNMINSTER PSA
renamed **1842 KIDDERMINSTER PSA**

1842 KIDDERMINSTER LJA
see **STAFFORDSHIRE AND WEST MERCIA** ....p. 119

1843 SOUTH WORCESTERSHIRE LJA
see **STAFFORDSHIRE AND WEST MERCIA** ....p. 119

1845 BEWDLEY BOROUGH DIVISION
combined with 1862 STOURPORT DIVISION to form (after boundary adjustment) **1871 BEWDLEY AND STOURPORT DIVISION**

1846 BROMSGROVE DIVISION
(after boundary adjustment) combined with 1860 REDDITCH DIVISION to form **1840 BROMSGROVE AND REDDITCH DIVISION**

1847 BROMYARD DIVISION
abolished wef 1/1/88: Majority absorbed into **1868 NORTH HEREFORDSHIRE DIVISION** *and remainder into* **1869 SOUTH HEREFORDSHIRE DIVISION**

1848 DORE AND BREDWARDINE DIVISION
abolished wef 1/1/88 and absorbed into **1869 SOUTH HEREFORDSHIRE DIVISION**

1849 DROITWICH DIVISION
combined with 1853 HUNDRED HOUSE DIVISION and 1866 WORCESTER (COUNTY) DIVISION to form (after boundary adjustment) **1872 MID-WORCESTER DIVISION**

1850 EVESHAM DIVISION
combined with 1859 PERSHORE DIVISION to form (after boundary adjustment) **1873 VALE OF EVESHAM DIVISION**

1851 CITY OF HEREFORD DIVISION
combined with 1868 NORTH HEREFORDSHIRE DIVISION and 1869 SOUTH HEREFORDSHIRE DIVISION to form **1841 HEREFORDSHIRE DIVISION**

1852 HEREFORD (COUNTY) DIVISION
abolished wef 1/1/88. Majority absorbed into **1869 SOUTH HEREFORDSHIRE DIVISION** *and remainder into* **1868 NORTH HEREFORDSHIRE DIVISION**

1853 HUNDRED HOUSE DIVISION
combined with 1849 DROITWICH DIVISION and 1866 WORCESTER (COUNTY) DIVISION to form (after boundary adjustment) **1872 MID-WORCESTERSHIRE DIVISION**

1854 KIDDERMINSTER DIVISION
combined with 1871 BEWDLEY AND STOURPORT DIVISION to form **1842 SEVERNMINSTER DIVISION**

1855 KINGTON DIVISION
absorbed into **1868 NORTH HEREFORDSHIRE DIVISION**

1856 LEDBURY DIVISION
absorbed into **1869 SOUTH HEREFORDSHIRE DIVISION**

1857 LEOMINSTER AND WIGMORE DIVISION
absorbed into **1868 NORTH HEREFORDSHIRE DIVISION**

1858 MALVERN DIVISION
combined with 1864 UPTON-ON-SEVERN DISTRICT to form (after boundary adjustment) **1870 MALVERN HILLS DIVISION**

1859 PERSHORE DIVISION
combined with 1850 EVESHAM DIVISION to form (after boundary adjustment) **1873 VALE OF EVESHAM DIVISION**

1860 REDDITCH DIVISION
combined with 1846 BROMSGROVE DIVISION (after boundary adjustment) to form **1840 BROMSGROVE AND REDDITCH DIVISION**

1861 ROSS DIVISION
absorbed into **1869 SOUTH HEREFORDSHIRE DIVISION**

1862 STOURPORT DIVISION
combined with 1845 BEWDLEY BOROUGH DIVISION to form (after boundary adjustment) **1871 BEWDLEY AND STOURPORT DIVISION**

1863 TENBURY DIVISION
absorbed into **1868 NORTH HEREFORDSHIRE DIVISION**

1864 UPTON-ON-SEVERN DIVISION
combined with 1858 MALVERN DIVISION to form (after boundary adjustment **1870 MALVERN HILLS DIVISION**

1865 CITY OF WORCESTER DIVISION
boundary with 1866 WORCESTER (COUNTY) DIVISION adjusted to form **1874 CITY OF WORCESTER DIVISION**

1866 WORCESTER (COUNTY) DIVISION
combined with 1849 DROITWICH DIVISION and 1853 HUNDRED HOUSE DIVISION to form (after boundary adjustment) **1872 MID-WORCESTERSHIRE DIVISION**

1867 WORCESTER (COUNTY) DIVISION (MOTORWAY)
abolished

1868 NORTH HEREFORDSHIRE DIVISION
combined with 1851 CITY OF HEREFORD DIVISION and 1869 SOUTH HEREFORDSHIRE DIVISION to form **1841 HEREFORDSHIRE DIVISION**

1869 SOUTH HEREFORDSHIRE DIVISION
combined with 1851 CITY OF HEREFORD DIVISION and 1868 HEREFORDSHIRE DIVISION to form **1841 HEREFORDSHIRE DIVISION**

1870 MALVERN HILLS DIVISION
combined with 1872 MID-WORCESTERSHIRE DIVISION (after boundary adjustment), 1873 VALE OF EVESHAM DIVISION and 1874 CITY OF WORCESTER DIVISION to form **1843 SOUTH WORCESTERSHIRE DIVISION**

1871 BEWDLEY AND STOURPORT DIVISION
combined with 1854 KIDDERMINSTER DIVISION to form **1842 SEVERNMINSTER DIVISION**

1872 MID-WORCESTERSHIRE DIVISION
(after boundary adjustment) combined with 1870 MALVERN HILLS DIVISION, 1873 VALE OF EVESHAM DIVISION and 1874 CITY OF WORCESTER DIVISION to form **1843 SOUTH WORCESTERSHIRE DIVISION**

1873 VALE OF EVESHAM DIVISION
combined with 1870 MALVERN HILLS DIVISION, 1872 MID-WORCESTERSHIRE DIVISION (after boundary adjustment) and CITY OF WORCESTER DIVISION to form **1843 SOUTH WORCESTERSHIRE DIVISION**

1874 CITY OF WORCESTER DIVISION
combined with 1870 MALVERN HILLS DIVISION, 1872 MID-WORCESTERSHIRE DIVISION (after boundary adjustment) and 1873 VALE OF EVESHAM DIVISION to form **1843 SOUTH WORCESTERSHIRE DIVISION**

1875 BISHOP'S STORTFORD DIVISION
combined with 1877 CHESHUNT DIVISION and 1888 HERTFORD AND WARE DIVISION to form **1888 EAST HERTFORDSHIRE DIVISION**

1876 BUNTINGFORD DIVISION
combined with 1888 HERTFORD AND WARE

1877 CHESHUNT DIVISION
combined with 1875 BISHOP'S STORTFORD DIVISION and 1888 HERTFORD AND WARE DIVISION to form **1888 EAST HERFORDSHIRE DIVISION**

1878 DACORUM PSA
combined with 1886 WATFORD PSA to form **1893 WEST HERTFORDSHIRE PSA**

1879 HATFIELD DIVISION
combined with 1887 WELWYN DIVISION to form **1890 MID HERTFORDSHIRE DIVISION**

1879 HATFIELD MAGISTRATES' COURT
see BEDFORDSHIRE AND HERTFORDSHIRE ....p. 143

1881 HITCHIN DIVISION
combined with 1882 ODSEY DIVISION to form **1889 NORTH HERTFORDSHIRE DIVISION**

1882 ODSEY DIVISION
combined with HITCHIN DIVISION to form **1889 NORTH HERTFORDSHIRE DIVISION**

1883 ST ALBAN'S PSA
combined with 1890 MID HERTFORDSHIRE PSA to form **1892 CENTRAL HERTFORDSHIRE PSA**

1884 SOUTH MIMMS DIVISION
abolished wef 3/9/93 and absorbed into **1877 CHESHUNT DIVISION and 1886 WATFORD DIVISION**

1885 STEVENAGE DIVISION
combined with 1889 North Hertfordshire Division to form one new division to be known as the **NORTH HERTFORDSHIRE DIVISION**

1886 WATFORD PSA
after boundary adjustment) combined with 1878 DACORUM PSA to form **1893 WEST HERTFORDSHIRE PSA**

1887 WELWYN DIVISION
combined with 1879 HATFIELD DIVISION to form **1890 MID HERTFORDSHIRE DIVISION**

1888 HERTFORD AND WARE DIVISION
combined with 1875 BISHOP'S STORTFORD DIVISION and 1877 CHESHUNT DIVISION to form **1888 EAST HERTFORDSHIRE DIVISION** *(retaining existing Court Code No.)*

1888 EAST HERTFORDSHIRE LJA
combined with 1889 NORTH HERTFORDSHIRE LJA to form **1911 NORTH AND EAST HERTFORDSHIRE LJA**

1889 NORTH HERTFORDSHIRE LJA
combined with 1888 EAST HERTFORDSHIRE LJA to form **1911 NORTH AND EAST HERFORDSHIRE LJA**

1890 MID HERTFORDSHIRE PSA
combined with 1883 ST ALBANS PSA to form **1892 CENTRAL HERTFORDESHIRE PSA**

1892 CENTRAL HERTFORDSHIRE LJA
combined with 1893 WEST HERTFORDSHIRE LJA to form **1910 WEST AND CENTRAL HERTFORDSHIRE LJA**

1893 WEST HERTFORDSHIRE LJA
combined with 1892 CENTRAL HERTFORDSHIRE LJA to form **1910 WEST AND CENTRAL HERTFORDSHIRE LJA**

1901 SOUTH HUNSLEY BEACON AND HOWDENSHIRE DIVISION
Part combined with part of 1928 EPWORTH AND GOOLE DIVISION to form **1928 GOOLE AND HOWDENSHIRE DIVISION** *and remainder becomin* **1901 SOUTH HUNSLEY BEACON DIVISION**

1901 SOUTH HUNSLEY BEACON PSA
combined with 1925 BEVERLEY PSA, parts of 1905 BAINTON, WILTON AND HOLME BEACON PSA and parts of DICKERING AND NORTH HOLDERNESS PSA to form **1942 BEVERLEY AND THE WOLDS PSA**

1902 SOUTH AND MIDDLE HOLDERNESS PSA
combined with 1933 KINGSTON UPON HULL PSA to form **1943 HULL AND HOLDERNESS PSA**

1903 SCUNTHORPE, BRIGG AND BARTON DIVISION
combined with part of 1928 EPWORTH AND GOOLE DIVISION to form **1903 NORTH LINCOLNSHIRE DIVISION**

1903 NORTH LINCOLNSHIRE LJA
see **HUMBER AND SOUTH YORKSHIRE** p. 126

1904 DICKERING AND NORTH HOLDERNESS PSA
Part combined with 1901 SOUTH HUNSLEY BEACON, 1925 BEVERLEY PSA and part of 1905 BAINTON, WILTON AND HOLME BEACON PSA to form **1942 BEVERLEY AND THE WOLDS PSA**
Remainder combined with remaining part of 1905 BAINTON WILTON AND HOLME PSA to form **1941 BRIDLINGTON PSA**

1905 BAINTON, WILTON AND HOLME BEACON PSA
Part combined with 1901 SOUTH HUNSLEY BEACON PSA, 1925 BEVERLEY PSA and part of 1904 DICKERING AND NORTH HOLDERNESS PSA to form **1942 BEVERLEY AND THE WOLDS PSA.**
Remainder combined with the remainder of DICKERING AND NORTH HOLDERNESS to form **1941 BRIDLINGTON PSA**

1910 WEST AND CENTRAL HERTFORDSHIRE LJA
see **BEDFORDSHIRE AND HERTFORDSHIRE** ....p. 143

1911 NORTH AND EAST HERTFORDSHIRE LJA
see **BEDFORDSHIRE AND HERTFORDSHIRE** ....p. 143

1920 BERKSHIRE LJA
see **THAMES VALLEY** ....p. 153

1921 BUCKINGHAMSHIRE LJA
see **THAMES VALLEY** ....p. 153

1922 OXFORDSHIRE LJA
see **THAMES VALLEY** ....p. 153

1923 BAINTON BEACON DIVISION
combined with 1939 WILTON BEACON DIVISION and 1931 HOLME BEACON DIVISION to form **1905 BAINTON, WILTON AND HOLME BEACON DIVISION**

1924 BARTON-UPON-HUMBER DIVISION
combined with 1936 SCUNTHORPE DIVISION and 1926 BRIGG DIVISION to form **1903 SCUNTHORPE, BRIGG AND BARTON DIVISION**

1925 BEVERLEY PSA
combined with 1901 SOUTH HUNSLEY BEACON PSA, part of 1905 BAINTON, WILTON AND HOLME BEACON PSA and part of 1904 DICKERING AND NORTH HOLDERNESS PSA to form **1942 BEVERLEY AND THE WOLDS PSA**

1926 BRIGG DIVISION
combined with 1936 SCUNTHORPE DIVISION and 1924 BARTON-UPON-HUMBER DIVISION to form **1903 SCUNTHORPE, BRIGG AND BARTON DIVISION**

1927 DICKERING DIVISION
combined with 1935 NORTH HOLDERNESS DIVISION to form **1904 DICKERING AND NORTH HOLDERNESS DIVISION**

1928 EPWORTH AND GOOLE DIVISION
Part combined with 1903 SCUNTHORPE, BRIGG AND BARTON DIVISION to form **1903 NORTH LINCOLNSHIRE DIVISION**; *Part combined with part of 1901 SOUTH HUNSLEY BEACON AND HOWDENSHIRE DIVISION to form* **1928 GOOLE AND HOWDENSHIRE DIVISION**

1928 GOOLE AND HOWDENSHIRE LJA
CLOSED wef 12/11

1929 GRIMSBY (BOROUGH) DIVISION
combined with 1930 CLEETHORPES DIVISION to form **1940 GRIMSBY AND CLEETHORPES DIVISION**

1930 GRIMSBY (COUNTY) DIVISION
renamed **CLEETHORPES DIVISION,** *see below*

1930 CLEETHORPES DIVISION
combined with 1929 GRIMSBY (BOROUGH) DIVISION to form **1940 GRIMSBY AND CLEETHORPES DIVISION**

1931 HOLME BEACON DIVISION
combined with 1923 BAINTON BEACON DIVISION and 1939 WILTON BEACON DIVISION to form **1905 BAINTON, WILTON AND HOLME BEACON DIVISION**

1932 HOWDENSHIRE DIVISION
combined with 1938 SOUTH HUNSLEY BEACON DIVISION to form **1901 SOUTH HUNSLEY BEACON AND HOWDENSHIRE DIVISION**

1933 KINGSTON UPON HULL PSA
combined with 1902 SOUTH AND MIDDLE HOLDERNESS PSA to form **1943 HULL AND HOLDERNESS PSA**

1934 MIDDLE HOLDERNESS DIVISION
combined with 1937 SOUTH HOLDERNESS DIVISION to form **1902 SOUTH AND MIDDLE HOLDERNESS DIVISION**

1935 NORTH HOLDERNESS DIVISION
combined with 1927 DICKERING DIVISION to form **1904 DICKERING AND NORTH HOLDERNESS DIVISION**

1936 SCUNTHORPE DIVISION
combined with 1926 BRIGG DIVISION and 1924 BARTON-UPON-HUMBER DIVISION to form **1903 SCUNTHORPE, BRIGG AND BARTON DIVISION**

1937 SOUTH HOLDERNESS DIVISION
combined with 1934 MIDDLE HOLDERNESS DIVISION to form **1902 SOUTH AND MIDDLE HOLDERNESS DIVISION**

1938 SOUTH HUNSLEY BEACON DIVISION
combined with 1932 HOWDENSHIRE DIVISION to form **1901 SOUTH HUNSLEY BEACON AND HOWDENSHIRE DIVISION**

1939 WILTON BEACON DIVISION
combined with 1923 BAINTON BEACON DIVISION and 1931 HOLME BEACON DIVISION to form **1905 BAINTON, WILTON AND HOLME BEACON DIVISION**

1940 GRIMSBY AND CLEETHORPES LJA
see **HUMBER AND SOUTH YORKSHIRE** ....p. 126

1941 BRIDLINGTON LJA
combined with 1942 BEVERLEY AND THE WOLDS LJA to form **2353 EAST YORKSHIRE LJA**

1942 BEVERLEY AND THE WOLDS LJA
combined with 1941 BRIDLINGTON LJA to form **2353 EAST YORKSHIRE LJA**

1943 HULL AND HOLDERNESS LJA
see **HUMBER AND SOUTH YORKSHIRE** ....p. 126

1945 ISLE OF WIGHT LJA
see **HAMPSHIRE, ISLE OF WIGHT AND WILTSHIRE** ....p. 159

1952 ASHFORD AND TENTERDEN DIVISION
combined with 1955 DOVER AND EAST KENT DIVISION and 1957 FOLKESTONE AND HYTHE DIVISION to form **1957 CHANNEL DIVISION**

1953 CANTERBURY LJA
combined with 1957 CHANNEL LJA and 1968 THANET LJA to form **1957 EAST KENT LJA**

1954 DARTFORD DIVISION
part combined with 1963 SEVENOAKS DIVISION, 1966 TUNBRIDGE WELLS AND CRANBROOK DIVISION and 1965 TONBRIDGE AND MALLING DIVISION (Part) to form **1963 WEST KENT DIVISION** – *balance remains under existing Court Code of 1954*

1954 DARTFORD DIVISION
combined with 1958 GRAVESHAM DIVISION to form **1969 DARTFORD AND GRAVESHAM DIVISION**

1955 DOVER AND EAST KENT DIVISION
combined with 1952 ASHFORD AND TENTERDEN DIVISION and 1957 FOLKESTONE AND HYTHE DIVISION to form **1957 CHANNEL DIVISION**

1956 FAVERSHAM DIVISION
combined with 1964 SITTINGBOURNE DIVISION to form **1967 FAVERSHAM AND SITTINGBOURNE DIVISION**

1957 FOLKESTONE AND HYTHE DIVISION
combined with 1952 ASHFORD AND TENTERDEN DIVISION and 1955 DOVER AND EAST KENT DIVISION to form **1957 CHANNEL DIVISION**

1957 CHANNEL LJA
combined with 1953 CANTERBURY LJA and 1968 THANET LJA to form **1957 EAST KENT LJA**

1957 EAST KENT LJA
see **KENT** ....p. 147

1958 GRAVESHAM DIVISION
combined with 1954 DARTFORD DIVISION to form **1969 DARTFORD AND GRAVESHAM DIVISION**

1959 MAIDSTONE DIVISION
combined with 1965 TONBRIDGE AND MALLING DIVISION (Part) to form **1959 MID KENT DIVISION**

1959 MID KENT
abolished and absorbed into **1960 CENTRAL KENT LJA**

1960 MARGATE DIVISION
combined with 1962 RAMSGATE DIVISION to form **1968 THANET DIVISION**

1960 CENTRAL KENT LJA
see **KENT** ....p. 147

1961 MEDWAY
combined with 1969 DARTFORD AND GRAVESHAM PSA to form **1966 NORTH KENT LJA**

1962 RAMSGATE DIVISION
combined with 1962 MARGATE DIVISION to form **1968 THANET DIVISION**

1963 SEVENOAKS DIVISION
combined with 1965 TONBRIDGE AND MALLING DIVISION (Part), 1966 TUNBRIDGE WELLS AND CRANBROOK DIVISION and 1954 DARTFORD DIVISION (Part) to form **1963 WEST KENT DIVISION**

1963 WEST KENT
abolished and absorbed into **1960 CENTRAL KENT LJA**

1964 SITTINGBOURNE DIVISION
combined with 1956 FAVERSHAM DIVISION to form **1967 FAVERSHAM AND SITTINGBOURNE DIVISION**

1965 TONBRIDGE AND MALLING DIVISION
part combined with 1959 MAIDSTONE DIVISION to form **1959 MID KENT DIVISION**: part combined with 1966 TUNBRIDGE WELLS AND CRANBROOK DIVISION, 1963 SEVENOAKS DIVISION and 1954 DARTFORD DIVISION (Part) to form **1963 WEST KENT DIVISION**

1965 EAST KENT LJA
see **KENT** ....p. 147

1966 TUNBRIDGE WELLS AND CRANBROOK DIVISION
combined with 1963 SEVENOAKS DIVISION, 1965 TONBRIDGE AND MALLING DIVISION (Part) and 1954 DARTFORD DIVISION (Part) to form **1963 WEST KENT DIVISION**

1966 NORTH KENT LJA (DARTFORD AND MEDWAY)
see **KENT** ....p. 147

1967 FAVERSHAM AND SITTINGBOURNE
abolished and absorbed into **1960 CENTRAL KENT LJA**

1968 THANET LJA
combined with 1953 CANTERBURY LJA and 1957 CHANNEL LJA to form **1957 EAST KENT LJA**

1969 DARTFORD AND GRAVESHAM PSA
combined with 1961 MEDWAY PSA to form **1966 NORTH KENT LJA**

1970 NORTH ESSEX LJA
see **CAMBRIDGESHIRE AND ESSEX** ....p. 145

1971 SOUTH ESSEX LJA
see **CAMBRIDGESHIRE AND ESSEX** ....p. 145

1972 NORFOLK LJA
see **NORFOLK AND SUFFOLK** ....p. 149

1992 FYLDE COAST LJA
see **CUMBRIA AND LANCASHIRE** ....p. 136

1994 ACCRINGTON DIVISION
combined with 1999 CHURCH DIVISION to form **2010 HYNDBURN DIVISION**

1995 BLACKBURN DIVISION
combined with 2000 DARWEN DIVISION and major part of 2008 RIBBLE VALLEY DIVISION to form
2012 BLACKBURN, DARWEN AND RIBBLE VALLEY DIVISION

1996 BLACKPOOL DIVISION
combined with 2001 FYLDE DIVISION to form **1996 BLACKPOOL AND FYLDE DIVISION**

1996 BLACKPOOL AND FYLDE PSA
combined with 2009 WYRE PSA to form **1992 FLYDE COAST PSA**

1997 BURNLEY DIVISION
combined with 2004 PENDLE DIVISION and part of 2008 RIBBLE VALLEY DIVISION to form **2011
BURNLEY AND PENDLE DIVISION**

1998 CHORLEY LJA
see **CUMBRIA AND LANCASHIRE** ....p. 136

1999 CHURCH DIVISION
combined with 1994 ACCRINGTON DIVISION to form **2010 HYNDBURN DIVISION**

2000 DARWEN DIVISION
*combined with 1925 BLACKBURN DIVISION and major part of 2008 RIBBLE VALLEY DIVISION to
form* **2012 BLACKBURN, DARWEN AND RIBBLE VALLEY DIVISION**

2001 FYLDE DIVISION
combined with 1996 BLACKPOOL DIVISION to form **1996 BLACKPOOL AND FYLDE DIVISION**

2002 LANCASTER LJA
see **CUMBRIA AND LANCASHIRE** ....p. 136

2003 ORMSKIRK LJA
see **CUMBRIA AND LANCASHIRE** ....p. 136

2004 PENDLE DIVISION
combined with 1997 BURNLEY DIVISION and part of 2008 RIBBLE VALLEY DIVISION to form **2011
BURNLEY AND PENDLE DIVISION**

2005 PRESTON LJA
see **CUMBRIA AND LANCASHIRE** ....p. 136

2006 ROSSENDALE PSA
combined with 2011 BURNLEY AND PENDLE PSA to form **2014 BURNLEY, PENDLE AND
ROSSENDALE PSA**

2007 SOUTH RIBBLE LJA
see **CUMBRIA AND LANCASHIRE** ....p. 136

2008 RIBBLE VALLEY DIVISION
abolished and absorbed into **2012 BLACKBURN, DARWEN AND RIBBLE VALLEY DIVISION, 2011
BURNLEY AND PENDLE DIVISION and 2005 PRESTON DIVISION**

2009 WYRE PSA
combined with 1996 BLACKPOOL AND FLYDE PSA to form **1992 FLYDE COAST PSA**

2010 HYNDBURN LJA
see **1725 EAST LANCASHIRE LJA**

2011 BURNLEY AND PENDLE PSA
combined with 2006 ROSSENDALE PSA to form **2014 BURNLEY, PENDLE AND ROSSENDALE PSA**

2012 BLACKBURN, DARWEN AND RIBBLE VALLEY LJA
see **1725 EAST LANCASHIRE LJA**

2014 BURNLEY, PENDLE AND ROSSENDALE LJA
see **CUMBRIA AND LANCASHIRE** ....p. 136

2038 ASHBY-DE-LA-ZOUCH DIVISION
subjected to boundary adjustment and renumbered **2047 ASHBY-DE-LA-ZOUCH DIVISION**

2039 LEICESTER (CITY) DIVISION
combined with 2040 LEICESTER (COUNTY) DIVISION to form (after boundary adjustment) **2048 LEICESTER DIVISION**

2040 LEICESTER (COUNTY) DIVISION
combined with 2039 LEICESTER (CITY) DIVISION to form (after boundary adjustment) **2048 LEICESTER DIVISION**

2041 LOUGHBOROUGH DIVISION
subjected to boundary adjustment and renumbered **2049 LOUGHBOROUGH DIVISION**

2042 LUTTERWORTH DIVISION
combined with 2044 MARKET HARBOROUGH DIVISION to form (after boundary adjustment **2051 MARKET HARBOROUGH AND LUTTERWORTH DIVISION**

2043 MARKET BOSWORTH DIVISION
subjected to boundary adjustment and renumbered **2050 MARKET BOSWORTH DIVISION**

2044 MARKET HARBOROUGH DIVISION
combined with 2042 LUTTERWORTH DIVISION to form (after boundary adjustment) **2051 MARKET HARBOROUGH AND LUTTERWORTH DIVISION**

2045 MELTON AND BELVOIR DIVISION
combined with 2046 RUTLAND DIVISION to form **2045 MELTON, BELVOIR AND RUTLAND DIVISION**

2045 MELTON, BELVOIR AND RUTLAND LJA
CLOSED wef 31/7/11

2046 RUTLAND DIVISION
combined with 2045 MELTON AND BELVOIR DIVISION to form **2045 MELTON, BELVOIR AND RUTLAND DIVISION**

2047 ASHBY-DE-LA-ZOUCH LJA
CLOSED wef 7/11

2048 LEICESTER LJA
see **LEICESTERSHIRE, RUTLAND, LINCOLNSHIRE, NORTHAMPTONSHIRE** ....p. 116

2049 LOUGHBOROUGH LJA
see **LEICESTERSHIRE, RUTLAND, LINCOLNSHIRE, NORTHAMPTONSHIRE** ....p. 116

2050 MARKET BOSWORTH LJA
see **LEICESTERSHIRE, RUTLAND, LINCOLNSHIRE, NORTHAMPTONSHIRE** ....p. 116

2051 MARKET HARBOROUGH AND LUTTERWORTH LJA
CLOSED wef 31/7/11

2053 ALFORD DIVISION
combined with 2064 LOUTH DIVISION and 2067 SPILSBY DIVISION to form **2070 LOUTH DIVISION** *and* **2071 SPILSBY AND SKEGNESS DIVISION**

2054 BOSTON DIVISION
subjected to boundary adjustments and renumbered **2073 BOSTON DIVISION**

2055 BOURNE DIVISION
combined with 2068 STAMFORD DIVISION to form **2074 BOURNE AND STAMFORD DIVISION**

2056 CAISTOR DIVISION
*combined with 2079 LINCOLN DISTRICT DIVISION and 2081 MARKET RASEN DIVISION to form
new* **2079 LINCOLN DISTRICT DIVISION**

2057 EAST ELLOE DIVISION
combined with 2069 WEST ELLOE DIVISION to form (after boundary adjustment) **2076 ELLOES
DIVISION**

2058 GAINSBOROUGH DIVISION
subjected to boundary adjustments and renumbered **2075 GAINSBOROUGH DIVISION**

2059 GRANTHAM DIVISION
subjected to boundary adjustments and renumbered **2077 GRANTHAM DIVISION**

2060 HORNCASTLE DIVISION
combined with 2070 LOUTH DIVISION to form (after boundary adjustments) **2078 WOLDS DIVISION**

2061 LINCOLN (CITY) DIVISION
combined with 2072 LINCOLN (COUNTY) DIVISION to form (after boundary adjustments) **2079
LINCOLN DISTRICT DIVISION**

2062 LINCOLN (KESTEVEN) DIVISION
combined with 2063 LINDSEY (LINCOLN AND WRAGBY) DIVISION to form **2072 LINCOLN
(COUNTY) DIVISION**

2063 LINDSEY (LINCOLN AND WRAGBY) DIVISION
*combined with 2062 LINCOLN (KESTEVEN) DIVISION to **form*** **2072 LINCOLN (COUNTY) DIVISION**

2064 LOUTH DIVISION
combined with 2053 ALFORD DIVISION and 2067 SPILSBY DIVISION to form **2070 LOUTH
DIVISION** *and* **2071 SPILSBY AND SKEGNESS DIVISION**

2065 MARKET RASEN DIVISION
subjected to boundary adjustments and renumbered **2081 MARKET RASEN DIVISION**

2066 SLEAFORD DIVISION
subjected to boundary adjustments and renumbered **2080 SLEAFORD DIVISION**

2067 SPILSBY DIVISION
combined with 2053 ALFORD DIVISION and 2064 LOUTH DIVISION to form **2070 LOUTH DIVISION**
and **2071 SPILSBY AND SKEGNESS DIVISION**

2068 STAMFORD DIVISION
combined with 2055 BOURNE DIVISION to form **2074 BOURNE AND STAMFORD** DIVISION

2069 WEST ELLOE DIVISION
combined with 2057 EAST ELLOE DIVISION to form (after boundary adjustments) **2076 ELLOES
DIVISION**

2070 LOUTH DIVISION
combined with 2060 HORNCASTLE DIVISION to form (after boundary adjustments) **2079 WOLDS
DIVISION**

2071 SPILSBY AND SKEGNESS DIVISION
subjected to boundary adjustments and renumbered **2082 SPILSBY AND SKEGNESS DIVISION**

2072 LINCOLN (COUNTY) DIVISION
combined with 2061 LINCOLN (CITY) DIVISION to form (after boundary adjustments) **2079 LINCOLN
DISTRICT DIVISION**

2073 BOSTON LJA
combined with 2082 SKEGNESS LJA to form **2085 EAST LINCOLNSHIRE LJA**

2074 BOURNE AND STAMFORD LJA
combined with ELLOES LJA to form **2076 ELLOES, BOURNE AND STAMFORD LJA**

2075 GAINSBOROUGH LJA
closed wef 31/7/11

2076 ELLOES, BOURNE AND STAMFORD LJA
combined with 2077 GRANTHAM AND SLEAFORD LJA to form **2084 SOUTH LINCOLNSHIRE LJA**

2077 GRANTHAM AND SLEAFORD LJA
combined with 2076 ELLOES, BOURNE AND STAMFORD LJA to form **2084 SOUTH LINCOLNSHIRE LJA**

2078 WOLDS DIVISION
combined with part of 2079 LINCOLN DISTRICT DIVISION to form enlarged **2078 WOLDS DIVISION**

2078 WOLDS LJA
abolished

2079 LINCOLN DISTRICT DIVISION
part combined with 2078 WOLDS DIVISION to form enlarged 2078 WOLDS DIVISION; remainder combined with 2056 CAISTOR DIVISION and 2081 MARKET RASEN DIVISION to form new **2079 LINCOLN DISTRICT DIVISON**

2079 LINCOLN DISTRICT LJA
now **2083 NORTH WEST LINCOLNSHIRE LJA**

2080 SLEAFORD LJA
combined with GRANTHAM LJA to form **2077 GRANTHAM AND SLEAFORD LJA**

2081 MARKET RASEN DIVISION
combined with 2056 CAISTOR DIVISION and 2079 LINCOLN DISTRICT DIVISION to form new **2079 LINCOLN DISTRICT DIVISION**

2082 SPILSBY AND SKEGNESS DIVISION
renamed **SKEGNESS DIVISION** *– see* **EAST MIDLANDS**

2082 SKEGNESS LJA
combined with 2073 BOSTON LJA to form **2085 EAST LINCOLNSHIRE LJA**

2083 NORTH WEST LINCOLNSHIRE LJA
see **LEICESTERSHIRE, RUTLAND, LINCOLNSHIRE, NORTHAMPTONSHIRE** ....p. 116

2084 SOUTH LINCOLNSHIRE LJA
see **LEICESTERSHIRE, RUTLAND, LINCOLNSHIRE, NORTHAMPTONSHIRE** ....p. 116

2085 EAST LINCOLNSHIRE LJA
see **LEICESTERSHIRE, RUTLAND, LINCOLNSHIRE, NORTHAMPTONSHIRE** ....p. 116

2266 KNOWSLEY LJA
CLOSED wef 12/11

2267 LIVERPOOL LJA
see **5730 LIVERPOOL AND KNOWSLEY LJA**

2268 ST HELENS LJA
see **CHESHIRE AND MERSEYSIDE** ....p. 133

2269 NORTH SEFTON DISTRICT LJA
CLOSED wef 9/11

2270 SOUTH SEFTON DISTRICT LJA
see **1728 SEFTON LJA**

2271 WIRRAL LJA
see **CHESHIRE AND MERSEYSIDE** ....p. 133

2320 BRACKLEY DIVISION
now amalgamated with **2327 TOWCESTER DIVISION**

2321 CORBY LJA
see **LEICESTERSHIRE, RUTLAND, LINCOLNSHIRE, NORTHAMPTONSHIRE** ....p. 116

2322 DAVENTRY LJA
CLOSED wef 31/3/11

2323 KETTERING LJA
see **LEICESTERSHIRE, RUTLAND, LINCOLNSHIRE, NORTHAMPTONSHIRE** ....p. 116

2324 MID NORTHANTS DIVISION
part amalgamated with **2322 DAVENTRY DIVISION**: *– part amalgamated with 2327* **TOWCESTER DIVISION**

2325 NORTHAMPTON LJA
see **LEICESTERSHIRE, RUTLAND, LINCOLNSHIRE, NORTHAMPTONSHIRE** ....p. 116

2326 OUNDLE AND THRAPSTON DIVISION
part amalgamated with **2321 CORBY DIVISION**: *– part amalgamated with* **2323 KETTERING DIVISION:** *– part amalgamated with* **2328 WELLINGBOROUGH DIVISION**

2327 TOWCESTER LJA
CLOSED wef 31/3/11

2328 WELLINGBOROUGH LJA
see **LEICESTERSHIRE, RUTLAND, LINCOLNSHIRE, NORTHAMPTONSHIRE** ....p. 116

2335 BAMBURGH WARD DIVISION
combined with **2339 EAST COQUETDALE WARD DIVISION** *to form* **2345 BAMBURGH AND EAST COQUETDALE DIVISION**

2336 BELLINGHAM DIVISION
combined with **2341 HEXHAM DIVISION** *to form* **2346 TYNEDALE DIVISION**

2337 BERWICK-UPON-TWEED DIVISION
combined with **2340 GLENDALE WARD DIVISION** *to form* **2348 BERWICK-UPON-TWEED DIVISION**

2338 BLYTH VALLEY DIVISION
combined with 2342 MORPETH WARD DIVISION and 2343 WANSBECK DIVISION to form **2349 SOUTH EAST NORTHUMBERLAND DIVISION**

2339 EAST COQUETDALE WARD DIVISION
combined with 2335 BAMBURGH WARD DIVISION to form **2345 BAMBURGH AND EAST COQUETDALE DIVISION**

2340 GLENDALE WARD DIVISION
combined with 2337 BERWICK-UPON-TWEED DIVISION to form **2348 BERWICK-UPON-TWEED DIVISION**

2341 HEXHAM DIVISION
combined with 2336 BELLINGHAM DIVISION to form **2346 TYNEDALE DIVISION**

2342 MORPETH WARD DIVISION
combined with 2338 BLYTH VALLEY DIVISION and 2343 WANSBECK DIVISION to form **2349 SOUTH EAST NORTHUMBERLAND DIVISION**

2343 WANSBECK DIVISION
combined with 2338 BLYTH VALLEY DIVISION and 2342 MORPETH WARD DIVISION to form **2349 SOUTH EAST NORTHUMBERLAND DIVISION**

2344 WEST COQUETDALE WARD DIVISION
combined with 2345 BAMBURGH AND EAST COQUETDALE DIVISION to form **2347 COQUETDALE DIVISION**

2345 BAMBURGH AND EAST COQUETDALE DIVISION
combined with 2344 WEST COQUETDALE WARD DIVISION to form **2347 COQUETDALE DIVISION**

2346 TYNEDALE LJA
CLOSED wef 31/3/11

2347 ALNWICK LJA
CLOSED wef 31/3/11

2348 BERWICK-UPON-TWEED LJA
see **NORTHUMBRIA** ....p. 131

2349 SOUTH EAST NORTHUMBERLAND LJA
see **NORTHUMBRIA** ....p. 131

2353 SOUTH EAST YORKSHIRE LJA
see **HUMBER AND SOUTH YORKSHIRE** ....p. 126

2522 ALLERTONSHIRE DIVISION
combined with 2523 BIRDFORTH DIVISION, 2528 GILLING EAST DIVISION (part), 2529 HALLIKELD DIVISION, 2530 HANG EAST DIVISION (part) and 2539 STOKESLEY DIVISION to form **2543 NORTHALLERTON DIVISION**

2523 BIRDFORTH DIVISION
combined with 2522 ALLERTONSHIRE DIVISION, 2528 GILLING EAST DIVISION (part), 2529 HALLIKELD DIVISION, 2530 HANG EAST DIVISION (part) and 2539 STOKESLEY DIVISION to form **2543 NORTHALLERTON DIVISION**

2524 BUCKROSE DIVISION
combined with 2542 MALTON DIVISION

2525 BULMER EAST DIVISION
combined with 2526 BULMER WEST DIVISION to form **2544 EASINGWOLD DIVISION**

2526 BULMER WEST DIVISION
combined with 2525 BULMER EAST DIVISION to form **2544 EASINGWOLD DIVISION**

2527 CLARO DIVISION
abolished wef 1/1/97 and, after adjustment of boundaries with 2541 YORK division, reformed without change of Court Code Number.

2527 CLARO DIVISION
combined with 2534 RIPON LIBERTY DIVISION, 2534 NORTHALLERTON DIVISION (part) and 2537 SELBY DIVISION (Parish of Wighill only) to form **2527 HARROGATE DIVISION**

2527 HARROGATE AND SKIPTON LJA
see **NORTH AND WEST YORKSHIRE** ....p. 128

2528 GILLING EAST DIVISION
part combined with 2522 ALLERTONSHIRE DIVISION, 2523 BIRDFORTH DIVISION, 2529 HALLIKELD DIVISION, 2530 HANG EAST DIVISION (part) and 2539 STOKESLEY DIVISION to form **2543 NORTHALLERTON DIVISION**: *– part combined with 2530 HANG EAST DIVISION (part), 2531 HANG WEST DIVISION and 2533 RICHMOND AND GILLING WEST DIVISION to form* **2545 RICHMOND DIVISION**

2529 HALLIKELD DIVISION
combined with 2522 ALLERTONSHIRE DIVISION, 2523 BIRDFORTH DIVISION, 2528 GILLING EAST DIVISION (part), 2530 HANG EAST DIVISION (part) and 2539 STOKESLEY DIVISION to form **2543 NORTHALLERTON DIVISION**

2530 HANG EAST DIVISION
part combined with 2522 ALLERTONSHIRE DIVISION, 2523 BIRDFORTH DIVISION, 2528 GILLING EAST DIVISION (part), 2529 HALLIKELD DIVISION and 2539 STOKESLEY DIVISION to form **2543 NORTHALLERTON DIVISION**: *– part combined with 2528 GILLING EAST DIVISION (part), 2531 HANG WEST DIVISION and 2533 RICHMOND AND GILLING WEST DIVISION to form* **2545 RICHMOND DIVISION**

2531 HANG WEST DIVISION
combined with 2528 GILLING EAST DIVISION (part), 2530 HANG EAST DIVISION (part), and 2533 RICHMOND AND GILLING WEST DIVISION to form **2545 RICHMOND DIVISION**

2533 RICHMOND AND GILLING WEST DIVISION
combined with 2528 GILLING EAST DIVISION (part), 2530 HANG EAST DIVISION (part), and 2531 HANG WEST DIVISION to form **2545 RICHMOND DIVISION**

2534 RIPON LIBERTY DIVISION
combined with 2527 CLARO DIVISION, 2543 NORTHALLERTON DIVISION (part) and 2537 SELBY DIVISION (Parish of Wighill only) to form **2527 HARROGATE DIVISION**

2535 RYEDALE DIVISION
combined with 2542 MALTON DIVISION to form **2546 RYEDALE DIVISION**

2536 SCARBOROUGH DIVISION
combined with 2540 WHITBY STRAND DIVISION, 2546 RYEDALE DIVISION and 2543 NORTHALLERTON DIVISION (part) to form **2536 SCARBOROUGH DIVISION**

2536 SCARBOROUGH LJA
see **NORTH AND WEST YORKSHIRE** ....p. 128

2537 SELBY DIVISION
abolished wef 1/1/97 and, after adjustment of boundaries with 2541 YORK DIVISION, reformed without change of Court Code Number

2537 SELBY LJA
closed wef March 2013, see **2541 YORK AND SELBY LJA**

2538 SKIPTON LJA
see **2527 HARROGATE AND SKIPTON LJA**

2539 STOKESLEY DIVISION
combined with 2522 ALLERTONSHIRE DIVISION, 2523 BIRDFORTH DIVISION, 2528 GILLING EAST DIVISION (part), 2529 HALLIKELD DIVISION and 2530 HANG EAST DIVISION (part) to form **2543 NORTHALLERTON DIVISION**

2540 WHITBY STRAND DIVISION
combined with 2536 SCARBOROUGH DIVISION, 2546 RYEDALE DIVISION and 2543 NORTHALLERTON DIVISION (part) to form **2536 SCARBOROUGH DIVISION**

2541 YORK DIVISION
abolished wef 1/1/97 and, after adjustment of boundaries with 2527 CLARO DIVISION and 2537 SELBY DIVISION and absorbing part of 2544 EASINGWOLD DIVISION, reformed without change to Court Code Number

2541 YORK LJA
see **NORTH AND WEST YORKSHIRE** ....p. 128

2542 MALTON DIVISION
combined with 2535 RYEDALE DIVISION to form **2546 RYEDALE DIVISION**

2543 NORTHALLERTON DIVISION
abolished wef 1/1/97 and reformed to include part of 2544 EASINGWOLD DIVISION, without change of Court Code Number

2543 NORTHALLERTON DIVISION
part combined with 2527 CLARO DIVISION and 2534 RIPON DIVISION and 2537 SELBY DIVISION (part) to form **2527 HARROGATE DIVISION**: *– part combined with 2536 SCARBOROUGH DIVISION, 2540 WHITBY STRAND DIVISION AND 2546 RYESDALE DIVISION to form* **2536 SCARBOROUGH DIVISION**: *– remainder combined with 2545 RICHMOND DIVISION to form* **2543 NORTHALLERTON AND RICHMOND DIVISION.**

2543 NORTHALLERTON AND RICHMOND LJA
see **NORTH AND WEST YORKSHIRE** ....p. 128

2544 EASINGWOLD DIVISION
abolished wef 1/1/97 – part combined with 2543 NORTHALLERTON DIVISION, part with 2546 RYEDALE DIVISION and part with 2541 YORK DIVISION

2545 RICHMOND DIVISION
combined with 2543 NORTHALLERTON DIVISION (part) to form **2543 NORTHALLERTON AND RICHMOND DIVISION**

RYEDALE DIVISION
abolished wef 1/1/97 and reformed to include part of 2544 EASINGWOLD DIVISION, without change of Court Code Number

2546 RYEDALE DIVISION
combined with 2536 SCARBOROUGH DIVISION, 2540 WHITBY STRAND DIVISION and 2543 NORTHALLERTON DIVISION (part) to form **2536 SCARBOROUGH DIVISION**

2552 BINGHAM DIVISION
combined with 2557 NOTTINGHAM (CITY) DIVISION and 2558 NOTTINGHAM (COUNTY) DIVISION to form (after boundary adjustments) **2568 NOTTINGHAM DIVISION**

2553 EAST RETFORD PSA
combined with 2560 WORKSOP PSA to form **2569 WORKSOP AND RETFORD PSA**

2554 MANSFIELD (BOROUGH) DIVISION
combined with 2555 MANSFIELD (COUNTY) DIVISION to form **2566 MANSFIELD DIVISION**

2555 MANSFIELD (COUNTY) DIVISION
combined with 2554 MANSFIELD (BOROUGH) DIVISION to form **2566 MANSFIELD DIVISION**

2556 NEWARK DIVISION
combined with 2559 *SOUTHWELL DIVISION to form* **2567 NEWARK AND SOUTHWELL DIVISION**

2557 NOTTINGHAM (CITY) DIVISION
combined with 2552 *BINGHAM DIVISION and 2558 NOTTINGHAM (COUNTY) DIVISION to form*
(after boundary adjustments) **2568 NOTTINGHAM DIVISION**

2558 NOTTINGHAM (COUNTY) DIVISION
combined with 2552 *BINGHAM DIVISION and 2557 NOTTINGHAM (CITY) DIVISION to form (after*
boundary adjustments) **2568 NOTTINGHAM DIVISION**

2559 SOUTHWELL DIVISION
combined with 2556 *NEWARK DIVISION to form* **2567 NEWARK AND SOUTHWELL DIVISION**

2560 WORKSOP PSA
combined with 2553 *EAST RETFORD PSA to form* **2569 WORKSOP AND RETFORD PSA**

2566 MANSFIELD LJA
see **DERBYSHIRE AND NOTTINGHAMSHIRE** ....p. 114

2567 NEWARK AND SOUTHWELL LJA
CLOSED wef 30/9/11

2568 NOTTINGHAM LJA
see **DERBYSHIRE AND NOTTINGHAMSHIRE** ....p. 114

2569 WORKSOP AND RETFORD LJA
see **DERBYSHIRE AND NOTTINGHAMSHIRE** ....p. 115

2570 CENTRAL LONDON LJA (ADULT)
see **LONDON – CENTRAL AND SOUTH (CRIME)** ....p. 105

2571 NORTH WEST LONDON LJA (ADULT)
see **LONDON – NORTH AND WEST (CRIME)** ....p. 108

2572 NORTH LONDON LJA (ADULT)
see **LONDON – NORTH AND WEST (CRIME)** ....p. 108

2573 NORTH EAST LONDON LJA (ADULT)
see **LONDON – NORTH AND WEST (CRIME)** ....p. 108

2574 EAST LONDON LJA (ADULT)
see **LONDON – NORTH AND WEST (CRIME)** ....p. 108

2575 SOUTH EAST LONDON LJA (ADULT)
see **LONDON – CENTRAL AND SOUTH (CRIME)** ....p. 106

2576 SOUTH LONDON LJA (ADULT)
see **LONDON – CENTRAL AND SOUTH (CRIME)** ....p. 105

2577 SOUTH WEST LONDON LJA (ADULT)
see **LONDON – CENTRAL AND SOUTH (CRIME)** ....p. 106

2578 WEST LONDON LJA (ADULT)
see **LONDON – NORTH AND WEST (CRIME)** ....p. 108

2631 CITY OF LONDON MAGISTRATES' COURT
see **2570/6570 CENTRAL LONDON LJA**

2641 BOW STREET MAGISTRATES' COURT
CLOSED

2642 CLERKENWELL MAGISTRATES' COURT
CLOSED

2643 GREENWICH MAGISTRATES' COURT
see **2575/6575 SOUTH EAST LONDON LJA**

2643 WOOLWICH MAGISTRATES' COURT
CLOSED wef 1/7/11

2644 MARLBOROUGH STREET MAGISTRATES' COURT
CLOSED

2646 MARYLEBONE MAGISTRATES' COURT
CLOSED

2648 OLD STREET MAGISTRATES' COURT
CLOSED

2649 SOUTH WESTERN MAGISTRATES' COURT
see **2577/6577 SOUTH WEST LONDON LJA**

2650 THAMES MAGISTRATES' COURT
see **2574/6574 EAST LONDON LJA**

2651 TOWER BRIDGE MAGISTRATES' COURT
CLOSED wef 2013

2652 WEST LONDON M.C.
combined with 2657 WALTON STREET M.C. to form **2658 WEST LONDON M.C.**

2653 WOOLWICH MAGISTRATES' COURT
renumbered 2643 see **GREATER LONDON**

2655 WELLS STREET MAGISTRATES' COURT
CLOSED

2656 CAMBERWELL GREEN MAGISTRATES' COURT
see **2576/6576 SOUTH LONDON LJA**

2657 WALTON STREET M.C.
combined with 2652 WEST LONDON M.C. to form **2658 WEST LONDON M.C.**

2658 WEST LONDON MAGISTRATES' COURT
see **2578/6578 WEST LONDON LJA**

2660 HORSEFERRY ROAD MAGISTRATES' COURT
renamed **CITY OF WESTMINSTER MAGISTRATES COURT**

2660 CITY OF WESTMINSTER MAGISTRATES' COURT
see **2570/6570 CENTRAL LONDON LJA**

2663 HIGHBURY CORNER MAGISTRATES' COURT
see **2572/6572 NORTH LONDON LJA**

2665 METROPOLITAN POLICE
(Fixed Penalty)

2667 ABINGDON (BOROUGH) DIVISION
combined with 2668 ABINGDON (COUNTY) DIVISION to form **2681 ABINGDON DIVISION**

2668 ABINGDON (COUNTY) DIVISION
combined with 2667 ABINGDON (BOROUGH) DIVISION to form **2681 ABINGDON DIVISION**

2669 BAMPTON EAST DIVISION
combined with 2670 BAMPTON WEST DIVISION to form **2703 WITNEY DIVISION**

2670 BAMPTON WEST DIVISION
combined with 2669 BAMPTON EAST DIVISION to form **2703 WITNEY DIVISION**

2671 BICESTER DIVISION
subjected to boundary adjustment and renumbered **2776 BICESTER DIVISION**

2672 BULLINGDON DIVISION
combined with 2680 WATLINGTON DIVISION to form **2717 EAST OXFORDSHIRE DIVISION**

2673 CHIPPING NORTON DIVISION
combined with 2677 NORTH OXFORDSHIRE DIVISION to form **2702 NORTH OXFORDSHIRE AND CHIPPING NORTON DIVISION**

2674 FARINGDON DIVISION
combined with 2679 WANTAGE DIVISION to form **2682 WANTAGE AND FARINGDON DIVISION**

2675 HENLEY DIVISION
combined with 2717 EAST OXFORDSHIRE DIVISION to form **2719 THAME AND HENLEY DIVISION**

2676 MORETON AND WALLINGFORD DIVISION
combined with 2682 WANTAGE AND FARINGDON DIVISION to form **2718 DIDCOT AND WANTAGE DIVISION**

2677 NORTH OXFORDSHIRE DIVISION
combined with 2673 CHIPPING NORTON DIVISION to form **2702 NORTH OXFORDSHIRE AND CHIPPING NORTON DIVISION**

2678 OXFORD DIVISION
subjected to boundary adjustment and renumbered **2777 OXFORD DIVISION**

2679 WANTAGE DIVISION
combined with 2674 FARINGDON DIVISION to form **2682 WANTAGE AND FARINGDON DIVISION**

2680 WATLINGTON DIVISION
combined with 2672 BULLINGDON DIVISION to form **2717 EAST OXFORDSHIRE DIVISION**

2681 ABINGDON DIVISION
combined with 2718 DIDCOT AND WANTAGE DIVISION to form (after boundary adjustment) **2774 ABINGDON, DIDCOT AND WANTAGE DIVISION**

2682 WANTAGE AND FARINGDON DIVISION
combined with 2676 MORETON AND WALLINGFORD DIVISION to form **2718 DIDCOT AND WANTAGE DIVISION**

2701 WOODSTOCK DIVISION
abolished and absorbed into **2775 BANBURY DIVISION, 2776 BICESTER DIVISION and 2779 WITNEY DIVISION**

2702 NORTH OXFORDSHIRE AND CHIPPING NORTON DIVISION
abolished and absorbed into **2779 WITNEY DIVISION and 2775 BANBURY DIVISION**

2703 WITNEY DIVISION
subjected to boundary adjustment and renumbered **2779 WITNEY DIVISION**

2704 FROME DIVISION
combined with 2707 SHEPTON MALLET DIVISION and 2710 WELLS DIVISION to form **2715 MENDIP DIVISION**

2705 ILMINSTER DIVISION
combined with 2708 SOMERTON DIVISION, 2712 WINCANTON DIVISION and 2713 YEOVIL DIVISION to form **2714 SOUTH SOMERSET DIVISION**

2706 SEDGEMOOR LJA
CLOSED wef April 2012

2707 SHEPTON MALLET DIVISION
combined with 2704 FROME DIVISION and 2710 WELLS DIVISION to form **2715 MENDIP DIVISION**

2708 SOMERTON DIVISION
combined with 2705 ILMINSTER DIVISION, 2712 WINCANTON DIVISION and 2713 YEOVIL DIVISION to form **2714 SOUTH SOMERSET DIVISION**

2709 TAUNTON DEANE PSA
renamed **2709 TAUNTON DEANE AND WEST SOMERSET PSA**

2709 TAUNTON DEANE AND WEST SOMERSET LJA
see 1030 SOMERSET lja

2710 WELLS DIVISION
combined with 2704 FROME DIVISION and 2707 SHEPTON MALLET DIVISION to form **2713 MENDIP DIVISION**

2711 WEST SOMERSET PSA
absorbed into 2709 TAUNTON DEANE PSA and renamed **2709 TAUNTON DEANE AND WEST SOMERSET PSA**

2712 WINCANTON DIVISION
combined with 2705 ILMINSTER DIVISION, 2708 SOMERTON DIVISION and 2713 YEOVIL DIVISION to form **2714 SOUTH SOMERSET DIVISION**

2713 YEOVIL DIVISION
combined with 2705 ILMINSTER DIVISION, 2708 SOMERTON DIVISION and 2712 WINCANTON DIVISION to form **2714 SOUTH SOMERSET DIVISION**

2714 SOUTH SOMERSET LJA
combined with 2715 MENDIP LJA to form **2716 (now 1030) SOUTH SOMERSET AND MENDIP LJA**

2715 MENDIP LJA
combined with 2714 SOUTH SOMERSET LJA to form **2716 (now 1030) SOUTH SOMERSET AND MENDIP LJA**

2716 SOUTH SOMERSET AND MENDIP LJA
see **1030 SOMERSET LJA**

2717 EAST OXFORDSHIRE DIVISION
combined with 2675 HENLEY DIVISION to form **2719 THAME AND HENLEY DIVISION**

2718 DIDCOT AND WANTAGE DIVISION
combined with 2681 ABINGDON DIVISION to form (after boundary adjustment) **2774 ABINGDON, DIDCOT AND WANTAGE DIVISION**

2719 THAME AND HENLEY DIVISION
subjected to boundary adjustment and renumbered **2778 THAME AND HENLEY DIVISION**

2721 STRATFORD MAGISTRATES' COURT
see **2574/6574 EAST LONDON LJA**

2722 WEST HAM MAGISTRATES' COURT
CLOSED

2723 ACTON MAGISTRATES' COURT
CLOSED wef 4/2011

2725 BARNET MAGISTRATES' COURT
CLOSED

2726 BRENTFORD MAGISTRATES' COURT
renumbered 2769

2727 BROMLEY MAGISTRATES' COURT
see **2575/6575 SOUTH EAST LONDON LJA**

2728 BEXLEY MAGISTRATES' COURT
see **2575/6575 SOUTH EAST LONDON LJA**

2731 WALLINGTON MAGISTRATES' COURT
combined with 2756 SUTTON M.C. to form **2733 SUTTON MAGISTRATES' COURT**

2732 CROYDON MAGISTRATES' COURT
see **2576/6576 SOUTH LONDON LJA**

2733 SUTTON MAGISTRATES' COURT
CLOSED wef 6/2011

2734 EALING MAGISTRATES' COURT
see **2578/6578 WEST LONDON LJA**

2740 HAMPSTEAD MAGISTRATES' COURT
CLOSED

2741 HENDON MAGISTRATES' COURT
see **2571/6571 NORTH WEST LONDON LJA**

2742 HARINGEY MAGISTRATES' COURT
see **2572/6572 NORTH LONDON LJA**

2755 BEACONTREE MAGISTRATES' COURT
renamed and renumbered **2815 REDBRIDGE MAGISTRATES' COURT**

2756 SUTTON MAGISTRATES' COURT
combined with 2731 WALLINGTON M.C. to form **2733 SUTTON M.C.**

2757 ENFIELD MAGISTRATES' COURT
see **2572/6572 NORTH LONDON LJA**

2760 HARROW MAGISTRATES' COURT
CLOSED wef 6/2011

2762 BRENT MAGISTRATES' COURT
see **2578/6578 WEST LONDON LJA**

2763 WIMBLEDON MAGISTRATES' COURT
see **2577/6577 SOUTH WEST LONDON LJA**

2766 UXBRIDGE MAGISTRATES' COURT
see **2578/6578 WEST LONDON LJA**

2768 RICHMOND-UPON-THAMES MAGISTRATES' COURT
see **2577/6577 SOUTH WEST LONDON LJA**

2769 FELTHAM MAGISTRATES' COURT
see **2578/6578 WEST LONDON LJA**

2769 BRENTFORD MAGISTRATES' COURT
CLOSED wef 12/2011

2774 ABINGDON, DIDCOT AND WANTAGE DIVISION
renamed **2774 SOUTHERN OXFORDSHIRE DIVISION**

2774 SOUTHERN OXFORDSHIRE LJA
combined with 2777 OXFORD LJA and 2775 NORTHERN OXFORDSHIRE LJA to form **1922 OXFORDSHIRE LJA**

2775 NORTHERN OXFORDSHIRE LJA
combined with 2777 OXFORD LJA and 2774 SOUTHERN OXFORDSHIRE LJA to form **1922 OXFORDSHIRE LJA**

2776 BICESTER DIVISION
combined with 2775 BANBURY DIVISION and 2779 WITNEY DIVISION to form **2775 NORTHERN OXFORDSHIRE DIVISION**

2777 OXFORD DIVISION
combined with 2778 THAME AND HENLEY DIVISION to form **2777 OXFORD PSA**

2777 OXFORD LJA
combined with 2775 NORTHERN OXFORDSHIRE LJA and 2774 SOUTHERN OXFORDSHIRE LJA to form **1922 OXFORDSHIRE LJA**

2778 THAME AND HENLEY DIVISION
combined with 2777 OXFORD DIVISION to form **2777 OXFORD DIVISION**

2779 WITNEY DIVISION
combined with 2775 BANBURY DIVISION and 2776 BICESTER DIVISION to form **2775 NORTHERN OXFORDSHIRE DIVISION**

2780 BURTON-UPON-TRENT PSA
combined with 2860 LICHFIELD AND TAMWORTH PSA to form **2860 SOUTH EAST STAFFORDSHIRE PSA**

2781 CANNOCK DIVISION
combined with 2789 SEISDON DIVISION to form **2859 CANNOCK AND SEISDON DIVISION**

2782 CHEADLE DIVISION
combined with 2784 LEEK DIVISION to form **2796 STAFFORDSHIRE MOORLANDS DIVISION**

2783 ECCLESHALL DIVISION
combined with 2790 STAFFORD DIVISION, 2792 STONE DIVISION and 2794 UTTOXETER DIVISION to form **2795 MID-STAFFORDSHIRE DIVISION**

2784 LEEK DIVISION
combined with 2782 CHEADLE DIVISION to form **2796 STAFFORDSHIRE MOORLANDS DIVISION**

2785 LICHFIELD DIVISION
combined with 2793 TAMWORTH DIVISION to form **2860 LICHFIELD AND TAMWORTH DIVISION**

2786 NEWCASTLE-UNDER-LYME DIVISION
combined with 2787 PIREHILL NORTH DIVISION to form **2797 NEWCASTLE-UNDER-LYME AND PIREHILL NORTH DIVISION**

2787 PIREHILL NORTH DIVISION
combined with 2786 NEWCASTLE-UNDER-LYME DIVISION to form **2797 NEWCASTLE-UNDER-LYME AND PIREHILL NORTH DIVISION**

2788 RUGELEY DIVISION
combined with 2795 MID STAFFORDSHIRE DIVISION to form **2799 MID STAFFORDSHIRE AND RUGELEY DIVISION**

2789 SEISDON DIVISION
combined with 2781 CANNOCK DIVISION to form **2859 CANNOCK AND SEISDON DIVISION**

2790 STAFFORD DIVISION
combined with 2792 STONE DIVISION, 2783 ECCLESHALL DIVISION and 2794 UTTOXETER DIVISION to form **2795 MID-STAFFORDSHIRE DIVISION**

2791 STOKE-ON-TRENT PSA
combined with 2798 NORTH STAFFORDSHIRE PSA to form **2791 NORTH STAFFORDSHIRE PSA**

2791 NORTH STAFFORDSHIRE LJA
see **STAFFORDSHIRE AND WEST MERCIA** p. 119

2792 STONE DIVISION
combined with 2790 STAFFORD DIVISION, 2783 ECCLESHALL DIVISION and 2794 UTTOXETER DIVISION to form **2795 MID-STAFFORDSHIRE DIVISION**

2793 TAMWORTH DIVISION
combined with 2785 LICHFIELD DIVISION to form **2860 LICHFIELD AND TAMWORTH DIVISON**

2794 UTTOXETER DIVISION
combined with 2790 STAFFORD DIVISION, 2792 STONE DIVISION and 2793 ECCLESHALL DIVISION to form **2795 MID-STAFFORDSHIRE DIVISION**

2795 MID-STAFFORDSHIRE DIVISION
combined with 2788 RUGELEY DIVISION to form **2799 MID STAFFORDSHIRE AND RUGELEY DIVISION**

2796 STAFFORDSHIRE MOORLANDS DIVISION
combined with 2797 NEWCASTLE-UNDER-LYME AND PIREHILL NORTH DIVISION to form **2798 NORTH STAFFORDSHIRE DIVISION**

2797 NEWCASTLE-UNDER-LYME AND PIREHILL NORTH DIVISION
combined with 2796 STAFFORDSHIRE MOORLANDS DIVISION to form **2798 NORTH STAFFORDSHIRE DIVISION**

2798 NORTH STAFFORDSHIRE PSA
combined with 2791 STOKE-ON-TRENT PSA to form **2791 NORTH STAFFORDSHIRE PSA**

2799 MID STAFFORDSHIRE AND RUGELEY PSA
combined with 2859 CANNOCK AND SEISDON PSA to form **2799 CENTRAL AND SOUTH WEST STAFFORDSHIRE PSA**

2799 CENTRAL AND SOUTH WEST STAFFORDSHIRE LJA
see **STAFFORDSHIRE AND WEST MERCIA** p. 119

2812 KINGSTON-UPON-THAMES MAGISTRATES' COURT
CLOSED wef 6/2011

2813 WALTHAM FOREST MAGISTRATES' COURT
see **2574/6574 EAST LONDON LJA**

2814 BARKING MAGISTRATES' COURT
CLOSED wef 9/2011

2815 REDBRIDGE MAGISTRATES' COURT
see **2573/6573 NORTH EAST LONDON LJA**

2816 BECCLES DIVISION
combined with 2822 LOWESTOFT DIVISION and 2831 SAXMUNDHAM DIVISION to form **2863 NORTH EAST SUFFOLK DIVISION**

2817 BLYTHING DIVISION
combined with portions of 2819 HARTISMERE DIVISION to form **2831 SAXMUNDHAM DIVISION**

2818 FELIXSTOWE DIVISION
combined with 2829 WOODBRIDGE DIVISION to form **2861 DEBEN DIVISION**

2819 HARTISMERE DIVISION
abolished – part absorbed into **2831 SAXMUNDHAM DIVISION**, *part into* **2832 ST EDMUNDSBURY DIVISION** *and remainder into* **2833 STOW DIVISION**

2820 IPSWICH DIVISION
combined with 2824 ORWELL DIVISION to form **2830 IPSWICH DIVISION**

2821 LACKFORD DIVISION
renamed **MILDENHALL DIVISION** – *see below*

2821 MILDENHALL DIVISION
combined with 2923 NEWMARKET DIVISION to form **2862 NORTH WEST SUFFOLK DIVISION**

2822 LOWESTOFT DIVISION
combined with 2816 BECCLES DIVISION and 2831 SAXMUNDHAM DIVISION to form **2863 NORTH EAST SUFFOLK DIVISION**

2823 NEWMARKET DIVISION
combined with 2021 MILDENHALL DIVISION to for **2862 NORTH WEST SUFFOLK DIVISION**

2824 ORWELL DIVISION
combined with 2820 IPSWICH DIVISION to form **2830 IPSWICH DIVISION**

2825 HAVERHILL DIVISION (FORMERLY RISBRIDGE DIVISION)
combined with 2828 SUDBURY DIVISION to form **2864 HAVERHILL AND SUDBURY DIVISION**

2826 ST EDMUNDSBURY DIVISION
combined with portions of 2819 HARTISMERE DIVISION to form **2832 ST EDMUNDSBURY DIVISION**

2827 STOW DIVISION
combined with portions of 2819 HARTISMERE DIVISION to form **2833 STOW DIVISION (now renamed STOWMARKET DIVISION)**

2828 SUDBURY DIVISION (FORMERLY SUDBURY AND COSFORD DIVISION)
combined with 2825 HAVERHILL DIVISION to form **2864 HAVERHILL AND SUDBURY DIVISION**

2829 WOODBRIDGE DIVISION
combined with 2818 FELIXSTOWE DIVISION to form **2861 DEBEN DIVISION**

2830 IPSWICH PSA
combined with 2861 DEBEN PSA to form **2866 SOUTH EAST SUFFOLK PSA**

2831 SAXMUNDHAM DIVISION
combined with 2816 BECCLES DIVISION and 2822 LOWESTOFT DIVISION to form **2863 NORTH EAST SUFFOLK DIVISION**

2832 ST EDMUNDSBURY DIVISION
combined with 2833 STOWMARKET DIVISION to form **2865 ST EDMUNDSBURY AND STOWMARKET DIVISION**

2833 STOWMARKET DIVISION (FORMERLY STOW DIVISION)
combined with 2932 ST EDMUNDSBURY DIVISION to form **2865 ST EDMUNDSBURY AND STOWMARKET DIVISION**

2835 CHERTSEY DIVISION
combined with 2844 WOKING DIVISION (after boundary adjustment and including parts of 2838 ESHER AND WALTON DIVISION and 2839 FARNHAM DIVISION) to form **2846 NORTH WEST SURREY DIVISION**

2836 DORKING DIVISION
combined with 2840 GODSTONE DIVISION and 2842 REIGATE DIVISION to form **2847 SOUTH EAST SURREY DIVISION**

2837 EPSOM DIVISION
combined with 2843 STAINES AND SUNBURY DIVISION and part of 2838 EASHER AND WALTON DIVISION to form **2845 NORTH AND EAST SURREY DIVISION**

2838 ESHER AND WALTON DIVISION
now absorbed into 2845 NORTH AND EAST SURREY DIVISION and **2846 NORTH WEST SURREY DIVISION**

2839 FARNHAM DIVISION
now absorbed into 2846 NORTH WEST SURREY DIVISION and **2848 SOUTH WEST SURREY DIVISION**

2840 GODSTONE DIVISION
combined with 2836 DORKING DIVISION and 2842 REIGATE DIVISION to form **2847 SOUTH EAST SURREY DIVISION**

2841 GUILDFORD DIVISION
boundary adjusted to include part of 2844 WOKING DIVISION and part of 2839 FARNHAM DIVISION to form **2848 SOUTH WEST SURREY DIVISION**

2842 REIGATE DIVISION
combined with 2836 DORKING DIVISION and 2840 GODSTONE DIVISION to form **2847 SOUTH EAST SURREY DIVISION**

2843 STAINES AND SUNBURY DIVISION
combined with 2837 EPSOM DIVISION and part of 2838 ESHER AND WALTON DIVISION to form **2845 NORTH AND EAST SURREY DIVISION**

2844 WOKING DIVISION
(after boundary adjustment and including parts of 2838 ESHER AND WALTON DIVISION and 2839 FARNHAM DIVISION) combined with 2835 CHERTSEY DIVISION to form **2846 NORTH WEST SURREY DIVISION**

2845 NORTH AND EAST SURREY DIVISION
boundary adjusted to include part of 2846 NORTH WEST SURREY TO FORM **2849 NORTH SURREY PSA**

2846 NORTH WEST SURREY DIVISION
boundary adjusted following absorption by NORTH SURREY of part of 2846 North West Surrey to form **2857 NORTH WEST SURREY PSA**

2847 SOUTH EAST SURREY DIVISION
boundary adjusted to include part of 2845 NORTH AND EAST SURREY to form **2856 SOUTH EAST SURREY PSA**

2853 SOUTH TYNESIDE DISTRICT LJA
see **NORTHUMBRIA** ....p. 131

2854 HOUGHTON-LE-SPRING LJA
CLOSED wef 31/3/11

2855 SUNDERLAND LJA
see **NORTHUMBRIA** ....p. 131

2856 SOUTH EAST SURREY LJA
see **SURREY AND SUSSEX** ....p. 151

2857 NORTH WEST SURREY LJA
CLOSED wef 31/12/11

2859 CANNOCK AND SEISDON PSA
combined with 2799 MID STAFFORDSHIRE AND RUGELEY PSA to form **2799 CENTRAL AND
SOUTH WEST STAFFORDSHIRE PSA**

2860 LICHFIELD AND TAMWORTH PSA
combined with 2780 BURONT-UPON-TRENT PSA to form **2860 SOUTH EAST STAFFORDSHIRE
PSA**

2860 SOUTH EAST STAFFORDSHIRE LJA
see **STAFFORDSHIRE AND WEST MERCIA** ....p. 119

2861 DEBEN PSA
combined with 2830 IPSWICH PSA to form **2866 SOUTH EAST SUFFOLK PSA**

2862 NORTH WEST SUFFOLK PSA
*combined with 2864 HAVERHILL AND SUDBURY PSA and 2865 ST EDMUNDSBURY AND
STOWMARKET PSA to form* **2867 WEST SUFFOLK PSA**

2863 NORTH EAST SUFFOLK LJA
see **NORFOLK AND SUFFOLK** ....p. 149

2864 HAVERHILL AND SUDBURY PSA
*combined with 2862 NORTH WEST SUFFOLK PSA and 2865 ST EDMUNDSBURY AND
STOWMARKET PSA to form* **2867 WEST SUFFOLK PSA**

2865 ST EDMUNDSBURY AND STOWMARKET PSA
*combined with 2862 NORTH WEST SUFFOLK PSA and 2864 HAVERHILL AND SUDBURY PSA to
form* **2867 WEST SUFFOLK PSA**

2866 SOUTH EAST SUFFOLK LJA
see **NORFOLK AND SUFFOLK** ....p. 149

2867 WEST SUFFOLK LJA
see **NORFOLK AND SUFFOLK** ....p. 149

2893 ALCESTER DIVISION
*combined with 2895 KINETON DIVISION, 2898 SHIPSTON-ON-STOUR DIVISION and 2900
STRATFORD-UPON-AVON DIVISION to form* **2902 SOUTH WARWICKSHIRE DIVISION**

2894 ATHERSTONE AND COLESHILL PSA
*combined with 2896 NENEATON PSA, 2897 RUGBY PSA, 2902 SOUTH WARWICKSHIRE PSA and
2903 MID-WARWICKSHIRE PSA to form* **2904 WARWICKSHIRE PSA**

2895 KINETON DIVISION
*combined with 2893 ALCESTER DIVISION, 2898 SHIPSTON-ON-STOUR DIVISION and 2900
STRATFORD-UPON-AVON DIVISION to form* **2902 SOUTH WARWICKSHIRE DIVISION**

2896 NUNEATON PSA
*combined with 2894 ATHERSTONE AND COLESHILL PSA, 2897 RUGBY PSA, 2902 SOUTH
WARWICKSHIRE PSA and 2903 MID-WARWICKSHIRE PSA to form* **2904 WARWICKSHIRE PSA**

2897 RUGBY PSA
*combined with 2894 ATHERSTONE AND COLESHILL PSA, 2896 NUNEATON PSA, 2902 SOUTH
WARWICKSHIRE PSA and 2903 MID-WARWICKSHIRE PSA to form* **2904 WARWICKSHIRE PSA**

2898 SHIPSTON-ON-STOUR DIVISION
combined with 2893 ALCESTER DIVISION, 2895 KINETON DIVISION and 2900 STRATFORD-UPON-AVON DIVISION to form **2902 SOUTH WARWICKSHIRE DIVISION**

2899 SOUTHAM DIVISION
combined with 2901 WARWICK DIVISION to form **2903 MID-WARWICKSHIRE DIVISION**

2900 STRATFORD-UPON-AVON DIVISION
combined with 2893 ALCESTER DIVISION, 2895 KINETON DIVISION and 2898 SHIPSTON-ON-STOUR DIVISION to form **2902 SOUTH WARWICKSHIRE DIVISION**

2901 WARWICK DIVISION
combined with 2899 SOUTHAM DIVISION to form **2903 MID-WARWICKSHIRE DIVISION**

2902 SOUTH WARWICKSHIRE PSA
combined with 2894 ATHERSTONE AND COLESHILL PSA, 2896 NUNEATON PSA, 2897 RUGBY PSA and 2903 MID-WARWICKSHIRE PSA to form **2904 WARWICKSHIRE PSA**

2903 MID-WARWICKSHIRE PSA
combined with 2894 ATHERSTONE AND COLESHILL PSA, 2896 NUNEATON PSA, 2897 RUGBY PSA and 2902 SOUTH WARWICKSHIRE PSA to form **2904 WARWICKSHIRE PSA**

2904 WARWICKSHIRE LJA
see **WEST MIDLANDS AND WARWICKSHIRE** ....p. 121

2908 BIRMINGHAM LJA
see **WEST MIDLANDS AND WARWICKSHIRE** ....p. 121

2909 SUTTON COLDFIELD LJA
CLOSED wef 30/6/11

2910 COVENTRY DISTRICT LJA
see **WEST MIDLANDS AND WARWICKSHIRE** ....p. 121

2911 DUDLEY LJA
combined with 2912 STOURBRIDGE AND HALESOWEN LJA to form **2921 DUDLEY AND HALESOWEN LJA**

2912 HALESOWEN DIVISION
combined with 2913 STOURBRIDGE DIVISION to form **2912 STOURBRIDGE AND HALESOWEN DIVISION**

2912 STOURBRIDGE AND HALESOWEN LJA
combined with 2911 DUDLEY LJA to form **2921 DUDLEY AND HALESOWEN LJA**

2913 STOURBRIDGE DIVISION
combined with 2912 HALESOWEN DIVISION to form **2912 STOURBRIDGE AND HALESOWEN DIVISION**

2914 WARLEY LJA
combined with 2915 WEST BROMWICH LJA to form **2920 SANDWELL LJA**

2915 WEST BROMWICH LJA
combined with 2914 WARLEY LJA to form **2920 SANDWELL LJA**

2916 SOLIHULL LJA
see **WEST MIDLANDS AND WARWICKSHIRE** ....p. 121

2917 WALSALL AND ALDRIDGE LJA
see **WEST MIDLANDS AND WARWICKSHIRE** ....p. 121

2918 WALSALL LJA
combined with 2917 ALDRIDGE AND BROWNHILLS PSA to form **2917 WALSALL AND ALDRIDGE LJA**

2919 WOLVERHAMPTON LJA
see **WEST MIDLANDS AND WARWICKSHIRE** ....p. 121

2920 SANDWELL LJA
see **WEST MIDLANDS AND WARWICKSHIRE** ....p. 121

2921 DUDLEY AND HALESOWEN LJA
see **WEST MIDLANDS AND WARWICKSHIRE** ....p. 121

2927   ARUNDEL PSA
combined with 2937 WORTHING AND DISTRICT PSA and 2936 CHICHESTER AND DISTRICT PSA
to form **2949 SUSSEX (WESTERN) PSA**

2928   CHICHESTER DIVISION
combined with 2931 MIDHURST DIVISION and 2933 PETWORTH DIVISION to form **2936 CHICHESTER AND DISTRICT DIVISION**

2929   CRAWLEY PSA
combined with 2930 HORSHAM PSA and 2932 MID-SUSSEX PSA to form **2947 SUSSEX (NORTHERN) PSA**

2930   HORSHAM PSA
combined with 2929 CRAWLEY PSA and 2932 MID-SUSSEX PSA to form **2947 SUSSEX (NORTHERN) PSA**

2931   MIDHURST DIVISION
combined with 2928 CRAWLEY PSA and 2930 HORSHAM DIVISION to form **2947 SUSSEX (NORTHERN) PSA**

2932   MID-SUSSEX PSA
combined with 2929 CRAWLEY PSA and 2930 HORSHAM DIVISION to form **2947 SUSSEX (NORTHERN) PSA**

2933   PETWORTH DIVISION
combined with 2928 CHICHESTER DIVISION and 2931 MIDHURST DIVISION to form **2936 CHICHESTER AND DISTRICT DIVISION**

2934   STEYNING DIVISION
abolished w.e.f. 1 April 1996 and absorbed into **2930 HORSHAM DIVISION and 2937 WORTHING AND DISTRICT DIVISION**

2935   WORTHING DIVISION
abolished w.e.f. 1 April 1996 and after adjustment of boundaries reconstituted as **2937 WORTHING AND DISTRICT DIVISION**

2936   CHICHESTER AND DISTRICT PSA
combined with 2927 ARUNDEL PSA and 2937 WORTHING AND DISTRICT PSA to form **2949 SUSSEX (WESTERN) PSA**

2937   WORTHING AND DISTRICT PSA
combined with 2927 ARUNDEL PSA and 2936 CHICHESTER AND DISTRICT PSA to form **2949 SUSSEX (WESTERN) PSA**

2947   SUSSEX (NORTHERN) LJA
see **SURREY AND SUSSEX** ....p. 151

2948   SUSSEX (EASTERN) LJA
see **SURREY AND SUSSEX** ....p. 151

2949   SUSSEX (WESTERN) LJA
see **SURREY AND SUSSEX** ....p. 151

2950   SUSSEX (CENTRAL) LJA
see **SURREY AND SUSSEX** ....p. 151

2978   BRADFORD AND KEIGHLEY LJA
see **NORTH AND WEST YORKSHIRE** ....p. 128

2979   KEIGHLEY LJA
CLOSED wef 4/12

2980   BRIGHOUSE DIVISION
combined with 2984 CALDER DIVISION and 2983 TODMORDEN DIVISION to form **2997 CALDERDALE DIVISION**

2981   CALDER DIVISION
combined with 2982 HALIFAX DIVISION to form **2984 CALDERDALE DIVISION**

2982   HALIFAX DIVISION
combined with 2981 CALDER DIVISION to form **2984 CALDER DIVISION**

2983 TODMORDEN DIVISION
combined with 2980 BRIGHOUSE DIVISION and 2984 CALDER DIVISION to form **2997 CALDERDALE DIVISION**

2984 CALDER DIVISION
combined with 2980 BRIGHOUSE DIVISION and 2983 TODMORDEN DIVISION to form **2997 CALDERDALE DIVISION**

2985 BATLEY DIVISION
combined with 2986 DEWSBURY DIVISION to form **2996 BATLEY AND DEWSBURY DIVISION**

2986 DEWSBURY DIVISION
combined with 2985 BATLEY DIVISION to form **2996 BATLEY AND DEWSBURY DIVISION**

2987 KIRKLEES LJA
see **NORTH AND WEST YORKSHIRE** ....p. 128

2988 LEEDS PSA
combined with 2989 MORLEY PSA, 2990 PUDSEY AND OTLEY PSA and 2991 SKYRACK AND WETHERBY PSA to form **2992 LEEDS DISTRICT PSA**

2989 MORLEY PSA
combined with 2988 LEEDS PSA, 2990 PUDSEY AND OTLEY PSA, and 2991 SKYRACK AND WETHERBY PSA to form **2992 LEEDS DISTRICT PSA**

2990 PUDSEY AND OTLEY PSA
combined with 2988 LEEDS PSA, 2989 MORLEY PSA and 2991 SKYRACK AND WETHERBY PSA to form **2992 LEEDS DISTRICT PSA**

2991 SKYRACK AND WETHERBY PSA
combined with 2988 LEEDS PSA, 2989 MORLEY PSA, 2990 PUDSEY AND OTLEY PSA to form **2992 LEEDS DISTRICT PSA**

2992 LEEDS DISTRICT LJA
see **NORTH AND WEST YORKSHIRE** ....p. 128

2994 PONTEFRACT LJA
closed wef March 2013, see **2995 WAKEFIELD AND PONTEFRACT LJA** ....p. 129

2995 WAKEFIELD AND PONTEFRACT LJA
see **NORTH AND WEST YORKSHIRE** ....p. 128

2996 BATLEY AND DEWSBURY LJA
CLOSED wef 4/12

2997 CALDERDALE LJA
see **NORTH AND WEST YORKSHIRE** p. 128

3005 BRADFORD-ON-AVON DIVISION
combined with 3013 MELKSHAM DIVISION, 3017 TROWBRIDGE DIVISION, 3018 WARMINSTER DIVISION (most), 3019 WESTBURY DIVISION and 3020 WHORWELLSDOWN DIVISION to form **3024 WEST WILTSHIRE DIVISION**

3006 CALNE DIVISION
combined with 3007 CHIPPENHAM DIVISION, 3008 CRICKLADE DIVISION and 3011 MALMESBURY DIVISION to form **3022 NORTH WILTSHIRE DIVISION**

3007 CHIPPENHAM DIVISION
combined with 3006 CALNE DIVISION, 3008 CRICKLADE DIVISION and 3011 MALMESBURY DIVISION to form **3022 NORTH WILTSHIRE DIVISION**

3008 CRICKLADE DIVISION
combined with 3006 CALNE DIVISION, 3007 CHIPPENHAM DIVISION and 3011 MALMESBURY DIVISION to form **3022 NORTH WILTSHIRE DIVISION**

3009 DEVIZES DIVISION
(most) combined with 3010 EVERLEY AND PEWSEY DIVISION (most) and 3011 MARLBOROUGH DIVISION to form **3025 KENNET DIVISION**

3010 EVERLEY AND PEWSEY DIVISION
(most) combined with 3009 DEVIZES DIVISION (most) and 3011 MARLBOROUGH DIVISION to form **3025 KENNET DIVISION**

3011 MALMESBURY DIVISION
combined with 3006 CALNE DIVISION, 3007 CHIPPENHAM DIVISION and 3008 CRICKLADE DIVISION to form **3022 WILTSHIRE DIVISION**

3012 MARLBOROUGH DIVISION
combined with 3009 DEVIZES DIVISION (most) and 3010 EVERLEY AND PEWSEY DIVISION (most) to form **3025 KENNET DIVISION**

3013 MELKSHAM DIVISION
combined with 3005 BRADFORD-ON-AVON DIVISION, 3017 TROWBRIDGE DIVISION, 3016 WARMINSTER DIVISION (most), 3019 WESTBURY DIVISION and 3020 WHORWELLSDOWN DIVISION to form **3024 WEST WILTSHIRE DIVISION**

3014 SALISBURY DIVISION
combined with 3018 TISBURY AND MERE DIVISION and parts of 3009 DEVIZES DIVISION, 3010 EVERLEY AND PEWSEY DIVISION and 3018 WARMINSTER DIVISION to form **3023 SALISBURY DIVISION**

3015 SWINDON LJA

3016 TISBURY AND MERE DIVISION
combined with 3014 SALISBURY DIVISION and parts of 3009 DEVIZES DIVISION, 3010 EVERLEY AND PEWSEY DIVISION and 3018 WARMINSTER DIVISION to form **3023 SALISBURY DIVISION**

3017 TROWBRIDGE DIVISION
combined with 3005 BRADFORD-ON-AVON DIVISION, 3013 MELKSHAM DIVISION, 3018 WARMINSTER DIVISION (most), 3019 WESTBURY DIVISION and 3020 WHORWELLSDOWN DIVISION to form **3024 WEST WILTSHIRE DIVISION**

3018 WARMINSTER DIVISION
most) combined with 3005 BRADFORD-ON-AVON DIVISION, 3013 MELKSHAM DIVISION, 3017 TROWBRIDGE DIVISION, 3019 WESTBURY DIVISION and 3020 WHORWELLSDOWN DIVISION to form 3024 WEST WILTSHIRE DIVISION

3019 WESTBURY DIVISION
combined with 3005 BRADFORD-ON-AVON DIVISION, 3013 MELKSHAM DIVISION, 3017 TROWBRIDGE DIVISION, 3018 WARMINSTER DIVISION (most) and 3020 WHORWELLSDOWN DIVISION to form **3024 WEST WILTSHIRE DIVISION**

3020 WHORWELLSDOWN DIVISION
combined with 3005 BRADFORD-ON-AVON DIVISION, 3013 MELKSHAM DIVISION, 3017 TROWBRIDGE DIVISION 3018 WARMINSTER DIVISION (most) and 3019 WESTBURY DIVISION to form **3024 WEST WILTSHIRE DIVISION**

3021 WILTSHIRE LJA

3022 NORTH WILTSHIRE DIVISION
combined with 3024 WEST WILTSHIRE DIVISION to form **3026 NORTH WEST WILTSHIRE DIVISION**

3023 SALISBURY DIVISION
combined with 3025 KENNET DIVISION to form **3027 SOUTH EAST WILTSHIRE DIVISION**

3024 WEST WILTSHIRE DIVISION
combined with 3022 NORTH WILTSHIRE DIVISION to form **3026 NORTH WEST WILTSHIRE DIVISION**

3025 KENNET DIVISION
combined with 3023 SALISBURY DIVISION to form **3027 SOUTH EAST WILTSHIRE DIVISION**

3026 NORTH WEST WILTSHIRE LJA

3027 SOUTH EAST WILTSHIRE LJA

3273 TELFORD AND SOUTH SHROPSHIRE LJA

6656 GREENWICH, LEWISHAM & SOUTHWARK YOUTH COURTS
see **6576 SOUTH LONDON LJA** ....p. 105

6700 INNER LONDON FAMILY PROCEEDINGS COURT
see **LONDON – FAMILY** ....p. 112

7021 WILTSHIRE LJA (YOUTH COURT)
see **HAMPSHIRE, ISLE OF WIGHT AND WILTSHIRE** ....p. 159

TBC   GREATER MANCHESTER PUBLIC LAW FAMILY PROCEEDINGS COURTS AND
  MANCHESTER CITY LJA PRIVATE LAW FAMILY PROCEEDINGS COURTS
see **GREATER MANCHESTER** ....p. 140

TBC   NORTH CAMBRIDGESHIRE LJA
see **CAMBRIDGESHIRE AND ESSEX** ....p. 145

TBC   SOUTH CAMBRIDGESHIRE LJA
see **CAMBRIDGESHIRE AND ESSEX** ....p. 145

WALES

3051 BERWYN DIVISION
abolished – functions transferred to 3052 COLWYN DIVISION, 3061 DENBIGHSHIRE DIVISION or
3058 WREXHAM MAELOR DIVISION

3052 COLWYN PSA
combined with 3237 ABERCONWY PSA to form **3062 CONWY PSA**

3053 DYFFRYN CLWYD DIVISION
part transferred to 3052 COLWYN DIVISION, remainder combined with 3057 RHUDDLAN DIVISION,
3051 BERWYN DIVISION (Part) and 3052 COLWYN DIVISION (Part) to form **3061 DENBIGHSHIRE**
DIVISION

3054 FLINT DIVISION
combined with 3055 HAWARDEN DIVISION, and 3056 MOLD DIVISION to form (after boundary
adjustment) **3059 FLINTSHIRE DIVISION**

3055 HAWARDEN DIVISION
combined with 3054 FLINT DIVISION and 3056 MOLD DIVISION to form (after boundary adjustment)
3059 FLINTSHIRE DIVISION

3056 MOLD DIVISION
combined with 3054 FLINT DIVISION, and 3055 HAWARDEN DIVISION to form (after boundary
adjustment) **3059 FLINTSHIRE DIVISION**

3057 RHUDDLAN DIVISION
combined with 3053 DYFFRYN CLWYD DIVISION (Part), 3051 BERWYN DIVISION (Part) and 3052
COLWYN DIVISION (Part) to form **3061 DENBIGHSHIRE DIVISION**

3058 WREXHAM MAELOR LJA
see **NORTH WALES** ....p. 164

3059 FLINTSHIRE LJA
see **NORTH WALES** ....p. 164

3060 ARFON PSA
combined with 3236 DWYFOR PSA and 3239 MEIRIONNYDD PSA to form **3244 GWYNEDD PSA**

3061 DENBIGHSHIRE LJA
see **NORTH WALES** p.164

3062 CONWY LJA
see **NORTH WALES** ....p. 164

3109 ABERAERON DIVISION
combined with 3118 LAMPETER DIVISION and 3121 LLANDYSSUL DIVISION to form **3134**
CEREDIGION GANOL DIVISION

3110 ABERYSTWYTH DIVISION
combined with 3131 TREGARON DIVISION to form **3135 GOGLEDD CEREDIGION DIVISION**

3111 AMMAN VALLEY DIVISION
combined with 3119 LLANDEILO DIVISION and 3120 LLANDOVERY DIVISION (part) to form **3140 DINEFWR DIVISION**

3112 CARDIGAN DIVISION
combined with 3128 RHYDLEWIS DIVISION to form **3136 DE CEREDIGION DIVISION**

3113 CARMARTHEN DIVISION
combined with 3129 ST CLEARS DIVISION and 3132 WHITLAND DIVISION to form **3138 CARMARTHEN SOUTH DIVISION**

3114 CEMAES DIVISION
combined with 3116 FISHGUARD DIVISION to form **3141 GOGLEDD PRESELI DIVISION**

3115 DEWSLAND DIVISION
combined with 3117 HAVERFORDWEST DIVISION to form **3133 DEWSLAND-HAVERFORDWEST DIVISION**

3116 FISHGUARD DIVISION
combined with 3114 CEMAES DIVISION to form **3141 GOGLEDD PRESELI DIVISION**

3117 HAVERFORDWEST DIVISION
combined with 3115 DEWSLAND DIVISION to form **3133 DEWSLAND-HAVERFORDWEST DIVISION**

3118 LAMPETER DIVISION
combined with 3109 ABERAERON DIVISION and 3121 LLANDYSSUL DIVISION to form **3134 CEREDIGION GANOL DIVISION**

3119 LLANDEILO DIVISION
combined with 3111 AMMAN VALLEY DIVISION and 3120 LLANDOVERY DIVISION (part) to form **3140 DINEFWR DIVISION**

3120 LLANDOVERY DIVISION
part combined with 3111 AMMAN VALLEY DIVISION and 3119 LLANDEILO DIVISION to form 3140 DINEFWR DIVISION and part combined with 3125 NEWCASTLE EMLYN DIVISION and PENCADER DIVISION to form **3137 CARMARTHEN NORTH DIVISION**

3121 LLANDYSSUL DIVISION
combined with 3109 ABERAERON DIVISION and 3118 LAMPETER DIVISION to form **3134 CEREDIGION DIVISION**

3122 LLANELLI LJA
combined with CARMARTHEN AND DINEFWR to form **3252 CARMARTHENSHIRE LJA**

3123 MILFORD HAVEN DIVISION
combined with 3133 DEWSLAND-HAVERFORDWEST DIVISION to form **3139 CLEDDAU DIVISION**

3124 NARBERTH DIVISION
combined with 3126 PEMBROKE DIVISION and 3130 TENBY DIVISION to form **3142 SOUTH PEMBROKESHIRE DIVISION**

3125 NEWCASTLE EMLYN DIVISION
combined with 3120 LLANDOVERY DIVISION (part) and 3127 PENCADER DIVISION to form **3137 CARMARTHEN NORTH DIVISION**

3126 PEMBROKE DIVISION
combined with 3124 NARBERTH DIVISION and 3130 TENBY DIVISION to form **3142 SOUTH PEMBROKESHIRE DIVISION**

3127 PENCADER DIVISION
combined with 3120 LLANDOVERY DIVISION (part) and 3125 NEWCASTLE EMLYN DIVISION to form **3137 CARMARTHEN NORTH DIVISION**

3128 RHYDLEWIS DIVISION
combined with 3112 CARDIGAN DIVISION to form **3136 DE CEREDIGION DIVISION**

3129 ST CLEARS DIVISION
combined with 3113 CARMARTHEN DIVISION and 3132 WHITLAND DIVISION to form **3138 CARMARTHEN SOUTH DIVISION**

3130 TENBY DIVISION
combined with 3124 NARBERTH DIVISION and 3126 PEMBROKE DIVISION to form **3142 PEMBROKESHIRE DIVISION**

3131 TREGARON DIVISION
combined with 3110 ABERYSTWYTH DIVISION to form **3135 GOGLEDD CEREDIGION DIVISION**

3132 WHITLAND DIVISION
combined with 3113 CARMARTHEN DIVISION and 3129 ST CLEARS DIVISION to form **3138 CARMARTHEN SOUTH DIVISION**

3133 DEWSLAND-HAVERFORDWEST DIVISION
combined with 3123 MILFORD HAVEN DIVISION to form **3139 CLEDDAU DIVISION**

3134 CEREDIGION GANOL DIVISION
combined with 3135 GOGLEDD CEREDIGION DIVISION and 3136 DE CEREDIGION DIVISION to form **3135 CEREDIGION DIVISION**

3135 GOGLEDD CEREDIGION DIVISION
combined with 3134 CEREDIGION GANOL DIVISION and 3136 DE CEREDIGION DIVISION to form **3135 CEREDIGION DIVISION**

3135 CEREDIGION LJA
combined with 3356 PEMBROKESHIRE LJA to form **3253 CEREDIGION AND PEMBROKESHIRE LJA**

3136 DE CEREDIGION DIVISION
combined with 3134 CEREDIGION GANOL DIVISION and 3135 GOGLEDD CEREDIGION DIVISION to form **3135 CEREDIGION DIVISION**

3137 CARMARTHEN NORTH DIVISION
combined with 3138 CARMARTHEN SOUTH DIVISION to form **3138 CARMARTHEN DIVISION**

3138 CARMARTHEN SOUTH DIVISION
combined with 3137 CARMARTHEN NORTH DIVISION to form **3138 CARMARTHEN DIVISION**

3138 CARMARTHEN LJA
combined with 3140 DINEFWR and LLANELLI to form **3252 CARMARTHENSHIRE LJA**

3139 CLEDDAU DIVISION
combined with 3141 GOGLEDD PRESELI DIVISION to form **3139 NORTH PEMBROKESHIRE DIVISION**

3139 NORTH PEMBROKESHIRE LJA
Combined with 3142 SOUTH PEMBROKESHIRE to form **3356 PEMBROKESHIRE LJA**

3140 DINEFWR LJA
combined with 3138 CARMARTHEN and 3122 LLANELLI to form **3252 CARMARTHENSHIRE LJA**

3141 GOGLEDD PRESELI DIVISION
combined with 3139 CLEDDAU DIVISION to form **3139 NORTH PEMBROKESHIRE DIVISION**

3142 SOUTH PEMBROKESHIRE LJA
combined with 3139 NORTH PEMBROKESHIRE to form **3356 PEMBROKESHIRE LJA**

3200 ABERGAVENNY DIVISION
combined with 3202 CWMBRAN DIVISION, 3203 CHEPSTOW DIVISION, 3204 MONMOUTH DIVISION, 3206 PONTYPOOL DIVISION and 3207 USK DIVISION to form **3208 EAST GWENT DIVISION**

3201 BEDWELLTY PSA (EXCEPT LLANELLY HILL)
combined with 3263 LOWER RHYMNEY VALLEY PSA and 3267 UPPER RHYMNEY VALLEY PSA to form **3209 NORTH WEST GWENT PSA**

3202 CWMBRAN DIVISION
combined with 3200 ABERGAVENNY DIVISION, 3203 CHEPSTOW DIVISION, 3204 MONMOUTH DIVISION, 3206 PONTYPOOL DIVISION and 3207 USK DIVISION to form **3208 EAST GWENT DIVISION**

3203 CHEPSTOW DIVISION
combined with 3200 ABERGAVENNY DIVISION, 3202 CWMBRAN DIVISION, 3204 MONMOUTH DIVISION, 3206 PONTYPOOL DIVISION and 3207 USK DIVISION to form **3208 EAST GWENT DIVISION**

3204 MONMOUTH DIVISION
combined with 3200 ABERGAVENNY DIVISION, 3202 CWMBRAN DIVISION, 3203 CHEPSTOW DIVISION, 3206 PONTYPOOL DIVISION and 3207 USK DIVISION to form **3208 EAST GWENT DIVISION**

3205 NEWPORT PSA
combined with 3208 EAST GWENT PSA (including Llanelly Hill) to form **3210 SOUTH EAST GWENT PSA**

3206 PONTYPOOL DIVISION
combined with 3200 ABERGAVENNY DIVISION, 3202 CWMBRAN DIVISION, 3203 CHEPSTOW DIVISION, 3204 MONMOUTH DIVISION and 3207 USK DIVISION to form **3208 EAST GWENT DIVISION**

3207 USK DIVISION
combined with 3200 ABERGAVENNY DIVISION, 3202 CWMBRAN DIVISION, 3203 CHEPSTOW DIVISION, 3204 MONMOUTH DIVISION AND 3206 PONTYPOOL DIVISION to form **3208 EAST GWENT DIVISION**

3208 EAST GWENT PSA (INCLUDING LLANELLY HILL)
combined with 3205 NEWPORT PSA to form **3210 SOUTH EAST GWENT PSA**

3209 NORTH WEST GWENT
combined with 3210 SOUTH EAST GWENT to form **3211 GWENT LJA**

3210 SOUTH EAST GWENT
combined with 3209 NORTH WEST GWENT to form **3211 GWENT LJA**

3211 GWENT LJA
see **SOUTH EAST WALES** ....p. 166

3220 ARDUDWY-IS-ARTRO DIVISION
combined with 3226 ESTIMANER DIVISION, 3230 PENLLYN DIVISION and 3233 TALYBONT DIVISION to form **3235 SOUTH MEIRIONNYDD DIVISION**

3221 NORTH MEIRIONNYDD DIVISION (FORMERLY ARDUDWY-UWCH-ARTRO DIVISION)
combined with 3235 SOUTH MEIRIONNYDD DIVISION to form **3239 MEIRIONNYDD DIVISION**

3222 BANGOR DIVISION
combined with 3234 CAERNARFON DIVISION to form (after boundary adjustment) **3060 ARDON DIVISION**

3223 CAERNARVON DIVISION
combined with 3227 GWYRFAI DIVISION to form **3234 CAERNARFON AND GWYRFAI DIVISION**

3224 CONWY AND LLANDUDNO DIVISION
combined with 3228 NANT CONWY DIVISION to form **3237 ABERCONWY DIVISION**

3225 EIFIONYDD DIVISION
combined with 3231 PWLLHELI DIVISION to form **3236 EIFIONYDD AND PWLLHELI DIVISION**

3226 ESTIMANER DIVISION
combined with 3220 ARDUDWY-IS-ARTRO DIVISION, 3230 PENLLYN DIVISION and 3233 TALYBONT DIVISION to form **3235 SOUTH MEIRIONNYDD DIVISION**

3227 GWYRFAI DIVISION
combined with 3223 CAERNARVON DIVISION to form **3234 CAERNARFON AND GWYRFAI DIVISION**

3228 NANT CONWY DIVISION
combined with 3224 CONWY AND LLANDUDNO DIVISION to form **3237 ABERCONWY DIVISION**

3229 NORTH ANGLESEY DIVISION
combined with 3232 SOUTH ANGLESEY DIVISION to form **3238 YNYS MON/ANGLESEY DIVISION**

3230 PENLLYN DIVISION
combined with 3220 ARDUDWY-IS-ARTRO DIVISION, 3226 ESTIMANER DIVISION and 3233 TALYBONT DIVISION to form **3235 SOUTH MEIRIONNYDD DIVISION**

3231 PWLLHELI DIVISION
combined with 3225 EIFIONYDD DIVISION to form **3236 EIFIONYDD AND PWLLHELI DIVISION**

3232 SOUTH ANGLESEY DIVISION
combined with 3229 NORTH ANGLESEY DIVISION to form **3238 YNYS MON/ANGLESEY DIVISION**

3233 TALYBONT DIVISION
combined with 3220 ARDUDWY-IS-ARTRO DIVISION, 3226 ESTIMANER DIVISION and 3230 PENLLYN DIVISION to form **3235 SOUTH MEIRIONNYDD DIVISION**

3234 CAERNARFON AND GWYRFAI DIVISION
combined with 3222 BANGOR DIVISION to form (after boundary adjustment) **3060 ARFON DIVISION**

3235 SOUTH MEIRIONNYDD DIVISION
combined with 3221 NORTH MEIRIONNYDD DIVISION to form **3239 MEIRIONNYDD DIVISION**

3236 EIFIONYDD AND PWLLHELI DIVISION
renamed **DWYFOR DIVISION**

3236 DWYFOR PSA
combined with 3060 ARFON PSA and 3239 MEIRIONNYDD PSA to form **3244 GWYNEDD PSA**

3237 ABERCONWY PSA
combined with 3052 COLWYN PSA to form **3062 CONWY PSA**

3238 YNYS MON/ANGLESEY LJA
see **NORTH WALES** ....p. 164

3239 MEIRIONNYD PSA
combined with 3060 ARFON PSA and 3236 DWYFOR PSA to form **3244 GWYNEDD PSA**

3244 GWYNEDD LJA
see **NORTH WALES** ....p. 164

3250 BRECKNOCK AND RADNORSHIRE LJA
see **MID AND WEST WALES** ....p. 161

3251 CARDIFF AND THE VALE OF GLAMORGAN LJA
see **SOUTH EAST WALES** ....p. 166

3252 CARMARTHENSHIRE LJA
see **MID AND WEST WALES** ....p. 161

3253 CEREDIGION AND PEMBROKESHIRE LJA
see **MID AND WEST WALES** ....p. 161

3262 CYNON VALLEY LJA
combined with 3264 MERTHYR TYDFIL LJA and 3265 MISKIN LJA to form **GLAMORGAN VALLEYS LJA**

3263 LOWER RHYMNEY VALLEY PSA
combined with 3267 UPPER RHYMNEY VALLEY PSA and 3201 BEDWELLTY PSA (except Llanelly Hill) to form **3209 NORTH WEST GWENT PSA**

3264 MERTHYR TYDFIL LJA
combined with 3262 CYNON VALLEY LJA and 3265 MISKIN LJA to form **GLAMORGAN VALLEYS LJA**

3265 MISKIN LJA
combined with 3262 CYNON VALLEY LJA and 3264 MERTHYR TYDFIL LJA to form **GLAMORGAN VALLEYS LJA**

3266 NEWCASTLE AND OGMORE LJA
see **SOUTH EAST WALES** ....p. 166

3267 UPPER RHYMNEY VALLEY PSA
combined with 3263 LOWER RHYMNEY VALLEY PSA AND 3201 BEDWELLTY PSA (except Llanelly Hill) to form **3209 NORTH WEST GWENT PSA**

3270 GLAMORGAN VALLEYS LJA
see **SOUTH EAST WALES** ....p. 166

3320 BRECON DIVISION
combined with 3324 DEFYNOCK DIVISION to form **3342 BRECON DIVISION**

3321 BUILTH DIVISION
combined with 3322 COLWYN DIVISION and 3335 PAINSCASTLE DIVISION to form **3345 BUILTH DIVISION**

3322 COLWYN DIVISION
combined with 3321 BUILTH DIVISION and 3335 PAINSCASTLE DIVISION to form **3345 BUILTH DIVISION**

3323 CRICKHOWELL DIVISION
combined with 3342 BRECON DIVISION (except for Ystradfellte) and 3338 TALGARTH DIVISION to form **3350 BRECON DIVISION**

3324 DEFYNOCK DIVISION
combined with 3320 BRECON DIVISION to form **3342 BRECON DIVISION**

3325 DEYTHEUR DIVISION
combined with 3328 LLANFYLLIN DIVISION and 3339 WELSHPOOL DIVISION to form **3341 WELSHPOOL DIVISION**

3326 KNIGHTON DIVISION
combined with 3343 EAST RADNOR DIVISION to form **3344 EAST RADNOR DIVISION**

3327 LLANDRINDOD WELLS DIVISION
combined with 3345 BUILTH DIVISION, 3344 EAST RADNOR DIVISION and 3337 RHAYADER DIVISION to form **3351 LLANDRINDOD WELLS DIVISION**

3328 LLANFYLLIN DIVISION
combined with 3325 DEYTHEUR DIVISION and 3339 WELSHPOOL DIVISION to form **3341 WELSHPOOL DIVISION**

3329 LLANIDLOES DIVISION
combined with 3347 NEWTOWN DIVISION to form **3352 NEWTOWN DIVISION**

3330 MACHYNLLETH DIVISION
combined with 3352 NEWTOWN DIVISION to form **3352 DE MALDWYN DIVISION** – see above

3331 MATHRAFAL DIVISION
combined with 3341 WELSHPOOL DIVISION to form **3346 WELSHPOOL DIVISION**

3332 MONTGOMERY DIVISION
combined with 3334 NEWTOWN DIVISION to form **3347 NEWTOWN DIVISION**

3333 NEW RADNOR DIVISION
combined with 3336 PRESTEIGNE DIVISION to form **3343 EAST RADNOR DIVISION**

3334 NEWTOWN DIVISION
combined with 3332 MONTGOMERY DIVISION to form **3347 NEWTOWN DIVISION**

3335 PAINSCASTLE DIVISION
combined with 3321 BUILTH DIVISION AND 3322 COLWYN DIVISION to form **3345 BUILTH DIVISION**

3336 PRESTEIGNE DIVISION
combined with 3333 NEW RADNOR DIVISION to form **3343 EAST RADNOR DIVISION**

3337 RHAYADER DIVISION
combined with 3345 BUILTH DIVISION, 3327 LLANDRINDOD WELLS DIVISION and 3344 EAST RADNOR DIVISION to form **3351 LLANDRINDOD WELLS DIVISION**

3338 TALGARTH DIVISION
combined with 3342 BRECON DIVISION (except for Ystradfellte) and 3323 CRICKHOWELL DIVISION TO FORM **3350 BRECON DIVISION**

3339 WELSHPOOL DIVISION
combined with 3325 DEYTHEUR DIVISION and 3328 LLANFYLLIN DIVISION to form **3341 WELSHPOOL DIVISION**

3340 YSRTADGYNLAIS DIVISION
combined with 3350 BRECON DIVISION to form **3350 DE BRYCHEINIOG DIVISION**

3341 WELSHPOOL DIVISION
combined with 3331 MATHRAFAL DIVISION to form **3346 WELSHPOOL DIVISION**

3342 BRECON DIVISION
(except for Ystradfellte) combined with 3323 CRICKHOWELL DIVISION and 3338 TALGARTH DIVISION to form **3350 BRECON DIVISION**

3343 EAST RADNOR DIVISION
combined with 3326 KNIGHTON DIVISION to form **3344 EAST RADNOR DIVISION**

3344 EAST RADNOR DIVISION
combined with 3345 BUILTH DIVISION, 3327 LLANDRINDOD WELLS DIVISION and 3337 RHAYADER DIVISION to form **3351 LLANDRINDOD WELLS DIVISION**

3345 BUILTH DIVISION
combined with 3327 LLANDRINDOD WELLS DIVISION, 3344 EAST RADNOR DIVISION and 3337 RHAYADER DIVISION to form **3351 LLANDRINDOD WELLS DIVISION**

3346 WELSHPOOL LJA
combined with 3352 DE MALDWYN LJA to form **3355 MONTGOMERYSHIRE LJA**

3347 NEWTOWN DIVISION
combined with 3329 LLANIDLOES DIVISION to form **3352 NEWTOWN DIVISION**

3348 CARDIFF LJA
combined with 3349 VALE OF GLAMORGAN LJA to form **CARDIFF AND THE VALE OF GLAMORGAN LJA**

3349 VALE OF GLAMORGAN LJA
combined with 3348 CARDIFF LJA to form **CARDIFF AND THE VALE OF GLAMORGAN LJA**

3350 BRECON DIVISION
combined with 3340 YSTRADGYNLAIS DIVISION to form **3350 DE BRYCHEINIOG DIVISION**

3350 DE BRYCHEINIOG LJA
combined with 3351 RADNORSHIRE AND NORTH BRECKNOCK to form **BRECKNOCK AND RADNORSHIRE LJA**

3351 LLANDRINDOD WELLS DIVISION
renamed **RADNORSHIRE AND NORTH BRECKNOCK DIVISION**

3351 RADNORSHIRE AND NORTH BRECKNOCK LJA
combined with 3350 DE BRYCHEINIOG to form **BRECKNOCK AND RADNORSHIRE LJA**

3352 NEWTOWN DIVISION
combined with 3330 MACHYNLLETH DIVISION to form **3352 DE MALDWYN DIVISION**

3352 DE MALDWYN LJA
combined with 3346 WELSHPOOL LJA to form **3355 MONTGOMERYSHIRE LJA**

3355 MONTGOMERYSHIRE LJA
see **MID AND WEST WALES** ....p. 161

3356 PEMBROKESHIRE LJA
combined with 3138 CEREDIGION to form **3253 CEREDIGION AND PEMBROKESHIRE LJA**

3357 PORT TALBOT DIVISION
combined with 3359 NEATH DIVISION to form **3359 NEATH PORT TALBOT DIVISION**

3358 LLIW VALLEY DIVISION
combined with 3360 SWANSEA DIVISION to form **3360 SWANSEA COUNTY DIVISION**

3359 NEATH DIVISION
combined with 3357 PORT TALBOT DIVISION to form **3359 NEATH PORT TALBOT DIVISION**

3359 NEATH PORT TALBOT LJA
see **MID AND WEST WALES** ....p. 161

3360 SWANSEA DIVISION
combined with 3358 LLIW VALLEY DIVISION to form **3360 SWANSEA COUNTY DIVISION**

NORTHERN IRELAND

9001 ANTRIM
Mrs L. Webster, Antrim Court Office, The Courthouse, 30 Castle Way, Antrim BT41 4AQ
Tel: 028 9446 2661
Fax: 028 9446 3301
Courts and times
Antrim
Adult: Fifth Monday in month, Tuesday 10:00
VC: Tuesday 09:30
YC: Second and fourth Monday in month 10:00
Dom: Third Monday in month 10:00
Dept: First Monday in month 10:00

9002 ARDS
Mr A. Heaney, Newtownards Court Office, The Courthouse, Regent Street, Newtownards BT23 4LP
Tel: 028 9181 4343
Fax: 028 9181 8024
Courts and times
Newtownards
Adult: Monday, Tuesday, Thursday 10:30
VC: Tuesday 11:00
YC: Second and fourth Tuesday in month, third Monday in month 10:30
FPC: First, second third and fourth Monday in month, Wednesday, first third and fourth Thursday in month 10:30
Dom: Fourth Thursday in month 10:30
Dept: Second Monday in month 10:30

9003 ARMAGH
Mrs M. Donaldson, Armagh Court Office, The Courthouse, The Mall, Armagh BT61 9DJ
Tel: 028 3752 2816
Fax: 028 3752 8194
Courts and times
Armagh
Adult: Second Monday in month, Tuesday 10:30
VC: Tuesday 10:00
YC: Second and fourth Friday in month 10:30
Dom: Fourth Friday in month 10:30
Dept: Third Friday in month 10:30

9004 BALLYMENA
Ms S. McCollum, Ballymena Court Office, The Courthouse, Albert Place, Ballymena, Co. Antrim BT43 5BS
Tel: 028 2564 9416
Fax: 028 2565 5371
Courts and times
Ballymena
Coleraine
Adult: Ballymena: Second Monday in month, fourth Tuesday in month, fifth Wednesday in month, Thursday 10:00

VC: Ballymena: Thursday 11:00
YC: Ballymena: First and third Tuesday in month 10:00
FPC: Ballymena: Friday 10:00**; Coleraine**: Second and fourth Monday in month, third Thursday in month 10:00
Dom: Ballymena: Second Tuesday in month 10:00
Dept: Ballymena: Fourth Tuesday in month 10:00 (alternate months)

9005 BALLYMONEY
combined with COLERAINE and MOYLE to form **The Petty Sessions District of NORTH ANTRIM**

9006 BANBRIDGE
Mrs G. Campbell, Banbridge Court Office, The Courthouse, 23 New Street, Newry BT35 6JD
Tel: 028 4062 362
Fax: 028 4062 3059
Courts and times
Newry
Adult: First Monday in month, first, third and fourth Thursday in month 10:30
YC: Third Monday in month 10:30
Dom: Third Monday in month 10:30
Dept: Second Thursday in month 10:30
FPC: First, third and fourth Thursday in month 12:00

9007/9008/9009 BELFAST AND NEWTOWNABBEY
Mrs P. McCourt, Laganside Courts, 45 Oxford Street, Belfast BT1 3LL
Tel: 028 9023 2721
Fax: 028 9031 5219
Courts and times
Laganside Courts, 45 Oxford Street, Belfast BT1 3LL
Old Town Hall Building, 80 Victoria Street, Belfast BT1 3FA
Adult: Laganside Courts: Weekdays 10:30
VC: Laganside Courts: Weekdays 09:45
Youth VC: Old Town Hall Building: Wednesday 11:00
YC: Old Town Hall Building: Monday, Wednesday, Friday 10:30
FPC: Old Town Hall Building: Monday, Tuesday, Thursday, Friday 09:45
Dom: Old Town Hall Building: First Tuesday in month, Wednesday 10:30
Dept: Laganside Courts: Tuesday 10:30

9010 CARRICKFERGUS AND NEWTOWNABBEY
renamed **NEWTOWNABBEY**

9012 CASTLEREAGH
Mr A. Heaney, Newtownards Court Office, The Courthouse, Regent Street, Newtownards BT23 4LP
Tel: 028 9181 4343
Fax: 028 9181 8024
Note: All business within this PS District has been incorporated into Ards PS District sittings.

9014 COLERAINE
combined with BALLYMONEY and MOYLE to form **The Petty Sessions District of NORTH ANTRIM**

9015 COOKSTOWN
combined with DUNGANNON to form **The Petty Sessions District of EAST TYRONE**

9016/9017 CRAIGAVON
Mr C. Cromie, Craigavon Court Office, The Courthouse, Central Way, Craigavon BT64 1AP
Tel: 028 3834 1324
Fax: 028 3834 1243
Courts and times
Craigavon Court Office, The Courthouse, Central Way, Craigavon BT64 1AP
The Courthouse, Railway Street, Lisburn
Adult: Craigavon: Fifth Monday in month, Wednesday, fifth Thursday in month, Friday 10:30
VC: Craigavon: Friday 09:45
YC: Craigavon: Second and fourth Tuesday in month 10:30
FPC: Craigavon: First, second , third and fourth Thursday in month 10:30**; Lisburn:** Second third and fourth Wednesday in month 10:30
Dom: Craigavon: First Monday in month, third Thursday in month 10:30
Dept: Craigavon: First Tuesday in month 10:30

9018 DOWN
Mr A. Heaney, Downpatrick Court Office, The Courthouse, English Street, Downpatrick BT30 6AB
Tel: 028 4461 4621
Fax: 028 4461 3969
Courts and times
Downpatrick Court Office, The Courthouse, English Street, Downpatrick BT30 6AB
Adult: Second and fourth Monday in month, Thursday, 10:00
VC: Thursday 09:30
YC: First and third Tuesday in month 10:00
Dom: Third Monday in month 10:00
Dept: First Monday in month 10:00

9019 DUNGANNON
combined with COOKSTOWN to form **The Petty Sessions District of EAST TYRONE**

EAST TYRONE
Miss R. Crockett, Dungannon Court Office, The Courthouse, 46 Killyman Road, Dungannon BT71 6DE
Tel: 028 8772 2992
Fax: 028 8772 8169
Courts and times
Dungannon Court Office, The Courthouse, 46 Killyman Road, Dungannon BT71 6DE
Adult: First, third and fourth Monday in month, third and fifth Tuesday in month, Wednesday, Friday 10:30
Dept: Second Monday in month 10:30
YC: First and third Tuesday in month 10:30
VC: Wednesday 12:00
Dom: Second Tuesday in month 10:30
FPC: Second and fifth Thursday in month, fourth Tuesday in month 10:30

9020 FERMANAGH
Mrs C. Deazley, Office Manager, Enniskillen Court Office, The Courthouse, East Bridge Street, Enniskillen BT74 7BP
Tel: 028 6632 2356
Fax: 028 6632 3636
Courts and times
Enniskillen Court Office, The Courthouse, East Bridge Street, Enniskillen BT74 7BP
Adult: First, fourth and fifth Monday in month, first and third Wednesday in month, first Tuesday in month 10:00
YC: Second Tuesday in month, fourth Wednesday in month 10:00
Dom: Third Tuesday in month 10:00
Dept: Second Monday in month, second Wednesday in month 10:00
VC: Monday 12:00

9024 LARNE
Ms S. McCollum, Ballymena Court Office, The Courthouse, Albert Place, Ballymena, Co. Antrim BT43 5BS
Tel: 028 2564 9416
Fax: 028 2565 5371
Courts and times
Ballymena
Adult: Second, third, fourth and fifth Friday in month 10:00
YC: Fourth Thursday in month 10:00
VC: Friday 10:30
Dom: Second Thursday in month 10:00
Dept: First Friday 10:00
Family: Third Thursday in month 10:00

9025 LIMAVADY
Clerk of Petty Sessions, Limavady Court Office, The Courthouse, Main Street, Limavady BT49 0EY
Tel: 028 7772 2688
Fax: 028 7776 8794

Courts and times
Limavady Court Office, The Courthouse, Main Street, Limavady BT49 0EY
Adult: First, second, fourth and fifth Wednesday in month 10:00
Dept: Third Wednesday in month 10:00

9026 LISBURN
Mrs S. Dougan, Lisburn Court Office, The Courthouse, Railway Street, Lisburn BT28 1XR
Tel: 028 9267 5336
Fax: 028 9260 4107

Courts and times
Lisburn Court Office, The Courthouse, Railway Street, Lisburn BT28 1XR
Adult: Monday, fifth Tuesday in month, fifth Wednesday in month, Thursday, second and fourth
Friday in month 10:30
VC: Tuesday 10:45
YC: First and third Friday in month 10:30
Dom: First Tuesday in month 10:30
Dept: Third Tuesday in month 10:30

9028 LONDONDERRY
Mr L. Millar, Court Administrator, Londonderry Court Office, The Courthouse, Bishop Street,
Londonderry BT48 6PQ
Tel: 028 7136 3448
Fax: 028 7137 2059

Courts and times
The Courthouse, Bishop Street, Londonderry BT48 6PQ
Adult: Monday, second and fifth Tuesday in month, Wednesday, first, second, fourth and fifth
Thursday in month, Friday 10:00
YC: First, third and fourth Wednesday in month 10:00
VC: Thursday 12:00
FPC: Second and fourth Thursday in month, Friday 10:00
Dom: Fourth Monday in month 10:00
Dept: Third Thursday in month 10:00

9029 MAGHERAFELT
Clerk of Petty Sessions, Magherafelt Court Office, The Courthouse, Hospital Road, Magherafelt BT45
5DG
Tel: 028 7963 2121
Fax: 028 7963 4063

Courts and times
The Courthouse, Hospital Road, Magherafelt BT45 5DG
Adult: First, second, third and fourth Wednesday in month 10:00
YC: Third Monday in month 10:00
Dom: Third Monday in month 11:00
VC: Wednesday 12:00
Dept: First Monday in month 10:00

9030 MOYLE
combined with COLERAINE and BALLYMONEY to form **The Petty Sessions District of NORTH
ANTRIM**

9032 NEWRY AND MOURNE
Mrs G. Campbell, Newry Court Office, The Courthouse, 23 New Street, Newry BT35 6JD
Tel: 028 3025 2040
Fax: 028 3026 9830

Courts and times
The Courthouse, 23 New Street, Newry BT35 6JD
Adult: Second, fourth and fifth Monday in month, Wednesday, third and fifth Thursday in month,
second, fourth and fifth Friday in month 10:30
VC: Wednesday 10:00
YC: First and third Friday in month 10:30
FPC: First Monday in month, Tuesday 10:30
Dom: First Thursday in month 10:30
Dept: Third Monday in month 10:30

9033 NEWTOWNABBEY
CLOSED – Business transferred to BELFAST AND NEWTOWNABBEY

NORTH ANTRIM
Mr S. Tosh, Coleraine Court Office, The Courthouse, 46A Mountsandel Road, Coleraine, Co. Londonderry BT52 1NY
Tel: 028 7034 3437
Fax: 028 7032 0156
Courts and times
The Courthouse, 46A Mountsandel Road, Coleraine, Co. Londonderry BT52 1NY
Adult: Monday, fifth Tuesday in month, Wednesday, second, third, fourth and fifth Friday in month 10:00
YC: Second and fourth Tuesday in month 10:00
VC: Monday 09:45
Dom: First Thursday in month 10:00
Dept: First Friday in month 10:00

9034 NORTH DOWN
Mr A. Heaney, Newtownards Court Office, The Courthouse, Regent Street, NewtownardsBangor BT23 4LP
Tel: 028 9187 4343
Fax: 028 8181 8024
Courts and times
The Courthouse, Regent Street, Newtownards BT23 4LP
Adult: Wednesday, first, second and fifth Friday in month 10:30
YC: Second and fourth Tuesday in month, third Monday in month 10:30
VC: Tuesday 11:00
Dom: Fourth Friday in month 10:30
Dept: Third Friday in month 10:30

9035 OMAGH
Mrs J. McGonigle, Omagh Court Office, The Courthouse, High Street, Omagh BT78 1DU
Tel: 028 8224 2056
Fax: 028 8225 1198
Courts and times
The Courthouse, High Street, Omagh BT78 1DU
Adult: Tuesday, fourth Friday in month, fifth Wednesday in month, second and fifth Thursday in month 10:00
FPC: Third Monday in month, first, third and fourth Thursday in month 10:30
YC: Third Wednesday in month, first Friday in month 10:00
Dom: First Friday in month 10:00
VC: Tuesday 12:00
Dept: Second Friday in month 10:00

9036 STRABANE
Mrs J. McGonigle, Strabane Court Office, The Courthouse, Derry Road, Strabane BT82 8DT
Tel: 028 7138 2544
Fax: 028 7138 3209
Courts and times
The Courthouse, Derry Road, Strabane BT82 8DT
Adult: First, third, fourth and fifth Thursday in month, fifth Wednesday in month, first, second and fourth Friday in month 10:00
YC: Third Friday in month 10:00
Dom: Third Friday in month 11:00
VC: Thursday in month 11:30
Dept: Second Thursday in month 10:00

SCOTLAND

Sheriff Principal: Craig A.L. Scott
Sheriffdom Business Manager: Steve Bain
Sheriffdom Legal Adviser: Patricia Wallace
Legal Advisers: Howard Rattray; Eliza Harkins
Fines Collection and Enforcement: tel: 0141 429 8888

9761 GLASGOW AND STRATHKELVIN SHERIFF, JUSTICE OF THE PEACE AND STIPENDIARY MAGISTRATE COURTS

Steve Bain, Sheriffdom Business Manager & Sheriff Clerk, Sheriff Court House, PO Box 23, 1 Carlton Place, Glasgow G5 9DA
Tel: 0141 429 8888
Fax: 0141 418 5244 (Admin Dept); 5248 (Civil Dept); 5270 (Solemn Criminal Dept); 5247 (Summary Criminal Dept); 5185 (JP/Stips); 5270 (Cashier Dept); 5398 (Fines Enforcement Office)
DX: 551020 (Sheriff Clerk); 551021 (Criminal Dept); 551022 (Sheriffs); 551023 (Small Claims and Commissary Dept); DX: 551024 (General Civil Dept)
Legal Post: LP-6 GLASGOW 2
Email: glasgow@scotcourts.gov.uk

Courts and times
Sheriff Court Hourse, 1 Carlton Place, Glasgow
Trial: Weekdays 10:00
Criminal Custody (Sheriff): Weekdays 13:00
Criminal Custody (JP): Weekdays 10:00
Summary Cause: Payments: Alternate Wednesdays 10:00; **Heritable:** Tuesday 10:00
Small Claims, Payments and Miscellaneous: Friday 10:00
Appeal: Tuesday, Wednesday, Thursday 10:00
Adults with Incapacity: Alternate Wednesdays 10:00
Debtors (Scotland) Act: Monday 10:00
Miscellaneous Civil: Monday 11:30
Options Hearings: Family: Tuesday 09:30; **Commercial:** Wednesday 10:00; **Ordinary:** Friday 10:00

SHERIFFDOM OF GRAMPIAN, HIGHLAND AND ISLANDS

Sheriff Principal: Derek Pyle
Sheriffdom Business Manager: Audrey Bayliss, Scottish Court Service, 6 Ardross Terrace, Inverness
    IV3 5NQ. Tel: 01463 251964
Sheriffdom Legal Adviser: Kay Polson, Aberdeen Justice of the Peace Court, Castle Street, Aberdeen
    AB10 1WP. Tel: 01224 657200
Legal Advisers: Alison Stone, James McPherson and Sheila Shepherd, Aberdeen Sheriff Court; Fiona
    Grant, Catriona MacDonald, Sandy Lorimer, Area Management Team Offices, 6 Ardross
    Terrace, as above
Fines Collection and Enforcement: tel: 0845 602 5228

9251 ABERDEEN SHERIFF COURT AND JUSTICE OF THE PEACE COURT
F. Hendry, Sheriff Clerk, Sheriff Court House, Castle Street, Aberdeen AB10 1WP
Tel: 01224 657200
Fax: 01224 657234
DX: 61 ABERDEEN
Legal Post: LP-7 ABERDEEN 1
Email: aberdeen@scotcourts.gov.uk

Courts and times
Court House, Castle Street, Aberdeen
Criminal: Weekdays 10:00
Civil: Wednesday 09:45
Family and Child Welfare Hearings: Friday 09:45
Summary Cause: Thursday 10:00
Small Claims: Thursday 10:00
Commercial: Alternate Fridays 12:00
JP: Weekdays 10:00

9252 BANFF SHERIFF COURT AND JUSTICE OF THE PEACE COURT
Tracey Reid, Sheriff Clerk Depute, Sheriff Court House, Banff AB45 1AU
Tel: 01261 812140
Fax: 01261 818394
DX: 521325 BANFF
Legal Post: LP-5 BANFF
Email: banff@scotcourts.gov.uk

Courts and times
Sheriff Court House, Banff AB45 1AU
Criminal: Alternate Tuesdays 10:00
Ordinary: Tuesday once a month 10:00
Summary Cause: Tuesday once a month 11:00
Small Claims: Tuesday once a month 11:00
JP: Wednesday once a month 10:00

9343 DINGWALL SHERIFF COURT AND JUSTICE OF THE PEACE COURT
Ken Kerr, Sheriff Clerk Depute, Sheriff Court House, Dingwall IV15 9QX
Tel: 01349 863153
Fax: 01349 863153
DX: 520584 DINGWALL
Legal Post: LP-4 DINGWALL
Email: dingwall@scotcourts.gov.uk

Courts and times
Sheriff Court House, Dingwall
Criminal: Second Thursday in month and as required
Ordinary: Second Thursday in month 10:00
Summary Cause: Second Thursday in month 10:00
JP: Fourth Tuesday and Friday in month 10:00

9344 DORNOCH SHERIFF COURT AND JUSTICE OF THE PEACE COURT
Mrs Ruth Thomson, Sheriff Clerk Depute, Sheriff Court House, Dornoch IV25 3SD
Tel: 01862 810224
Fax: 01862 810224
Legal Post: LP-2 DORNOCH

Email: dornoch@scotcourts.gov.uk

Courts and times
Sheriff Court House, Dornoch
Criminal: Fourth Monday in month 10:00
Ordinary: Fourth Monday in month 10:00
Summary Cause: Fourth Monday in month 10:00
JP: Wednesday every eight weeks or as required

9341 ELGIN SHERIFF COURT AND JUSTICE OF THE PEACE COURT
Richard Cantwell, Sheriff Clerk, Sheriff Court House, Elgin IV30 1BU
Tel: 01343 542505
Fax: 01343 559517
DX: 520652 ELGIN
Legal Post: LP-8 ELGIN
Email: elgin@scotcourts.gov.uk

Courts and times
Sheriff Court House, Elgin
Criminal: Cited cases: Thursday 10:00, other days as required
Ordinary: Alternate Fridays 10:30
Summary Cause: Alternate Fridays 10:00
JP: Tuesday 10:00

9345 FORT WILLIAM SHERIFF COURT AND JUSTICE OF THE PEACE COURT
Verona MacDonald, Sheriff Clerk Depute, Sheriff Court House, High Street, Fort William PH33 6EE
Tel: 01397 702087
Fax: 01397 706214
DX: 531405 FORT WILLIAM
Legal Post: LP-2 FORT WILLIAM
Email: fortwilliam@scotcourts.gov.uk

Courts and times
Sheriff Court House, High Street, Fort William
Criminal: Monthly 10:00
Ordinary: Fourth Friday in month 10:00
Summary Cause: Fourth Friday in month 10:00
JP: Every four weeks 10:00

9346 INVERNESS SHERIFF COURT AND JUSTICE OF THE PEACE COURT
Mrs Frances MacPherson, Sheriff Clerk, Sheriff Court House, Inverness IV2 3EG
Tel: 01463 230782
Fax: 01463 710602
DX: IN25
Legal Post: LP-15
Email: inverness@scotcourts.gov.uk

Courts and times
Sheriff Court House, Inverness
Criminal: Weekdays 10:00 and Tuesday 10:30
Ordinary: Alternate Wednesdays 10:00
Summary Cause: Alternate Wednesdays 10:00
JP: Alternate Mondays, Wednesday, Friday 10:00

9805 KIRKWALL SHERIFF COURT
Gail Edwards, Sheriff Clerk Depute, Sheriff Court House, Kirkwall KW15 1PD
Tel: 01856 872110
Fax: 01856 874835
Legal Post: LP-7
Email: kirkwall@scotcourts.gov.uk
Note: No JP Court in Kirkwall

Courts and times
Sheriff Court House, Kirkwall
Criminal: Second Wednesday in month 10:00
Ordinary: Second Friday in month 10:00
Summary Cause: Second Friday in month 10:00
Small Claims: Second Friday in month 10:00

9812 LERWICK SHERIFF COURT
Sheriff Clerk Depute, Sheriff Court House, Lerwick ZE1 0HD
Tel: 01595 693914
Fax: 01595 693340
Email: lerwick@scotcourts.gov.uk
Note: No JP Court in Lerwick

Courts and times
Sheriff Court House, Lerwick
Criminal: Thursday 10:00
Trials: Wednesday 10:00
Ordinary: Second Tuesday 10:00
Summary Cause: Second Tuesday 10:00

9814 LOCHMADDY SHERIFF COURT
Margaret Campbell, Sheriff Clerk Depute, Sheriff Court House, Lochmaddy HS6 5AE
Tel: 01478 612191
Fax: 0844 561 3015
Email: lochmaddy@scotcourts.gov.uk

Courts and times
Sheriff Court House, Lochmaddy
Criminal: Fourth Tuesday in month and as required
Ordinary: Fourth Tuesday in month 10:30
Summary Cause: Fourth Tuesday in month 10:30

9253 PETERHEAD SHERIFF COURT AND JUSTICE OF THE PEACE COURT
Elaine McLeod, Sheriff Clerk, Sheriff Court House, Queen Street, Peterhead AB42 1TP
Tel: 01779 476676
Fax: 01779 472435
DX: 521376 PETERHEAD
Legal Post: LP-3 PETERHEAD
Email: peterhead@scotcourts.gov.uk

Courts and times
Sheriff Court House, Queen Street, Peterhead
Intermediate Diet: Second Wednesday in month 10:00
Criminal: Thursday 10:00
Trials: First and third Monday and Tuesday in month, third Friday in month 09:30
Custody: Weekdays 12:00
Ordinary: First and fourth Friday in month 09:30
Summary Cause: First and fourth Friday in month 11:30
JP: Fourth Monday and Friday in month 10:00

9347 PORTREE SHERIFF COURT AND JUSTICE OF THE PEACE COURT
Margaret Campbell, Sheriff Clerk Depute, Sheriff Court House, Portree IV51 9EH
Tel: 01478 612191
Fax: 01478 613203
Email: portree@scotcourts.gov.uk

Courts and times
Sheriff Court House, Portree
Criminal: Fourth Monday in month and as required
Ordinary: Fourth Monday in month 10:00
Summary Cause: Fourth Monday in month 10:00

9254 STONEHAVEN SHERIFF COURT AND JUSTICE OF THE PEACE COURT
Sheriff Clerk, Sheriff Court House, Stonehaven AB39 2JH
Tel: 01569 762758
Fax: 01569 762132
DX: 521023 STONEHAVEN
Legal Post: LP-3 STONEHAVEN
Email: stonehaven@scotcourts.gov.uk

Courts and times
Sheriff Court House, Stonehaven
Criminal: Alternate Wednesdays 10:00
Ordinary: Alternate Thursdays 10:00
Summary Cause: Alternate Thursdays 10:00 (same day as ordinary court)

Small Claims: Alternate Thursdays 10:00 (same day as ordinary court)
JP: Alternate Tuesdays 10:00

9384 STORNOWAY SHERIFF COURT AND JUSTICE OF THE PEACE COURT
Kenneth Finnie, Sheriff Clerk Depute, Sheriff Court House, 9 Lewis Street, Stornoway HS1 2JF
Tel: 01851 702231
Fax: 01851 704296
Email: stornoway@scotcourts.gov.uk
Courts and times
Sheriff Court House, 9 Lewis Street, Stornoway
Criminal: As required
Ordinary: Alternate Thursdays 10:00
Summary Cause: Alternate Thursdays 10:00
JP: Fourth Tuesday in month 10:00

9348 TAIN SHERIFF COURT AND JUSTICE OF THE PEACE COURT
Donna Jack, Sheriff Clerk Depute, Sheriff Court House, Tain IV19 1AB
Tel: 01862 892518
Fax: 01862 892518
Email: tain@scotcourts.gov.uk
Courts and times
Sheriff Court House, Tain
Criminal: Trials: Thursday/Friday once a month; **Cited:** Monday once a month 10:00
Ordinary: Fourth Thursday in month 10:00
Summary Cause: Fourth Thursday in month 11:00
JP: Fourth Thursday in month 10:00

9891 WICK SHERIFF COURT AND JUSTICE OF THE PEACE COURT
Janet McEwan MBE, Sheriff Clerk Depute, Sheriff Court House, Wick KW1 4AJ
Tel: 01955 602846
Fax: 01955 602846
Legal Post: LP-4
Email: wick@scotcourts.gov.uk
Courts and times
Sheriff Court House, Wick
Criminal: Cited Cases: Alternate Fridays 10:00; **Others:** As required
Ordinary: Alternate Mondays 10:00
Summary Cause: Alternate Mondays 10:00
JP: Fourth Thursday in month 10:00

SHERIFFDOM OF LOTHIAN AND BORDERS

Sheriff Principal: Mhairi M. Stephen
Sheriffdom Business Manager: David Shand, Edinburgh Sheriff Court, 27 Chamber Street, Edinburgh EH1 1LB. Tel: 0131 225 2525
Sheriffdom Legal Adviser: David Kemp, Edinburgh Justice of the Peace Court, 27 Chamber Street, Edinburgh EH1 1LB. Tel: 0131 225 2525
Legal Advisers: Deirdre Morrison, Margaret Dundas, Alison Brown, Julia Dunbar, Anne Mainland, Angela Ward, Michael Wright
Fines Collection and Enforcement: tel: 0131 247 2566

9729 DUNS SHERIFF COURT
Mark Kubeczka, Sheriff Clerk, Sheriff & JP Court House, 8 Newtown Street, Duns TD11 3DT
Tel: 01835 863231
Fax: 01835 864110
DX: 581222 JEDBURGH
Legal Post: LP-3 JEDBURGH
Email: jedburgh@scotcourts.gov.uk
Note: This court is only open on court sitting days. Staff are located in Jedburgh and administration of the business is carried out in Jedburgh.

Courts and times
Sheriff & JP Court House, 8 Newtown Street, Duns
Criminal: Alternate Wednesdays 10:00
Civil: Alternate Wednesdays 10:00
Summary Cause: Alternate Wednesdays 10:00

9350 DUNS JUSTICE OF THE PEACE COURT
Sheriff & JP Court House, 8 Newtown Street, Duns TD11 3DT
Tel: 01835 863231
Fax: 01835 864110
Legal Post: LP-3 JEDBURGH
Email: jedburgh@scotcourts.gov.uk
Note: This court is only open on court sitting days. Staff are located in Jedburgh and administration of the business is carried out in Jedburgh.

Courts and times
Sheriff & JP Court House, 8 Newtown Street, Duns TD11 3DT
JP: Alternate Tuesdays 10:00 and as required

9741 EDINBURGH SHERIFF COURT
David Shand, Sheriff Clerk, Sheriff Court House, 27 Chambers Street, Edinburgh EH1 1LB
Tel: 0131 225 2525
Fax: 0131 225 4422
DX: 550308 ED 37 (Admin/Crime/Cash); 550312 ED 37 (Civil); 550313 ED37 (Commissary)
Legal Post: LP-2 EDINBURGH 10
Email: edinburgh@scotcourts.gov.uk

Courts and times
Sheriff Court House, 27 Chambers Street, Edinburgh
Criminal: Weekdays 10:00
Ordinary: Weekdays 10:00
Options: Weekdays 10:00
Family: Weekdays 12:00
Summary Cause: Wednesday and Friday 09:45 or as required
Small Claims – Preliminary Hearings: Wednesday and Friday 10:30

9478 EDINBURGH JUSTICE OF THE PEACE COURT
David Kemp, Sheriffdom Legal Advisor, Sheriff Court House, 27 Chambers Street, Edinburgh EH1 1LB
Tel: 0131 225 2525
Fax: 0131 225 4422
DX: 550308 ED 37
Legal Post: LP-2 EDINBURGH 10
Email: edinburgh@scotcourts.gov.uk

Courts and times
Sheriff Court House, 27 Chambers Street, Edinburgh
JP: Weekdays 10:00

9771 HADDINGTON SHERIFF COURT
John O'Donnell, Sheriff Clerk, Sheriff Court House, Court Street, Haddington EH41 3HN
Tel: 01620 822325 822936
Fax: 01620 826350
DX: 540732 HADDINGTON
Email: haddington@scotcourts.gov.uk
Courts and times
Sheriff Court House, Court Street, Haddington
Criminal: Wednesday, Thursday, Friday
Ordinary: Alternate Mondays 11:30
Summary Cause: Alternate Mondays 11:30

9270 HADDINGTON JUSTICE OF THE PEACE COURT
John O'Donnell, Sheriff Clerk, Sheriff & JP Court House, Court Street, Haddington EH41 3HN
Tel: 01620 822325; 822936
Fax: 01620 825350
DX: 540732 HADDINGTON
Email: haddington@scotcourts.gov.uk
Courts and times
Sheriff & JP Court House, Court Street, Haddington
JP: Tuesday 10:00

9791 JEDBURGH SHERIFF COURT
Mark Kubeczka, Sheriff Clerk, Sheriff Court House, Castlegate, Jedburgh TD8 6AR
Tel: 01835 863231
Fax: 01835 864110
DX: 581222 JEDBURGH
Legal Post: LP-3 JEDBURGH
Email: jedburgh@scotcourts.gov.uk
Courts and times
Sheriff Court House, Castlegate, Jedburgh
Criminal: Thursday and Friday 10:00
Civil: Tuesday 10:00
Summary Cause: Tuesday 10:00

9351 JEDBURGH JUSTICE OF THE PEACE COURT
Sheriff & JP Court House, Castlegate, Jedburgh TD8 6AR
Tel: 01835 863231
Fax: 01835 864110
DX: 581222 JEDBURGH
Legal Post: LP-3 JEDBURGH
Email: jedburgh@scotcourts.gov.uk
Courts and times
Sheriff & JP Court House, Castlegate, Jedburgh
JP: Alternate Tuesdays 10:00. Additional sittings as required

9815 LIVINGSTON SHERIFF COURT
D. Fyfe, Sheriff Clerk, The Civic Centre, Howden South Road, Livingston EH54 6FF
Tel: 01506 402400
Fax: 01506 415262
DX: 552062 LIVINGSTON 7
Legal Post: LP-2 LIVINGSTON 2
Email: livingston@scotcourts.gov.uk
Courts and times
The Civic Centre, Howden South Road, Livingston
Ordinary: Wednesday

9380 LIVINGSTON JUSTICE OF THE PEACE COURT
Sheriff and JP Court, The Civic Centre, Howden South Road, Livingston EH54 6FF
Tel: 01506 402400
Fax: 01506 415262

DX: 552062 LIVINGSTON 7
Legal Post: LP-2 LIVINGSTON 2
Email: livingston@scotcourts.gov.uk
Courts and times
The Civic Centre, Howden South Road, Livingston
JP: Tuesday and Thursday

9852 PEEBLES SHERIFF COURT
Mrs M. McCabe, Sheriff Clerk, c/o Sheriff Court Selkirk, Ettrick Terrace, Selkirk TD1 1TB
Tel: 01750 721269
Fax: 01750 722884
DX: 581011 SELKIRK
Legal Post: LP-2 SELKIRK
Email: peebles@scotcourts.gov.uk
Note: Peebles Sheriff Court is only open on court sitting days. Staff are located in Selkirk and
administration of the business is carried out in Selkirk Sheriff Court.

Courts and times
Sheriff Court Selkirk, Ettrick Terrace, Selkirk
Criminal: First Wednesday in month 10:00
Ordinary: Third Wednesday in month 10:00
Summary Cause: Third Wednesday in month 10:00
Small Claims: Third Wednesday in month 10:00

9352 PEEBLES JUSTICE OF THE PEACE COURT
c/o Sheriff Court Selkirk, Etbrick Terrace, Selkirk TD1 1TB
Tel: 01750 721269
Fax: 01750 722884
DX: 581011 SELKIRK
Email: peebles@scotcourts.gov.uk
Note: Peebles JP Court is only open on court sitting days. Staff are located in Selkirk and
administration of the business is carried out in Selkirk Sheriff Court.

Courts and times
Sheriff Court Selkirk, Etbrick Terrace, Selkirk
JP: Thursday once a month 10:00

9871 SELKIRK SHERIFF COURT
M. McCabe, Sheriff Clerk, Sheriff Court House, Etbrick Terrace, Selkirk TD7 4LE
Tel: 01750 721269
Fax: 01750 722884
DX: 581011 SELKIRK
Legal Post: LP-2 SELKIRK
Email: selkirk@scotcourts.gov.uk

Courts and times
Sheriff Clerk, Sheriff Court House, Etbrick Terrace, Selkirk
Criminal: Monday 10:00, alternate Tuesdays 10:00
Ordinary: Alternate Thursdays 10:00 during session
Summary Cause: Alternate Thursdays 10:00 during session
Small Claims: Alternate Thursdays 10:00 during session

9353 SELKIRK JUSTICE OF THE PEACE COURT
Sheriff & JP Court House, Etbrick Terrace, Selkirk TD7 4LE
Tel: 01750 721269
Fax: 01750 722884
DX: 581011 SELKIRK
Legal Post: LP-2 SELKIRK
Email: selkirk@scotcourts.gov.uk

Courts and times
Sheriff & JP Court House, Etbrick Terrace, Selkirk
JP: Alternate Thursdays 10:00 and as required

SHERIFFDOM OF NORTH STRATHCLYDE

Sheriff Principal: Bruce A. Kerr QC
Sheriffdom Business Manager: Lisa Davis, Paisley Sheriff Court, St James' Street, Paisley PA3 2HW.
    Tel: 0141 887 5291
Sheriffdom Legal Adviser: Anne Hilland, Paisley Justice of the Peace Court, St James' Street, Paisley
    PA3 2HW. Tel: 0141 887 5291
Legal Advisers for Dumbarton, Greenock and Paisley: Eileen Burns, Angela Devine, Kathleen
    Graham, Vivian Lindsay, Peter Livingstone, Catriona Sagar
Legal Advisers for Irvine and Kilmarnock: Angus Livingstone, Kevin Walsh
Legal Adviser for Dunoon, Oban, Campbeltown and Lochgilphead: Frances Roberts
Fines Collection and Enforcement: tel: 01475 787073

9716 CAMPBELTOWN SHERIFF COURT AND JUSTICE OF THE PEACE COURT
Graham Whitelaw, Sheriff Clerk Depute, Sheriff Court House, Castlehill, Campbeltown PA28 6AN
Tel: 01586 552503
Fax: 01586 554967
Legal Post: LP-3 CAMPBELTOWN
Email: campbeltown@scotcourts.gov.uk

Courts and times
Sheriff Court House, Castlehill, Campbeltown
Criminal: As required
Ordinary: Fourth Friday in month 10:00
Summary Cause: Fourth Friday in month 10:00

9376 DUMBARTON JUSTICE OF THE PEACE COURT
JP Administration, Senior Legal Advisor, Dumbarton JP Court, Church Street, Dumbarton G82 1QR
Tel: 01389 763266
Fax: 01389 764085
DX: 500597 DUMBARTON
Email: dumbarton@scotcourts.gov.uk

Courts and times
Dumbarton JP Court, Church Street, Dumbarton
JP: Tuesday, Wednesday, Thursday 10:00

9723 DUMBARTON SHERIFF COURT
Sheriff Clerk, Sheriff Court House, Church Street, Dumbarton G82 1QR
Tel: 01389 763266
Fax: 01389 764085
DX: 500597 DUMBARTON
Email: dumbarton@scotcourts.gov.uk

Courts and times
Sheriff Court House, Church Street, Dumbarton
Criminal: Weekdays
Ordinary: Thursday 10:00
Summary Cause: Alternate Wednesdays 10:00

9728 DUNOON SHERIFF COURT AND JUSTICE OF THE PEACE COURT
Kim Wilson, Sheriff Clerk Depute, Sheriff Court House, George Street, Dunoon PA23 8BQ
Tel: 0300 790 0049
Fax: 01369 702191
DX: 591655 DUNOON
Legal Post: LP-2 DUNOON
Email: dunoon@scotcourts.gov.uk

Courts and times
Sheriff Court House, George Street, Dunoon
Criminal: As required
Ordinary: Alternate Tuesdays 10:00
Summary Cause: Alternate Tuesdays 11:00

9762 GREENOCK SHERIFF COURT AND JUSTICE OF THE PEACE COURT
Allister Wilson, Sheriff Clerk, Sheriff Court House, 1 Nelson Street, Greenock PA15 1TR
Tel: 01475 787073

Fax: 01475 729746
DX: GR16 GREENOCK
Legal Post: LP-5 GREENOCK 1
Email: greenock@scotcourts.gov.uk

Courts and times
Sheriff Court House, 1 Nelson Street, Greenock
Criminal: As required
Ordinary: Monday 10:00
Summary Cause: Monday 11:00

9354 IRVINE JUSTICE OF THE PEACE COURT
St Marnock Street, Kilmarnock KA1 1ED
Tel: 01563 550024
Fax: 01563 543568
DX: KK20 KILMARNOCK
Legal Post: LP-5 KILMARNOCK
Email: irvine@scotcourts.gov.uk

Courts and times
St Marnock Street, Kilmarnock
JP: Wednesday and Thursday 10:00

9801 KILMARNOCK SHERIFF COURT AND JUSTICE OF THE PEACE COURT
Chris McGrane, Sheriff Clerk, Sheriff Court House, St Marnock Street, Kilmarnock KA1 1ED
Tel: 01563 550024
Fax: 01563 543568
DX: KK20 KILMARNOCK
Legal Post: LP-5 KILMARNOCK
Email: kilmarnock@scotcourts.gov.uk

Courts and times
Sheriff Court House, St Marnock Street, Kilmarnock
Criminal: Weekdays
Ordinary: Wednesday 10:00
Summary Cause: Alternate Fridays 10:00
Small Claims: Alternate Fridays 10:00
JP: Monday 12:00, Tuesday and Friday 10:00

LOCHGILPHEAD JUSTICE OF THE PEACE COURT
Police Buildings, Lochnell Street, Lochgilphead PA31 8JJ
Email: dunoon@scotcourts.gov.uk
Note: Court staff only attend when the court is sitting. Staff can be contacted at Dunoon Sheriff Court.

9841 OBAN SHERIFF COURT AND JUSTICE OF THE PEACE COURT
Graham Whitelaw, Sheriff Clerk Depute, Sheriff Court House, Albany Street, Oban PA34 4AL
Tel: 01631 562414
Fax: 01631 562037
DX: OB8 OBAN
Legal Post: LP-4 OBAN
Email: oban@scotcourts.gov.uk

Courts and times
Sheriff Court House, Albany Street, Oban
Criminal: As required
Ordinary: Fourth Thursday in month 10:00
Summary Cause: Fourth Thursday in month 10:00

9851 PAISLEY SHERIFF COURT AND JUSTICE OF THE PEACE COURT
Fiona Fraser, Sheriff Clerk, Sheriff Court House, St James' Street, Paisley PA3 2HW
Tel: 0141 887 5291
Fax: 0141 887 6702
DX: PA48 PAISLEY
Legal Post: LP-12 Paisley
Email: paisley@scotcourts.gov.uk

Courts and times
Sheriff Court House, St James' Street, Paisley
Criminal: Weekdays
Ordinary: Monday 10:00
Summary Cause: Friday 09:30
JP: Weekdays 10:00

9861 ROTHESAY SHERIFF COURT

Allister Wilson, Sheriff Clerk, (Greenock), Eaglesham House, Mount Pleasant Road, Rothesay, Isle of Bute PA20 9HQ
Tel: 01700 502982; 01475 787073
Fax: 01700 504112
DX: GR16 GREENOCK
Legal Post: LP-5 GREENOCK 1
Email: rothesay@scotcourts.gov.uk
All administration for Rothesay Sheriff Court is conducted by Greenock Sheriff Court.

Courts and times
Eaglesham House, Mount Pleasant Road, Rothesay, Isle of Bute
Criminal: Monday (and at Greenock Sheriff Court other days)
Ordinary: Alternate Mondays 10:00
Summary Cause: Alternate Mondays 10:00

SHERIFFDOM OF SOUTH STRATHCLYDE, DUMFRIES AND GALLOWAY

Sheriff Principal: Brian A. Lockhart

Sheriffdom Business Manager: Sheila Hindes, Airdrie Sheriff Court, Graham Street, Airdrie ML6 6EE. Tel: 01236 751121

Sheriffdom Legal Adviser: Phyllis Hands, Airdrie Sheriff Court, Graham Street, Airdrie ML6 6EE. Tel: 01236 751121

Legal Advisers: Fiona Ross, Dumfries Sheriff Court; Alan Rosamund, Ayr Sheriff Court; Valerie Dorans, Airdrie Sheriff Court; John Donnelly, Ronald Bain, Angus Livingston, Hamilton JP Court

Fines Collection and Enforcement: contact individual courts

9702 AIRDRIE SHERIFF COURT

Miss A. Currie, Sheriff Clerk, Sheriff Court House, Graham Street, Airdrie ML6 6EE

Tel: 01236 751121

Fax: 01236 747497

DX: 570416 AIRDRIE

Legal Post: LP-7 AIRDRIE

Email: airdrie@scotcourts.gov.uk

Courts and times

Sheriff Court House, Graham Street, Airdrie

Criminal: Weekdays

Civil: Thursday 10:00

Summary Cause: Alternate Tuesdays 10:00

9704 AYR SHERIFF COURT

Alan Johnston, Sheriff Clerk, Sheriff Court House, Wellington Square, Ayr KA7 1EE

Tel: 01292 268474/292200

Fax: 01292 292249

DX: AY16 AYR

Legal Post: LP-6 AYR

Email: ayr@scotcourts.gov.uk

Courts and times

Sheriff Court House, Wellington Square, Ayr

Criminal: Weekdays

Ordinary: Thursday 10:00

Summary Cause: Alternate Fridays 10:00

Small Claims: Alternate Fridays 10:00

9560 AYR JUSTICE OF THE PEACE COURT

Alan Johnston, Sheriff Clerk, Sheriff Court House, Wellington Square, Ayr KA7 1EE

Tel: 01292 268474/292200

Fax: 01292 292249

DX: AY16 AYR

Legal Post: LP-6 AYR

Email: ayr@scotcourts.gov.uk

Courts and times

Sheriff Court House, Wellington Square, Ayr

Criminal: Friday 10:00

Trial and Intermediate Diets: Three Tuesdays in four, Thursday 10:00

Custody: Monday 14:30, Wednesday 11:00

9355 COATBRIDGE JUSTICE OF THE PEACE COURT

Miss A. Currie, Sheriff Clerk, Sheriff Court House, Graham Street, Airdrie ML6 6EE

Tel: 01236 751121

Fax: 01236 747497

DX: 570416 AIRDRIE

Legal Post: LP-7 AIRDRIE

Email: airdrie@scotcourts.gov.uk

Courts and times

435 Main Street, Coatbridge

JP: Monday, Tuesday, Thursday

9531 CUMBERNAULD JUSTICE OF THE PEACE COURT
Miss A. Currie, Sheriff Clerk, Sheriff Court House, Graham Street, Airdrie ML6 6EE
Tel: 01236 751121
Fax: 01236 747497
DX: 570416 AIRDRIE
Legal post: LP-7 Airdrie
Email: airdrie@scotcourts.gov.uk
Courts and times
Bron Way, Cumbernauld
JP: Friday

9724 DUMFRIES SHERIFF COURT AND JUSTICE OF THE PEACE COURT
Miss E. S. O. Young, Sheriff Clerk, Sheriff Court House, Dumfries DG1 2AN
Tel: 01387 262334
Fax: 01387 262357
DX: 580617 DUMFRIES
Legal Post: LP-5 DUMFRIES
Email: dumfries@scotcourts.gov.uk
Courts and times
Sheriff Court House, Dumfries
Criminal: Weekdays 10:00
Ordinary: First, second and third Thursday in month 10:00
Summary Cause: Fourth Thursday in month 10:00
Small Claims: Fourth Thursday in month 10:00
Dumfries JP: Tuesday, fourth Wednesday in month 10:00
Annan JP: Alternate Thursdays 10:00

9772 HAMILTON SHERIFF COURT
Maureen McLean, Sheriff Clerk, Sheriff Court House, 4 Beckford Street, Hamilton ML3 0BT
Tel: 01698 282957
Fax: 01698 201365 (Criminal); 201366 (Fines)
Civil Department, Birnie House, Caird Park, Hamilton Business Park, Caird Street, Hamilton ML3 0AL
Tel: 01698 201375
Fax: 01698 284870
DX: HA16 HAMILTON
Legal Post: LP-4 HAMILTON 2
Email: hamilton@scotcourts.gov.uk
Courts and times
Sheriff Court House, 4 Beckford Street, Hamilton
Criminal: Weekdays
Options Hearing: Tuesday 14:00
Summary Cause Heritable: Monday 11:00
Summary Cause: Thursday 10:00
Small Claims: Thursday 10:00
Ordinary: Wednesday 10:00

9566 HAMILTON JUSTICE OF THE PEACE COURT
Maureen McLean, Sheriff Clerk, Sheriff Clerk's Office, Sheriff Court House, 4 Beckford Street, Hamilton ML3 0BT
Tel: 01698 282957
Fax: 01698 201365
DX: HA16 HAMILTON
Legal Post: LP-4 HAMILTON
Email: hamilton@scotcourts.gov.uk
Courts and times
Sheriff Court House, 4 Beckford Street, Hamilton
Trials: Monday 10:00, alternate Wednesdays and Fridays
Cited: Alternate Wednesdays and Fridays 10:00

9532 MOTHERWELL JUSTICE OF THE PEACE COURT
Maureen McLean, Sheriff Clerk, Sheriff Court House, 4 Beckford Street, Hamilton ML3 0BT
Tel: 01698 282957
Fax: 01698 201365
DX: HA16 HAMILTON
Legal Post: LP-4 HAMILTON 2

Email: hamilton@scotcourts.gov.uk

Courts and times
Sheriff Court House, 4 Beckford Street, Hamilton
Civic Centre, Windmill Street, Motherwell ML1 1AB. Tel: 0131 248 1810. Fax: 01698 267495. Email: motherwell@scotcourts.gov.uk
Trials: Hamilton: Monday, Thursday, alternate Fridays 10:00
Cited: Civic Centre, Motherwell: times on application

9804 KIRKCUDBRIGHT SHERIFF COURT AND JUSTICE OF THE PEACE COURT
Sheriff Clerk Depute, Sheriff Court House, Kirkcudbright DG6 4JW
Tel: 01557 330574
Fax: 01557 331764
DX: 580812 KIRKCUDBRIGHT
Legal Post: LP-2 KIRKCUDBRIGHT
Email: kirkcudbright@scotcourts.gov.uk

Courts and times
Sheriff Court House, Kirkcudbright
Criminal: Thursday
Ordinary: Thursday
Summary Cause: Second and fourth Thursday in month 10:00
Small Claims: Second and fourth Thursday in month 10:00
JP: One Wednesday in four

9811 LANARK SHERIFF COURT AND JUSTICE OF THE PEACE COURT
John G. Foy, Sheriff Clerk, Sheriff Court House, 24 Hope Street, Lanark ML11 7NE
Tel: 01555 661531
Fax: 01555 664319
DX: 570832 LANARK
Legal Post: LP-2 LANARK
Email: lanark@scotcourts.gov.uk

Courts and times
Sheriff Court House, 24 Hope Street, Lanark
Custody: Monday 14:00, Tuesday, Wednesday, Thursday, Friday 12:30
Criminal: Tuesday, Wednesday, Thursday 10:00
Ordinary: Alternate Tuesdays 11:00
Summary Cause: Alternate Tuesdays 10:00
JP: Three Wednesdays in four

9875 STRANRAER SHERIFF COURT AND JUSTICE OF THE PEACE COURT
B.J. Lindsay, Sheriff Clerk, Sheriff Court House, Stranraer DG9 7AA
Tel: 01776 702138; 706135
Fax: 01776 706792
DX: 581261 STRANRAER
Legal Post: LP-2 STRANRAER
Email: stranraer@scotcourts.gov.uk

Courts and times
Sheriff Court House, Stranraer
Criminal: Monday, Tuesday, Wednesday 10:00
Ordinary: Second and fourth Friday in month 10:00
Small Claims: Second and fourth Friday in month 10:00
Summary Cause: Second and fourth Friday in month 10:00
JP: Alternate Thursdays 10:00

SHERIFFDOM OF TAYSIDE, CENTRAL AND FIFE

Sheriff Principal: R.A. Dunlop QC

Sheriffdom Business Manager: Pam McFarlane, Stirling Sheriff Court, Viewfield Place, Stirling FK8 1NH. Tel: 01786 462191

Sheriffdom Legal Adviser: Alison Comiskey, Dundee Justice of the Peace Court, 6 West Bell Street, Dundee DD1 9AD. Tel: 01382 229961

Legal Advisers: Hilary Stephen, Kirkcaldy Sheriff Court; Jean Davis, Dunfermline Sheriff Court; Joyce Horsman and Iain Lockhart, Perth Sheriff Court; Tracey Scott, Stirling Sheriff Court; Amanda Inglis, Falkirk Sheriff Court; Stephen Wilson, Dundee Justice of the Peace Court

Fines Collection and Enforcement: tel: 01382 318251

9703 ALLOA SHERIFF COURT AND JUSTICE OF THE PEACE COURT
David Graham, Sheriff Clerk, Sheriff Court House, 47 Drysdale Street, Alloa FK10 1JA
Tel: 01259 722734
Fax: 01259 219470
DX: 560433 ALLOA
Legal Post: LP-3 ALLOA
Email: alloa@scotcourts.gov.uk

Courts and times
Sheriff Court House, 47 Drysdale Street, Alloa
Criminal: As required
JP: Alternate Tuesdays 10:00
Ordinary: Alternate Fridays 10:00
Summary Cause: Alternate Fridays 10:00
Small Claims: Alternate Fridays 10:00

9705 ARBROATH SHERIFF COURT AND JUSTICE OF THE PEACE COURT
Sheriff Clerk, Sheriff Court House, 88–92 High Street, Arbroath DD11 1HL
Tel: 01241 876600
Fax: 01241 874413
DX: 530442 ARBROATH
Legal Post: LP-3 ARBROATH
Email: arbroath@scotcourts.gov.uk

Courts and times
Sheriff Court House, 88–92 High Street, Arbroath
Criminal: Tuesday, Wednesday, Thursday 10:00
Ordinary: Monday 10:00
Summary Cause: Monday 10:00
Small Claims: Monday 10:00
JP: Friday 10:00

9717 CUPAR SHERIFF COURT AND JUSTICE OF THE PEACE COURT
Nicola Fraser, Sheriff Clerk, Sheriff Court House, Cupar KY15 4LX
Tel: 01334 652121
Fax: 01334 656807
DX: 560545 CUPAR
Legal Post: LP-11 CUPAR
Email: cupar@scotcourts.gov.uk

Courts and times
Sheriff Court House, Cupar
Criminal: Thursday
Ordinary: Alternate Wednesdays 10:00
Summary Cause: Alternate Wednesdays 14:00
Small Claims: Alternate Wednesdays 14:00
JP: Alternate Fridays 10:00

9726 DUNDEE SHERIFF COURT AND JUSTICE OF THE PEACE COURT
L. McIntosh, Sheriff Clerk, Sheriff Court House, Dundee DD1 9AD
Tel: 01382 229961
Fax: 01382 318222
DX: DD33 DUNDEE
Legal Post: LP-21 Dundee

Email: dundee@scotcourts.gov.uk

Courts and times
Sheriff Court House, Dundee
Criminal: Weekdays 09:30
Ordinary: Tuesday 10:00
Family: Thursday 10:00
Summary Cause: Monday 10:00
Small Claims: Monday 10:00
JP: Weekdays 10:00

9727 DUNFERMLINE SHERIFF COURT AND JUSTICE OF THE PEACE COURT
Johanne White, Sheriff Clerk, Sheriff Court House, 1–6 Carnegie Drive, Dunfermline KY12 7HJ
Tel: 01383 724666
Fax: 01383 621205
DX: DF17 DUNFERMLINE
Legal Post: LP-5 DUNFERMLINE
Email: dunfermline@scotcourts.gov.uk

Courts and times
Sheriff Court House, 1–6 Carnegie Drive, Dunfermline
Criminal: Weekdays 10:00
Ordinary: Monday 10:00
Summary Cause: Friday every four weeks 09:45
Small Claims: Friday every four weeks 10:00
JP: Tuesday, alternate Fridays 10:00

9751 FALKIRK SHERIFF COURT AND JUSTICE OF THE PEACE COURT
Dennis McCall, Sheriff Clerk, Sheriff Court House, Camelon, Falkirk FK1 4AR
Tel: 01324 620822
Fax: 01324 678238
DX: 552070 FALKIRK
Legal Post: LP 2 FALKIRK
Email: falkirk@scotcourts.gov.uk

Courts and times
Sheriff Court House, Camelon, Falkirk FK1 4AR
Criminal: Weekdays
Ordinary: Wednesday 10:00
Summary Cause: Wednesday 09:30 and 12:00
Small Claims: Wednesday 09:30
JP: Monday and Thursday 10:00

9752 FORFAR SHERIFF COURT AND JUSTICE OF THE PEACE COURT
Christine M. Petch, Sheriff Clerk, Sheriff Court House, Market Street, Forfar DD8 3LA
Tel: 01307 462186
Fax: 01307 462268
DX: 530674 FORFAR
Email: forfar@scotcourts.gov.uk

Courts and times
Sheriff Court House, Market Street, Forfar
Criminal: Thursday 10:00 and as required
Ordinary: Wednesday 10:00
Summary Cause: Wednesday 09:45
Small Claims: Wednesday 09:45
JP: Alternate Wednesdays 10:00

9803 KIRKCALDY SHERIFF COURT AND JUSTICE OF THE PEACE COURT
Gail Smith, Sheriff Clerk, Sheriff Court House, Whytescauseway, Kirkcaldy KY1 1XQ
Tel: 01592 260171
Fax: 01592 642361
DX: KY17 KIRKCALDY
Legal Post: LP-7 KIRKCALDY
Email: kirkcaldy@scotcourts.gov.uk

Courts and times
Sheriff Court House, Whytescauseway, Kirkcaldy
Criminal: Weekdays 10:00

Ordinary: Alternate Fridays 09:30
Options Hearings: Alternate Fridays 09:30
Child Welfare Hearings: Wednesday 09:30
Summary Cause: Friday 11:30
Summary Cause Heritable: Alternate Fridays 14:00
Small Claims: Friday 11:30
JP: Monday and Thursday 10:00

9853 PERTH SHERIFF COURT AND JUSTICE OF THE PEACE COURT
Mr A. Nicol, Sheriff Clerk, Sheriff Court House, Perth PH2 8NL
Tel: 01738 620546
Fax: 01738 623601
DX: PE20 PERTH
Legal Post: LP-8 PERTH
Email: perth@scotcourts.gov.uk
Courts and times
Sheriff Court House, Perth PH2 8NL
Criminal: As required
Ordinary: Alternate Wednesdays 10:00
Summary Cause: Alternate Wednesdays 10:00
Small Claims: Alternate Wednesdays 10:00
JP: Tuesday and Thursday 10:00

9872 STIRLING SHERIFF COURT AND JUSTICE OF THE PEACE COURT
Anne Reid, Sheriff Clerk, Sheriff Court House, Stirling FK8 1NH
Tel: 01786 462191
Fax: 01786 470456
DX: ST15 STIRLING
Legal Post: LP-6 STIRLING
Email: stirling@scotcourts.gov.uk
Courts and times
Sheriff Court House, Stirling
Criminal: Weekdays
Ordinary: Alternate Tuesdays 10:00
Summary Cause: Alternate Tuesdays 10:00
Small Claims: Alternate Tuesdays 10:00
JP: Wednesday and Friday 10:00

NUMERICAL INDEX TO COURT CODES OF SHERIFF COURTS

NUMERICAL INDEX TO COURT CODES OF JUSTICES OF THE PEACE COURTS

Index of the Justice of the Peace Courts created by the Criminal Proceedings etc. (Reform) (Scotland) Act 2007.

HISTORICAL INDEX TO COURT CODES OF DISTRICT COURTS (NOW DISESTABLISHED)

in use after 1 September 1998

Court No	
9400	Aberdeen (City of) DC (DISESTABLISHED)
9405	Aberdeenshire DC at Banff
9407	Aberdeenshire DC at Inverurie (DISESTABLISHED)
9408	Aberdeenshire DC at Peterhead (DISESTABLISHED)
9409	Aberdeenshire DC at Stonehaven (DISESTABLISHED)
9415	Angus DC at Arbroath (DISESTABLISHED)
9417	Angus DC at Forfar (DISESTABLISHED)
9426	Argyll & Bute DC at Campbeltown (DISESTABLISHED)
9427	Argyll & Bute DC at Dunoon (DISESTABLISHED)
9428	Argyll & Bute DC at Helensburgh (DISESTABLISHED)
9429	Argyll & Bute DC at Lochgilphead (DISESTABLISHED)
9430	Argyll & Bute DC at Oban (DISESTABLISHED)
9440	Clackmannanshire DC at Alloa (DISESTABLISHED)
9445	Dumfries and Galloway DC at Annan (DISESTABLISHED)
9446	Dumfries and Galloway DC at Dumfries (DISESTABLISHED)
9447	Dumfries and Galloway DC at Kirkcudbright (DISESTABLISHED)
9449	Dumfries and Galloway DC at Sanquhar (CLOSED)
9450	Dumfries and Galloway DC at Stranraer (DISESTABLISHED)
9456	Dundee (City of) DC (DISESTABLISHED)
9460	East Ayrshire DC at Cumnock (DISESTABLISHED)
9461	East Ayrshire DC at Kilmarnock (DISESTABLISHED)
9465	East Dunbartonshire DC at Kirkintilloch (DISESTABLISHED)
9466	East Dunbartonshire DC at Milngavie (DISESTABLISHED)
9474	East Renfrewshire DC at Giffnock (DISESTABLISHED)
9478	Edinburgh (City of) DC (DISESTABLISHED)
9482	Falkirk DC (DISESTABLISHED)
9485	Fife DC at Cupar (DISESTABLISHED)
9486	Fife DC at Dunfermline (DISESTABLISHED)
9487	Fife DC at Kirkcaldy (DISESTABLISHED)
9495	Glasgow (City of) DC (DISESTABLISHED)
9500	Highland DC at Dingwall (DISESTABLISHED)
9501	Highland DC at Dornoch (DISESTABLISHED)
9502	Highland DC at Fort William (DISESTABLISHED)
9503	Highland DC at Inverness (DISESTABLISHED)
9504	Highland DC at Kingussie (DISESTABLISHED)
9505	Highland DC at Nairn (DISESTABLISHED)
9506	Highland DC at Portree (DISESTABLISHED)
9508	Highland DC at Wick (DISESTABLISHED)
9509	Highland DC at Tain (DISESTABLISHED)
9514	Inverclyde DC at Greenock (DISESTABLISHED)
9518	Midlothian DC at Loanhead (DISESTABLISHED)
9522	Moray DC at Elgin (DISESTABLISHED)
9526	North Ayrshire DC at Irvine (DISESTABLISHED)
9530	North Lanarkshire DC at Coatbridge (DISESTABLISHED)
9531	North Lanarkshire DC at Cumbernauld (DISESTABLISHED)
9532	North Lanarkshire DC at Motherwell (DISESTABLISHED)
9538	Perth & Kinross DC at Perth (DISESTABLISHED)
9542	Renfrewshire DC at Paisley (DISESTABLISHED)
9560	South Ayrshire DC at Ayr (DISESTABLISHED)
9561	South Ayrshire DC at Girvan (DISESTABLISHED)
9565	South Lanarkshire DC at East Kilbride (DISESTABLISHED)
9566	South Lanarkshire DC at Hamilton (DISESTABLISHED)

HISTORICAL INDEX TO COURT CODES OF DISTRICT COURTS
(NOW DISESTABLISHED)
in use prior to 1 September 1998

Court No	
9901	Angus DC at Arbroath (DISESTABLISHED)
	Angus DC at Forfar (DISESTABLISHED)
9902	Dumfries and Galloway DC at Annan (DISESTABLISHED)
9903	Argyll and Bute DC at Campbeltown (DISESTABLISHED)
	Argyll and Bute DC at Dunoon (DISESTABLISHED)
	Argyll and Bute DC at Helensburgh (DISESTABLISHED)
	Argyll and Bute DC at Lochgilphead (DISESTABLISHED)
	Argyll and Bute DC at Oban (DISESTABLISHED)
9904	Highland DC at Kingussie (DISESTABLISHED)
9905	Aberdeenshire DC at Banff (DISESTABLISHED)
	Aberdeenshire DC at Peterhead (DISESTABLISHED)
9906	East Dunbartonshire DC at Milngavie (DISESTABLISHED)
9907	Scottish Borders DC at Duns (DISESTABLISHED)
9908	Highland DC at Wick (DISESTABLISHED)
9909	Clackmannanshire DC at Alloa (DISESTABLISHED)
9910	West Dunbartonshire DC at Clydebank (DISESTABLISHED)
9911	North Lanarkshire DC at Cumbernauld (DISESTABLISHED)
9912	East Ayrshire DC at Cumnock (DISESTABLISHED)
9913	North Ayrshire DC at Irvine (DISESTABLISHED)
9914	West Dunbartonshire DC at Dumbarton (DISESTABLISHED)
9915	Dundee, (City of) DC (DISESTABLISHED)
9916	Fife DC at Dunfermline (DISESTABLISHED)
9917	South Lanarkshire DC at East Kilbride (DISESTABLISHED)
9918	East Lothian DC at Haddington (DISESTABLISHED)
9919	East Renfrewshire DC at Giffnock (DISESTABLISHED)
9920	Edinburgh, (City of) DC (DISESTABLISHED)
9921	Scottish Borders DC at Selkirk (Ettrick & Lauderdale Division) (DISESTABLISHED)
9922	Falkirk DC (DISESTABLISHED)
9923	Glasgow, (City of) DC (DISESTABLISHED)
9924	Aberdeenshire DC at Inverurie (DISESTABLISHED)
9925	South Lanarkshire DC at Hamilton (DISESTABLISHED)
9926	Inverclyde DC at Greenock (DISESTABLISHED)
9927	Highland DC at Inverness (DISESTABLISHED)
9928	East Ayrshire DC at Kilmarnock (DISESTABLISHED)
9929	Aberdeenshire DC at Stonehaven (DISESTABLISHED)
9930	Fife DC at Kirkcaldy (DISESTABLISHED)
9931	South Ayrshire DC at Ayr (DISESTABLISHED)
	South Ayrshire DC at Girvan (DISESTABLISHED)
9932	South Lanarkshire DC at Lanark (DISESTABLISHED)
9933	Highland DC at Fort William (DISESTABLISHED)
9935	North Lanarkshire DC at Coatbridge (DISESTABLISHED)
9936	Moray DC at Elgin (DISESTABLISHED)
9937	North Lanarkshire DC at Motherwell (DISESTABLISHED)
9938	Highland DC at Nairn (DISESTABLISHED)
9939	Dumfries and Galloway DC at Dumfries (DISESTABLISHED)
	Dumfries and Galloway DC at Sanquhar (CLOSED) (DISESTABLISHED)
9940	Fife DC at Cupar (DISESTABLISHED)
9941	Perth and Kinross DC at Perth (DISESTABLISHED)
9942	Renfrewshire DC at Paisley (DISESTABLISHED)
9943	Highland DC at Dingwall (DISESTABLISHED)
9944	Scottish Borders DC at Jedburgh (Roxburgh Division) (DISESTABLISHED)
9945	Highland DC at Portree (DISESTABLISHED)

INDEX TO ALL COURTS OF SUMMARY JURISDICTION

B

Part IV

Coroners and Coroners' Officers

CORONERS AND CORONERS' OFFICERS

CHIEF CORONER OF ENGLAND AND WALES
His Honour Judge Peter Thornton QC

THE ROYAL HOUSEHOLD
Senior Coroner: M.J.C. Burgess
49 Ormond Avenue, Hampton, Middlesex TW12 2RY

AVON

AVON
Coroner: Ms M.E. Voisin
Coroner's Court, The Courthouse, Old Weston Road, Flax Bourton, Bristol BS48 1UL
Tel: 01275 461920
Fax: 01275 462749
Email: coroners.officers@bristol.gov.uk

BEDFORDSHIRE

BEDFORDSHIRE & LUTON
Coroner: to be confirmed
Tel: 0300 300 6559 (Secretary)
Coroner's Offices:
Coroner's Office, The Court House, Woburn Road, Ampthill MK45 2HZ
Tel: 0300 300 6557/6558
Fax: 01234 273014
Coroner's Office, Jansel House, Hitchin Road, Luton LU2 7XH
Tel: 0300 300 6157/6158
Fax: 01582 481261

BERKSHIRE

BERKSHIRE
Coroner: Peter J. Bedford
Yeomanry House, 131 Castle Hill, Reading RG1 7TA
Tel: 0118 937 3528
Fax: 0118 937 5448
Email: peter.bedford@reading.gov.uk
Coroner's Officers:
Thames Valley Police, Bracknell Police Station, Bracknell
Tel: 01344 823432
Fax: 01344 823499
Royal Berkshire Hospital, Craven Road, Reading RG1 5AN
Tel: 0118 986 3116
Fax: 0118 975 6594
Wexham Park Hospital, Wexham Street, Slough SL2 4HL
Tel: 01753 633732
Fax: 01753 5780733

BUCKINGHAMSHIRE

BUCKINGHAMSHIRE
Coroner: R.A. Hulett
29 Windsor End, Beaconsfield HP9 2JJ

Tel: 01494 475505
Fax: 01494 673760
DX: 34502 BEACONSFIELD
Email: coroners@buckscc.gov.uk
Coroner's Officers:
As above

MILTON KEYNES
Coroner: Thomas Osborne
Postal address: Coroner's Office, Milton Keynes Council, 1 Saxon Gate East, Central Milton Keynes MK9 3EJ
Court address: HM Coroner's Court, Crownhill Crematorium Site, Dansteed Way, Milton Keynes MK8 0AH
Tel: 01908 254327
Fax: 01908 253636
DX: 31406 MILTON KEYNES
Email: coroners.office@milton-keynes.gov.uk
Coroner's Officer:
As above

CAMBRIDGESHIRE

NORTH & EAST CAMBRIDGESHIRE
Coroner: William R. Morris
Coroner's Office, Lawrence Court, Princes Street, Huntingdon PE29 3PA
Tel: 0345 045 1364
Fax: 01480 372777
Email: hmcoroners.cambridge@cambridgeshire.gov.uk

SOUTH & WEST CAMBRIDGESHIRE
Coroner: David S. Morris
Coroner's Office, Lawrence Court, Princes Street, Huntingdon PE29 3PA
Tel: 0345 045 1364
Fax: 01480 372777
Email: hmcoroners.cambridge@cambridgeshire.gov.uk

PETERBOROUGH
Coroner: David Heming
Town Hall, Bridge Street, Peterborough PE7 1HG
Tel: 01733 452275; mob: 07920 160718
Fax: 0870 238 4085
Email: hmcoroner@peterborough.gov.uk
Coroner's Officers:
Lesley Edmonds
Tel: 01733 452373
Email: lesley.edmonds@peterborough.gov.uk
Gemma James
Tel: 01733 452372
Email: gemma.james@peterborough.gov.uk

CHESHIRE

CHESHIRE
Coroner: N.L. Rheinberg
The West Annexe, Town Hall, Sankey Street, Warrington WA1 1UH
Tel: 01925 444216
Fax: 01925 444219
Email: nrheinberg@warrington.gov.uk

CORNWALL

CORNWALL
Coroner: Dr E.E. Carlyon
14 Barrack Lane, Truro, Cornwall TR1 2DW
Tel: 01872 261612
Fax: 01872 262738
Email: cornwallcoroner@cornwall.gov.uk
Coroner's Officers:
Truro Police Station, Tregolls Road, Truro TR1 1PY
Tel: (enquiries) 01872 326075; (to report a death) 01872 326207
Fax: 01872 326024

ISLES OF SCILLY
Coroner: I.M. Arrow
Cary Chambers, 1 Palk Street, Torquay TQ2 5EL
Tel: 01803 380705
Fax: 01803 380704
Email: hmcoroner@torbay.gov.uk

CUMBRIA

NORTH & WEST CUMBRIA
Coroner: David Ll. Roberts
Unit 5D/5E Lakeland Business Park, Lamplugh Road, Cockermouth CA13 0QT
Tel: 01900 706902
Fax: 01900 706915
Email: hmcoroner.northwest@cumbria.gov.uk

SOUTH & EAST CUMBRIA
Coroner: Ian Smith
Central Police Station, Market Street, Barrow-in-Furness LA14 2LE
Tel: 01229 848966
Fax: 01229 848953

DERBYSHIRE

DERBY & SOUTH DERBYSHIRE
Coroner: Dr Robert Hunter
St Katherine's House, St Mary's Wharf, Mansfield Road, Derby DE1 3TQ
Tel: 01332 343225
Fax: 01332 294942
Email: derby.coroner@derbyshire.gov.uk

SCARSDALE & HIGH PEAK
Coroner: Dr Robert Hunter
Coroner's Court, Ground Floor, 5–6 Royal Court, Basil Close, Chesterfield S41 7SL
Tel: 01246 201391
Fax: 01246 273058

DEVON

EXETER & GREATER DEVON
Coroner: Dr Elizabeth Ann Earland
Room 226, Devon County Hall, Topsham Road, Exeter EX2 4QD
Tel: 01392 383636
Fax: 01392 383635
Email: coroner@exgd-coroner.co.uk

PLYMOUTH & SOUTH WEST DEVON
Coroner: I.M. Arrow
3 The Crescent, Plymouth PL1 3AB
Tel: 01752 204636
Fax: 01752 313297
Email: hmcoroner@plymouth.gov.uk

TORBAY & SOUTH DEVON
Coroner: I.M. Arrow
Cary Chambers, 1 Palk Street, Torquay TQ2 5EL
Tel: 01803 380705
Fax: 01803 380704
Email: hmcoroner@torbay.gov.uk

DORSET

DORSET, BOURNEMOUTH & POOLE
Coroner: S.S. Payne
The Coroner's Court, Stafford Road, Bournemouth BH1 1PA
Tel: 01202 310049
Fax: 01202 780423
DX: 156942 BOURNEMOUTH 3
Email: coroner@bournemouth.gov.uk
Coroner's Officers:
Tel: 01202 789057/879/353/154
Fax: 01202 780423
Coroner's Office – West Dorset
Dorchester Police Station, Weymouth Avenue, Dorchester DT1 1QZ
Tel: 01305 224780 Fax: 01305 226897
Email: coroners.office.west@dorset.pnn.police.uk

COUNTY DURHAM

DARLINGTON & SOUTH DURHAM
Coroner: Andrew Tweddle
HM Coroner's Office, Fourth Floor, Civic Centre, North Terrace, Crook DL15 9ES
Postal address: HM Coroner's Office, PO Box 282, Bishop Auckland DL14 4FY
Tel: 01388 761564
Fax: 01388 765430
Email: hmcoroner@durham.gov.uk
Coroner's Officers:
Police Office, Wesleyan Road, Spennymoor DL16 6FB
Tel: 0345 606 0365
Fax: 01325 742732

NORTH DURHAM
Coroner: Andrew Tweddle
HM Coroner's Office, Fourth Floor, Civic Centre, North Terrace, Crook DL15 9ES
Postal address: HM Coroner's Office, PO Box 282, Bishop Auckland DL14 4FY
Tel: 01388 761564
Fax: 01388 765430
Email: hmcoroner@durham.gov.uk
Coroner's Officers:
Police Office, Wesleyan Road, Spennymoor DL16 6FB
Tel: 0345 606 0365
Fax: 01325 742732

HARTLEPOOL
Coroner: C.W.M. Donnelly
c/o Donnelly McArdle Adamson, Solicitors, 155 York Road, Hartlepool TS26 9EQ
Tel: 01429 861563
Fax: 01429 260199

EAST YORKSHIRE

EAST RIDING & KINGSTON-UPON-HULL
Coroner: Prof. Paul V. Marks
Coroner's Office & Court, The Guildhall, Kingston-upon-Hull HU1 2AA
Tel: 01482 613009
Fax: 01482 613020

ESSEX

ESSEX & THURROCK
Coroner: Mrs Caroline Beasley-Murray
New Bridge House, 60–68 New London Road, Chelmsford CM2 0PD
Tel: 01245 506837
Fax: 01245 506839/840
Email: coroner@essex.gov.uk

SOUTHEND & SOUTH EAST ESSEX
Deputy Coroner: Yvonne Blake
New Bridge House, 60–68 New London Road, Chelmsford CM2 0PD
Tel: 01245 506837
Fax: 01245 506839/840
Email: coroner@essex.gov.uk

GLOUCESTERSHIRE

GLOUCESTERSHIRE
Coroner: Alan C. Crickmore
Gloucestershire Coroner's Court, Corinium Avenue, Barnwood, Gloucester GL4 3DJ
Tel: 01452 305661
Fax: 01452 412618
Email: coroner@gloucestershire.gov.uk

GREATER MANCHESTER

MANCHESTER
Coroner: N.S. Meadows
HM Coroner's Office, Crown Square, Deansgate, Manchester M60 1PR
Tel: 0161 830 4222
Fax: 0161 274 7329
Email: coroners@manchester.gov.uk

MANCHESTER NORTH
Coroner: Simon R. Nelson
Coroner's Office, The Phoenix Centre, Church Street, Heywood OL10 1LR
Tel: 01706 924815
Fax: 0844 963 2383
Email: coroners@rochdale.gov.uk

MANCHESTER SOUTH
Coroner: J.S. Pollard
Mount Tabor, Mottram Street, Stockport SK1 3PA
Tel: 0161 474 3993
Fax: 0161 474 3994
Email: john.pollard@stockport.gov.uk

MANCHESTER WEST
Coroner: Mrs Jennifer Leeming
Paderborn House, Civic Centre, Howell Croft North, Bolton BL1 1JW
Tel: 01204 338799

Fax: 01204 338798
Email: jennifer.leeming@bolton.gov.uk

HAMPSHIRE

CENTRAL HAMPSHIRE
Coroner: G.A. Short
c/o Blake Lapthorn, New King's Court, Chandlers Ford, Eastleigh SO53 3LG
Tel: 023 8090 8090
Fax: 0844 620 3412
Email: centralhants-coroner@bllaw.co.uk

NORTH EAST
Coroner: A.M. Bradley
Goldings, London Road, Basingstoke RG21 4AN
Tel: 01256 478119
Fax: 01256 814292
Coroner's Officer: David Richards
As above

PORTSMOUTH & SOUTH EAST HAMPSHIRE
Coroner: David Clark Horsley
The Guildhall, Guildhall Square, Portsmouth PO1 2AB
Tel: 023 9268 8326
Fax: 023 9268 8331
Email: coroners.office@portsmouthcc.gov.uk

SOUTHAMPTON & NEW FOREST
Coroner: K. St J. Wiseman
Coroner's Court, 12–18 Hulse Road, Southampton SO15 2JX
Tel: 023 8071 0452
Fax: 023 8067 4479
Coroner's Officers:
Tel: 023 8067 4266

HEREFORDSHIRE

HEREFORDSHIRE
Coroner: H.G.M. Bricknell
36/37 Bridge Street, Hereford HR4 9DJ
Tel: 01432 355301
Fax: 01432 356619
DX: 17207 HEREFORD
Email: mb@lambecorner.co.uk

HERTFORDSHIRE

HERTFORDSHIRE
Coroner: E.G. Thomas
The Old Courthouse, St Albans Road East, Hatfield AL10 0ES
Tel: 01707 292707
Fax: 01707 897399
DX: 100702 HATFIELD
Email: coroner.service@hertfordshire.gov.uk
Coroner's Officers:
As above

ISLE OF WIGHT

ISLE OF WIGHT
Coroner: Mrs C. Sumeray
3–9 Quay Street, Newport, Isle of Wight PO30 5BB
Tel: 01983 520697
Fax: 01983 527678
Email: coroners@iow.gov.uk

KENT

CENTRAL & SOUTH EAST KENT
Coroner: Rachel Redman
Elphicks Farmhouse, Hunton, Maidstone ME15 0SB
Tel: 01622 820412
Fax: 01622 820800
Email: rredman@kentcoroner.co.uk
Coroner's Officers:
Ashford Police Station, Tufton Street, Ashford TN23 1BT
Tel: (Ashford) 01233 896242; (Folkestone/Hythe) 896171; (Dover; Faversham) 896172
Fax: 01233 896249

MID KENT & MEDWAY
Coroner: Patricia Harding
The Archbishop's Palace, Mill Street, Maidstone ME15 6YE
Tel: 01622 701927
Fax: 01622 663690
Coroner's Officers (Maidstone):
Police Station, Palace Avenue, Maidstone ME15 6NF
Tel: 01622 604115/6
Fax: 01622 604119
Coroner's Officers (Medway):
Medway Maritime Hospital, Windmill Road, Gillingham ME7 5NY
Tel: 01634 848773
Fax: 01634 845092

NORTH EAST KENT
Coroner: Rebecca Cobb
5 Lloyd Road, Broadstairs CT10 1HX
Tel: 01843 863260
Fax: 01843 603927
Coroner's Officers:
Margate Police Station, Fort Hill, Margate
Tel: 01843 222170/1/3/5
Fax: 01843 222172

NORTH WEST KENT
Coroner: Roger Hatch
The White House, Melliker Lane, Hook Green, Meopham DA13 0JB
Tel: 01474 815747
Fax: 01474 815356
Email: nwkentcoroner@aol.com
Coroner's Officers:
Tunbridge Wells Police Station, Crescent Road, Tunbridge Wells TN1 2LU
Tel: 01892 502171/137
Fax: 01892 502172
North Kent Police Station, Thames Way, Northfleet DA11 8BD
Tel: 01474 366481/2
Fax: 01474 366489

LANCASHIRE

BLACKBURN, HYNDBURN AND RIBBLE VALLEY
Coroner: M.J.H. Singleton
King George's Hall, Northgate, Blackburn BB2 1AA
Tel: 01254 588680; mob: 07968 326068
Fax: 01254 588681
Email: michael.singleton@blackburn.gov.uk
Coroner's Officers: John Clucas; Jayne Morant; Darren Wingrove
The Royal Blackburn Hospital, Haslingden Road, Blackburn BB2 3HH
Tel: 01254 734116; mob: 07983 016369; 07940 93955

BLACKPOOL/FYLDE
Coroner: Alan Anthony Wilson
Municipal Buildings, Blackpool Council, Corporation Street, Blackpool FY1 1GB
Tel: 01253 477128
Fax: 01253 477129
Email: kerry.hall@blackpool.gov.uk
Coroner's Officers:
Lancashire Constabulary, Montague Street, Blackpool
Tel: 01253 604207
Fax: 01253 604200

EAST LANCASHIRE
Coroner: Richard G. Taylor
6a Hargreaves Street, Burnley BB11 1ES
Tel: 01282 438446/446519
Fax: 01282 446525
DX: 23860 BURNLEY
Coroners Officers:
Tel: 01282 446519
Email: cheryl.grice@lancashire.gov.uk

PRESTON & WEST LANCASHIRE
Coroner: Dr James Adeley
2 Faraday Court, Faraday Drive, Fulwood, Preston PR2 9NB
Tel: 01772 703700
Fax: 01772 704422
Coroner's Officers:
Royal Preston Hospital, Sharoe Green Lane North, Fulwood, Preston
Tel: 01772 524740
Fax: 01772 524361
Chorley Police Station, St Thomas's Road, Chorley
Tel: 01257 246207
Fax. 01257 246348
Royal Lancaster Infirmary, Ashton Road, Lancaster LA1 4RP
Tel: 01524 516353
Fax: 01524 516059

LEICESTERSHIRE

LEICESTER CITY & SOUTH LEICESTERSHIRE
Coroner: C.E. Mason
The Town Hall, Leicester LE1 9BG
Tel: 0116 225 2534/2535/2509
Fax: 0116 225 2537
Email: leicester.coroner@leicester.gov.uk

RUTLAND & NORTH LEICESTERSHIRE
Coroner: T.H. Kirkman
Coroner's Office, Southfield Road, Loughborough LE11 2TR
Tel: 0116 305 7732
Fax: 01509 550473
Email: hmcoroner@leics.gov.uk

LINCOLNSHIRE

CENTRAL LINCOLNSHIRE
Coroner: S.P.G. Fisher
Lindum House, 10 Queen Street, Spilsbury PE23 5JE
Tel: 01522 552500
Fax: 01522 516055
Email: lincscoroner@lincolnshire.gov.uk
Coroner's Officers:
Area Police HQ, West Parade, Lincoln LN1 1YP
Tel: 01522 885217
Fax: 01522 885344
Area Police HQ, Grantham NG31 9DD
Tel: 01476 403217
Fax: 01476 403217
N.J. Jones, County Police Station, The Wong, Horncastle LN9 6EB
Tel: 01205 312330
Fax: 01205 312310

NORTH LINCOLNSHIRE & GRIMSBY
Coroner: Paul Kelly
HM Coroner's Office, The Town Hall, Knoll Street, Cleethorpes DN35 8LN
Tel: 01472 324005
Fax: 01472 324007
Email: coroners@nelincs.gov.uk

SOUTH LINCOLNSHIRE
Coroner: A.R.W. Forrest
Unit 1, Gilbert Drive, Endeavour Park, Boston PE21 7QT
Tel: 01522 552064
Coroner's Officer: J. Bradwell
County Police Station, Lincoln Lane, Boston PE21 8QS
Tel: 01205 312217; mob: 07768 503329
Fax: 01205 312353
Email: james.bradwell@lincs.pnn.police.uk

LONDON

CITY OF LONDON
Coroner: Paul Matthews
City of London Coroner's Court, Walbrook Wharf, 78–83 Upper Thames Street, London EC4R 3TD
Tel: 020 7332 1598
Fax: 020 7332 1800
Email: paul.major@cityoflondon.gov.uk

EASTERN DISTRICT OF GREATER LONDON
Coroner: Mr Chinyere Inyama
Coroner's Court, Queens Road, Walthamstow E17 8QP
Tel: 020 8496 5000
Fax: (Barking, Dagenham, Havering, Romford) 020 8496 3378; (Newham, Redbridge, Walthamstow) 020 8496 3379
Email: sue.hardie@walthamforest.gov.uk

INNER NORTH LONDON
Coroner: Ms Mary E. Hassell
St Pancras Coroner's Court, Camley Street, London NIC 4PP
Tel: 020 7387 4882
Fax: 020 7383 2485
Poplar Coroner's Court, 127 Poplar High Street, London E14 0AE
Tel: 020 7538 1201
Fax: 020 7538 0565

INNER SOUTH LONDON
Coroner: Dr Andrew Harris
Southwark Coroner's Court, 1 Tennis Street, London SE1 1YD
Tel: 020 7525 4200
Fax: 020 7525 6356
Email: andrew.harris@southwark.gov.uk

INNER WEST LONDON
Coroner: Fiona J. Wilcox
Westminster Coroner's Court, 65 Horseferry Road, London SW1P 2ED
Tel: 020 7802 4750
Fax: 020 7828 2837
Battersea Office, City of Westminster, City Hall, 5th Floor, Victoria Street, London SW1E 6QP
Tel: 020 7641 5305
Fax: 020 7641 5351

NORTH LONDON
Coroner: Andrew Walker
29 Wood Street, Barnet, London EN5 4BE
Tel: 020 8447 7680
Fax: 020 8447 7689/7690
Coroner's Clerk: Jacqueline Reid
Tel: 020 8447 7693; mob: 07772 137993
Email: jacqueline.reed@hmc-northlondon.co.uk

SOUTHERN DISTRICT OF GREATER LONDON
Coroner: Dr Roy Palmer
Croydon Coroner's Court, Barclay Road, Croydon CR9 3NE
Tel: 020 8681 3275
Fax: 020 8680 0999
Email: info@southlondoncoroner.org
Website: www.southlondoncoroner.org
Coroner's officers:
St Blaise Building, Bromley Civic Centre, Stockwell Close, Bromley BR1 3UH
Tel: 020 8313 1883
Fax: 020 8313 3673

WEST LONDON
Coroner: to be confirmed
25 Bagleys Lane, Fulham, London SW6 2QA
Tel: 020 8753 6800/02
Fax: 020 8753 6803
Email: hmcoroner@lbhf.gov.uk

MERSEYSIDE

LIVERPOOL
Coroner: A.J.A. Rebello OBE
HM Coroner's Court, St George's Hall, St George's Place, Liverpool L1 1JJ
Tel: 0151 225 5770/5057/5058
Fax: 0151 703 6838
Email: coroner@liverpool.gov.uk

SEFTON, KNOWSLEY & ST HELENS
Coroner: Christopher Kent Sumner
Southport Town Hall, Lord Street, Southport PR8 1DA
Tel: 0151 934 2746/9
Fax: 01704 534321
Email: coroner@sefton.gov.uk
Sefton North, Sefton South
Southport Police Station, Law Courts, Southport
Tel: 0151 777 3480
Fax: 01704 512784
Email: coroner@sefton.gov.uk
Knowsley & St Helens

Coroner's Office, Whiston Hospital, Whiston, Merseyside
Tel: 0151 430 1238
Fax: 0151 426 6694
Email: coroner@sefton.gov.uk

WIRRAL
Coroner: Christopher W. Johnson
South Annexe, Town Hall, Brighton Street, Wallasey, Wirral CH48 8ED
Tel: 0151 691 8648
Fax: 0151 691 8474
Email: hmcoroner@wirral.gov.uk

NORFOLK

NORFOLK
Coroner: Mrs Jacqueline Lake (wef October 2013)
Office: 69–75 Thorpe Road, Norwich NR1 1UA
Court: Eastgate House, 122 Thorpe Road, Norwich NR1 1RT
Tel: 01603 663302
Fax: 01603 665511
Email: norfolk@coroner.norfolk.gov.uk
Coroner's Officers:
King's Lynn Police Station, St James Street, King's Lynn, Norfolk PE30 5DE
Tel: 01553 665088
Fax: 01553 665017

NORTH YORKSHIRE

EASTERN DISTRICT
Coroner: M.D. Oakley
Rose Cottage, Oswaldkirk, York YO62 5XT
Tel: 01439 788339; mob: 07860 789957
Coroner's Officers:
Police Station, Northway, Scarborough YO12 7AD
Tel: 01723 509332
Fax: 01723 509030
Police Station, 72 High Street, Northallerton DL7 8BR
Tel: 01609 789458
Fax: 01609 789413

WESTERN DISTRICT
Coroner: R. Turnbull
21 Grammar School Lane, Northallerton DL6 1DF
Tel: 01609 533805; 533843 (Secretary)
Fax: 01609 780793
Email: coronersadmin@northyorks.gov.uk
Coroner's Officers:
Police Station, North Yorkshire Police, Beckwith Head Road, Beckwith, Harrogate HG1 1FR
Tel: 01423 539332
Fax: 01423 539302
Police Station, 72 High Street, Northallerton DL7 8ES
Tel: 01609 789458
Fax: 01609 789413
Police Station, Otley Street, Skipton BD23 1EZ
Tel: 01423 539731
Fax: 01423 539701
Police Station, Portholme Road, Selby YO8 4QQ
Tel: 01904 669654
Fax: 01904 669651

TEESSIDE
Coroner: M.J.F. Sheffield
Register Office, Corporation Road, Middlesbrough, Cleveland TS1 2DA
Tel: 01642 729350
Fax: 01642 729948
DX: 60532 MIDDLESBROUGH 1
Email: gail_walls@middlesbrough.gov.uk

YORK
Senior Coroner: W.D.F. Coverdale
Sentinel House, Peasholme Green, York YO1 7PP
Tel: 01904 716000
Fax: 01904 716100
DX: 61510 YORK
Email: donald.coverdale@warekay.co.uk
Coroner's Officers:
North Yorkshire Police Divisional HQ, Fulford Road, York YO1 4BY
Tel: 01904 669332
Fax: 01904 479965

NORTHAMPTONSHIRE

NORTHAMPTONSHIRE
Coroner: Mrs A. Pember
110 Whitworth Road, Northampton NN1 4HJ
Tel: 01604 624732
Fax: 01604 623681
Email: coroners@northantscoroner.com
Coroner's Officers:
Campbell Square Police Station, Northampton NN1 3EL
Tel: 03000 111 222
Fax: 01604 888801
Kettering Police Station, London Road, Kettering NN15 7PQ
Tel: 03000 111 222
Fax: 01604 888729

NORTHUMBERLAND

NORTH NORTHUMBERLAND
Coroner: Tony Brown
Deputy Coroner: Paul Dunn
Assistant Deputy Coroner: David Mitford
17 Church Street, Berwick-upon-Tweed TD15 1EE
Tel: 01289 304318
Fax: 01289 303591
Email: jane.tait@northumberland.gov.uk
Coroner's Officer:
Northumbria Police, Lintonville Terrace, Ashington NE63 9JX
Tel: 01661 861654
Fax: 01661 861658

SOUTH NORTHUMBERLAND
Coroner: E. Armstrong
3 Stanley Street, Blyth NE24 2BS
Tel: 01670 354777
Fax: 01670 797891
DX: 62601 BLYTH
Email: ann.battensby@northumberland.gov.uk

NOTTINGHAMSHIRE

NOTTINGHAMSHIRE
Coroner: Miss M. Casey
HM Coroner's Office, The Council House, Old Market Square, Nottingham NG1 2DT
Tel: 0115 841 5553
Fax: 0115 876 5689
Email: coroners@nottinghamcity.gov.uk

OXFORDSHIRE

OXFORDSHIRE
Coroner: D.M. Salter
Court: Coroner's Court, County Hall, New Road, Oxford OX1 1ND
Office: Oxfordshire Coroner's Office, Oxford Register Office, 2nd Floor, 1 Tidmarsh Lane, Oxford OX1 1NS
Tel: 01865 815020
Fax: 01865 783391
Email: coroners.oxfordshire@oxfordshire.gov.uk

SHROPSHIRE

MID & NORTH-WEST SHROPSHIRE
Coroner: J.P. Ellery
HM Coroner's Service, Third Floor, Guildhall, Frankwell Quay, Shrewsbury SY3 8HQ
Tel: 01743 281297/8
Fax: 01743 2812890
Email: john.ellery@shropshire.gov.uk
Coroner's Officer:
West Mercia Police, Police HQ, Clive Road, Monkmoor, Shrewsbury SY2 5RW
Tel: 01743 237445
Fax: 01743 264879

SOUTH SHROPSHIRE
Coroner: J.P. Ellery
HM Coroner's Service, Third Floor, Guildhall, Frankwell Quay, Shrewsbury SY3 8HQ
Tel: 01743 281297/8
Fax: 01743 2812890
Email: john.ellery@shropshire.gov.uk
Coroner's Officers:
Ludlow Police Station, Lower Galdeford, Ludlow, Shropshire SY8 1SA
Tel: 0300 333 3000 ext. 4608
Fax: 01584 879302

TELFORD & WREKIN BOROUGH COUNCIL
Coroner: J.P. Ellery
HM Coroner's Service, Third Floor, Guildhall, Frankwell Quay, Shrewsbury SY3 8HQ
Tel: 01743 281297/8
Fax: 01743 2812890
Email: john.ellery@shropshire.gov.uk
Coroner's Officers:
West Mercia Police, Wellington Police Station, Victoria Road, Wellington, Telford TF1 1LQ
Tel: 01743 791937/792863
Fax: 01743 792248

SOMERSET

EASTERN SOMERSET
Coroner: T. Williams
22 Bath Street, Frome BA11 1DL

Tel: 0117 973 4259
Fax: 0117 973 6430
Email: info@hmcoroner.co.uk

WESTERN SOMERSET
Coroner: Michael Richard Rose
Blackbrook Gate, Blackbrook Park Avenue, Taunton TA1 2PG
Tel: 0845 209 1796
Fax: 01845 209 2572
DX: 97175 TAUNTON (Blackbrook)
Email: coroner@clarkewillmott.com
Coroner's Officers:
The Police Station, Shuttern, Taunton TA1 3QA
Tel: 01823 363271
Fax: 01823 363103

SOUTH YORKSHIRE

EAST DISTRICT
Coroner: Ms Nicola J. Mundy
Coroner's Court & Office, 5 Union Street, off St Sepulchre Gate West, Doncaster DN1 3AE
Tel: 01302 320844
Fax: 01302 364833
Email: hmc.doncaster@doncaster.gov.uk
Coroner's Officers:
The Police Station, Main Street, Rotherham S60 1QU
Tel: 01709 832031
Fax: 01709 832145

WEST DISTRICT
Coroner: C.P. Dorries OBE
Medico-Legal Centre, Watery Street, Sheffield S3 7ET
Tel: 0114 273 8721
Fax: 0114 272 6247
Email: medico-legalcentre@sheffield.gov.uk
Coroner's Officers:
Barnsley Police Station, Churchfield, Barnsley
Tel: 0122 673 6031
Fax: 0122 673 6295

STAFFORDSHIRE

STAFFORDSHIRE SOUTH
Coroner: A.A. Haigh
Coroner's Office, 1 Staffordshire Place, Stafford ST16 2LP
Tel: 01785 276127
Fax: 01785 276128
DX: 712320 STAFFORD 5
Email: sscor@staffordshire.gov.uk
Coroner's Officers:
Justice Department, Block 9, Weston Road Police Complex, Stafford ST18 0YY
Tel: (Stafford) 01785 235537; (Burton-on-Trent) 01785 235510; mob: 07870 684969; (Cannock) 01785 235524

STOKE-ON-TRENT & NORTH STAFFORDSHIRE
Coroner: I.S. Smith
Coroner's Court & Chambers, 547 Hartshill Road, Hartshill, Stoke-on-Trent ST4 6HF
Tel: 01782 234777
Fax: 01782 232074
Email: coroners@stoke.gov.uk

SUFFOLK

SUFFOLK
Coroner: Dr Peter Dean
Bury St Edmunds Police Station, Raingate Street, Bury St Edmunds IP33 2AP
Tel: 01284 774167
Fax: 01284 774204
Email: coroner_bury@suffolk.pnn.police.uk
Coroner's Officers:
Coroner's Office, First Floor, Landmark House, 4 Egerton Road, Ipswich IP1 5PF
Tel: 01473 613888 ext. 3167/3159
Fax: 01473 613619
Suffolk Police, Old Nelson Street, Lowestoft
Tel: 01986 835167
Fax: 01986 835174

SURREY

SURREY
Coroner: R. Travers
HM Coroner's Court, Station Approach, Woking GU22 7AP
Tel: 01483 776138
Fax: 01483 765460
Coroner's Officers:
Tel: 01483 637300
Fax: 01483 634814

SUSSEX (EAST)

CITY OF BRIGHTON & HOVE
Coroner: Veronica Hamilton-Deeley
The Coroner's Office, Woodvale, Lewes Road, Brighton BN2 3QB
Tel: 01273 292046
Fax: 01273 292047
Coroner's Officers:
Brighton Police Station, John Street, Brighton BN2 2LA
Tel: 01273 665525
Fax: 01273 404042

EAST SUSSEX
Coroner: A.R. Craze
28/29 Grand Parade, St Leonard's-on-Sea TN37 6DR
Tel: 01424 200144
Fax: 01424 200145
Email: eastsussex.coroner@eastsussex.gov.uk
Coroner's Officers:
Hammonds Drive Patrol Centre, Hammonds Drive, Eastbourne BN23 1PW
Tel: 01273 475432
Fax: 01273 404300
The Police Station, Bohemia Road, Hastings TN34 1BT
Tel: 01273 404371
Fax: 01273 404394

SUSSEX (WEST)

WEST SUSSEX
Coroner: Penelope A. Schofield
County Record Office, Orchard Street, Chichester PO19 1DD
Tel: 0330 222 7100
Fax: 01243 753644

Coroner's Officers:
Centenary House, Durrington Lane, Worthing
Tel: 01243 404012/3
Fax: 01243 404020
Police Station, Hurst Road, Horsham
Tel: 01243 404163
Fax: 01243 404186
Email: hm.coroner@westsussex.gov.uk

TYNE AND WEAR

GATESHEAD & SOUTH TYNESIDE
Coroner: T. Carney
35 Station Road, Hevvurn NE31 1LA
Tel: 0191 483 8771
Fax: 0191 428 6699
Email: t.carney@terence-carney.co.uk
Coroner's Officers (Gateshead):
35 Station Road, as above
Tel: 0191 483 8192
Fax: 0191 483 9069
Coroner's Officers (South Tyneside):
35 Station Road, as above
Tel: 0191 483 8189
Fax: 0191 483 9761

NEWCASTLE-UPON-TYNE
Coroner: Karen Lorraine Dilks
Coroner's Department, Civic Centre, Barras Bridge, Newcastle-upon-Tyne NE1 8PS
Tel: 0191 277 7280
Fax: 0191 261 2952
Email: karen.dilks@newcastle.gov.uk

NORTH TYNESIDE
Coroner: E. Armstrong
3 Stanley Street, Blyth NE24 2BS
Tel: 01670 354777
Fax: 01670 797891
DX: 62601 BLYTH
Email: ann.battensby@northumberland.gov.uk

CITY OF SUNDERLAND
Coroner: D. Winter
Civic Centre, Burdon Road, Sunderland SR2 7DN
Tel: 0191 561 7843
Fax: 0191 553 7803
Email: derek.winter@sunderland.gov.uk

WARWICKSHIRE

WARWICKSHIRE
Coroner: S. McGovern
HM Coroner Office, Warwickshire Justice Centre, Newbold Terrace, Leamington Spa CV32 4EL
Tel: 01926 684065
Fax: 01926 682513
Email: coronerofficer@warwickshire.pnn.police.uk
Coroner's Officers (Southern Area):
Southern Area HM Coroner Office, Warwickshire Justice Centre, as above
Tel: 01926 684228/4229/4065
Fax: 01926 682513
Coroner's Officers (Northern Area – Bedworth & Nuneaton):
Bedworth Police Station, High Street, Bedworth CV12 8NH

Tel: 02476 483361/8
Fax: 02476 483392

WEST MIDLANDS

BIRMINGHAM/SOLIHULL
Coroner: Aidan Keith Cotter
Coroner's Court, 50 Newton Street, Birmingham B4 6NE
Tel: 0121 303 3228
Fax: 0121 233 4841
Email: coronercotter@birmingham.gov.uk

COVENTRY
Coroner: Sean P. McGovern
Police HQ, Little Park Street, Coventry CV1 2JX
Tel: 02476 539017
Fax: 02476 539804
Email: coroner@coventry.gov.uk

BLACK COUNTRY
Coroner: Robin J. Balmain
Smethwick Council House, High Street, Smethwick B66 3NT
Tel: 0845 352 7483
Fax: 0121 569 5384
Email: barbara_powles@sandwell.gov.uk
Coroner's Officers:
Tel: 0845 352 7480/1/4/5/8/9

WEST YORKSHIRE

EASTERN DISTRICT
Coroner: D. Hinchliff
Coroner's Office, 71 Northgate, Wakefield WF1 3BS
Tel: 01924 302180
Fax: 01924 302184
Coroner's Officers:
Symons House, Belgrave Street, Leeds LS2 8DD
Tel: 0113 397 0600/0602/0607
Fax: 0113 245 4892
Email: leedscoroner@wakefield.gov.uk
71 Northgate, Wakefield WF1 3BS
Tel: 01924 293270; 292683; 292684; 293265
Fax: 01924 302184
Email: hmcoroner@wakefield.gov.uk

WESTERN DISTRICT
Acting Coroner: Prof. Paul V. Marks
Coroner's Office, The City Courts, Bradford BD1 1LA
Tel: 01274 391362
Fax: 01274 721794
Email: hmc@bradford.gov.uk
Coroner's Officers:
Lawcroft House, Lilycroft Road, Bradford BD9 5AF
Tel: 01274 475299
West Yorkshire Police, Keighley Division, Keighley
Tel: 01535 615788
West Yorkshire Police, Dewsbury Division, Aldams Road, Dewsbury
Tel: 01924 431070
West Yorkshire Police, Huddersfield Division, Civic Centre, Huddersfield
Tel: 01484 436700
HM Coroner's Office, 8 Carlton Street, Halifax HX1 2AL

Tel: 01422 354606
Fax: 01422 380153

WILTSHIRE

WILTSHIRE & SWINDON
Coroner: David W.G. Ridley
Wiltshire & Swindon Coroner's Court, 26 Endless Street, Salisbury SP1 1DP
Tel: 01722 438900
Fax: 01722 332223
Email: wscoronersoffice@wiltshire.gov.uk
Coroner's Officers:
Divisional Police HQ, Wilton Road, Salisbury SP2 7HR
Tel: 01722 435293
Fax: 01722 435240
Divisional Police HQ, Police Station, Gablecross, Shrivenham Road, South Marston, Swindon SN3 4RB
Tel: 01793 507841
Fax: 01793 507840

WORCESTERSHIRE

WORCESTERSHIRE
Coroner: G.U. Williams
The Court House, Bewdley Road, Stourport-on-Severn DY13 8XE
Tel: 01299 824029
Fax: 01299 879238
Email: coroner@worcestershire.gov.uk
Coroner's Officers:
Police Station, Castle Street, Worcester WR1 3AD
Tel: 01905 331026
Fax: 01905 331025
Police Station, Grove Street, Redditch B98 8DD
Tel: 01527 586186
Fax: 01527 586116

WALES

BRIDGEND & GLAMORGAN VALLEYS [PEN-Y-BONT & CHYMOEDD MORGANWG]
Coroner: Louise Hunt
The Coroner's Office, Rock Grounds, Aberdare CF44 7AE
Tel: 01685 885202
Fax: 01685 885250
Email: coroner.admin@rctcbc.gov.uk
Coroner's Officer: Patrick Williams
Police Station, Swan Street, Merthyr Tydfil
Tel: 01685 724228
Coroner's Officer: Stuart Griffiths
Police Station, 1–3 Heol y Gyfraith, Talbot Green, Rhondda Cynon Taff
Tel: 01443 743698
Coroner's Officer: Mark Adams
Police Station, Pandy Road, Aberkenfig, Bridgend
Tel: 01656 762968

CARDIFF & THE VALE OF GLAMORGAN [CAERDYDD & BRO MORGANNWG]
Coroner: to be confirmed
Coroner's Court and Offices, Central Police Station, Cathays Park, Cardiff CF10 3NN
Tel: 029 2022 2111 ext. 30697/8/9
Fax: 029 2023 3886

CARDIGANSHIRE [SIR ABERTEIFI]
Coroner: P.L. Brunton
6 Upper Portland Street, Aberystwyth, Ceredigion SY23 2DU
Tel: 01970 612567; 617931
Fax: 01970 615572
Email: peter.brunton@bruntonandco.co.uk
Coroner's Officer:
Aberystwyth Police Station, Boulevard St Brieuc, Aberystwyth SY23 1PH
Tel: 01970 612791
Fax: 01970 625174

CARMARTHENSHIRE [SIR GAERFYRDDIN]
Coroner: Mark Layton
The Town Hall, Hamilton Terrace, Milford Haven SA73 3JW
Tel: 01646 698129
Fax: 01646 690607
Email: hmcpembs1@btconnect.com

GWENT
Coroner: D.T. Bowen
Victoria Chambers, 11 Clytha Park Road, Newport NP20 4PB
Tel: 01633 264194
Fax: 01633 841146
Email: davidtbowen@colbornex.org.uk

NEATH & PORT TALBOT [CASTELL-NEDD & PHORT TALBOT]
Coroner: Mr Philip Rogers
The Coroner's Office, The Civic Centre, Oystermouth Road, Swansea SA1 3SN
Tel: 01792 636237
Fax: 01792 636603
Email: coroner@swansea.gov.uk
Coroner's Officer:
Neath Police Station, Gnoll Park Road, Neath SA11 3BN
Tel: 01792 562784

NORTH WALES (EAST AND CENTRAL) [GOGLEDD CYMRU (DWYRIAN A CANOL)]
Coroner: John Gittins
County Hall, Wynnstay Road, Ruthin LL15 1YN
Tel: 01824 708047
Fax: 01824 708048
DX: 21839 RUTHIN
Email: coroner@denbighshire.gov.uk
Coroner's Officers:
North Wales Police, Central Division Headquarters, Ffordd William Morgan, St Asaph Business Park, St Asaph, Denbighshire LL17 0HQ
Tel: 01745 588607
Eastern Control Room, Police Station, Bodhyfryd, Wrexham LL12 7BW
Tel: 01978 348555

NORTH WEST WALES [GOGLEDD GORLLEWIN CYMRU]
Coroner: D. Pritchard Jones
37 Castle Square, Caernarfon, Gwynedd LL55 2NN
Tel: 01286 672804
Fax: 01286 675217
Email: coroner@pritchardjones.co.uk

PEMBROKESHIRE [SIR BENFRO]
Coroner: Mark Layton
The Town Hall, Hamilton Terrace, Milford Haven SA73 3JW
Tel: 01646 698129
Fax: 01646 690607
Email: hmcpembs1@btconnect.com
Coroner's Officer: Jeremy Davies
The Police Station, Charles Street, Milford Haven SA73 2HP
Tel: 01646 690799
Fax: 01646 698873

POWYS [POWYS]
Coroner: Louise Hunt
Coroner's Office, 1st Floor Rock Ground, Aberdare, Rhondda-Cynnon-taf CF44 7AE
Tel: 01685 885202
Fax: 01685 885250
Coroner's Officer:
Email: gavin.lindsay@dyfed-powys.pnn.police.uk

CITY AND COUNTY OF SWANSEA [ABERTAWE]
Coroner: Philip Rogers
The Coroner's Office, Civic Centre, Oystermouth Road, Swansea SA1 3SN
Tel: 01792 636237
Fax: 01792 636603
Coroner's Officer:
Central Police Station, Grove Place, Swansea
Tel: 01792 450698

ALPHABETICAL INDEX TO CORONERS' DISTRICTS

Part V

PROBATE REGISTRARS AND PROBATE COURTS

Probate Registrars and Probate Courts

Website: www.justice.gov.uk/courts/probate/probate-registries

All registries are open Monday to Friday. Most are open from 09:30–16:00 (London 10:00–16:00).

BIRMINGHAM (DISTRICT REGISTRY)
Registrar: Ms P. Walbeoff
Probate Manager: Mrs J. O'Dwyer
The Priory Courts, 33 Bull Street, Birmingham B4 6DU
Tel: 0121 681 3400
DX: 701990 BIRMINGHAM 7

BODMIN (SUB-REGISTRY)
Registrar: Mrs B. Phillips (Bristol DPR)
Probate Manager: Mrs Emma Sherwin
The Law Courts, Launceston Road, Bodmin, Cornwall PL31 2AL
Postal address: The Civil Justice Centre, 2 Redcliff Street, Bristol BS1 6GR
Tel: 01208 261581
Fax: 01208 77542
DX: 136847 BODMIN 2

BRIGHTON (DISTRICT REGISTRY)
Registrar: Miss H. Whitby
Probate Manager: Mr M. Hussain
William Street, Brighton BN2 0RF
Tel: 01273 573510
Fax: 01273 625845
DX: 98073 BRIGHTON 3

BRISTOL (DISTRICT REGISTRY)
Registrar: Mrs B. Phillips
Court Manager: Mrs Christine Chelton
The Civil Justice Centre, 2 Redcliff Street, Bristol BS1 6GR
Tel: 0117 366 4960/4961
DX: 94400 BRISTOL 5

CAERNARFON (SUB-REGISTRY)
Registrar: Mrs F. C. Herdman (Cardiff DPR)
Probate Manager: Mr R. Perry
Criminal Justice Centre, Llanberis Road, Caernarfon, Gwynedd LL55 2DF
Postal address: 3rd Floor, Cardiff Magistrates' Court, Fitzalan Place, Cardiff CF24 0RZ
Tel: 01286 669755
Fax: 01286 671509
DX: 744381 CAERNARFON 6

CARDIFF PROBATE REGISTRY OF WALES
Registrar: Mrs F. C. Herdman
Probate Manager: Mrs Yvette Owen
3rd Floor, Cardiff Magistrates' Court, Fitzalan Place, Cardiff CF24 0RZ
Tel: 029 2047 4373
Fax: 029 2045 6411
DX: 743940 CARDIFF 38

CARLISLE (SUB-REGISTRY)
Registrar: Mr Keiron Murphy (Newcastle DPR)
Courts of Justice, Earl Street, Carlisle, Cumbria CA1 1DJ
Postal address: Newcastle DPR, No 1 Waterloo Square, Newcastle-upon-Tyne NE1 4DR
Tel: 0191 211 2170
DX: 63034 CARLISLE
Office open by appointment only

CARMARTHEN (SUB-REGISTRY)
Registrar: Mrs F.C. Herdman (Cardiff DPR)
Probate Manager: Mrs Yvette Owen
Carmarthen Hearing Centre, Hill House, Picton Terrace, Carmarthen SA31 3BS
Postal address: 3rd Floor, Cardiff Magistrates' Court, Fitzalan Place, Cardiff CF24 0RZ
Tel: 01267 242560

Fax: 01267 245047
DX: 99574 CARMARTHEN 2

CHESTER (SUB-REGISTRY)
Registrar: Mr Keiron Murphy (Manchester DPR)
Chester Civil Justice Centre, Trident House, Little St John Street, Chester CH1 1SN
Postal address: Liverpool District Probate Registry, Queen Elizabeth II Law Courts, Derby Square, Liverpool L2 1XA
Tel: 0151 236 8264
Fax: 0151 227 4634
DX: 702470 CHESTER 18
Office open by appointment only

EXETER (SUB-REGISTRY)
Registrar: Mrs B. Phillips (Bristol DPR)
Probate Manager: Mr G.R. Bower
1st Floor, Exeter Crown and County Courts, Southernhay Gardens, Exeter EX1 1UH
Postal address: Bristol District Probate Registry, The Civil Justice Centre, 2 Redcliff Street, Bristol BS1 6GR
Tel: 01392 415370
Fax: 01392 415608
DX: 98442 EXETER 2

GLOUCESTER (SUB-REGISTRY)
Registrar: Mrs F.C. Herdman (Oxford DPR)
Probate Manager: Mrs Samantha Jenkins
2nd Floor, Combined Court Building, Kimbrose Way, Gloucester GL1 2DG
Postal address: Oxford District Probate Registry, Combined Court Building, St Aldates, Oxford OX1 1LY
Tel: 01452 834966
Fax: 01452 834970
DX: 98663 GLOUCESTER 5

IPSWICH (DISTRICT REGISTRY)
Registrar: Miss H. Whitby
Office Manager: Miss C. Buckingham
Ground Floor, 8 Arcade Street, Ipswich IP1 1EJ
Tel: 01473 284260
Fax: 01473 231951
DX: 97733 IPSWICH 3

LANCASTER (SUB-REGISTRY)
Registrar: Mr Keiron Murphy (Manchester DPR)
Room 111, Mitre House, Church Street, Lancaster LA1 1HE
Postal address: Queen Elizabeth II Law Courts, Derby Square, Liverpool L2 1XA
Tel: 0151 236 8264
Fax: 0151 227 4634
DX: 145883 LANCASTER 2
Open by appointment only

LEEDS (DISTRICT REGISTRY)
Registrar: Mr Keiron Murphy
Probate Manager: Mrs Sally Holding
York House, 31 York Place, Leeds LS1 2BA
Tel: 0113 389 6133
Fax: 0113 389 6123
DX: 26451 LEEDS PARK SQUARE

LEICESTER (SUB-REGISTRY)
Registrar: Mrs F.C. Herdman (Oxford DPR)
Crown Court Building, 90 Wellington Street, Leicester LE1 6HG
Postal address: Oxford District Probate Registry, Combined Court Building, St Aldates, Oxford OX1 1LY
Tel: 0116 285 3380
DX: 17403 LEICESTER 3

LINCOLN (SUB-REGISTRY)
Registrar: Mr Keiron Murphy (Leeds DPR)
Probate Manager: Mr N. Kitching
360 High Street, Lincoln LN5 7PS
Postal address: Leeds District Probate Registry, York House, York Place, Leeds LS1 2BA
Tel: 01522 523648
Fax: 01522 539903
DX: 703231 LINCOLN 6

LIVERPOOL (DISTRICT REGISTRY)
Registrar: Mr Keiron Murphy
Probate Manager: Mrs D. Shone
Queen Elizabeth II Law Courts, Derby Square, Liverpool L2 1XA
Tel: 0151 236 8264
Fax: 0151 227 4634
DX: 14246 LIVERPOOL 1

LONDON PROBATE DEPARTMENT
Registrar: Miss H. Whitby
Probate Manager: Tina Constantinou
London Probate Department, PRFD, First Avenue House, 42–49 High Holborn, 7th Floor, London WC1V 6NP
Tel: 020 7947 6939; (Probate Helpline) 0845 302 0900
Fax: 020 7947 6946
DX: 160011 KINGSWAY 7
Email: londonpersonalapplicationenquiries@hmcts.gsi.gov.uk;
londonsolicitorsenquiries@hmcts.gsi.gov.uk

MAIDSTONE (SUB-REGISTRY)
Registrar: Miss H. Whitby (Brighton DPR)
The Law Courts, Barker Road, Maidstone ME16 8EQ
Postal address: Brighton District Probate Registry, William Street, Brighton, East Sussex BN2 0RF
Tel: 01273 573510
DX: 130066 MAIDSTONE 7
Office open by appointment only

MANCHESTER (DISTRICT REGISTRY)
Registrar: Mr Keiron Murphy
Probate Manager: Stephen Howard
Manchester Civil Justice Centre, Ground Floor, 1 Bridge Street West, PO Box 4240, Manchester M60 1WJ
Tel: 0161 240 5700/2
DX: 724784 MANCHESTER 44

MIDDLESBROUGH (SUB-REGISTRY)
Registrar: Mr Keiron Murphy (Newcastle DPR)
Probate Manager: Mr Mark Burden (at Newcastle DPR)
Teesside Combined Court Centre, Russell Street, Middlesbrough TS1 2AE
Postal address: 1 Waterloo Square, Newcastle-upon-Tyne NE1 4DR
Tel: 0191 211 2170
Open by appointment only

NEWCASTLE-UPON-TYNE (DISTRICT REGISTRY)
Registrar: Mr Keiron Murphy
Probate Manager: Mr Mark Burden
1 Waterloo Square, Newcastle-upon-Tyne NE1 4DR
Tel: 0191 211 2170
Fax: 0191 211 2184
DX: 61081 NEWCASTLE-UPON-TYNE 14

NORWICH (SUB-REGISTRY)
Registrar: Miss H. Whitby (Ipswich DPR)
Probate Manager: Mr T. Harvey
Combined Court Building, The Law Courts, Bishopgate, Norwich NR3 1UR
Postal address: Ipswich District Probate Registry, Ground Floor, 8 Arcade Street, Ipswich IP1 1EJ
Tel: 01603 728267
DX: 97390 NORWICH 5

NOTTINGHAM (SUB-REGISTRY)
Registrar: Ms P. Walbeoff (Birmingham DPR)
60 Canal Street, Nottingham NG1 7EJ
Postal address: Birmingham District Probate Registry, The Priory Courts, 33 Bull Street, Birmingham B4 6DU
Tel: 0121 681 3400
Open by appointment only

OXFORD (DISTRICT REGISTRY)
Registrar: Mrs F.C. Herdman
Probate Manager: Diane Rice
Combined Court Building, St Aldates, Oxford OX1 1LY
Tel: 01865 793050/5
DX: 96454 OXFORD 4

PETERBOROUGH (SUB-REGISTRY)
Registrar: Miss H. Whitby (Ipswich DPR)
1st Floor, Crown Building, Rivergate, Peterborough PE1 1EJ
Postal address: Ipswich District Probate Registry, Ground Floor, 8 Arcade Street, Ipswich IP1 1EJ
Tel: 01473 284260
DX: 97733 IPSWICH 3
Open by appointment only

SHEFFIELD (SUB-REGISTRY)
Registrar: Mr Keiron Murphy (Leeds DPR)
Probate Manager: Ms Lisa Joel
PO Box 832, The Law Courts, 50 West Bar, Sheffield S3 8YR
Tel: 0114 281 2596
Fax: 0114 273 0848
DX: 742916 SHEFFIELD 6

STOKE-ON-TRENT (SUB-REGISTRY)
Registrar: Ms P. Walbeoff (Birmingham DPR)
Combined Court Centre, Bethesda Street, Hanley, Stoke-on-Trent ST1 3BP
Postal address: Birmingham District Probate Registry, The Priory Courts, 33 Bull Street, Birmingham B4 6DU
Tel: 0121 681 3400
DX: 703363 HANLEY 3

WINCHESTER (DISTRICT REGISTRY)
Registrar: Mr A. Butler
Probate Manager: Julie Kingdom
4th Floor, Cromwell House, Andover Road, Winchester SO23 7EW
Tel: (solicitors' enquiries) 01962 897024; (personal applications) 01962 897029
DX: 96900 WINCHESTER 2

YORK (SUB-REGISTRY)
Registrar: Mr Keiron Murphy (Leeds DPR)
Piccadilly House, 55 Piccadilly, York YO1 9WL
Postal address: York House, 31 York Place, Leeds LS1 2BA
Tel: 0113 389 6133
DX: 26451 LEEDS PARK SQUARE
Open by appointment only

Part VI

THE CROWN PROSECUTION SERVICE (CPS)

CROWN PROSECUTION SERVICE (CPS)

The Crown Prosecution Service is the government department responsible for prosecuting criminal cases investigated by the police and other investigative authorities, including the Serious & Organised Crime Agency (SOCA), Independent Police Complaints Commission (IPCC), UK Borders Agency (UKBA), Department for Environment, Food and Rural Affairs (Defra), Department of Work and Pensions (DWP), and Department of Health and Her Majesty's Revenue & Customs (HMRC) in England and Wales.

As the principal prosecuting authority in England and Wales, the Crown Prosecution Service is responsible for: advising on and reviewing cases; determining any charges in more serious or complex cases; preparing cases for court; presenting cases at court.
Rose Court, 2 Southwark Bridge, London SE1 9HS
Tel: 020 3357 0000
Email: enquiries@cps.gsi.gov.uk
Website: www.cps.gov.uk
Director of Public Prosecutions: Keir Starmer QC (to October 2013)
Chief Executive: Peter Lewis CB
Principal Legal Advisor: Alison Levitt QC

CPS AREAS

CYMRU/WALES
Twentieth Floor, Capital Tower, Greyfriars Road, Cardiff CF10 3PL
Tel: 029 2080 3800
Chief Crown Prosecutor: Ed Beltrami
Area Business Manager: Mike Grist

EAST MIDLANDS
CPS East Midlands, 2 King Edward Court, King Edward Street, Nottingham NG1 1EL
Tel: 0115 852 3300
Chief Crown Prosecutor: Steve Chappell
Area Business Manager: Adele Clarke

EAST OF ENGLAND
CPS East of England HQ, County House, 100 New London Road, Chelmsford, Essex CM2 0RG
Tel: 01245 455800
Chief Crown Prosecutor: Grace Ononiwu
Area Business Manager: Susan Stovell

LONDON
CPS London, Rose Court, Fifth Floor, 2 Southwark Bridge, London SE1 9HS
Tel: 020 3357 0000
Chief Crown Prosecutor: Alison Saunders
Area Business Manager: Jean Ashton

MERSEY-CHESHIRE
CPS Mersey-Cheshire HQ, Seventh Floor, Royal Liver Building, Pier Head, Liverpool L3 1HN
Tel: 0151 239 6400
Chief Crown Prosecutor: Claire Lindley
Area Business Manager: Angela Walsh

NORTH EAST
CPS North East HQ, St Ann's Quay, 122 Quayside, Newcastle-upon-Tyne NE1 3BD
Tel: 0191 260 4200
Chief Crown Prosecutor: Wendy Williams
Area Business Manager: Ian Brown

NORTH WEST
CPS North West, PO Box 237, 8th Floor, Sunlight House, Quay Street, Manchester M60 3PS
Tel: 0161 827 4700
Chief Crown Prosecutor: Nazir Afzal
Area Business Manager: Louise Rice

SOUTH EAST
CPS South East HQ, Priory Gate, 29 Union Street, Maidstone ME14 1PT
Tel: 01622 356300
Chief Crown Prosecutor: Roger Coe-Salazar
Area Business Manager: Julie Heron

SOUTH WEST
CPS South West, 5th Floor, Kite Wing, Temple Quay House, 2 The Square, Bristol BS1 6PN
Tel: 0117 930 2800
Chief Crown Prosecutor: Barry Hughes
Area Business Manager: Sarah Trevelyan

THAMES AND CHILTERN
CPS Thames and Chiltern HQ, Eaton Court, 112 Oxford Road, Reading RG1 7LL
Tel: 0118 951 3600
Chief Crown Prosecutor: Baljit Ubhey
Area Business Manager: Karen Sawitzki

WESSEX
CPS Wessex HQ, Black Horse House, 8–10 Leigh Road, Eastleigh SO50 9FH
Tel: 023 8067 3800
Chief Crown Prosecutor: Kate Brown
Area Business Manager: Denise Meldrum

WEST MIDLANDS
CPS West Midlands, Colmore Gate, 2 Colmore Row, Birmingham B3 2QA
Tel: 0121 262 1300
Chief Crown Prosecutor: Harry Ireland
Area Business Manager: Laurence Sutton

YORKSHIRE AND HUMBERSIDE
CPS Yorkshire and Humberside, 27 Park Place, Leeds LS1 2SZ
Tel: 0113 290 2700
Chief Crown Prosecutor: Martin Goldman
Area Business Manager: Karen Wright

CPS DIRECT
Sixth Floor, United House, Piccadilly, York YO1 9PQ
Tel: 01904 545592
Chief Crown Prosecutor: Nick Hawkins
Area Business Manager: Claire Toogood

Part VII

CROWN OFFICE AND PROCURATOR FISCAL SERVICE (SCOTLAND) (COPFS)

CROWN OFFICE AND PROCURATOR FISCAL SERVICE (SCOTLAND) (COPFS)

The Crown Office and Procurator Fiscal Service (COPFS) is Scotland's sole prosecution service. It is also responsible for the investigation of deaths that require further explanation, and for investigating allegations of criminal conduct against police officers.

COPFS is brigaded into four federations: National, North, West and East. The National Federation comprises Corporate Services and Serious Casework, headed by the Deputy Chief Executive and Director of Serious Casework (see below).

CROWN OFFICE

25 Chambers Street, Edinburgh EH1 1LA
Tel: 0844 561 2000
Fax: 0844 561 4089
Website: www.copfs.gov.uk
Crown Agent/Chief Executive: Catherine Dyer
Deputy Chief Executive: Peter Collings
Director of Serious Casework: David Harvie
COPFS National Enquiry Point: Tel: 0845 561 3000

COPFS

Procurator Fiscal Service

EAST FEDERATION

29 Chambers Street, Edinburgh EH1 1LD
Tel (all offices): 0844 561 3000 (from a landline); 01389 739557 (from a mobile)
Website: www.copfs.gov.uk
Procurator Fiscal for the East of Scotland: John Logue
Head of Business Management for the East of Scotland: Nancy Darroch
Procurator Fiscal for High Court for the East of Scotland: Michelle MacLeod
Procurator Fiscal for Sheriff and Jury for the East of Scotland: Moira Orr
Procurator Fiscal for Summary for the East of Scotland: Andrew Richardson
Procurator Fiscal for Initial Case Processing for the East of Scotland: Ruth McQuaid

ALLOA
Sheriff Court, Alloa FK10 1HR
Sheriff and JP Court
Alloa

CUPAR
Sheriff Court, Cupar KY15 4LS
Sheriff and JP Court
Cupar

DUMFERMLINE
Sheriff Court, Carnegie Drive, Dunfermline KY12 7HW
Sheriff and JP Court
Dunfermline

EDINBURGH
29 Chambers Street, Edinburgh EH1 1LB
Sheriff and JP Court
Edinburgh

FALKIRK
Mansionhouse Road, Camelon, Falkirk FK1 4LW
Sheriff and JP Court
Falkirk

HADDINGTON
10–12 Court Street, Haddington EH41 3JA
Sheriff and JP Court
Haddington

JEDBURGH
Sheriff Court, Jedburgh TD8 6AR
Sheriff and JP Court
Jedburgh

KIRKCALDY
Wing D, Carlyle House, Carlyle Road, Kirkcaldy KY1 1DB
Sheriff and JP Court
Kirkcaldy

LIVINGSTON
West Lothian Civic Centre, Howden South Road, Livingston EH54 6FF
Sheriff and JP Court
Livingston

SELKIRK
Sheriff Court, Selkirk TD7 4LE

Sheriff and JP Court
Selkirk

STIRLING
Carseview House, Castle Business Park, Stirling FK9 4SW

Sheriff and JP Court
Stirling

NORTH FEDERATION

c/o Caledonian House, Greenmarket, Dundee DD1 4QA

Tel (all offices): 0844 561 3000 (from a landline); 01389 739557 (from a mobile)

Website: www.copfs.gov.uk

Procurator Fiscal for the North of Scotland: Liam Murphy

Head of Business Management for the North of Scotland: Rosemary Fallon

Procurator Fiscal for High Court for the North of Scotland: Andrew Shanks

Procurator Fiscal for Sheriff and Jury for the North of Scotland: Andrew McIntyre

Procurator Fiscal for Summary for the North of Scotland: Andrew Laing

Procurator Fiscal for Initial Case Processing for the North of Scotland: Andrew Shanks

ABERDEEN
Atholl House, 84–88 Guild Street, Aberdeen AB11 6QA
Sheriff and JP Court
Aberdeen

ARBROATH
Aitken House, 15 Hill Street, Arbroath DD1 1BR
Sheriff and JP Court
Arbroath

BANFF
Sheriff Court, Banff AB4 1AU
Sheriff and JP Court
Banff

DINGWALL
County Buildings, Ferry Road, Dingwall IV15 9QX
Sheriff and JP Court
Dingwall

DORNOCH
Sheriff Court, Dornoch IV25 3FD
Sheriff and JP Court
Dornoch

DUNDEE
Caledonian House, Greenmarket, Dundee DD1 1QX
Sheriff and JP Court
Dundee

ELGIN
48 South Street, Elgin IV30 1BU
Sheriff and JP Court
Elgin

FORFAR
Sheriff Court, Forfar DD8 3LA
Sheriff and JP Court
Forfar

FORT WILLIAM
2nd Floor, Tweeddale, High Street, Fort William PH33 6EU
Sheriff and JP Court
Fort William

INVERNESS
Great Glen House, Leachkin Road, Inverness IV3 8NW
Sheriff and JP Court
Inverness

KIRKWALL
Sheriff Court, Kirkwall KW15 1PD
Sheriff Court
Kirkwall

LERWICK
Sheriff Court, Lerwick ZE1 0HD
Sheriff Court
Lerwick

LOCHMADDY
Sheriff Court, Lochmaddy HS6 5AE
Sheriff Court
Lochmaddy

PERTH
82 Tay Street, Perth PH1 5TR
Sheriff and JP Court
Perth

PETERHEAD
70 St Peter Street, Peterhead AB4 6QD
Sheriff and JP Court
Peterhead

PORTREE
Sheriff Court, Portree IV51 9EH
Sheriff and JP Court
Portree

STONEHAVEN
Sheriff Court, Stonehaven AB3 2JD
Sheriff and JP Court
Stonehaven

STORNOWAY
Sheriff Court Buildings, Lewis Street, Stornoway HS1 2JF
Sheriff and JP Court
Stornoway

TAIN
11 Stafford Street, Tain IV19 1BP
Sheriff and JP Court
Tain

WICK
Sheriff Court, Wick KW1 4AJ
Sheriff and JP Court
Wick

WEST FEDERATION

10 Ballater Street, Glasgow G5 9PS

Tel (all offices): 0844 561 3000 (from a landline); 01389 739557 (from a mobile)

Website: www.copfs.gov.uk

Procurator Fiscal for the West of Scotland: John Dunn

Head of Business Management for the West of Scotland: Paul Lowe

Procurator Fiscal for High Court for the West of Scotland: Anthony McGeehan

Procurator Fiscal for Sheriff and Jury for the West of Scotland: Anthony McGeehan

Procurator Fiscal for Initial Case Processing and Summary for the West of Scotland: Geri Watt

AIRDRIE
87A Graham Street, Airdrie ML6 6DE
Sheriff and JP Court
Sheriff Court: Airdire
JP Court: Coatbridge

AYR
37 Carrick Street, Ayr KA7 1NS
Sheriff and JP Court
Ayr

CAMPBELTOWN
Sheriff Court, Campbeltown PA28 6AN
Sheriff and JP Court
Campbeltown

DUMBARTON
St Mary's Way, Dumbarton G82 1NL
Sheriff and JP Court
Dumbarton

DUMFRIES
44 Buccleuch Street, Dumfries DG1 2AP
Sheriff and JP Court
Dumfries

DUNOON
Sheriff Court, Dunoon PS23 8BQ
Sheriff and JP Court
Dunoon

GLASGOW
10 Ballater Street, Glasgow G5 9PS
Sheriff and JP Court
Sheriff Court: Glasgow & Strathkelvin
JP Court: Glasgow

GREENOCK
Victory Court, Cartsburn Maritime, Arthur Street, Greenock PA15 4RT
Sheriff and JP Court
Greenock

HAMILTON
Cameronian House, 3/5 Almada Street, Hamilton ML3 0HG
Sheriff and JP Court
Sheriff Court: Hamilton
JP Court: Hamilton / Motherwell

KILMARNOCK
St Marnock Street, Kilmarnock KA1 1DZ

Sheriff and JP Court
Kilmarnock

KIRKCUDBRIGHT
Sheriff Court, Kirkcudbright DG6 4JW

Sheriff and JP Court
Kirkcudbright

LANARK
Sheriff Court, 24 Hope Street, Lanark ML11 7NE

Sheriff and JP Court
Lanark

OBAN
Third Floor, Boswell House, Argyll Square, Oban PA34 4BD

Sheriff and JP Court
Oban

PAISLEY
1 Love Street, Paisley PA3 2DA

Sheriff and JP Court
Paisley

ROTHESAY
Sheriff Court, Rothesay PA20 9AB

Sheriff Court
Rothesay

STRANRAER
Sheriff Court, Stranraer DG9 7AA

Sheriff and JP Court
Stranraer

Part VIII

NATIONAL OFFENDER MANAGEMENT SERVICE AND PENAL ESTABLISHMENTS

National Offender Management Service

ENGLAND AND WALES

NATIONAL OFFENDER MANAGEMENT
SERVICE AND PENAL ESTABLISHMENTS

HEADQUARTERS

Clive House, 70 Petty France, London SW1H 9EX
Email: public.enquiries@noms.gsi.gov.uk
Website: www.justice.gov.uk/about/noms/index
Chief Executive Officer: Michael Spurr. Tel: 0300 047 5163.
Director of Finance & Analysis: Andrew Emmett. Tel: 0300 047 6730
Director of HR: Carol Carpenter. Tel: 0300 047 5161
Director of NOMS ICT & Change: Martin Bellamy. Tel: 0300 047 5165
Director of Commissioning & Commercial (Interim): Ian Blakeman. Tel: 0300 047 5318
Director of Public Sector Prisons: Phil Copple. Tel: 0300 047 5152
Director of Probation & Contracted Services: Colin Allars. Tel: 0300 047 5157
Director of National Operational Services: Digby Griffith. Tel: 0300 047 5868

REGIONS

For prison details, categories, etc, see the table beginning on p 320.

EAST MIDLANDS

Public Sector Prisons (NOMS), HMYOI & RC Glen Parva, Tigers Road, Wigston, Leicester LE18 4TN
Tel: 0116 228 4005
Fax: 0116 228 4160
Deputy Director of Custody: Neil Richards (Acting)
Secretary: Antoinette Steele. Tel: 0116 228 4005
Operations Manager: Barbara White. Tel: 0116 228 4006

Prisons

Foston Hall	Nottingham
Gartree	Onley
Glen Parva	Ranby
Leicester	Stocken
Lincoln	Sudbury
Morton Hall	Whatton
North Sea Camp	

EAST OF ENGLAND

Stirling House, Bury Road, Stradishall, Suffolk CB8 9YL
Tel: 01440 7432775
Deputy Director of Custody: Adrian Smith

Prisons

Bedford	Littlehey
Blundeston	The Mount
Bure	Norwich
Chelmsford	Warren Hill
Highpoint	Wayland
Hollesley Bay	

GREATER LONDON

Red Zone, Point 6.01, Sixth Floor, Clive House, 70 Petty France, London SW1H 9EX
Tel: 0300 047 5868
Deputy Director of Custody: Nick Pascoe
Secretary: Jackie Wright. Tel: 0300 047 5887
Operations Manager: Gary Poole. Tel: 0300 047 5874

Prisons

Brixton	Isis
Coldingley	Pentonville
Downview	Send
Feltham	Wandsworth
Highdown	Wormwood Scrubs
Holloway	

KENT & SUSSEX

80 Sir Evelyn Road, Rochester, Kent ME1 3NF
Fax: 01634 673029
Deputy Director Custody: Michelle Jarman-Howe. Tel: 01634 673011
Secretary: Pauline Kidney. Tel: 01634 673010
Operations Manager: Jonathan Christopher. Tel: 01634 673022

Prisons

Blantyre House	Lewes
Cookham Wood	Maidstone
Dover	Rochester
East Sutton Park	Sheppey Cluster
Ford	

NORTH EAST

Forest House, Aykley Heads Business Park, Aykley Heads, Durham DH1 5TS
Tel: 0191 376 6803
Fax: 0191 376 6801
Deputy Director of Custody: Alan Tallentire. Tel: 0191 376 6803
Secretary: Gillian Beeston. Tel: 0191 376 6803
Operations Manager: Neil Evans. Tel: 0191 3766816

Prisons

Deerbolt	Kirklevington Grange
Durham	Low Newton
Holme House	

NORTH WEST

Wymott Conference Centre, Ulnes Walton Lane, Leyland PR26 8LT
Postal address: PO Box 368, Leyland PR25 9EJ
Tel: 01772 442442
Fax: 01772 442083
Deputy Director of Custody: Alan Scott. Tel: 01772 442442
Secretary: Kathryn Bullock. Tel: 01772 442 442
Operations Managers: Eileen Fenerly-Lyons. Tel: 01772 442444

Prisons

Buckley Hall	Liverpool
Garth	Preston
Haverigg	Risley
Hindley	Styal
Kennet	Thorn Cross
Kirkham	Wymott
Lancaster Farms	

SOUTH CENTRAL

South Central Office HMP Winchester, Romsey Road, Winchester SO22 5DF
Deputy Director of Custody: Claudia Sturt. Tel: 0754 573 2731
Business Manager: Rachel Hardy. Tel: 01962 723090
Operations Manager: Neil Howard. Tel: 07973 457492
Area Estates Manager: Phil Harle. Tel: 01296 442706

Prisons

Aylesbury	Haslar
Bullingdon	Huntercombe
Grendon/Spring Hill	Isle of Wight

Reading   Winchester

SOUTH WEST
1 Tortworth Road, Leyhill, Wotton-under-Edge, Gloucestershire GL12 8BQ
Deputy Director of Custody: Ferdie Parker. Tel: 01454 264271
Secretary: Vacant. Tel: 01454 264271
Operations Manager: Lucy Young. Tel: 01454 264272

Prisons

Bristol   Exeter
Channings Wood   Guys Marsh
Dartmoor   Leyhill
Dorchester   Portland
Eastwood Park   The Verne
Erlestoke

WEST MIDLANDS
West Midlands DDC Team, Regional Office, c/o HMP Stafford, 54 Gaol Road, Stafford ST16 3AW
Tel: 01785 773077
Deputy Director of Custody: Luke Serjeant
Secretary: Sarah Keay. Tel: 01785 773077.
Office Co-ordinator: Michelle Thomas Tel: 01785 773278
Operations Manager: Debbie Lewis. Tel: 01785 773148

Prisons

Brinsford   Stafford
Drake Hall   Stoke Heath
Featherstone   Swinfen Hall
Hewell   Werrington

YORKSHIRE & HUMBERSIDE
DDC Office, HMP Askham Grange, Main Street, Askham Richard, York YO23 3FT
Tel: 01904 772000
Fax: 01904 772145
Deputy Director of Custody: Paul Baker. Tel: 01904 772056
Secretary: Clare Burton. Tel: 01904 772056
Operations Manager: Andy Crofts

Prisons

Askham Grange   New Hall
Everthorpe   Northallerton
Hull   Wealstun
Leeds   Wetherby
Lindholme   Wolds
Moorland & Hatfield

WALES
Deputy Director of Custody Office, 3rd Floor, Churchill House, Churchill Way, Cardiff CF10 2HH
Fax: 029 2067 8338
Deputy Director of Custody: Ian Mulholland. Tel: 029 2067 8385; mob: 07968 907607
Secretary: Elaine Eliot. Tel: 029 2067 8385

Prisons

Cardiff   Usk/Prescoed
Swansea

HIGH SECURITY
Clive House, 70 Petty France, London SW1H 9EX
Deputy Director of Custody: Richard Vince. Tel: 0300 047 6104
Secretary: Denise Gayle. Tel: 0300 047 5152

Prisons

Belmarsh	Manchester
Frankland	Wakefield
Full Sutton	Whitemoor
Long Lartin	Woodhill

DIRECTORATE OF PROBATION AND CONTRACTED SERVICES

Room 1.15, First Floor, Clive House, 70 Petty France, London SW1H 9EX
Tel: 0300 047 5157
Fax: 0300 047 6819
Deputy Director of Contracted Custodial Services: Brian Pollett. Tel: 0300 047 5889
Operations Manager: Pauline Skinner. Tel: 0300 047 5889

Contracted Prisons

Altcourse	Lowdham Grange
Ashfield	Northumberland
Birmingham	Oakwood
Bronzefield	Parc
Doncaster	Peterborough
Dovegate	Rye Hill
Forest Bank	Thameside

YOUTH JUSTICE BOARD FOR ENGLAND AND WALES

1 Drummond Gate, London SW1V 2QZ.
Tel: 020 3372 8000. Fax: 020 3372 8002.
Website: www.yjb.gov.uk

PENAL ESTABLISHMENTS ENGLAND AND WALES (WITH CATEGORIES)

*	contracted prison
ABCD	prisoner categories (see Prison Service Order 0900 Categorisation)
CL	closed
F	females
HC	holding centre
IRC	immigration removal centre
J	juveniles
L	local
M	males
O	open
RC	remand centre
RES	resettlement
S-O	semi-open
YOI	young offenders' institution

Further information can be found on the prison service website www.justice.gov.uk/about/hmps

HMP ALTCOURSE*
Higher Lane, Fazakerley, Liverpool L9 7LH
Tel: 0151 522 2000. Fax: 0151 522 2121
(M, L)

HMP ASHFIELD*
Shortwood Road, Pucklechurch, Bristol BS16 9QJ
Tel: 0117 303 8000. Fax: 0117 303 8001
(M, C)

HMP/YOI ASKHAM GRANGE
Askham Richard, York YO23 3FT
Tel: 01904 772000. Fax: 01904 772001
(F, O)

HMYOI AYLESBURY
Bierton Road, Aylesbury, Buckinghamshire HP20 1EH
Tel: 01296 444000. Fax: 01296 444001
(YOI(M), A, CL, RES)

HMP BEDFORD
St Loyes Street, Bedford MK40 1HG
Tel: 01234 373000. Fax: 01234 273568
(M, L)

HMP BELMARSH
Western Way, Thamesmead, London SE28 0EB
Tel: 020 8331 4400. Fax: 020 8331 4401
(M, A, CL)

HMP BIRMINGHAM*
Winson Green Road, Birmingham B18 4AS
Tel: 0121 345 2500. Fax: 0121 345 2501
(M, L)

HMP BLANTYRE HOUSE
Goudhurst, Cranbrook, Kent TN17 2NH
Tel: 01580 213200. Fax: 01580 213201
(M, C, S-O)

HMP BLUNDESTON
Lowestoft, Suffolk NR32 5BG
Tel: 01502 734500. Fax: 01502 734501
(M, C, CL)

HMP/YOI BRINSFORD
New Road, Featherstone, Wolverhampton WV10 7PY
Tel: 01902 533450. Fax: 01902 533451
(YOI, J, CL, RC)

HMP BRISTOL
19 Cambridge Road, Bristol BS7 8PS
Tel: 0117 372 3100. Fax: 0117 372 3113
(M, L)

HMP BRIXTON
PO Box 269, Jebb Avenue, Brixton, London SW2 5XF
Tel: 020 8588 6000. Fax: 020 8588 6191
(M, B, L)

HMP BRONZEFIELD*
Woodthorpe Road, Ashford, Middlesex TW15 3JZ
Tel: 01784 425690. Fax: 01784 425691
(F)

HMP BUCKLEY HALL
Buckley Road, Rochdale, Lancashire OL12 9DP
Tel: 01706 514300. Fax: 01706 514399
(M, C)

HMP BULLINGDON
PO Box 50, Bicester, Oxfordshire OX25 1PZ
Tel: 01869 353100. Fax: 01869 353101
(M, C, CL, L)

HMP BURE
Jaguar Drive, Scottow, Norwich NR10 5GB
Tel: 01603 326000. Fax: 01603 326001
(M, C)

HMP/RC CARDIFF
Knox Road, Cardiff CF24 0UG
Tel: 029 2092 3100. Fax: 029 2092 3318
(M, L, RC)

HMP CHANNINGS WOOD
Denbury, Newton Abbot, Devon TQ12 6DW
Tel: 01803 814600. Fax: 01803 814601
(M, C, CL)

HMP/YOI CHELMSFORD
200 Springfield Road, Chelmsford CM2 6LQ
Tel: 01245 552000. Fax: 01245 552001
(M, L, RC)

HMP COLDINGLEY
Shaftesbury Road, Bisley, Woking, Surrey GU24 9EX
Tel: 01483 344300. Fax: 01483 344427
(M, C, CL)

HMP COOKHAM WOOD
Sir Evelyn Road, Rochester, Kent ME1 3LU
Tel: 01634 202500. Fax: 01634 202501
(J, CL)

HMP DARTMOOR
Princetown, Yelverton, Devon PL20 6RR
Tel: 01822 322000. Fax: 01822 322001
(M, C, CL)

HMYOI DEERBOLT
Bowes Road, Barnard Castle, Co. Durham DL12 9BG
Tel: 01833 633200. Fax: 01833 633201
(YOI, CL)

HMP/YOI DONCASTER*
Off North Bridge Road, Marshgate, Doncaster DN5 8UX
Tel: 01302 760870. Fax: 01302 760851
(M, L)

HMP DORCHESTER
North Square, Dorchester, Dorset DT1 1JD
Tel: 01305 714500. Fax: 01305 714501
(M, L, RC)

HMP DOVEGATE*
Uttoxeter, Staffordshire ST14 8XR
Tel: 01283 829400. Fax: 01283 820066
(M, B, CL)

IRC DOVER
The Citadel, Western Heights, Dover, Kent CT17 9DR
Tel: 01304 246400. Fax: 01304 246401
(CL, IR, C)

HMP DOWNVIEW
Sutton Lane, Sutton, Surrey SM2 5PD
Tel: 020 8196 6300. Fax: 020 8196 6301
(F, C, CL)

HMP/YOI DRAKE HALL
Eccleshall, Staffordshire ST21 6LQ
Tel: 01785 774100. Fax: 01785 774010
(F, S-O, YOI)

HMP DURHAM
Old Elvet, Durham DH1 3HU
Tel: 0191 332 3400. Fax: 0191 332 3401
(M, CL, L)

HMP/YOI EAST SUTTON PARK
Sutton Valence, Maidstone, Kent ME17 3DF
Tel: 01622 785000. Fax: 01622 785001
(F, O)

HMP ELMLEY (SHEPPEY CLUSTER)
Church Road, Eastchurch, Sheerness, Kent ME12 4DZ
Tel: 01795 882000. Fax: 01795 882001
(M, B, CL, L, YOI)

HMP ERLESTOKE
Devizes, Wiltshire SN10 5TU
Tel: 01380 814250. Fax: 01380 814273
(M, C, CL)

HMP EVERTHORPE
1a Beck Road, Brough, East Yorkshire HU15 1RB
Tel: 01430 426500. Fax: 01430 426501
(M, C, CL)

HMP/YOI EXETER
New North Road, Exeter, Devon EX4 4EX
Tel: 01392 415650. Fax: 01392 415691
(M, L, RC)

HMP FEATHERSTONE
New Road, Featherstone, Wolverhampton WV10 7PU
Tel: 01902 703000. Fax: 01902 703001
(M, C, CL)

HMP/YOI FELTHAM
Bedfont Road, Feltham, Middlesex TW13 4ND
Tel: 020 8844 5000. Fax: 020 8844 5001
(M, CL, RC)

HMP FORD
Arundel, West Sussex BN18 0BX
Tel: 01903 663000. Fax: 01903 663001
(M, D, O)

HMP/YOI FOREST BANK*
Agecroft Road, Pendlebury, Salford M27 8FB
Tel: 0161 925 7000. Fax: 0161 925 7001
(M, L, YOI)

HMP/YOI FOSTON HALL
Foston, Derbyshire DE65 5DN
Tel: 01283 584300. Fax: 01283 584301
(F, CL)

HMP FRANKLAND
Brasside, Durham DH1 5YD
Tel: 0191 376 5000. Fax: 0191 376 5001
(M, A, CL)

HMP FULL SUTTON
Full Sutton, York YO41 1PS
Tel: 01759 475100. Fax: 01759 371206
(M, A, CL)

HMP GARTH
Ulnes Walton Lane, Leyland, Lancashire PR26 8NE
Tel: 01772 443300. Fax: 01772 443301
(M, B, CL)

HMP GARTREE
Gallow Field Road, Market Harborough, Leicestershire LE16 7RP
Tel: 01858 426600. Fax: 01858 426601
(M, B, CL)

HMYOI & RC GLEN PARVA
Tigers Road, Wigston, Leicestershire LE18 4TN
Tel: 0116 228 4100. Fax: 0116 228 4000
(CL, RC, YOI)

HMP GRENDON
Grendon Underwood, Aylesbury, Buckinghamshire HP18 0TL
Tel: 01296 445000. Fax: 01296 445001
(M, B, CL)

HMP/YOI GUYS MARSH
Shaftesbury, Dorset SP7 0AH
Tel: 01747 856400. Fax: 01747 856401
(M, C, CL)

IRC HASLAR
2 Dolphin Way, Gosport, Hampshire PO12 2AW
Tel: 023 9260 4000. Fax: 023 9260 4001
(HC)

HMP HAVERIGG
Millom, Cumbria LA18 4NA
Tel: 01229 713000. Fax: 01229 713001
(M, C, CL)

HMP HEWELL
Hewell Lane, Redditch, Worcestershire B97 6QS
Tel: 01527 785000. Fax: 01527 785001
(M, B, C, D)

HMP HIGH DOWN
Sutton Lane, Sutton, Surrey SM2 5PJ
Tel: 020 7147 6300. Fax: 020 7147 6301
(M, L)

HMP HIGHPOINT
Stradishall, Newmarket, Suffolk CB8 9YG
Tel: 01440 743100. Fax: 01440 743092
(M, C, CL)

HMYOI HINDLEY
Gibson Street, Bickershaw, Wigan, Lancashire WN2 5TH
Tel: 01942 663100. Fax: 01942 663101
(RC, CL, YOI)

HMP HOLLESLEY BAY
Woodbridge, Suffolk IP12 3JW
Tel: 01394 412400. Fax: 01394 410115
(M, D, O, YOI(CL))

HMP/YOI HOLLOWAY
Parkhurst Road, Holloway, London N7 0NU
Tel: 020 7979 4400. Fax: 020 7979 4401
(F, L)

HMP HOLME HOUSE
Holme House Road, Stockton-on-Tees, Cleveland TS18 2QU
Tel: 01642 744000. Fax: 01642 744001
(M, CL, L)

HMP HULL
Hedon Road, Hull HU9 5LS
Tel: 01482 282200. Fax: 01482 282400
(M, L, YOI(CL))

HMP HUNTERCOMBE
Huntercombe Place, Nuffield, Henley-on-Thames, Oxfordshire RG9 5SB
Tel: 01491 643100. Fax: 01491 643101
(CL)

HMP ISIS
Western Way, Thamesmead, London SE28 0NZ
Tel: 020 3356 4000. Fax: 020 3356 4001
(C, YOI)

HMP ISLE OF WIGHT
Clissold Road, Newport, Isle of Wight PO30 5RS
Tel: 01983 556300. Fax: 01983 556362
(M, B, C)

HMP KENNET
Parkbourn, Maghull, Liverpool L31 1HX
Tel: 0151 213 3000. Fax: 0151 213 3103
(M, C)

HMP KIRKHAM
Freckleton Road, Kirkham, Preston, Lancashire PR4 2RN
Tel: 01772 675400. Fax: 01772 675401
(M, D, O)

HMP KIRKLEVINGTON GRANGE
Yarm, Cleveland TS15 9PA
Tel: 01642 792600. Fax: 01642 792601
(M, C, D, RES)

HMP/YOI LANCASTER FARMS
Stone Row Head, off Quernmore Road, Lancaster LA1 3QZ
Tel: 01524 563450. Fax: 01542 563451
(J, YOI, RC, CL)

HMP LEEDS
Gloucester Terrace, Armley, Leeds LS12 2TJ
Tel: 0113 203 2600. Fax: 0113 203 2601
(M, L)

HMP LEICESTER
116 Welford Road, Leicester LE2 7AJ
Tel: 0116 228 3000. Fax: 0116 228 3001
(M, L)

HMP/YOI LEWES
1 Brighton Road, Lewes, East Sussex BN7 1EA
Tel: 01273 785100. Fax: 01273 785101
(M, L, YOI(CL))

HMP LEYHILL
Wotton-under-Edge, Gloucestershire GL12 8BT
Tel: 01454 264000. Fax: 01454 264001
(M, D, O)

HMP LINCOLN
Greetwell Road, Lincoln LN2 4BD
Tel: 01522 663000. Fax: 01522 663001
(M, L)

HMP IRC LINDHOLME
Bawtry Road, Hatfield Woodhouse, Doncaster, South Yorkshire DN7 6EE
Tel: 01302 524700. Fax: 01302 524750
(M, C, CL, O, IRC)

HMP LITTLEHEY
Perry, Huntingdon, Cambridgeshire PE28 OSR
Tel: 01480 333000. Fax: 01480 333070
(M, C, CL)

HMP LIVERPOOL
68 Hornby Road, Liverpool L9 3DF
Tel: 0151 530 4000. Fax: 0151 530 4001
(M, C, CL)

HMP LONG LARTIN
South Littleton, Evesham, Worcestershire WR11 8TZ
Tel: 01386 295100. Fax: 01386 295101
(M, A, CL)

HMYOI LOW NEWTON
Brasside, Durham DH1 5YA
Tel: 0191 376 4000. Fax: 0191 376 4001
(F, L, CL)

HMP LOWDHAM GRANGE*
Old Epperstone Road, Lowdham, Nottingham NG14 7DA
Tel: 0115 966 9200. Fax: 0115 966 9220
(M, B, CL)

HMP MAIDSTONE
36 County Road, Maidstone, Kent ME14 1UZ
Tel: 01622 775300. Fax: 01622 775301
(M, C, CL) (HMP Maidstone is a Foreign National Establishment)

HMP MANCHESTER
Southall Street, Manchester M60 9AH
Tel: 0161 817 5600. Fax: 0161 817 5601
(M, A, CL)

HMPYOI MOORLAND & HATFIELD
Bawtry Road, Hatfield Woodhouse, Doncaster, South Yorkshire DN7 6BW
Tel: 01302 523000. Fax: 01302 523001
(M, C, CL, YOI)
Thorne Road, Hatfield, Doncaster DN7 6EL
Tel: 01405 746500. Fax: 01405 746501.
(M, D, O, YOI)

HMP MORTON HALL
Swinderby, Lincoln LN6 9PT
Tel: 01522 666700. Fax: 01522 666750
(F, O, IRC)

HMP THE MOUNT
Molyneaux Avenue, Bovingdon, Hemel Hempstead, Hertfordshire HP3 0NZ
Tel: 01442 836300. Fax: 01442 836301
(M, C, CL)

HMP/YOI NEW HALL
Dial Wood, Flockton, Wakefield, West Yorkshire WF4 4XX
Tel: 01924 803000. Fax: 01924 803001
(F, CL, YOI(CL))

HMP NORTH SEA CAMP
Freiston, Boston, Lincolnshire PE22 0QX
Tel: 01205 769300. Fax: 01205 769301
(M, D, O)

HMYOI NORTHALLERTON
15a East Road, Northallerton, North Yorkshire DL6 1NW
Tel: 01609 785100. Fax: 01609 785101
(YOI CL)

HMP/YOI NORTHUMBERLAND*
Morpeth, Northumberland NE65 9XG
Tel: 01670 383100. Fax: 01670 383101
(CL, C, M)

HMP/YOI NORWICH
Knox Road, Norwich NR1 4LU
Tel: 01603 708600. Fax: 01603 708601
(M, L, YOI(CL))

HMP NOTTINGHAM
Perry Road, Sherwood, Nottingham NG5 3AG
Tel: 0115 872 4000. Fax: 0115 872 4001
(M, L)

HMP OAKWOOD*
Oak Road, Featherstone WV10 7PU
Tel: 01902 799700. Fax: 01902 703001
(M, C)

HMP ONLEY
Willoughby, Rugby, Warwickshire CV23 8AP
Tel: 01788 523400. Fax: 01788 523401
(J, CL)

HMP/YOI PARC*
Heol Hopcyn John, Bridgend, Mid Glamorgan CF35 6AP
Tel: 01656 300200. Fax: 01656 300201
(M, B, L, YOI(CL, RC))

HMP PENTONVILLE
Caledonian Road, London N7 8TT
Tel: 020 7023 7000. Fax: 020 7023 7001
(M, L)

HMP PETERBOROUGH*
Saville Road, Westwood, Peterborough PE3 7PD
Tel: 01733 217500. Fax: 01733 217501
(M, F, L, RC)

HMYOI PORTLAND
104 The Grove, Easton, Portland, Dorset DT5 1DL
Tel: 01305 715600. Fax: 01305 715601
(M, C, CL, YOI)

HMP/YOI PRESCOED
Coed-y-Paen, Pontypool, Gwent NP4 0TB
Tel: 01291 675000. Fax: 01291 675158
(M, C, CL, D, O, YOI(O))

HMP PRESTON
2 Ribbleton Lane, Preston, Lancashire PR1 5AB
Tel: 01772 444550. Fax: 01772 444551
(M, L)

HMP RANBY
Retford, Nottinghamshire DN22 8EU
Tel: 01777 862000. Fax: 01777 862001
(M, C, CL)

HMP/YOI READING
Forbury Road, Reading, Berkshire RG1 3HY
Tel: 0118 908 5000. Fax: 0118 908 5001
(YOI RC)

HMP RISLEY
Warrington Road, Risley, Warrington, Cheshire WA3 6BP
Tel: 01925 733000. Fax: 01925 733001
(M, C, CL)

HMYOI ROCHESTER
1 Fort Road, Rochester, Kent ME1 3QS
Tel: 01634 803100. Fax: 01634 803101
(YOI, C CL)

HMP RYE HILL*
Willoughby, Rugby, Warwickshire CV23 8SZ
Tel: 01788 523300. Fax: 01788 523311
(M, B)

HMP SEND
Ripley Road, Send, Woking, Surrey GU23 7LJ
Tel: 01483 471000. Fax: 01483 471001
(F, CL)

HMP SPRING HILL
Grendon Underwood, Aylesbury, Buckinghamshire HP18 0TL
Tel: 01296 445000. Fax: 01296 445001
(M, D, O)

HMP STAFFORD
54 Gaol Road, Stafford ST16 3AW
Tel: 01785 773000. Fax: 01785 773001
(M, C, CL)

HMP STANDFORD HILL (SHEPPEY CLUSTER)
Church Road, Eastchurch, Sheerness, Kent ME12 4AA
Tel: 01795 884500. Fax: 01795 884638
(M, D, O)

HMP STOCKEN
Stocken Hall Road, Stretton, Oakham, Rutland LE15 7RD
Tel: 01780 795100. Fax: 01780 410767
(M, C, CL)

HMYOI STOKE HEATH
Market Drayton, Shropshire TF9 2JL
Tel: 01630 636000. Fax: 01630 636001
(J, YOI, CL)

HMP/YOI STYAL
Wilmslow, Cheshire SK9 4HR
Tel: 01625 553000. Fax: 01625 553001
(F, CL, L)

HMP SUDBURY
Ashbourne, Derbyshire DE6 5HW
Tel: 01283 584000. Fax: 01283 584001

HMP SWALESIDE (SHEPPEY CLUSTER)
Brabazon Road, Eastchurch, Isle of Sheppey, Kent ME12 4AX
Tel: 01795 804100. Fax: 01795 804200
(M, B, CL)

HMP SWANSEA
200 Oystermouth Road, Swansea SA1 3SR
Tel: 01792 485300. Fax: 01792 485430
(M, L, RC(YOI))

HMYOI SWINFEN HALL
Swinfen, Lichfield, Staffs WS14 9QS
Tel: 01543 484000. Fax: 01543 484001
(YOI CL)

HMP THAMESIDE*
Griffin Manor Way, Thamesmead, London SE28 0FJ
Tel: 020 8317 9777
(M, YOI, L)

HMYOI THORN CROSS
Arley Road, Appleton Thorn, Warrington, Cheshire WA4 4RL
Tel: 01925 805100. Fax: 01925 805101
(J, YOI, O)

HMP USK
47 Maryport Street, Usk, Monmouth NP15 1XP
Tel: 01291 671600. Fax: 01291 671752
(M, C, CL)

HMP THE VERNE
The Verne, Portland, Dorset DT5 1EQ
Tel: 01305 825000. Fax: 01305 825001
(M, C, CL)

HMP WAKEFIELD
5 Love Lane, Wakefield, West Yorkshire WF2 9AG
Tel: 01924 612000. Fax: 01924 612001
(M, A)

HMP WANDSWORTH
PO Box 757, Heathfield Road, Wandsworth, London SW18 3HS
Tel: 020 8588 4000. Fax: 020 8588 4001
(M, L)

HMYOI WARREN HILL
Hollesley, Woodbridge, Suffolk IP12 3JW
Tel: 01394 633400. Fax: 01394 633401
(YOI CL)

HMP WAYLAND
Griston, Thetford, Norfolk IP25 6RL
Tel: 01953 804100. Fax: 01953 804220
(M, C, CL)

HMP WEALSTUN
Church Causeway, Thorp Arch, Wetherby, West Yorkshire LS23 7AZ
Tel: 01937 444400. Fax: 01937 444401
(M, C, CL, D, O)

HMYOI WERRINGTON
Ash Bank Road, Stoke-on-Trent, Staffordshire ST9 0DX
Tel: 01782 463300. Fax: 01782 463301
(J)

HMYOI WETHERBY
York Road, Wetherby, West Yorkshire LS22 5ED
Tel: 01937 544200. Fax: 01937 544201
(J, CL)

HMP WHATTON
New Lane, Whatton, Nottinghamshire NG13 9FQ
Tel: 01949 803200. Fax: 01949 803201
(M, C, CL)

HMP WHITEMOOR
Longhill Road, March, Cambridgeshire PE15 0PR
Tel: 01354 602350. Fax: 01354 602351
(M, A)

HMP WINCHESTER
Romsey Road, Winchester, Hampshire SO22 5DF
Tel: 01962 723000. Fax: 01962 723001
(M, B, L)

HMP WOLDS
Everthorpe, Brough, East Yorkshire HU15 2JZ
Tel: 01430 428000. Fax: 01430 428001
(M, L)

HMP WOODHILL
Tattenhoe Street, Milton Keynes, Buckinghamshire MK4 4DA
Tel: 01908 722000. Fax: 01908 867063
(M, A, L)

HMP WORMWOOD SCRUBS
PO Box 757, Du Cane Road, London W12 0AE
Tel: 020 8588 3200. Fax: 020 8588 3201
(M, L)

HMP WYMOTT
Ulnes Walton Lane, Leyland, Preston, Lancashire PR26 8LW
Tel: 01772 442000. Fax: 01772 442001

SPECIAL HOSPITALS

ASHWORTH
Ashworth Hospital, Parkbourn, Maghull, Liverpool L31 1HW
Tel: 0151 473 0303

BROADMOOR
Broadmoor Hospital, Crowthorne, Berkshire RG11 7EG
Tel: 01344 773111

RAMPTON
Rampton Hospital, Retford, Nottinghamshire DN22 0PD
Tel: 01777 248321

NORTHERN IRELAND

HEADQUARTERS ESTABLISHMENTS

HEADQUARTERS
Prison Service Headquarters, Dundonald House, Upper Newtownards Road, Belfast BT4 3SU
Tel: 028 9052 5065
Email: info@niprisonservice.gov.uk
Website: www.dojni.gov.uk/index/ni-prison-service.htm

PRISON SERVICE COLLEGE
Woburn House, Millisle, Co. Down BT22 2HS
Tel: 028 9186 3000. Fax: 028 9186 3022

PRISONS

MAGHABERRY
Old Road, Ballinderry Upper, Lisburn BT28 2PT
Tel: 028 92611888. Fax: 028 9261 9516

MAGILLIGAN
Point Road, Limavady, Co. Londonderry BT49 0LR
Tel: 028 7776 3311. Fax: 028 7772 0307

YOUNG OFFENDERS CENTRE AND PRISON

HYDEBANK WOOD
Hospital Road, Belfast BT8 8NA
Tel: 028 9025 3666. Fax: 028 9025 3668

SCOTLAND

SCOTTISH PRISON SERVICE HEADQUARTERS

HEADQUARTERS
Calton House, 5 Redheughs Rigg, Edinburgh EH12 9HW
Tel: 0131 244 8745
Email: gaolinfo@sps.pnn.gov.uk
Website: www.sps.gov.uk

PRISON SERVICE COLLEGE

SCOTTISH PRISON SERVICE COLLEGE
Head of College, Scottish Prison Service College, Newlands Road, Brightons, Falkirk, Stirlingshire FK2 0DE
Tel: 01324 710400. Fax: 01324 710401

PRISONS

HMP ABERDEEN
Craiginches, 4 Grampian Place, Aberdeen AB11 8FN
Tel: 01224 238300. Fax: 01224 896209

HMP ADDIEWELL (SODEXO JUSTICE SERVICES)
9 Station Road, Addiewell, West Lothian EH55 8QF
Tel: 01506 874500. Fax: 01506 874501

HMP BARLINNIE
Barlinnie, 81 Lee Avenue, Glasgow G33 2QX
Tel: 0141 770 2000. Fax: 0141 770 2060

HMP OPEN ESTATE – CASTLE HUNTLY
Open Estate – Castle Huntly, Longforgan, Nr Dundee DD2 5HL
Tel: 01382 319333. Fax: 01382 319350

HMP/HMYOI CORNTON VALE
Cornton Vale, Cornton Road, Stirling FK9 5NU
Tel: 01786 832591. Fax: 01786 833597

HMP DUMFRIES
Terregles Street, Dumfries DG2 9AX
Tel: 01387 261218. Fax: 01387 264144

HMP EDINBURGH
33 Stenhouse Road, Edinburgh EH11 3LN
Tel: 0131 444 3000. Fax: 0131 444 3045

HMP GLENOCHIL
King O'Muir Road, Tullibody, Clackmannanshire FK10 3AD
Tel: 01259 760471. Fax: 01259 762003

HMP GREENOCK
Gateside, Greenock, Renfrewshire PA16 9AH
Tel: 01475 787801. Fax: 01475 783154

HMP INVERNESS
Duffy Drive, Inverness IV2 3HH
Tel: 01463 229000. Fax: 01463 229010

HMP KILMARNOCK (SERCO)
Mauchline Road, Kilmarnock KA1 5AA
Tel: 01563 548800. Fax: 01563 548801

HMP LOW MOSS
Crosshill Road, Bishopbriggs, Glasgow G64 2QB
Tel: 0141 762 9500

HMP PERTH
3 Edinburgh Road, Perth PH2 8AT
Tel: 01738 458100. Fax: 01738 630545

HMP PETERHEAD
Peterhead, Aberdeenshire AB42 2YY
Tel: 01779 479101. Fax: 01779 470529

HMP SHOTTS
Scott Drive, Shotts, Lanarkshire ML7 4LE
Tel: 01501 824000. Fax: 01501 824022

YOUNG OFFENDER INSTITUTIONS

HMYOI CORNTON VALE
Cornton Vale, Cornton Road, Stirling FK9 5NU
Tel: 01786 832591. Fax: 01786 833597

HMYOI POLMONT
Brightons, Falkirk, Stirlingshire FK2 0AB
Tel: 01324 711558. Fax: 01324 714919

STATE HOSPITAL

STATE HOSPITAL
Carstairs, Lanark ML11 8RP
Tel: 01555 840293
Fax: 01555 840024
Email: tsh.info@nhs.net
Website: www.tsh.scot.nhs.uk

INDEX TO PENAL ESTABLISHMENTS